STAR MOMS SHINE…

Eva Jagger on Mick:
He's still your son. He's still your little kid. You brought him up. I don't grasp it. It isn't that I'm not proud of him; I think it's marvelous.

Georgia Holt on Cher:
I know Cher invites reaction with her flamboyant and sometimes outrageous sense of style, but she's just having fun—playing "dress up" like she did as a child…only now she does it as a grown-up.

Joe Collins on Joan:
Joan's relationships with men have often left me astonished at her naiveté. She has never manipulated any man, nor played off one man against another. In this respect, Alexis would despise Joan as a stupid little ninny.

Catrine Domenique on Cyndi Lauper:
She's such a gutsy girl, she really is. Sometimes she amazes me. No matter what Cyndi does, no matter how outrageous, the funny thing is, I can't wait for the next one because I think she's so terrific.

S0-ADG-628

STAR Mothers

The Moms Behind the Celebrities

GEORGIA HOLT
and
PHYLLIS QUINN
with SUE RUSSELL

ST. MARTIN'S PRESS/NEW YORK

Published by arrangement with Simon & Schuster Inc.

STAR MOTHERS

ISBN: 0-312-91540-3 Can. ISBN: 0-312-91541-1

Printed in the United States of America

Simon & Schuster edition published 1988
First St. Martin's Press mass market edition/May 1989

10 9 8 7 6 5 4 3 2 1

ACKNOWLEDGMENTS

MY DEEPEST THANKS TO KATHERINE (AMAZING) GRACE for her splendid, indefatigable assistance. To Robert Kerman for his loving support and ideas. Joni Evans for her faith in the book. Eddie Sanderson for his encouragement and deft camera work. Stacey Slaughter, Joyce Quarrie, and Norman Chapman for their research. Robert Gottlieb, my literary agent; Donna Colabella; Jane Lovelle Drache; Jack Dwosh; Bob Carr; Dave Schwartz; Dr. Frank Bredice; Sandra Bredesen; Rhonda Johnson; and the Margaret Herrick Library of the Academy of Motion Picture Arts & Sciences, for their invaluable contributions. My own mother, Bridget; and all the star mothers who shared their personal stories. And very special thanks to Robert Asahina, our incisive and insightful editor, who made it a better book.

—S.R.

MY PERSONAL THANKS TO ALL OF THE ABOVE. To my dear friends, the members of Screen Smart Set and Motion Picture Mothers. My wonderful children who made a motion picture mother out of me: Bob, Debra, Diane and Ted, who at the age of four, aptly made famous the line, "Mothers are like that!" Jim, Casey and Jamie Davis; Peggy Quinn; Ruth Bullington; Marion Lederer; Paul Shefrin; Harry Langdon; Ross Sheldon, for their help. Lillian McEdward for impetus; and to Dick and Kari Clark, Al Schwartz and Barry Adelman, for believing in the project. Jim Quinn, who allowed me to grow, still my high school sweetheart after all these years. My dear mother, Lucille, who always thought I could do anything. Most of all, I want to thank Sue Russell, who brought my long-time dream to fruition.

—P.Q.

Acknowledgments

To my daughters, Cher and Georganne LaPiere; my mother, Lynda Walker; Rev. Rosalyn Bruyere; my manager, Paul Cohen, and his assistant, Jennifer Ruiz; José Eber; John Forbess; Nola Johnson; Ann Rafkin; Paul Rosenfeld; Craig Spencer; my literary agent, Jan Miller, for her enthusiasm and support for this, my first book; and all the wonderful mothers who gave us their time and their memories.

—G.H.

Contents

Introduction:
A Star in the Family

Dear Reader:

Of all the thrills Cher's stardom has brought me, a very special one was watching her perform at the Hollywood Bowl—was it *really* twenty years ago?—in a concert to aid the blind. I remember my father gripping my arm tightly and saying, "That's you up there! That's you up there made over!" (Daddy had brought me to Los Angeles from Oklahoma City when I was ten. Because of my singing, everyone there told him I could be a star.) And here I am enjoying it all through my own child.

That night, I was also shown the terrifying side of stardom when suddenly all the teenagers in the audience stormed the stage. Cher acted completely calm. She couldn't possibly have felt it after her experience in Phoenix, where the kids had stormed the stage and she collapsed. (Big Jim, the bodyguard, had to hit teenagers with his fist just to reach her, then carry her to safety on his shoulders.) The guards at the Hollywood Bowl couldn't possibly have held the kids back, so Cher was incredibly brave when she just put her mike down and said, "Hey you guys, unless you sit down, I'm not going to sing, we're just going to stand here." I was so proud of her when everyone quietly went back to their seats. To me, that was real star power.

No feeling on earth can equal the rush of pure pleasure and adrenaline when your child does something truly special. Zelma Bullock, Tina Turner's mom, was sitting up in bed watching the 1984 Grammys on TV when Tina scooped the awards with her comeback album, *Private Dancer*. She was so filled with emotion, she felt sure she would burst. That night, Zelma was truly a mom in a million.

Imagine being handed a key to the most exclusive club in the world! A club into which no amount of money or fancy platinum credit card can buy you entry! Being a star mom is rather like that. But it's something over which you have no control whatsoever. When your child becomes a star, a ripple effect—more like a tidal wave, really!—sweeps the entire family along as well. My life changed just as irrevocably as Cher's. But while it has been glamorous at times, my life is far from being all premieres and chauffeur-driven limousines.

I quickly realized how bittersweet stardom is after Cher first became famous. We moms just have to take the constant criticism directed at our kids—whom we rarely see, by the way! We try not to be hurt by out-and-out lies about them in the press. I know Cher invites reaction with her flamboyant and sometimes outrageous sense of style, but she's just having fun—playing "dress up" like she did as a child . . . only now she does it as a grown-up. People at times were blatantly rude about her—people who have never even met her.

When we were just starting to gather the stories for this book, I received a letter from one star mom who had a profound impact on me. She wrote to tell me how much it helped to know there was at least one person who realized that her son hadn't just sprung on the scene one day, a full-fledged star, and that the love and nurturing of mom had also played a part in his accomplishments. She was feeling completely left out. I was so touched by that letter. Most star moms would admit that when your child is a star you not only touch the heights, you also plummet to the depths of despair.

Goldie Hawn and Tina Turner may appear to have little in common, but their moms, and *all* moms whose kids have become household names, share a special bond. We have a unique perspective on those the world has singled out to love and admire. For better or for worse, we played key roles in their development —and what bond is closer than the one between a mother and the child to whom she has given birth?

By talking to star moms, we learned why Barbra Streisand is

not bookkeeping in Brooklyn, and why Cyndi Lauper is not just singing in her shower. We encountered all kinds of life-styles, from the poverty and struggle of Dolly Parton's mom, Avie Lee, who raised twelve children in a cold-water shack, to the affluence of Patty Micci, Cybill Shepherd's mom, who hasn't had to work a day in her life and is a stunning Southern lady. Irrespective of background, finances, race, color, or creed, we women who gave birth to stars share so much.

We do have fun and laughs and luxuries, but we also have fears, heartaches, and a lot of worry. We share a sense of loss, too, because one big sting in the tail of stardom is loneliness. In a sense, we give up our kids to the world, to share them with fame and with fans—of course, we don't have much choice! Loneliness is a high price to pay. Yes, there is pride, but there is also pain, and we wouldn't be human if there weren't times when we wished we could turn back the clock and just be ordinary families; there is so much stress and strain.

You find out that a star is always a star, and even at intimate family gatherings, people treat stars differently. They just can't help it. In most families, the brothers and sisters are just as highly thought of, yet people somehow always tiptoe around The Star. When people are given too much power and turned into deities (and that's what stars are), they sometimes start thinking they can do no wrong. If someone comes along who tells them the truth, they sometimes just don't want to hear it.

I learned this almost overnight. In 1965, Cher was eighteen years old, and suddenly a star. My daughter was a complicated, dramatic teenager—a child without a real father—and she was also an international sensation. A role model, a fashion plate—and still my daughter! In 1948, I had won a plum part in John Huston's *The Asphalt Jungle* when one week later, before shooting began, Marilyn Monroe materialized and took the part. There went that dream. Now my own daughter was being handed that elusive prize—stardom. Only I, unlike most star moms, had already had a glimpse of the reality.

Imagine how hard it was for Cher to have a mother who knew; you only have to imagine how any teenager resists advice. Then think about Cher being Cher—independent, outspoken, smart about herself. And here was her mother who loved her, and was sensitive. And yet wary . . . very wary.

Storm clouds? Yes, and stormy weather and lots of teary mother-daughter scenes. The full range of emotions got played out. Months of separation, moments of anxiety and resentment, compassion and confusion—yet great love expressed and unexpressed.

Any mother knows these feelings; a star mother knows them more than most. It's the emotional truth of a star that draws us in as an audience—and it had to come from somewhere. Even if it's an imperfect, painful childhood. My fellow star mothers (in their own individual, quiet ways) will know what I'm talking about. If I had not heard it from Laura Hawn's own lips, I would find it hard to believe that Goldie was an unhappy wallflower when she was a teenager. And who can imagine Pia Zadora suffering from excruciating shyness? In the course of compiling this book, we looked at the childhoods of over 150 stars and found a thread of emotional pain running through the majority of them. Like Cher, many were very dissatisfied with their looks. However much I tried to reassure Cher that she was special in her own way, she wanted the California "golden girl" look that was in vogue at that time. I have often joked with her about where she'd be now had she been that blue-eyed, golden-haired dream. I was considered quite beautiful as a young woman and a "blonde," and that was hard on Cher, though I didn't realize it then (not that I could have done anything about it if I had).

The aim of this book is to let you know what being a star's mother is like—what it means, how it feels, how it changes everything forever. Like life itself, our book touches extremes. The normally reticent Brandy Foster spoke about Jodie's horrible ordeal as the target of presidential assailant John Hinckley's obsession. To our surprise, even Annette Funicello's mom, Virginia, talked a lot about security fears; it seems not even Mouseketeers are safe. Gerry Dreyfuss spoke of Richard's "miracle" car crash; her Oscar-winning son was found with cocaine in his possession, but as it turned out, the horrifying experience probably saved his life.

The book goes from the complete and utter devastation of a

murdered child, to Frances Bergen admitting that her beautiful daughter Candice went through a hurtful "smart-ass period," to the ultimate in froth. It covers reclusive star moms like John Lennon's surrogate mother, Auntie Mimi, and those like Ally Sheedy's literary agent mother, Charlotte Sheedy, who won't let being a star mom overshadow their own identity. In the majority, though, are the moms who relish the celebrity, like Maria Gurdin, who talks constantly about her beloved Natalie Wood. Knowing that Natalie is still loved by millions helps Maria cope with her grief. David Janssen's mom, Berniece, wants to live to see her late son receive a star on Hollywood's Walk of Fame . . . and we are rooting for her.

There's another thing star moms have to get used to: the "This-is-Cher's-mom" routine. When you are no longer introduced as a person but always as an appendage, you know you have a star in the family, and it can sometimes be upsetting. (Especially when people only care about you as "the star's mother.") I *am* Cher's mom, and I am proud to be her mom, but I am also Georgia Holt.

Watching our other children struggle on the edge of the limelight searching for appreciation for their own talents causes many star moms a lot of heartache. My other daughter, Georganne LaPiere, has had her own success as an actress, playing Heather on the TV serial "General Hospital" for over two years; she still has her fan club going from it.

For this book, we gathered very personal reminiscences from star moms, not just in Hollywood but also in far-flung places. In New York, Cyndi Lauper's mom talked about how she felt when Cyndi dyed her hair green and then shaved her head; in her motherly love, Catrine even came to accept the bald look and called it cute. In England, Eva Jagger now wonders why Mick's ear-covering hairdo caused such a universal furor. Looking back, it seems so tame. In Palm Springs, California, Elizabeth Taylor's spirited ninety-year-old mom, Sara, pedals around the grounds of her home on a three-wheeled bicycle. Since Sara is still as pretty as a picture, it's not hard to see where Elizabeth gets her lasting beauty. And in New York, George Hamilton's mom, Anne—such a character, and definitely the source of George's humor—reveals why she wants to be buried topless.

From extensive research and more than fifty interviews with star moms, stars themselves, and psychological experts, one thing became crystal clear: above all else, the star mothers are a unique and special group of ladies. They are flamboyant and funny—and adventurous. Each of them is colorful and full of life in their own way. In fact, when you look at them you can see their "star child."

I hope you enjoy and appreciate them as much as we do. They are the Peter Pan in all of us—longing to fly, and remaining forever young.

Most sincerely,
Georgia Holt

1 The Thrill of It All?

The next best thing to firsthand fame must surely be stardom by proxy? Stardom confers status not only upon stars, but upon an entire tapering chain of those in its proximity. Its power is such that even very tenuous links bring a little buzz of attention— "Guess who sat at the next table at Chasen's last night? George Burns!" So, imagine the thrill for moms who, courtesy of their offspring, are one tiny step from center stage. Who can blame those who relish every moment, basking in the spotlight, warming themselves in the glow of reflected glory?

Admiring the fur-collared coat of a total stranger in a Manhattan hotel lobby, George Hamilton's mom cannot resist proffering not only her favorable fashion judgment but also her star credentials (both entirely unsolicited) to a startled—but rapidly charmed—couple. Anne's girlish glee, however, remains delightfully infectious . . . in the "Aren't I lucky? Isn't this fun?" vein.

Some star moms have but one topic of conversation: their star child. And mothers whose identities are entirely entwined with those of their celebrity children are not always viewed with admiration. Yet it would be churlish not to smile at an anecdote Milton Berle wrote in his autobiography about his mom, Sandra, to whom he spoke daily. Berle once paged her at New York's Essex House, and this, in his words, is how she responded from the very public hotel lobby: "I heard the lobby phone pick up. Mama said, 'Hello?' I said hello back, and I heard Mama say in a loud voice so that the whole lobby could hear, 'Is this my son, Milton Berle?' "

By contrast, Debbie Reynolds' mom, Maxene, gives a most pragmatic reason for having kept quiet about her famous daughter for years at a stretch. "If the doctors or anybody find it out, the prices double, and I'd just as soon be known for myself." She was a volunteer at the Palm Springs, California, Desert Hospital for five years before the connection was discovered. "They said, 'Why didn't you tell us?' I said, 'Why should I? You've got kids. I don't know your daughter's name.' So it's no big deal; so I had a kid who's dumb enough to get into the movies!"

Laura Hawn did not have fans making pilgrimages to her home as did Eva Jagger and John Lennon's Aunt Mimi; Goldie Hawn's fame was not of the clothes-shredding variety experienced by rock stars. Even so, finding herself the mother of "the dumbest, dizziest blonde" was not entirely thrilling for Laura, who bristled when people asked, "Is she *really* that dumb?" Laura's retort was, "She had to be pretty smart to be that dumb!" Mrs. Hawn was equally disappointed with "Laugh-In" as a showcase for Goldie's talents, complaining, "Every time I thought she was going to dance, she would fall in the hole."

For Goldie, the transition from unknown to star was not without trauma. "Goldie had a little trouble getting used to all the fame overnight," admits Laura, who viewed the changes with utter amazement. "It was unreal. One day you walked into a supermarket—the next day it was impossible." As Goldie, or rather the image of "Goldie," became larger than life, the real Goldie started to suffer nonspecific anxiety attacks; her weight dipped to ninety-six pounds and she felt, rather than acted, dizzy in public places.

"Goldie saw a psychiatrist for a long time," her mother admits. "Longer than I felt was necessary. She would call me crying, saying, 'I don't want to be a star! I don't want to be a star!' It was the lack of privacy. She wasn't able to do anything without having people . . . you would have to be around it to see what they do to you."

Goldie found this new role in life confusing—her new power, her new friends, her new work situations. "I was very, very frightened. I couldn't go into a restaurant without throwing up," she told Fred Robbins of *McCall's* magazine. The situation was aggravated by the sudden nature of her fame, but Goldie was not the only one with problems.

"I had trouble with people thinking I wasn't quite human," says her mother, with a wry smile. Initial introductions were fine apparently, then she would suddenly be aware of a shift in gears, a change in the attitudes of her new acquaintances. She knew immediately that they had just been apprised of the fact she was Goldie's mother. "Then I would get hostile. I guess—I hope!—that is normal."

All too aware of the strain on Goldie, Laura rose to shield her from being harassed, clucking and flapping like the proverbial mother hen. "We are all protective of our children and I got very ugly. She couldn't afford to—but I could," Laura says defiantly, relating the story of one Christmas morning when they had gone out for breakfast in the obviously mistaken belief that theirs would be the only family in America to venture away from hearth and home. No sooner was their breakfast served than a woman approached the table to speak to Goldie. Goldie put down her knife and fork and listened politely while the woman chattered on endlessly, either oblivious to or uncaring about the fact that she was intruding. Finally, aware that Goldie's food was considerably chillier than the Christmas clime, Laura snapped, "Would you *kindly* let her eat her breakfast!" Laura chuckles, remembering Goldie's horrified reaction. "She said, 'Mother! How could you do that?' I just said, 'Very easy!'"

Goldie is now even more recognizable in all corners of the globe, yet nothing since has matched "Laugh-In"'s quirky cult status. To Laura's immense relief, in California her daughter is now rarely approached in the street or restaurants.

"I tried never to make my life change," Laura says. "It is her life, not mine, and I have tried very, very hard to keep it very separate, I really have—and I think I have done pretty well. I don't know how much money Goldie has and I don't care. I don't make that my business. I would care if she had *no* money. And I'm no longer involved in her business, choosing films or anything, it's just not something we even talk about anymore.

"We did in the beginning. That is when it was very exciting for me. Her climb. It didn't take very long. Things happened very,

very fast. My phone would ring at two or three in the morning—she never realized there is a three-hour difference between L.A. and Washington—and she would say, 'Oh, Mother, I think they like me!' It was so exciting."

Eva Jagger, in the throes of Rolling Stones mania, actively restrained herself from talking about Mick. "It was just a feeling you got," she explains. "I suppose you didn't want to feel bigheaded, so you went in the opposite direction. You didn't want people to think you were puffed up."

At the height of the sixties madness, even Mick's mom was inundated with personalized fan letters—too many to make individual replies practicable. She still receives autograph requests, but she does not see enough of Mick herself and hates pestering him for autographs when she does.

Walking down the street behind Mick, seeing the double takes, hearing the excited hisses—"Was that Mick Jagger? Was it?"—Eva admits, "I'm dying to say, 'Yes, that was Mick Jagger! Did you see him?' " It astounds her when she gives her name in stores and the response is not, "Any relation to Mick Jagger?" but merely an abbreviated, "Any relation?" If she is feeling naughty, she cannot resist the retort: "Yes, I'm his grandmother." Occasionally, she resorts to false names: "I think, 'Oh, I can't be bothered.' " It's not that she objects to the connection, but rather that when she *does* admit to being Mick's mom, she is not always believed.

"I think there is a certain amount of reflected glory," she agrees. "I suppose one should be pleased." Yet she cannot suppress a little mirth at the I've-touched-Mick-Jagger's-mother syndrome. A friend said her daughter would be excited and proud to hear she had occupied the same car seat in which Mick Jagger had deposited his famous frame. To Eva, that was hilarious. He is just Mick, after all, her own flesh and blood.

The mom who once was less envied than pitied ("Imagine having one of those long-haired louts in the family?" parents cried) concedes that it was strange reconciling herself to the fact that her son was an idol to millions. "He's still your son. He's still your little kid. You brought him up. I don't grasp it. It isn't that I'm not proud of him; I think it's marvelous." She suspects the more famous the family member, the greater the temptation to play it down.

"Meeting celebrities doesn't alter your life"—that is Eva's philosophy. "I've never been overawed by people. It doesn't mean I don't admire them for what they do—or what they are. It's just I don't believe in treating people like gods. This is what people think, I suppose, on the outside, about Mick—he's so different. He's no different as a person from anybody else. He might be to the outside world—but he's just a friendly, homey person."

The same might be said of Eva and Joe Jagger, who, when they had an extension built onto their three-bedroom home on the southern coast of England, were treated to the architect's open amazement that they were so down-to-earth. Eva's reaction: "Well, how do you expect us to act? He *could* have said, 'You're very ordinary.' That's probably what he meant," she adds wryly.

Mick Jagger and Jerry Hall's visits to his folks' home turf are conducted with the minimum of fuss. They can consume fondue at a Swiss restaurant or drinks at a small local pub and their privacy will be respected with typical British reserve, despite the fact that the most famous Rolling Stone is at their table. They are just another family out together, Eva says, although Mick complies politely with odd autograph requests. "I've never known him to say, 'Oh, go away.' "

The only time his fame could truly be called intrusive is when the family is engrossed in a cricket match at Lords ground in London. "It is a bit of a nuisance when people come up when you are trying to enjoy something," Eva concedes. But she and Joe Jagger (who is chairman of the local Residents' Association) find it all rather fun. "We lead a very ordinary life—highlighted, I must admit."

When Anna Cosby visits the West Coast it is generally with her sister-in-law, Clara, for some serious, around-the-clock bridge action. But in 1987, while vacationing at son Bill Cosby's magnificent Pacific Palisades home, she threw a luncheon party to meet some of the other star moms. It was staggeringly elegant by California's informal standards, and very festive, from the linen and lace placemats to the exquisite china and of course the food itself, prepared by Mr. Cosby's longtime personal chef and served by the chef's daughter, attired in starched cap and apron. Later, pictures were taken in Bill's English flower garden to commemorate the occasion.

Anna's guests were Georgia Holt; Maria Gurdin; John's mom, Dorothy Ritter; Ron's mom, Jean Howard; Barbra Streisand's mom, Diana Kind; Tina Turner's mom, Zelma Bullock; Diahann Carroll's mom, Mabel Johnson; Billy Dee's mom, Loretta Williams; Tom's mom, Martha Selleck, Anna's sister-in-law, Clara; and Phyllis Quinn. Son Bob Cosby, who arrived after luncheon to find his mother seated at the head of the table, says the dozen women present seemed more like forty women as he suddenly felt as if he were three years old again and was expected to be on his best behavior.

"I had to stand there as they introduced themselves to me—and, of course, everyone wanting to be famous and glamorous and popular. And every time I looked up to my mother, she was acting natural, like there was nothing to it. I just looked at her and said to myself, 'Well, that's mom!' "

According to Bob, Anna Cosby is the only person in a Bill Cosby audience who does not laugh at Bill's routine. The first time he noticed this phenomenon was when he glanced at her during a Las Vegas show. He promptly stopped laughing too, thinking something must be amiss. Not so. It is just that Anna studies Bill so intently, scrutinizing what Bob calls "all the little mother things. Bill is either losing too much weight or he is not getting enough sleep. Maybe sometimes she gets flashbacks: this is something she raised from when he was in diapers."

Bill's success has hardly changed Anna, who says, "I take it in my stride. People come up and say, 'Oooh, you're a celebrity.' I don't want to be that! I just want to be me. I say, 'Just consider me Anna.' " She points earthward and says firmly, "I want to be down there, I don't want to be up there."

Sometimes mom becomes an essential cog in the wheel that perpetuates stardom and takes an active part in the ramifications of fame. Raquel Welch's mother answers Raquel's mail, Philip Michael Thomas's mom runs the "Miami Vice" star's fan club, Dolly Parton's sister Cassie heads hers. R. J. Wagner keeps it in the family; Natalie Wood's mom helps take care of his mail and still sends pictures of Natalie to fans from England, Italy, Israel, and all points of the globe. The spirit of Natalie lives on through her mother, whose home is like a shrine to her late daughter, with Natalie's presence strikingly in evidence amidst the multitudinous family photographs, portraits, and memorabilia.

Martha Selleck is realistic about the effect of Tom's fame on her life. It has not escaped her notice that people sometimes make a beeline to talk to her. "I sometimes think, 'Am I getting this attention because I am Martha Selleck, or is it because I am Tom's mother?' I suppose it would be ridiculous if you didn't stop and think, 'It's got to be that!' "

There *are* shrinking violets in the fame-by-association game, but they are not in evidence among the collection of Hollywood star moms (Tom Selleck's, Natalie Wood's, and John Ritter's among them) who are members of the Motion Picture Mothers group and Screen Smart Set.

Sheer flamboyance and much camera-ready, practiced glamour is the order of the day for a meeting of the most celebrated bunch of over-fifties in town. There is no eastern sobriety at their luncheon and fashion show. Rather, it is as if a West Coast artist had run amok with a brush and paint palette across all their primary-color frills and flounces. Under the star moms' spell, the famed Beverly Hills restaurant Jimmy's metamorphoses into a perfumed oasis of California chic. The air is light, frothy, and festive, alive with tinkling laughter.

Theirs is a universe quite unlike any other. They frolic and splash in a pond where it does not matter who you are, only whose *mom* you are. And because the pond is populated by others of their ilk, they eliminate the risk of appearing self-centered (via their star) when they chatter about their super successful kids.

Martha Selleck admits that that is the appeal the moms' groups hold for her: "You have so much in common that you can sit and talk about your son—or their son or daughter—as much as you want and not feel like you might be intruding or boring anyone." In fact, there is less conversational focus on whose kid is doing what than on issues like the remarkably gargantuan appetites of Tippi Hedren's eighty-five big cats, with food bills of two thousand dollars a week plus, and something of a contrast to the aesthetically pleasing nouvelle nosh being consumed for luncheon.

There is much milling and mingling. Dorothy Ritter, a froth of pink with silvery-platinum hair. Martha Selleck, in a Diane Freis floral number (not new, she confides apologetically, but it can be rolled into a tiny ball and revived in seconds). Even the darkly intense Maria Gurdin is sporting florals. Mabel Johnson, Diahann Carroll's statuesque mom, dignity personified, adds a rare dash of neutral beige Ultrasuede. Everyone stops by to pay respect to Greer Garson and philanthropist Sybil Brand, after whom Los Angeles's women's prison was named.

The moms appreciatively applaud a parade of designer confections; the catwalk twirls expertly executed by minuscule-waisted Janet Leigh, in emerald green (a star herself, and star mom to Jamie Lee Curtis); coolly regal Frances Bergen (Candice's mom) in a rose pink Chanel suit; Jean Peters (Howard Hughes's ex) in a Bob Mackie original; and perky Tippi Hedren (daughter Melanie Griffith has made Hitchcock's protégée a star mom), swathed in animal print—what else?

Discretion is not the better part of these ladies' valor. They are bon vivants, every one. They positively thrive on the surrounding social whirl, but they also work very hard to raise funds for the Motion Picture and TV Country House and Hospital in Woodland Hills, California. Were it not for this broader spectrum, they might seem unforgivably frivolous. As it is, their charitable activities allow for a little levity, star moms—style. This is Hollywood, after all.

Images flash across the landscape of memory, of a host of monthly meetings attended by dozens of mothers of stars past and present. Like MPM's seventeenth anniversary celebration in 1956, marked by a jaunty Western costume dance at the Hollywood Roosevelt Hotel, with, to name but a few, the moms of Joan Crawford, Betty Hutton, and Gary Cooper in attendance. At a 1971 luncheon at the Beverly Hills Hotel's Crystal Room, singer Vivian Duncan put across the message, "I'm old enough for Medicare, but not too old for men to care." Gatherings resound with that kind of humor.

Olive Abbott, sister of the late Bud Abbott, is MPM's historian and the last living member of the original one hundred MPMs, whose lineup included the mothers of Tyrone Power, Judy Garland, Joan Crawford, and Fred MacMurray. Olive's mother rode circus elephants, son Norman is a director, and daughter Betty is a respected script supervisor. Olive will turn ninety-three on MPM's fiftieth birthday in 1989. On her ninetieth birthday, she received a letter from Ronald Reagan (whose mom was a member) on White House stationery. It included this message: "It is a real treat for me to share this happy occasion with a friend of Mother's. She always spoke very fondly of you and your association in the MPM Club." Framed, the letter goes nicely with the plaque Olive received for performing in front of Queen Victoria and King Edward with Barnum & Bailey.

Motion Picture Mothers was originally formed in 1939 to unite women with common interests who, by virtue of their children's Hollywood careers, found themselves adrift in a new town. Some suffered financial hardship, and at Christmas, the founding members had baskets of food delivered anonymously to the doors of hungry actors and their families. Fifty years on, that spirit of sharing is still served.

The motto of the Motion Picture and TV Fund is "We Take Care of Our Own," and the moms do. A tremendous support system kicks in when one of their members is ill. Individual friendships blossom and there are birthday parties, get-togethers for the taping of their star kids' shows, bridge parties, you name it.

At current lively lunches, participants include Billy Dee Williams' mom, Loretta; Natalie Wood's mom, Maria Gurdin; Anson Williams' mom, Riki Heimlick; Jack Haley Jr.'s mom, Flo Haley; Lisa Hartman's mom, Jonni; Dennis Dugan's mom, Marion; Mariette Hartley's mom, Polly; Deborah Raffin's mom, Trudy Marshall; Diahann Carroll's mom, Mabel Johnson; Gena Rowlands' mom, Mary Allen Rowlands; David Cassidy's mom, Evelyn Ward; and Pat Van Patten, mother of Nels, Jimmy, and Vince.

Some members, like Martha Selleck, Dorothy Ritter, and Berniece Janssen, need no further introduction than their distinctive last names. June Haver MacMurray's mom, Maria Haver, remains perennially glamorous in her wheelchair, her hair still jet black. (Although he is not an official member, the others delight in Maria's constant companion, the tiny poodle she keeps in her purse.)

Sorely missed are past members like Jim Nabors' late mom, Mavis. In the early, golden days of MPM, eminences included the mothers of major movie stars like Dorothy Lamour (Carmen Castleberry); Lucille Ball (DeDe Ball); Bing Crosby (Catherine Crosby); Robert Cummings (Elizabeth Cummings); Maureen O'Hara (Rita Fitzsimmons); Mitzi Gaynor (Pauline Gerber); Piper Laurie (Charlotte Jacobs); Joan Crawford (Annie LeSueur, a.k.a. Anna Cassin); Jane Withers (Ruth Boonshaft); Tyrone Power (Patia Power); Cesar Romero (Maria Romero); and Freddy Bartholomew (Millicent Bartholomew). And lest we forget, even Ronald Reagan's mother, Nell, was a fully paid-up member.

Jack Lemmon's mom, Millie, first escorted George Hamilton's mom, Anne, to a meeting over twenty years ago. The two became pals when both lived in Boston, where Millie's husband was in the donut-manufacturing business. Anne was fascinated by moms like Gary Cooper's mother, Alice (a founding member), whom she describes as "a western *grande dame,* absolutely the most divine woman, very tall and very dignified." (Alice Cooper was uniformed and involved in the war effort when she first joined MPM; Gary's father often attended luncheons too, enjoying himself immensely amongst the ladies.) Mickey Rooney's mom, Nell Pankey, was, according to Anne, a female replica of Mickey. (Pankey was given to introducing herself as "the mother of the Alimony Kid" at the expense of her son's notorious marital track record.) Also present was Tony Curtis's mom, Helen Schwartz, eye-catching in a green hat with a red flower. "She was so cute, a little dark-haired thing, adorable," says Anne.

Lillian McEdward, Blake Edwards' mom and Julie Andrews' mother-in-law, remembers Helen Schwartz too. She recalls all too vividly the time Tony Curtis bought his mother her first car and Helen excitedly rounded up some of the mothers to accompany her on a trip to Palm Springs; to Lillian's unmitigated horror, it rapidly became clear that Helen had absolutely no previous experience in passing other cars on a highway. Lillian, for one, quickly made alternative arrangements for the return journey.

It is Alma Day, Doris Day's late mother, who died in 1977, whom Phyllis Quinn remembers most fondly. "Alma was a real character, just kicked up her heels and had a good time. She loved to do things that would get in Doris's hair. She loved to be naughty, occasionally uttering an off-color word or two with the admonition—and a twinkle in her eye—'Now don't tell Doris!' "

Phyllis has had twenty-five years of involvement with star moms through Motion Picture Mothers and Screen Smart Set. She became involved when her two sons, Teddy and Bob, and two daughters, Diane and Debby, were successful child actors and she was managing their busy careers. (Teddy played the sons of Doris Day in *The Ballad of Josie,* Lana Turner in *Madame X,* and Orson Welles in *Necromancy,* besides appearing in countless TV shows like "Bonanza," "Bewitched," and "Dr. Kildare.")

Alma did not consider herself a stage-motherish presence in Doris's life. She told a reporter, "I didn't butt into anything. If she wanted to work in a dime store that was okay with me. I'm not the bossy type." Alma was chauffeured to a 1975 party only because "Doris won't let me drive at night. In the day I fly all over." Quite simply, many of her friends remember Alma in this vein: "She could be such a devil." Olive likes to remember Alma from the good old days when you could "give Alma two champagnes and she'd get up and do the shuffle!"

Today's Hollywood weaves no less incestuous and tangled a web than that of the golden era, and there are sometimes intriguing undercurrents to these mothers' meetings. Witness Elena Bairo (Jon Peters' mother) talking animatedly to Margot Warren (mother of Jon's ex-wife, Lesley-Anne Warren) and Diana Kind (mother of Jon's ex-lover, Barbra Streisand, who followed Lesley-Anne amidst a blaze of headlines). There must have been far touchier moments for this triangle, but as Margot Warren explains it, "We share a wonderful grandson, Chris."

In 1968, Lillian McEdward and Jill St. John's mother, Betty Oppenheim, branched out from MPM to form the Screen Smart Set, with an eye to attracting a younger, broader-reaching group from the film and TV industries. (Phyllis Quinn has spent six of the past twelve years as president of Screen Smart Set.) Lillian and Betty reactivated the thrift shop idea first started by Mary Pickford in the 1930s and founded the Cinema Glamour Shop.

The shop, which brings in more than a quarter of a million dollars a year, is frequently staffed by a star mom doing her bit for the cause—members like Ted Wass's mom, Gail; Deborah Raffin's mom, Trudy Marshall; Lesley-Anne Warren's mom, Margot; or Anson Williams' mom, Riki Heimlick. The racks include donated clothing from the likes of Julie Andrews, Barbara Stanwyck, Kenny Rogers, Bob Newhart, Frances and Candy Bergen, Cyd Charisse, Don Rickles, Elizabeth Taylor, and Tony Bennett. Robert and Dorothy Mitchum and Rhonda Fleming (also a past president of Screen Smart Set) are famous for their generosity. The money raised is bolstered by the annual October auction held at the Beverly Wilshire hotel when prize items are modeled by celebrities and their moms. Not only fashions go on the block, but also jewelry and antiques—and when Mary Pickford died, Phyllis Quinn and Lillian McEdward were invited to visit her Pickfair estate along with Mary's niece (and adopted daughter), Gwynne Pickford Ornstein, to pack up treasures like a silver tea service which Mary had left to the fund.

Lillian McEdward has kept up her passionate, energetic involvement with SSS and MPM, and she remains SSS's mainstay despite a slight stroke in 1987. She has staged lavish fashion shows and (with Phyllis Quinn) compiled *A Cookbook of the Stars* for MPM comprising recipes from members' children; in 1984, she was honored with a "Lillian McEdward Day" in Los Angeles and she received messages from President and Nancy Reagan.

No one was more surprised than Golden Girls' Betty White when her mother Tess and Lucille Ball's mother DeDe joined the mothers' groups. Tess and DeDe's friendship had been cemented over the years, yet, says Betty, "They were not social animals at all. But everybody kept leaning on them, so finally DeDe said, 'All right, we will join, but no work!' Mom said, 'Do you really want to?' DeDe, who was a very strong lady herself, said 'Yup!', so they went in. Well! My nonjoining mother, she was very popular. The next thing I know, she is treasurer. The next thing I know, she is turning down being president.

"She worked like a beaver for them; she was working her tail off. But what she loved about the silly Motion Picture Mothers —they had such a sense of fun. They were all a little off-the-wall. There was a little never-growing-up about it that made it such fun. And dignity was not their longest suit—which was great."

Betty White did not once hear Tess White gloat about her stardom-by-association. "Oh, dear God, save me from that!" Tess loved to be included, "but a star she was not. Thank God I did not have that problem." Betty says it took the combined strength of her and Mike Douglas to corral her mother into appearing on his show: "I practically got a noose around her neck." Tess also had to be coerced into appearing on "Password" when Betty's late husband, Allen Ludden, was the TV show's host. "Mom wound up creaming all of us. And I was never so thrilled in all my life. We were competitive. I was really trying, working like a thief, but she won. And I—reluctantly—was very proud of her."

In White's opinion, Tess trod the happy middle ground. She was neither militant nor defensive about being her own person, and while she took enormous pride and joy in Betty's success, she had her own life too. Realistically, Betty is sure her name somehow cropped up in conversation, but she cannot imagine Tess ever blatantly broadcasting the fact that she was Betty White's mother. Betty feels sure that when Tess dropped her name, it was more from pride than an attempt to seek privileges. Cher's mom, Georgia Holt, frankly admits to occasionally dropping the name of the star in her family: "If I want to get my vacuum cleaner repaired in a hurry, I might! It always seems to do the trick," she says with a smile.

2 Star Moms: The Dynamics of Inspiration

We were curious: where does a star come from? Why does the lightning stike? What forces synthesize to propel forth the chosen few from the anonymous mainstream? Most particularly, what is Mom's role in all this? Should she receive the credit? And if so, how much?

For look behind many a superstar, and the first thing you find is a mother—not as redundant an observation as it might at first sound, since she is very often not just a mother, but a MOTHER, whose mark of influence is stamped on her offspring as indelibly as if she had branded it there with a sizzling iron. Which does not mean to say that she is perfection personified.

Mothers work their magic in mysterious ways. Their power seems somehow to transcend their individual presence, character, or actions. Good or bad, weak or strong, faultless or fallible, cuddly or awe-inspiring—without exception, in their roles as Mother they are greater than the sum of their human parts. The very weight of their influence can be terrifying in its dimensions.

Raid the childhood closets of stars and the skeletons come tumbling out—there is a prevalence of heartache in their early lives. Absent parents, broken homes, poverty, death, disruption crop up again and again. Sources as notable as Katharine Hepburn and Bette Davis consider pain essential in the formation of great actors, the grain of sand with which to irritate the oyster into producing its pearl. Yet it would be a gross oversimplification and false generalization to assert that such pain was an indispensable ingredient, a prerequisite for stardom.

34

Stars of Bob Dylan's magnitude—Mick Jagger, Tom Selleck, Goldie Hawn, and Jon Voight among them—cleave that theory with a fracture a mile wide. Their stable childhoods and those of others like them accounted for one quarter of the more than one hundred and fifty stars whose backgrounds we scrutinized, swiftly eroding the anticipated landslide majority for the pain theory.

These superstars emerged from childhoods with no immediately visible tension—no handicaps to overcome, no overwhelming odds against which to battle, no overt suffering to endure— no grains of angst to irritate the oyster into producing its pearl. And yet the pearls exist.

Clearly, there is a diametric polarity between the happy, family origins of Tom Selleck and the tumultuous background of Steve McQueen. Like Richard Pryor, Tina Turner, and Cher, McQueen entered show business after graduating difficult life-experience classes, his report cards ticked in subjects like parental divorce, financial hardship, residential uncertainty, parental alcoholism, and combinations thereof.

The tides of Steve McQueen's love-hate feelings for his mother, Julian, would haunt him always. Although Julian was a chronic alcoholic, an unreliable, intermittent presence in his life, and a far cry from the storybook ideal, Julian positively shone as a model of maternal responsibility when held up for comparison with Steve's father, Terrence William McQueen, who left her almost immediately after Steve's birth in Beech Grove, Indiana, on March 24, 1930.

Julian was of that all-too-common variety—a mother before her time. She was young, beautiful, and ill equipped to cope with the all-too-real responsibility of another human being. For want of a better plan, she farmed her young son out to a kindly although undemonstrative great-grand-uncle, Claude Thompson. She made a valiant attempt to reclaim Steve at one point, to merge his growing life and its demands into her wildly unstructured one, taking him home to Indianapolis with her, but was soon forced to admit she could not cope.

To concede her failure to Uncle Claude, who stalwartly took Steve back for a few more years, was doubtless a humiliating experience for Julian. Yet its repercussions were no real hardship for her son, as Uncle Claude represented the sole stable figure in young Steve's life and a deep, if rarely expressed, fondness grew between them. It was away from Uncle Claude that Steve's troubles multiplied.

When he was with Julian he suffered abuse, sometimes physical, at the hands of the men with whom she became involved, and notably the man she married when he was twelve. Steve called him Berri, defying intimacy by unconvincingly claiming to have forgotten his stepfather's first name.

When Berri moved in, Julian had to take action to protect Steve from his stepfather and to curb her son's accelerating delinquency. Sadly for Steve, she was unwilling to face the humiliation of returning him yet again to his Uncle Claude. Instead, in a devastating move, she chose to send him to a home for wayward boys, the California Junior Boys' Republic in Chino. Not unnaturally, Steve perceived this as yet another rejection, another betrayal by Julian, who could not even manage to write him regular letters or to have him home for vacations. Steve would be left at school for the duration of the holidays, often the sole forgotten son. And so the desire in him grew for attention and fame, along with a desperate need to compensate for being ignored, first by his father and then by his mother.

The crucial development of self-esteem is badly handicapped if a child does not receive enough of what psychiatrists now call mirroring. Mirroring is the message reflected back to children about themselves via the smiles of pleasure and acceptance they see in the faces of their parents and other key figures, the reinforcement that assures them "You are okay, you're valuable, you're a good person, I'm proud of you, I enjoy being around you." If, as psychiatrists believe, very early experiences of mirroring are internalized, positive messages become an intrinsic part of the child's psychological make-up, reducing his need to seek that kind of input from the outside world. Tumultuous childhoods like Steve's, on the other hand, are notoriously short on such messages. If a child is abused, neglected, deprived, abandoned, or rejected by a parent, they grow into an adult who is in constant pursuit of a mirror to provide that missing "You are okay" message.

Steve McQueen's ex-wife Neile, who met Julian in 1956 when she first knew Steve and all three were living in New York, remembers the scars that the isolation and feeling of abandonment of those school vacations had left on her husband: "There he would wander the grounds alone, barely able to contain the pain that tore his heart."

"Without question, fame—or notoriety, for that matter—could be a mechanism by which those who achieve it strive to be accepted in a way they were not in their early lives. It is an attempt to build the incomplete self-esteem," says Dr. R. Barkley Clark, Assistant Clinical Professor of Psychiatry at the University of Colorado Health Sciences Center, and Psychiatric Consultant to the Denver Public Schools. "The void with which they are left, the sense of emptiness inside them, is temporarily hidden by fame. If people view you with awe and admiration, by default you feel better about yourself, more whole or more complete. The stereotypic mirror might be this famous position in life where everyone looks at you with a sense of awe."

(The danger, as Dr. Clark and his fellow psychiatrists are quick to point out, lies in the almost inevitable, eventual fall: the recession of the fame, the withdrawal of the admiration and the adulation. It can be a very big fall indeed for someone who has a dearth of internal resources on which to fall back. To survive, a star must possess the internal strength to keep the "You are okay" message in place once fame's artificial level recedes. Without that strength, the fallen famous are highly vulnerable to depression and plummeting feelings of self-worth.)

Neile McQueen took a considerably more charitable view of Steve's mother's shortcomings than did her husband, and she often asked him what else, rationally, he thought Julian might have done. "I said, 'She was nineteen years old at the time she had you, it was the Depression. She didn't know a thing! She had no skills of any kind, she had to dump you someplace!' Julian had the worst taste in men, and of course, that had a terrible effect on Steve. She did the best she could in that situation, too. When she put him in reform school, it was actually to get him away from the stepfather."

The good intention was lost on Steve. He was never able to

surmount his enormous anger toward Julian, nor quiet his rage at having been abandoned. At the same time—the power of Mom —Julian was never far from his mind. The effects of his disrupted childhood were glaringly apparent to Neile when she met Steve.

"He was just trying to get himself out of the gutter, so to speak. Julian was living in the Village too, and she would be in the bar —at the time, she was an alcoholic—he would be trying to get a little respect among his peers, and there she'd be, drunk. And of course, as a child, it was the embarrassment and the horror of it all."

Steve was torn emotionally between his disappointment and disgust and his intrinsic humanitarian sense that his mother needed his help. He did what little he could for her, but his deeply conflicting emotions about Julian would not be resolved while she was alive.

Neile recollects a period when Steve, suddenly grabbed by an urge to find his father, would instigate pilgrimages to find him. One, made in 1959 within months of the birth of their daughter, led them to nearby Silverlake in Los Angeles. Their search had been hampered by the fact that Julian did not like the name Terry and had taken to calling Steve's father Bill (his middle name was William), a vital nugget of information which she had omitted to pass on, and they arrived too late. Terry McQueen had suffered a fatal heart attack three months earlier.

Taller than Steve, his father had spent time in the Marine Corps and later in life worked for the Flying Tigers Cargo Company— a truth that would be embroidered upon by a son desperate for a heroic figure in his life. McQueen Sr. had been an avid watcher of the "Wanted . . . Dead or Alive" TV show and wondered if its star might be his son. Perhaps it was as well they were fated not to meet, for although Steve searched for his father, he hated the man who had deserted him perhaps more than he hated his mother.

Once, Julian tearfully asked Neile if she thought Steve had forgiven her. Recognizing her suffering, Neile swallowed hard and assured Julian that he had. However, there was no doubt in Neile's mind as to the truth of the matter: Steve would never forgive Julian, although he could not seem to cut their tie entirely.

Near the end of her life, Julian moved to San Francisco, where Neile would visit her periodically with Julian's grandchildren, Chad and Terry. She was a wonderful seamstress and made dresses for Neile and Terry. Steve was not entirely happy about these visits, but Neile's heart went out to his mother. She chose to tread the fine line and see Julian, but not often enough to anger Steve.

In 1965 Julian suffered a cerebral brain hemorrhage. Within twenty-four hours of being admitted to the hospital, she lapsed into a coma and died. It fell to Neile to arrange her funeral.

"It was the first time I had ever seen Steve unable to cope. Julian's death produced heart-wrenching sobs and left him guilt-stricken and bereft. He had hoped she would recover, if only to ask for her forgiveness for the unhappiness he had caused her."

Neile, to whom McQueen was married for more than fifteen years, was not exempt from the legacy of Steve's relationship with his mother. Eventually, she came to realize that his need for her transcended his love for her. He was desperately dependent upon his family (his first real family) for his happiness and security, but his rampant infidelity led to their divorce in 1972.

The preponderance of stars like Steve McQueen with tumult (albeit varying degrees of tumult) in their childhoods presents a confounding night-and-day contrast when viewed up against those of the Jagger contingent's ilk. Jagger & Co. burst forth from what is by comparison the torpid, bland, stagnant "normality" of middle-class family units. Yet burst forth they did, with all their creative juices intact and flowing freely.

Unlike stars who took a walk on the wild side by virtue of their birthright and childhood environment, stars like Jagger and Dylan sought it out later—on the world stage. Their careers were ignited by some mysterious ingredient found within the carpeted rooms of respectable suburbia. Stability itself—such anathema to hormone-ravaged teenagers—can prove just as effective a propellant, then, firing fantasy lives and a longing for other worlds. There is no slick, packaged answer to what makes stardom strike, any more than there is a hard and fast definition of the mother who acts as a catalyst. There is, however, a clean line of demarcation separating stars who were born great, or made darned sure they became great, from those whose "greatness" was merely thrust upon them almost as if by accident, or as the result of a transient quirk of that notoriously fickle item, public appetite.

Certainly the stardom of those plucked from obscurity by the sheer grace of their good looks—if the face fits, put it on a magazine cover—is cut from vastly different cloth than that which fashioned Cher or Faye Dunaway or Dustin Hoffman. It simply does not come from the same place as stardom which has been desperately strived for, sought out as urgently as if it were the oxygen supply itself. It was not any old success, nor even wealth, which superstars like Dustin Hoffman and Barbra Streisand chased—rather they seemed driven to meet that need in themselves to be loved by the world. They sought fame specifically. Celebrity, stardom, applause on the grandest scale.

Sylvester Stallone likened the burning need for expression and acceptance thus when talking to Nancy Collins of *Rolling Stone:* "It's like walking around with a present that no one wants. That's the way I felt as a child. A lot of actors felt that way, I think, and now, luckily, there's an outlet for it."

What the Steve McQueens and Tom Sellecks, from their vastly divergent backgrounds, do share is that they had the enduring drive to make it to the top. Tom could have opted for his father's real estate business, where the rewards were not inconsiderable and were more easily won, but he would not give up. As his mother, Martha, chides all who think he was some kind of overnight wonder with "Magnum, P.I.": "Remember, it took him thirteen years to be an overnight success with 'Magnum'! There was a struggle, and he did have thirteen years of doing pilots and commercials."

Martha Selleck is enormously proud of his star on Hollywood Boulevard's tourist attraction, the Walk of Fame, but what is less well-known is that Tom has equal reason to be proud of Mom: she was honored in 1985 as California Mother of the Year. A gentle, sunny woman, Martha was always Tom's unflinching supporter, even managing to conjure up a sincere smile when emerging from one of his early, skeleton-in-the-closet films like *Daughters of Satan*. "To see her come out with a big smile and say, 'You were great!'—that's where I got my acting ability," Tom says with a grin.

Martha and her husband, Bob Selleck, raised Tom and his brother Bob Jr., and then Dan and sister Marty (theirs is a two-tier family with eight years between tiers), in the San Fernando Valley, within sniffing distance of the star-making machine. When the boys were small and the Sellecks, recently arrived from Michigan and building a new life, were still a one-car family, Martha frequently took them on the bus through the Cahuenga Pass to meet their father when he finished work at Coldwell Banker Real Estate. Funnily enough, Tom's star would later be positioned very close to that office on Hollywood Boulevard.

In fact, Martha and Bob sometimes took Tom and Bob Jr. (who are just nineteen months apart in age) to Graumann's when they were kids, and vividly remember their delighted faces when they saw John Wayne's footprints, Roy Rogers'—and Trigger's. None of the Sellecks envisioned Tom one day joining those he so idolized as a youngster, but now the tables are turned, and thousands of Tom's own fans line the street to see his star, captured in the cement for posterity.

"That's what makes it so unbelievable but exciting," Martha exclaimed on Tom's big day, adding that she had not slept for two nights, she was so excited. (The weather was somewhat chilly and Martha wondered if Tom would dress warmly enough. She is that kind of mom.) Martha's enthusiasm was buoyant and she and Tom joked that they would take turns in dropping by to polish his star.

Tom's mom was born in Pennsylvania. Her own hardworking dad, Fred Jagger (no, Martha has not traced back to see if there is any connection, even though she has English ancestry), was a miner. Fred and his wife, Martha Sr., moved their family up in the world and on to Michigan when daughter Martha was five. Fred then went to work for Zenith Carburetor, where he became general manager and stayed with the company for the rest of his working life.

Martha had four brothers and four sisters, and each of the siblings held part-time jobs while in high school, to aid the family finances. Martha and her fraternal twin, Maggie, who is twenty minutes younger, worked after school and on Saturdays in the S.S. Kresge's five-and-ten enjoying shifting from the candy counter to hosiery to dinnerware. "It didn't hurt us a bit," she says emphatically, with a traceable touch of nostalgia. Both she and Maggie attended business college, then Martha became a private secretary to the chief engineer of Fisher Body, while Maggie worked at General Motors. The look-alike, dress-alike twins married young, and when Maggie's marriage ended in divorce almost a decade later, in 1955, the willowy brunette went to New York and became a top model.

Now, while Martha's life is to all intents and purposes perfect, her twin Maggie has been battling throat cancer and enduring great pain. Maggie, who moved in with Martha and Bob for almost two years when she underwent surgery, is progressing well and swallowing, speaking, and eating baby food. Martha is full of admiration for her courage and cannot help but be aware of the inequities.

"I know that I have so much to be thankful for. I have a family, four wonderful children, and a husband. And Maggie has supported herself, and isn't married, and doesn't have any children. She chose to have her surgery here in California with us. The doctor said she would need a lot of love, and she certainly has received it, all the family just love her.

"You wonder sometimes," she admits. "The faith in God, it's brought me through. He's been right here and He's answered a lot of my prayers, because that's all I could do. There were moments that I didn't see how I could even get through it. Maggie's attitude is good, she's fighting, and she's up and around and doing things, but it's not easy."

Martha Selleck met Tom's father while still in high school. They were drawn together by a mutual love of dancing—waltzing, the fox-trot, the jitterbug—and in the classic tradition went steady, became engaged, and then in 1942 rounded it off with a big wedding. Bob Sr. went into the Army Air Corps five days after their first child, Bob Jr., was born. Martha and her baby went to live with her in-laws (her parents' house being filled to capacity), and that is where they spent the majority of the six years that passed before they could afford their first home. It was a surprisingly harmonious arrangement, Martha says, because "it just seemed to me that I knew exactly when to pack up the boys and go to Mother's for the day!"

Bob Sr. was finally discharged in 1945, when Tom was about eleven months old. The family's move to Hollywood three years later was not prompted by show business, but California real estate, in which Bob's brother George had first blazed the trail, then encouraged Bob to join him. Twenty-seven-year-old Martha had monumental misgivings. Martha Sr. told her in no uncertain terms that it was a wife's place to follow her husband's wishes. And Mom Selleck made the journey across country with them and stayed for six weeks because (as she told Martha years later) she had a strong suspicion her daughter-in-law might otherwise have turned right around and hotfooted it back to Michigan.

Martha vividly remembers that historic first night in Los Angeles, when they all sat in a restaurant and it really struck her that this strange place was to be her new home. Suddenly, she could not contain the tears, and right there at the restaurant table she just cried and cried. She admits, "It was maybe a couple of years before I actually got over being *real* lonesome. But [Sherman Oaks in the San Fernando Valley] turned out to be the nicest, warmest, happiest neighborhood that anyone could raise their children in."

Martha traces her closeness to her children back to those early "pioneer" days. They were inseparable and all became extensively involved in their neighborhood's new Congregational Church— another big step for Martha, who was raised Episcopalian. She felt that the change was justified because of the warmth of the congregation and the fact that Bob Sr., who was a Methodist, would attend.

Tom was a sensitive boy who suffered when his dad took him, at ten years old, to hunt rabbits. When he hit a bird with a BB gun and had to watch it die, the little tough guy ran to his room and cried. He was an awkward adolescent, uncomfortable with girls. Prior to one date, he was hit in the groin with a baseball. It fell to Martha to explain to the girl's mother why their date had to be canceled, because poor Tom could not find the words.

To Martha's amusement, Tom claims to have been the easiest child to raise, the smallest—and the most considerate. (He used to help Martha diaper his younger brother and sister.) She is enthusiastic about having raised what amounted to two different families. "It just seemed like when my husband was through with Babe Ruth and Little League with Bob and Tom, there was Dan. We kept them involved in sports, and Marty was involved in modeling school as a youngster and then later took guitar lessons, and was in the Brownies. That's what I think kept us so close— and also kept them out of trouble."

Martha and Bob Selleck managed to instill in each of their children an internal right-from-wrong meter and discipline was never a problem. Not that they were perfect (Tom once chased his mom around the house with a mouse), but they respected their parents' wishes. Martha and Bob issued them challenges, like offering the reward of a gold watch when they turned twenty-one if they stayed away from smoking, drinking, and swearing (*not* a Rolex watch as has been printed). Keeping those vows laid the boys open to considerable teasing from their peers, their mom concedes, but this promised prize was also a sizable carrot to dangle before children who had never possessed a watch.

Bob and Tom can recall the wait for their father to receive his first big check for a real estate sale, and certainly, selling strictly on commission, with mouths to feed and a mortgage to pay, was stressful. There was struggle, but Martha now looks back to those days of counting pennies and thinks, "It wouldn't hurt to be that way through all the years. You just appreciate everything so much."

By the time it was Marty and Dan's turn to receive watches, Bob Sr. had become very successful and the family's status had elevated accordingly. All three boys attended USC and Marty went to Cal State University, Northridge, as an art major. (The Selleck boys all followed Bob Sr. into real estate, and even Tom shares a business with his brother Bob.)

Martha, who stands five feet seven and a half, ended up being the family shrimp. She is surrounded by strapping males, with Bob Jr. and Dan six feet seven, and Tom, like his father, six feet four—even her daughter Marty is five feet ten. (Twins often skip a generation, and Martha, who has eleven grandchildren, is a grandmother to identical twelve-year-olds courtesy of Bob and his wife, Laurie.)

When Tom announced his decision to become an actor, the

Sellecks encouraged him. If all else failed, they thought, he had his education to fall back on. It was not his work in TV pilots, most of which, depressingly, ended up on the cutting room floor, but a basketball commercial for USC that finally led to "The Dating Game." "He was never chosen, he always laughs about that." That in turn led to the Twentieth Century–Fox contract which seemed headed nowhere. Until "Magnum, P.I."

Martha readily admits that her life was affected by Tom's fame. For the most part, she has enjoyed every moment of it, all the more so because she knows how much intense pleasure it has given Tom after the long drought. Martha's horizons have been broadened by the people she has met and the wonderful trips with Tom to Hawaii, Yugoslavia, London, Venice—places she and Bob Sr. might never have seen. Appearing on television as "Tom's Mom" has been a particular personal triumph since she is rather shy. "Things that I never thought that I would do or could do, I've managed to get by, and that makes me very proud," she says.

Inevitably, there is the negative side of fame. Tom is one star who becomes extremely aggravated by his press coverage. Martha and the entire Selleck clan were annoyed, for instance, by *Star* magazine's use of a picture from Tom's Walk of Fame ceremony on its cover after Tom's wedding; the picture had no caption, but by omission it misled readers into believing they were looking at a wedding picture, and those had not been made public. Martha concedes that it is also upsetting when lies are printed—and not just for Tom. She pointedly avoids reading offending articles, but hates to think that tabloid readers believe what is there just because it is in black and white. "I don't blame Tom for being upset, I get upset *for* him," she says.

When Tom's image was emblazoned everywhere as that of a sexy hunk, Martha did not find that demeaning, however. "I *always* thought he was sexy! Women of all ages come up to me and tell me how wonderful and sexy Tom is. Some get embarrassed and say, 'I'm sorry, I'm older, but that's the way I feel,' and I say, 'I think it's *great!*' But it never did irritate me. I really never have asked Tom how he's felt about it. I imagine he would get a little tired of hearing it."

Martha Selleck was the constant supportive presence in Tom's life that Julian McQueen blatantly was not in Steve McQueen's. Freud believed that a boy who was the undisputed apple of his mother's eye went out into the world as a man with a feeling of triumph and confidence in success, a feeling which frequently led to actual success in the real world. (And why should girls be any different?) Yet McQueen presents resounding proof that not every star ventured out into the world equipped with that kind of maternally instilled inner confidence.

It seems it is time to stop trying to judge books by their covers. Time, too, that the Norman Rockwell illusion was bade a fond farewell, and for good reason. The physical, geographical, and material trappings which affluence can secure might create the traditional idea of a normal, stable environment, but they cannot stave off that possibility of internal instability. The most seemingly stable of families can play host to an unstable child should that be part of the heredity pattern, since a genetic predisposition can lie dormant and skip generations, waiting to emerge when hatched by an appropriate environment. Conversely, a child can emerge from the most chaotic of backgrounds with the ability to survive, cope, and be enormously successful. So the walls of so-called normality have come crumbling down.

Eminent California psychoanalyst James Grotstein, M.D., who is Clinical Professor of Psychiatry at UCLA and coeditor of a book on borderline personality disorders, is unable to define a normal family; how can you define that which you have never seen? After thirty or so years in practice, he has yet to come face to face with a living, breathing example of this endangered species. Of course, he does not doubt it exists—somewhere. "But there are more skeletons in the closet than we have ever thought," he says.

There is not a family between Santa Cruz and Hyannis which does not have some hidden agenda of issues—whether those issues are kept tucked away under the cloak of what society has come to accept as normality, whether they are simply dealt with effectively, or whether they exist unrecognized for what they are.

Besides personality, the other heredity factor is biochemical. Research has shown that areas like literature and the arts are heavily populated with people with disorders in the manic-depressive spectrum: manic-depression itself (now called bi-polar affective disorder), and the milder cyclothymia and hypo-mania, for instance. None of these conditions precludes fame (Vivien Leigh was manic-depressive; Patty Duke is; Ringo Starr described himself that way in the Beatles' heyday), although the severity of manic-depression itself is such that it is unlikely sufferers could sustain a career through its disruptions without diagnosis and treatment.

Manic-depressives, in their manic highs—as opposed to the terribly depressed or suicidal lows to which they eventually swing—can exhibit incredibly driven behavior. They can be hyperactive, euphoric, and bursting with ideas, and their inflated sense of self and extreme grandiosity can reach such a fever pitch that they lose touch with reality. But not necessarily. Their very grandiose and omnipotent view of themselves can work to their advantage. "They may actually be able to pull off a picture of themselves as being supersophisticated and supercompetent and catch people's eyes in that regard," says Dr. Clark.

Mental disorders aside, those in the general population with "Type A" personalities—extroverts whose high energy level often feeds off risk-taking—are frequently drawn to show business and other high-stress careers. So are counterphobics, people whose potentially paralyzing fears are masked behind a pattern of behavior that persistently seeks out the very dangerous situation of which they are most afraid. The paradoxical prevalence of shy actors and performers is explained thus. The insecure, like Neil Diamond and Elton John, are constantly drawn to the cliff's edge to confront their worst fears—each concert could be their last. It is no accident that Sheila Farebrother, Elton's mother, describes her son as "a Jekyll-and-Hyde character." Such duality is not uncommon.

Where else does the drive to become famous begin? Some stars' mothers could take credit for their son's or daughter's fame by sheer virtue of the fact that they were desperately ambitious for their children and undoubtedly force-fed that message right along with the creamed spinach. But then again, some moms were fiercely opposed to the mere suggestion of a show business career.

Barbra Streisand's mother anxiously tried to convince her daughter to train as a stenographer; she could not imagine that Barbra
might succeed as an actress or singer. John Lennon's Aunt Mimi,
who raised him, repeated almost daily that his guitar was all right,
but he would never make a living at it.

Charlotte Sheedy, whose daughter Ally Sheedy starred in *The
Breakfast Club* and *War Games,* sees childhood as a *Rashomon*
experience. Dr. Grotstein agrees that life is more like *Rashomon*
than not: four people will deliver at least six different eye-witness
accounts of events, be it an accident on the highway or a mother-
child relationship, and a patient's version of his or her childhood
will change noticeably throughout analysis. Sally Field said, "I
think I had a very tumultous childhood, yet I was the only one in
the family who did [think so]."

In the final analysis, you could say that for the right child, the
grain of sand with which to irritate that oyster exists in any home
environment—either too much love or not enough; too little
caring; suffocation; boredom; an abundance of tension and tur-
bulence. Hence the fact that Bob Dylan and Mick Jagger found
as much to propel them out of their comfortable environments
and onto the road to success as did Steve McQueen in his more
overtly difficult, angst-ridden scenario, and James Dean, whose
mother died and "left" him when he was nine.

Georgia Holt observes that Cher describes her childhood as
much tougher than it was. To Georgia, Cher's childhood was an
immeasurable leap forward from her own: "I was always so proud
to give birthday parties for her. The only one I ever remember
having was one my Aunt Zella gave me on my twelfth birthday."
Yet that achievement was lost on Cher (as parental progress is
invariably lost on children), who was doubtless busy rating her
parties against those of her friends.

Charlotte Sheedy, an activist, literary agent, and hardworking
single mother who operates out of her Manhattan apartment, was
described by her daughter Ally as a mentally absent parent who
was totally preoccupied with her work, political causes, and financial survival. Not altogether successful in the mothering department, then? Yet Ally, the end-product daughter, would not
classify Charlotte as anybody's idea of a failure as a parent.

Charlotte believes that children attribute powers to their parents which they simply do not possess—that they create a mythical figure based upon what is of necessity incomplete information: "That we all survive all of this is amazing to me. I wanted my children to have a pain-free existence. First of all, it's not possible, and second of all, they feel their lives are just the opposite. And they feel that I was responsible for helping create that! I think the primary impulse is to spare and to make their lives good. And you make mistakes, because what they want is never what we're giving and it's an impossible chore."

Robert Redford's father was a milkman by day, an accountant in the evenings. Sacrifices were made for young Robert by caring parents, and yet he felt stifled, restless, increasingly anxious to escape his pleasantly innocuous suburban home, his mind meandering over romantic notions of becoming an artist or an outlaw.

Redford was drawn to direct his Oscar-winning film *Ordinary People* for various reasons, one of which was that he saw in it an admittedly dramatized version of his own childhood scenario, what he called "the camouflage of feelings, the inability of people to get in touch with themselves." He told a group of reporters, "I had real problems with that when I was younger. I had good parents—they were perfectly fine—but I just heard different sounds, I guess, and that bothered people. As a result, I didn't feel I was being heard, which made me doubt my own sanity."

Many narcissists are drawn to seek fame, and for very powerful reasons, says Dr. Grotstein. Only if a mother gives unconditional love which she reaffirms while pushing her children away and allowing them to achieve their separate individuality, only then can they come to peace with their specialness, and their own human neediness. We all must live with both.

"But narcissists," Dr. Grotstein explains, "are addicted to being special and hate the ordinary neediness they see in themselves. They can become magnificent actors or celebrities by virtue of their enormous drive to remain extraordinary, and to have the mirror that comes with that. Narcissists are addicted to mirrors."

Dr. Clark agrees: "They are constantly searching for an excitement, a high, in a stereotypic mirroring. Like unhappy adolescents, who don't tolerate depression well, they fend off unhappy feelings by generating excitement in their lives, as much as they can, as fast as they can. For the adolescent, that will probably take the form of risk-taking, crazy driving, stimulants, drugs, and hypersexual behavior. For the narcissist in show business, the excitement could stem from the glitter, the lights, the fuss and fanfare and overall razzamatazz."

Chaim Potok wrote of Barbra Streisand in a predominantly complimentary fashion in *Esquire* magazine, but noted: "I sense about her something of the narcissistic personality; alluring, playing at being charming, centered on one's own self, laboring relentlessly and expecting the same of others, too soon bored with achievement, too quickly disdainful of permanence, grasping at opposites, at times impatient to near-ruthlessness with those of smaller mind or lesser vision."

Since there can be no consensus on what makes the lightning rod of stardom strike, one cannot overlook that intangible quality, that magical unknown quantity. The idea that it is a godlike hand which reaches down and bestows star status might not satisfy everyone, but while there inevitably remains a mystery about stardom, you can rest assured that at the core of it Mother looms large—probably larger than life.

Dr. Grotstein, who has made a study of famous people and their fans, gives credence to the notion of the "X factor." Besides drive and a capacity for focus and for ambition, he has observed among the famous a kind of knowledge of their future, a sense of destiny. Barbra Streisand, for all her monumental insecurities, also admits that she felt as if she were "chosen." So assured was she on some level of her future success that when she worked as a theater usher, she took the precaution of concealing her face from those she escorted to their seats, lest they should remember her and know her humiliating past once she became a star.

John Lennon, as a youngster who wrote poetry and painted, wondered whether he was a genius or whether he was mad; since no men in white coats appeared to cart him away, he concluded he must be a genius. To John, genius meant pain, and creativity was an escape valve for that pain. It was always entirely obvious to him that he was different, and he was angry even in adolescence that this seemed unrecognized by others. In fact, while Auntie

Mimi denigrated his chance of financial success with his guitar, she also recognized early that there was something special about John: "The main reason he was such a worry to me while he was growing up was because I knew he had *something*. *He* knew he had it too. But he didn't know where exactly to put this talent he had, or where it might lead him."

"I didn't become something when the Beatles made it, or when you heard about me, I've been like this all my life," he complained to Jann Wenner of *Rolling Stone* magazine in 1970. "That's been my hang-up, you know—continually trying to be Shakespeare or whatever it is. That's what I'm doing, I'm not pissing about. I consider I'm up against *them*. I'm not competing myself against Elvis. Rock just happens to be the media which I was born into."

Music critics seemed to Lennon an irritating repetition of those unseeing schoolteachers—inferiors who knew less than he, but who were in a position to judge his work. Although Lennon had a shyer side and was far more sensitive than ever he would wish to admit, this egotistical-sounding opinion is not unusual among stars—although perhaps few have voiced it so bluntly.

"They seem to have a rendezvous with some sense of greatness about themselves," says Dr. Grotstein. "And it may have been handed to them—usually by the mother or father, or both. Or maybe somebody in the early environment like a teacher, an uncle, or a grandparent. But there is that sense.

"Churchill, no matter how much of a slouch he was as a child, always seemed to have a sense of destiny. It was with him, it rode with him. He was kissed by fate, and always knew it. A child knows that he can create the world, then later on finds out that he did not. But sometimes it never gets fully given up. There is a sense of having power over one's life."

Not only is that sense of power connected to the mother, she is precisely the point at which it begins. She is its source.

3

Laughter Lines:
You Don't Have to Be Crazy,
but It Helps

Eccentric, quirky, hilarious, daring, outrageous, unconventional, bizarre, comical, and preposterous. Williams and Hamilton are all of the aforementioned, besides being the owners of warmly wicked senses of humor. No, not Robin Williams and George Hamilton—their moms, Laurie and Anne. Laurie Williams and Anne Stevens Potter Hamilton Hunt Spalding are two Southern belles. ("All women in the South are Southern belles, from the cradle to the grave; it's just a way of life, like Southern fried chicken," goes the gospel according to Laurie.) Coincidentally, they also share more than a passing acquaintance with an opulent life-style and a love of laughter. Their humor, albeit diverse in style, is a legacy each has passed on to her superstar son—in glorious abundance.

It is hard to believe that the irreverent Robin Williams grew up addressing his parents as "Sir" and "Ma'am." But the formality is deceptive; "Ma'am," you see, was a little unconventional. Robin, it transpires, was raised under the influence of a woman whom he describes as "out there," a woman who did not blanch at the prospect of pulling halved rubber bands (preferably red ones) from her nostrils on national television. Not only is that atypical maternal behavior, it is also precisely the trick that Laurie Williams' late husband, Robert Fitzgerald Williams (a man so imposing, Robin nicknamed him the Lord Viceroy of India), so abhorred that it once drove him to threaten to go somewhere, anywhere, as long as there was no rubber of any kind.

Both are aficionados and champions of flirting, but by contrast to Laurie, Anne Hamilton is positively demure, discussing nothing more risqué on British television than her wish to be buried topless—an admittedly unusual topic for a near-octogenarian. But then, how many ladies do you know who edge toward eighty still wearing high heels? Dinner conversation with George's mom is charming and rather refined; alive with tales of first kisses and love letters and Anne's shocking near-sacrifice on the Hollywood casting couch—or on reclining car seats, to be more precise.

Laurie Williams is an equally spritely, fizzy woman who is now in her mid-sixties. She raised her son in a chain of softly cushioned (frequently Whoopee-cushioned) environments. Daddy, the wry one, with the dry, subtle humor, worked as an executive for Ford Motor Company, a job that had his family ricocheting between Detroit and Chicago. (Sadly, Mr. Williams passed away in 1987, shortly after this interview.) Laurie still gets goosebumps thinking about one home—rented—a forty-room-mansion estate with a twelve-car garage, set in twenty acres in Detroit's swanky Bloomfield Hills suburb. "It had two oil burners—it was like heating up the *Queen Mary*."

The help left, convinced the place was haunted. Laurie herself once heard heavy footsteps emanating from the third floor and, convinced she would be "a yellow-bellied rat" for the rest of her life if she did not investigate, ran upstairs to check. In the absence of any disturbing evidence, the Williamses decided they could live in harmony with who or whatever it was.

Just as Robin was entering his senior year, Laurie's husband retired and chose to move his family to a remodeled 1901 summer house in Tiburon, the toniest of San Francisco suburbs—where having it tough means no Porsche until age sixteen. For Robin, the switch from formal boys' school regalia to co-ed Redwood High's uniform of blue jeans and socks optional provided the greatest culture shock.

The product of two second marriages, Robin came along in 1951, by which time he had the silk-lined nest to himself. (Laurie's son Lauren, now a physics professor in Memphis, was only eight when Robin was born but preferred to stay in the private boys' school where he was happily ensconced, near his Alabama-based grandmother, when Laurie remarried. Laurie's stepson Todd, thirteen years Robin's senior, is in the restaurant business.)

Living in a neighborhood devoid of children, the lad had no choice but to invent a rich fantasy life. Robin played with the family maid's son and the dog, Duke, and frequently retreated to the attic, where he executed battles as involved as chess games, with battalions of strategically placed tin soldiers. He created his own world with its own population: "Can I come out and play?" "I don't know, I'll have to ask myself."

It was a world where Carl the turtle reigned as king, until Robin, who was around four at the time, was hit by an overwhelming desire to let Carl taste freedom. He has had second thoughts and a healthy ration of nightmares since, but too late. Laurie jovially reassures him, "Don't have the guilties anymore about that turtle you flushed down the toilet. It's all right. He's in heaven." Robin is not so easily placated, suspecting that somewhere in the Chicago sewer system there lurks a two-hundred-pound turtle who badly wants to talk to him.

Mother and son's repartee is highly entertaining. However, their shared love of Whoopee cushions and insistence upon discussing the finer points of the effect of filling them with water did not go down well with Williams Sr.

"Picture George Burns and Gracie Allen looking like Alistair Cooke and Audrey Hepburn and that's what my parents are like," Robin once said, when attempting to describe the family dynamics to Lawrence Linderman of *Playboy* magazine.

Besides rubber bands and Whoopee cushions, there is also Laurie Williams' nice line in nasty poems, jokes, and tales, all laced with her off-the-wall trademark. Robin is especially fond of a book title his mother told him about, supposedly written by a nineteenth-century English princess who was a famed party-giver, entitled *Balls I Have Held*. Laurie says Robin has rather mangled that one; the author was a Chicago philanthropist.

His mom is anxious to dispel one myth that Robin has promulgated. He was not a fat little boy. Nor a fat older boy. She has a picture to show to prove it to the world. When the record has been as distorted as it clearly has (at the mercy of Robin's creative license), it is not surprising that Laurie is keen to straighten out a few points. He was hardly the little orphan child he sometimes paints himself as having been, although Laurie admits that has more drama than the truthful tale of his happy childhood. Robin's birthplace was *not* Edinburgh, Scotland, but the lobby of Wesley Memorial Hospital in Chicago. Well, perhaps not the lobby, *almost* the lobby.

The hospital staff was so preoccupied with the red-tape formalities of form-filling that it was a near-miss, averted only by Robin's father raising his voice and demanding that his wife be taken to her room. Shortly thereafter, a fine baby boy was born. A day later the three wisemen showed up, bearing, Robin quips, "myrrh, frankincense, and Valium."

Rarely serious, Robin claims that his own joke-telling began in seventh grade; like Michael J. Fox, he found humor a good deflector for the pubescent aggression of his swarthier schoolmates. Laurie believes that her court-jester son was sent to bring joy to the world; he loves to make people happy, and there is no cruel streak in his humor. She has seen him show mercy to the most destructive of hecklers, whom he could so easily have annihilated with his devastating wit. Instead, he showed kindness. He is extremely sensitive to other people's pain, to the point where it used to worry Laurie how he would fare in such a tough business. Now she has given up worrying and tells him, without sounding saccharine, "Your sweetness is like a suit of armor."

Neither parent was Jewish, but Robin was made an honorary Jew after attending fourteen bar mitzvahs in one year while at a private boys' school in Detroit. ("I saw more ice melt than the captain of the *Titanic* that year.") He is therefore qualified to point out the difference between Laurie and a Jewish mother. The Jewish mother, Robin explains, says, " 'Go ahead, eat, eat,' " whereas his mother tells him, " 'Here, here's a tiny piece of mesquite fish. Don't be afraid. It's a Marin thing.' "

Laurie was touched to learn that Robin (who has fond memories of the time she cooked the Thanksgiving turkey, complete with the giblets in their plastic bag) credited her and Jonathan Winters with being the two major influences on his life—along with being dropped on his head. "Well, I'm sorry he fell on his head. He bounced, but I caught him," she deadpans, not in the least disconcerted. (In fact, it was his nurse who dropped him.)

Modestly, she claims that her mother and husband were the

source of Robin's comedic talent. Shortly before his death, Laurie described her enormously confident and slightly cynical husband, Rob, as having a unique and brilliant humor "that just blows your mind. Here is this dignified, elegant man, and you think, 'I didn't hear right.' Never vulgar. But funny."

Grandma? She had a fondness for tuning her television to wrestling at midnight to watch men do unspeakable things to one another, so Grandma would doubtless have approved of Robin's defensive decision to learn how to wrestle and, Laurie feels sure, of his comedic career. The senior Williams flunked this one— worried about his son's future, he suggested Robin take up welding. Robin, Laurie notes, is a very good all-around athlete who partakes in cross-country running and karate.

Robin's maternal great-great-grandfather was governor of Mississippi and a U.S. senator (Laurie hopes her ethical son will foray into politics eventually). Robin's Grandma Laura was a Southern belle and Laurie grew up in New Orleans. Her parents divorced when she was three; her mother remarried; and Laurie, being legally adopted by her banker stepfather, went from the cachet of Laurie Janin to plain old Punky Smith. She never forgave her stepdaddy for that.

An only child, she used to tell her mother, "If you have another baby, I'm going to flush it down the toilet." Some years ago, Laurie wrote off to Jackson, Mississippi, asking for her birth certificate from September 24, 1923, and was shocked by the response, which ran along these lines: *Dear Madam. You were born September 24, 1922.*

Immediately, Laurie broached this discrepancy with her mother. "I said, 'Laura, you told me I was born in 1923. I was born in 1922!' She said, 'Oh, no, Punky, you were born in 1925.' Still trying to knock a couple of years off so she could be a Southern belle!"

Laurie was always proud of Robin's scholastic brilliance (a straight-A student, he was in the honorary scholastic fraternity and had a flair for languages), but not of his humor. There was nothing to be proud of—in those days he was introverted, and deadly serious. She suspected he was funny among his peers but that his behavior at home was tempered by the presence of his stern, disciplinarian father, a member of the old children-should-be-seen-and-not-heard school. "I realized he was gifted. But I didn't realize his other flair," she explains.

Robin thinks he is much like his mom, particularly in his streak of wildness. And who could remain unaffected by her notorious rubber band trick? "You don't forget that for a while. Like, well, that's your *mom*, man, with the rubber bugger." A legendary saying of hers, which also made a definite impact on Robin, was "Laughter is an enema for the soul." Sounding a little vague, she claims, "I had a bad automobile accident and I don't remember some things. I did a little brain damage."

Perhaps her son did not have an entirely normal childhood, she wonders, as if it is the first time the possibility has crossed her mind. It was not entirely normal, but Robin clearly loves her. He teasingly "reminds" Laurie of the time she and his father kept moving, changing their address and not letting him know where they were. They giggle with disarming affection for one another remembering a tabloid article which implied that Robin's humor came from being a neglected, unloved child.

What *is* telling is that Laurie herself once had theatrical ambitions. She was about twenty years old when she went to work in the Weather Bureau in Washington, during World War II. She was close to New York and envisioned herself heading next for the Big Apple, where she would "just knock 'em off their feet." Instead, she met and married a handsome naval officer sixteen years her senior, which signaled the end of her theatrical career before it had even begun. But no regrets: "You know the old saying, 'Take the cash, and let the credit go'?"

When her husband was posted to the Pacific, she waited it out in San Francisco and enrolled in art school. "Actually I was ashamed of myself, I was having the time of my life. I behaved myself, but oh, man, was I having fun." Once, Robin's father made a surprise trip home to the Los Angeles area and telephoned Laurie, asking her to fly down and meet him. When told the airline had just one ticket left, she pulled her coat over the flimsy slip she happened to be wearing at the time and sped off to the airport. "I was so hot, and I was sitting next to this guy who kept saying, 'Hey, don't you want to take that coat off?' "

Laurie's first inkling of Robin's talent came when he sang solo with the Episcopal church choir—unfortunately, she arrived late and missed it. (Seriously, that piece of tardiness remains her one big regret about his childhood.) Her first real taste of what makes him special came when she saw him perform in *Snoopy* ("I didn't realize he was such a dancer") at the College of Marin. Unlike most of us, Laurie has even seen Robin Williams tackle Shakespeare—he played Malvolio in *Twelfth Night* and had a full scholarship to Juilliard. Laurie did not doubt that he would make it, once she saw the reception he got doing a little mime routine in the lobby of New York's snooty Plaza Hotel.

Her favorite piece of his work is his first movie, *Popeye*. The film fared better in far-flung territories; in fact, being Popeye's mom did much for Laurie's status in a Chinese grocery. She believes in years to come it will be recognized as a classic. Unlike Robin, she does not run the tape backwards so that it has a happy ending. One of a multitude of memorable moments that come part and parcel with being Robin Williams' mom was the film's Los Angeles premiere. They exited the theater to see a fifty-foot can of spinach outside, and a re-creation of the film's Maltese village location.

Laurie will go to any premiere of Robin's to which she is invited. She breaks out in goosebumps at the thought of those for *The World According to Garp* and *Moscow on the Hudson*; during the filming of the latter, she spent a week in Munich with her son. There is no denying her excitement about his success. She tells him that she is living vicariously through him, and she is sure Grandma is too. Robin needs no further prompting to launch into a squeaky imitation (one of Laurie's favorites) of his Grandma telephoning from the dead; she is up there with Elvis, baking him some cakes.

Now Laurie has a small grandson, Zachary (who has a precocious taste for Caesar salad), but she still sees Zachary's dad once or twice a week and Robin describes the interchange on these visits home thus: " 'Take care. Thanks. Got an egg. I'm out of here.' Just like the old days, man. Sneak into the house, muss up your bed, and split."

He believes his mother when she tells him that she is meant to live until she is one hundred and thirty-nine. That is fine by him. Would he care to assess her? "She is, in many ways, a mother," he says formally. "She's a very elegant woman, living here in Marin with a Southern tradition, yet among the mesquite grills. Mother carries on—serving the rum cakes and black-eyed peas."

Pete Townshend of the Who is immensely loony and credits his mother with teaching him the intricate techniques of the art, saying, "Weaned by a loony!" That somehow seems an appropriate summary of the Williams duo.

The relationship between Anne Hamilton and her mahogany-skinned, perennially dapper son George is considerably more formal, but since his lounge lizard act is always laced with humor, no less amusing. Clearly, it is not his addiction to sun alone that has rendered George Hamilton a touch eccentric; all the "washed" blood in the world (Hamilton has had the supposedly rejuvenating treatment) cannot change that.

Believe it or not, there was stunningly simple logic behind Anne Hamilton's aforementioned desire to be buried topless. She articulated it for the benefit of millions of British TV viewers some years ago when their crusty interviewer Alan Whicker descended on Palm Beach intent upon exposing its shocking excess and its cosmetically reconstructed, older inhabitants for his sardonic travelogue, "Whicker's World." Even the jaded Mr. Whicker was doubtless unprepared for his guest Anne Hamilton, a status-conscious socialite who makes the modest claim to have known "everybody on earth." In Palm Beach she was a veritable oasis of self-deprecating frivolity, buoyant amidst a sea of pure pomposity.

Aided by a martini—or two—consumed to alleviate the tedium while waiting to go on camera, she was suitably responsive when her friend Grace prompted Whicker to enquire about Anne's recent bosom lift. The thrust of Anne's diatribe was that having given birth to three children and lived with "these things" all those years, she had finally had her figure rejuvenated by a skilled cosmetic surgeon and was determined not to let his efforts go to waste. "I told my children, with my luck I'll probably die tomorrow. But if I do, I want to be buried topless, because God knows I want *somebody* to see them before I go."

It stands to reason, does it not? Yet Palm Beach society was not a bit amused by this piece of undignified and unsolicited publicity. By contrast, Anne was inundated with congratulatory fan mail from Britain, whose inhabitants lauded the levity she brought to a land where face-tightening and surgical lifting and pleating are taken desperately seriously. Anne chortles at the memory of her embarrassing revelation, then confides that the now world-famous boob-lift was not, anyhow, a great success. Anne is far from averse to physical improvement. Her age does not deter her from daily rigors with a Gutbuster, whose virtues she extolls with enthusiasm.

Anne, who is nicknamed Teeny, lives in extreme but tasteful splendor in George's Manhattan apartment. She emerges from her boudoir dressed for dinner, a thirties-glamour study in midnight blue and inky black, from her long, sleek hair and the skull cap it is tucked under, to her chic, knee-revealing suit, sheer stockings, and perilous, high-heeled court shoes. Perilous, given that outside her centrally heated domain, Manhattan is doing its annual impersonation of Antarctica and 99.9 percent of its inhabitants have taken refuge inside boots, furs, and the kind of coats that look like walking sleeping bags. The task at hand is to reach the hotel restaurant which lies just catty-corner across snowy Park Avenue. No matter, a limousine awaits and the trip is chauffeur-driven.

Anne Hamilton's daunting elegance (haughty haute) is ameliorated entirely by her frisky personality and impish humor. It is hard to be intimidated by a woman who says she knew George was special the moment he was born because he promptly "pee-peed in the doctor's eye." Or a woman who is bemused but completely unperturbed when quizzed about George's wedding to Alana Stewart (which she did not attend), at which a dog reportedly gave the bride away: "I never heard that one, but it suits me fine." Or a woman who looks positively gleeful upon spotting the *National Enquirer* outside her apartment and is so plainly enjoying the burst of tabloid coverage (much of it fictional) about her son's relationship with Elizabeth Taylor.

George's idea of style was ordering 365 roses from the White House florist, one to be laid daily upon the pillow of his then-girlfriend, Lynda Bird Johnson. His old-world, chivalrous charm is legendary, as is his wardrobe, which at one tally included over 350 made-to-measure suits and 500 shirts. What does his proud mother think when she hears it said that he is also too handsome, too rich, too much of a womanizer, and too self-involved? "That he's a horse's ass, in other words?" It is hard to fault her grasp of a situation, so one listens when she also says, "George has a tremendous sense of humor. He is so bright, I cannot tell you. He is the next thing to a genius, he really is. I cannot believe how many things he can absorb. I want to slap him in the face." Everyone assumes he is a stuffed shirt because of the way he dresses and his gentlemanly behavior, but he is far from it.

Fortified by a martini, after dinner she is intent upon traversing the Park Avenue intersection minus the burly chauffeur and limousine. Rather, she insists upon negotiating kamikaze-style what once was snow but now is glass, teetering upon her spindly heels and clutching the arm of her not very surefooted companion. Her bravado is infectious.

Upon closer inspection, her exquisitely furnished dining room's curious décor comes into focus as a rendition of Napoleon's tent —Anne's late and dearly beloved first-born son, Bill, an interior decorator, felt a strong affinity for Napoleon. Should there be such a thing as past lives, Napoleon's world, she suspects, was Bill's world. She has been told she was once a rich and powerful woman in Germany. "I'm glad I was rich somewhere."

In this incarnation she was born in Hopkinsville, Kentucky. Her folk were one of the First Families of Virginia. They might have been workers (usually candid, she fudges a trifle here), but nevertheless Anne envisions them sipping mint juleps. She had "the most wonderful childhood of anybody in the world." She was the adored only child of a doctor who took more comfort from Christian Science than his Christian Scientist wife did—an embarrassing secret he insisted be kept within the family

A leading player in Anne's childhood was Annie Finney White Gaines Hubbard, her grandmother, a great beauty and "a darling little thing" of five-foot two. She was rumored to have been engaged forty-nine times and was also accused of considering it beneath her to put her foot on the ground. She had a carriage, and a walkway to her house, so her retort to that was, "Why *should* I put my foot on the ground?" She was the perfect sounding board for Anne's romantic adventures and teenage heartaches, which she would spill out after taking refuge in Grandma's bed. (Anne's idea of heartache might be another woman's bliss—being madly in love with Bill Potter in New York and equally madly in love with "whatever his name was in Oklahoma City.")

Anne, who was herself a great beauty, first fell madly in love in the eighth grade with a skinny-bottomed boy whose pants she wore in the school play and who introduced her to her first proper kiss on the upstairs balcony at the cinema. "It was one of those kisses that I had never known about," she says with a naughty glimmer in her eye. "And my God, the movie house shook and the balcony almost fell down. Of course I was mad about him. His family owned a laundry and cleaners there. Mother teased me, 'Well, of course you could always have your laundry and cleaning free.'"

Intent upon averting more serious repercussions, Mother arranged for Anne to jump the lengthy waiting list into Principia, a Christian Science school in St. Louis. She was banished at the end of the year, along with four of her closest comrades, for wearing rouge to school—they had dampened red tissue paper and rubbed it on their cheeks. Later, they were shown leniency and reinstated.

Her sunny disposition was marred only by a fear that her parents might die, which meant she shared Mother's bed. "I've always said that's why I never had any brothers or sisters, because poor Daddy never got near her!" she says wickedly.

She made her debut in Memphis at seventeen, at a splendid affair with all the girls dressed to the teeth in beautiful gowns, their mamas having gone all out to outdo one another. Then she was packed off to Mrs. Semples' finishing school in New York to learn to pour tea, a skill for which there was limited call: "I'd have done better if they'd taught me how to mix cocktails. My mother always thought, you know, that I'd be a lady in a drawing room. You weren't taught to do anything. And I took her word for it."

Her bloodline (which from her description is almost pure English, with a soupçon of Irish and a dash of Scottish) was once rather affluent. Great-grandfather General John Gaines fought in the Civil War and was terribly rich ("He had something like a thousand slaves; in those days slaves were worth one thousand dollars apiece"). Grandfather was merely very rich, and by Anne's generation the fortune was depleted. "The awful thing was, even though we hadn't known General Gaines or lived with him, we still had his grandiose ideas."

A dyed-in-the-silk nomad, she has lived in New York, California, Memphis, and Boston, with much to-ing and fro-ing. "We never lived anywhere over two minutes, six months, a year. It bored me."

Their lives were somewhat schizophrenic, veering from extreme affluence to hardship (after one divorce they retired to a Mexican hotel and subsisted on avocados and popcorn), yet neither Anne nor the three boys could bear to live anywhere but at the finest addresses. A maid was not a luxury, but a sheer necessity. "I used to pay the maid and borrow back from her the next week—it was awful," she says, wrinkling her pert nose in amusement. "We just had a hell of a struggle. When George was very little he used to say to me, 'I can't bother picking up my clothes. I can make money while those clothes are being picked up. I'll pay somebody to pick them up.' And he was so right."

Quite how she managed this life-style with no money and, she insists, with no charitable donations from ex-husbands or suitors remains unclear. No amount of prodding can secure one solid nugget of information. She promises to reveal all in a book of her life to be called *How to Live Well on Nothing*, but is first engaged in securing a collaborator with a suitable sense of the ridiculous, "because my life has been rather ridiculous," she says, peering out from underneath those lashes.

Naturally, she grew up expecting to be a movie star; she perused movie books and saw herself. "I had no idea it wouldn't happen. I'm a Virgo, and Virgos don't push, don't pursue, unfortunately. That's the worst thing. I miss more boats than have ever been on the ocean." She did not lack for opportunities, however, coming within a doorknob's turn of a chance to join the Ziegfeld Follies. She got cold feet. While in Hollywood some years later, she had other opportunities, but since she had no experience in show business, she was disadvantaged and they were opportunities of the wrong kind. A supposed agent invited her to a nightclub near her hotel.

"We weren't two blocks away, and we were in the woods. We were in a European car, and he pushed a button—and I was lying flat on my back! Well, I panicked. I don't know how I got out of that one, but I did. But it was just everybody," she says, complaining of the producer who threw her the line that since she had been married she needed to keep . . . well, stimulated. "And you knew that if you did the movie thing, it would be—the cameraman, director, producer, blah, blah, blah. By the time you were through with the movie, you'd have been so worn out, such an old sort of nothing, that you would have hated yourself."

She met Bill Potter, the first husband in her string of less-than-durable marital matches, at a ball she attended while at Mrs. Semples' finishing school in New York. Potter was entranced by the Southern belle, and she was equally besotted with this tall, dark, handsome young man whose hips were so narrow she would ask him incredulously, "How can you sit on that tiny little thing?"

Bill was a doctor's son, but their baby Bill was born in the South ("his father was a hernia specialist—he couldn't do me much good") and with great difficulty. He weighed ten and a half pounds and measured twenty-four and a half inches. "I almost died," Anne says dramatically. A few months after his birth, amid the 1929 crash, the marriage ended and she went South to her parents.

Six years later she married George's and David's father, George "Spike" Hamilton, a Dartmouth graduate and society band leader of the Barbary Coast Orchestra, who had initially pronounced her "very attractive, but a little Hollywoodish." It was a love match, until Anne caught him flagrante delicto. She did not, as George Jr. has said, see him, she heard him. She blames herself for insisting that he have a girl singer with the band. He took her literally, hiring a tall blonde who, she says, walked like a leopard but played helpless.

"And of course, stupid me, I was never helpless. I was home fixing the children's bicycles. *She* was having all sorts of problems,

'And what would you do, George?' " she simpers. "Well, I think that's what men really want, but I didn't know that. They should give you sons before you have any husbands, because you can take lessons from them, what they bite on, how stupid they are. You sit there and you watch another woman, and every move she makes, you know what she's doing. *He* doesn't. He's loving it. He likes that little woman that just sits there and rolls her eyes and is pathetic and needs help."

At dinner one night with Anne and her friend Elvera, Sammy Davis Jr.'s mom, the conversation inevitably turns to men. Elvera does not hold them in the highest regard, as faithful-husband-and-provider material, that is; in fact she denounces them as dogs. Initially, Anne, the Southern belle, looks horrified, but as the discussion continues, rife with tales of their dastardly deeds to which she herself contributes, she seems to weaken. A short while later she says to her companions, smiling, "You're right, they're dogs."

Anne believes George Sr. loved her, but that he got into a mess from which he was unable to extricate himself. On hearing his mistress was pregnant, Anne sent the woman her leftover birth-announcement stationery, with a note saying she hoped it arrived in time.

She is not proud of her checkered marital history—four husbands in nine years. "Well, I think it's dreadful! What a waste of a woman who could have just absolutely loved being married." She is so gregarious, she *should* have a companion. But Anne has lived alone since the death of her favorite son, Bill (who was nine years older than George), a few years ago; alcohol killed him.

She now occupies herself by worrying about David and George, especially George: his sun consumption, his vitamin consumption (at one point, one hundred and twenty tablets a day), his frequent flying. When George was a fledgling star and had an altercation with his younger brother, David, Anne was heard to cry, "Don't hit him in the face, he's an actor!"

She had not made it in Hollywood and she could not imagine that George would. George, however, who fashioned his career on Cary Grant rather than Marlon Brando and whom Anne believes has yet to fully exploit his Grant-esque comedic potential, has always managed very nicely, thank you, for a man who attended twenty-five prep schools and did not graduate.

Brother Bill used to say you could throw George into the ocean and he would reappear aboard a yacht. Early in his career, he employed a wily negotiation tactic of which his mother is proud. On being made a purely average contract offer by an MGM executive, George declined. He said he needed a new Rolls—and pointed to the one he had rented for the occasion, which sported a neighbor's gardener dressed up as a chauffeur. How could he go home to his mother and say that he could not afford the car he had gone to get the contract in, George wanted to know? The contract offer was doubled on the spot.

Anne has plenty of memories for company, not least of which are the romantic variety. Old letters from her suitors, many of whom were "divine," are both a comfort and a prickly reminder of what might have been. Most went unanswered, discarded in the feast before the famine, when she had her pick, "I had a million, at least a million." Laughing, she remembers the "terribly attractive" suitor who fell off his chair and went to sleep just as they were about to get amorous. He was swiftly relegated to the imperfect category.

She examines one letter which turns out to bear the date 1945. A little quick arithmetic shocks her. Its author, she says, "must be a hundred and five by this point. My God, he's got to be dead by now! I'd love to send out a little bulletin and say, 'I'm doing a survey; I'm writing to see if any of you are still alive. Are you still there? If you have a wife, forget it. If you are still there, I'm sure you're just en route to the cemetery, but if you're not, call me quick, I'd love to see you. Maybe we can spend our last two minutes together.'"

4 *May the Force Be with You*

The Gabor matriarch, Jolie, who is now almost ninety, was and is an enormously domineering presence in the lives of her daughters Zsa Zsa, Eva, and Magda. Her opening gambit when making her daily telephone calls to Zsa Zsa is nothing so kindly as "How are you?" It is an unrelenting "How fat are you?"

Zsa Zsa recalls her mama being one of the first women in Budapest to showcase her family in a grey convertible Mercedes with plush red leather upholstery. Zsa Zsa was seven, Eva five, and Magda eleven when Jolie lined her impeccably dressed daughters along the front seat beside her, put her impeccably groomed pooch in the back, and chauffeured them all around the Concorde D'Elégance.

Zsa Zsa does not question that her mother loved them, but says Jolie definitely saw them as beautiful props: "If we had not been pretty, I think we would have been drowned like little dogs. That's my mother!"

Traditionally, the label "strong mother" carries with it some extra adjectival baggage, most of which has less-than-appealing connotations. Words like domineering, bossy, overbearing, and meddlesome have edged the forceful mother up against mother-in-law into the most-maligned category. Even psychotherapists have added their weight to such popular opinion, although "misconception" might be a more appropriate word, since the force of a strong mother behind a child is clearly not the detrimental burden commonly believed.

Excluding those stars, like Michael Douglas and Jamie Lee Cur-

tis, whose success might have been influenced by a dynastic predisposition rather than the presence or lack of a strong mother,
over 90% of the remainder had come under the influence of a
strong maternal force. Perhaps some of those mothers deserve all
the criticism inherent in the aforementioned adjectives. But the
presence of those qualities in moderate doses can be actively beneficial, and infinitely preferable to, say, a wishy-washy mother
with a negative, defeatist approach to life. Successful people frequently emerge from the nests of high-achievers.

General MacArthur had a driving mother, as did President
Lyndon Johnson. The strong mother not only has her place, but
has much to commend her, particularly to anyone who would be
famous. An opinionated, purposeful mother who is strong, and
yes, perhaps even domineering, who has an agenda for her children's lives but also sees them as people in their own right and
tries lovingly to nurture their uniqueness, is healthy, says Dr.
Grotstein.

"*Or*, she can project her own unfulfilled ambitions onto the
child—which we think is a terrible thing to do. But there is the
flip side to that. The children may grow up bearing this burden
that they 'have to do it to please mother,' but while they are
pleasing mother they often, without admitting it, tend to like it.
And also become *very* famous."

After more than eight decades on this planet, Jolie Gabor remains unable to boil an egg. According to Zsa Zsa, Mother
would not be able to boil the pan of water in which to drop the
egg. A dubious achievement, one might think, but the underlying
strength beneath this apparently shameful incompetency stands
out a mile. Jolie made a deliberate and manipulative choice to
remain totally inept in the culinary arts. (It is not her intention to
starve, since she employs not one but two cooks.) The message
she passed on to her daughters is crystal clear, according to Zsa
Zsa: "Any girl of mine who cannot afford a cook should not be
allowed to exist."

Jolie Gabor is a perfect example of steely resolve camouflaged
behind a cloud of ostrich feathers and feminine frou-frou. Her
husband, Major Vilmos Gabor, lost his fortune when World War
II broke out. Jolie, knowing her daughters were no longer safe in

Hungary, packed all three off to exclusive boarding schools in Vienna and Lausanne.

As it was, Jolie lost both her mother, Francesca Tilleman, and her brother Alexander; they were killed by the Russians. Jolie prays that her mother died first and did not have to witness Alexander being shot. Vilmos Gabor had warned Jolie to hide her mother in a convent, but according to Jolie, irrespective of the possible repercussions, Francesca found such spartan accommodations an unpalatable prospect.

"My mother said my grandmother would not be comfortable anywhere but the Hotel Ritz," Zsa Zsa explains. "And the Russians shot and killed her right there in the Ritz. She was a very rich lady and they would have shot you for a gold bracelet or a coat. We still can't talk to my mother about that."

Equally forceful, but a contrast to Jolie in every other way imaginable, is Debbie Reynolds' mother, Maxene. Where Jolie is a fantasy figure dripping with diamonds and furs, Maxene is too economically minded to drip anything more than her outspoken, no-nonsense views on life.

There was nothing romantic about the Reynolds family's move from El Paso, Texas, to Burbank, California, in 1941. "It was for bread and butter," Maxene says matter-of-factly. Her husband Ray, whom she married when she was sixteen, died in May 1986, just three months short of their fifty-seventh wedding anniversary. Not once did they consider divorce. "Divorce, never; murder, yes."

Ray, a carpenter on the railroads and a retiring man, headed west a year ahead of his family. He went hungry and slept on benches in MacArthur Park while he worked and saved money. Nothing romantic about that. But in 1948, Ray and Maxene's daughter won a screen test in a contest at Burbank High School. A golden opportunity that Debbie Reynolds—who twirled the baton, played the French horn, and aspired to teach gymnastics —knows would not have come her way had her father not sought a better life and unwittingly moved his family into the shadows of the film studios. "Cinderella. It just does not happen today," Debbie says.

She considers herself lucky that Maxene, who was raised strict

Nazarene, did not believe in the religion's hard line and allowed her to sing, dance, and go to the cinema. The family was very poor, yet Maxene managed to eke a living out of Ray's impossibly small earnings and also to save a dime here, a penny there. "She was very strong, and she was uneducated, never finished high school. But she went to night school later. Mother had to be serious in her life. Nothing came easy," says Debbie, who describes her mother as an extraordinary but exacting woman, while seemingly unaware that the same might be said of her.

"There was no 'gimme' in my day," Maxene says cheerily. Implicit in that one phrase is the distinct impression that she will not gladly suffer fools, the idle, or the weak. "You either done without or you scratched chicken feed for a living. I think they should throw out every bit of welfare there is right now, food stamps and all, and let people scratch for a living."

When Maxene Reynolds imparts the information that she was given six months to live fifteen whole years ago, she does so with not inconsiderable pride at having fooled "them" and "outlived a whole bunch of them." She suffered several cardiac arrests and is currently fitted with a pacemaker.

"I guess the good Lord wasn't ready for me. There's still something for me to do, and I've got to get busy and find out what the heck it is. . . ."

Maxene is used to being ridiculed for this, but swears by aloe vera juice, the virtues of which she discovered when her heart medication clashed with her stomach ulcer medicine. She replaced the latter with aloe vera, which she notes is mentioned in the Bible, and says that in two weeks her ulcer had gone. When she lost her sight a few years ago (due to a variety of problems), Maxene used aloe vera as eye drops. People can laugh all they want, she says, but she now holds a California driver's license.

When Debbie went into show business, Maxene taught herself to sew and subsequently saved her daughter vast sums of money by making the elaborately beaded gowns Debbie needed for her stage act. She toured with Debbie and is proud of her honesty and professionalism, but complains that she is too trusting.

Maxene never minces her words. "I couldn't give you two cents for any of the industry. To me, it's a big bag of nothing, just a lot of hard work. They do make big money, but there's no privacy, there's no nothin'. You couldn't pay me to put up with the trash they put up with.

"She gets screwed so many times, you wouldn't believe it. Somebody tells her the moon is made out of green cheese, she still believes them. And you know—we know better now. That's the ole Texas upbringing. Your word was your bond."

Not that Debbie Reynolds is any pushover. She is a trooper and has inherited Maxene's formidable strength. She needed it to survive the break-up of her marriage to Eddie Fisher, which took place amidst an overwhelming blaze of publicity that only added to the pain. She was even spitefully mailed scrapbooks chronicling her errant husband's departure with Elizabeth Taylor when Carrie was just a year and a half old, Todd a baby.

Debbie Reynolds is both star and star mom, of course, since Carrie Fisher is now a star in her own right. From her parents, Debbie learned, "If you start the job, you finish it. You can't say you can't, because you can—and you must. And if you don't, you should kill yourself. Those were the rules." Much of Debbie's resultant feeling about stardom, her old-school sense of responsibility to it, bleeds over to Carrie.

Carrie's legacy from her is, Debbie says, first being born, second her humor ("Carrie is extraordinarily glib"), third her ear. "Now, naturally she and Todd have a father. Although not a good one. But he nevertheless was there. He had no influence on the children, but they were born with what he was born with—which was great vocal prowess."

Debbie imagines that Carrie's voice, which was aired briefly at age thirteen in her mother's nightclub act, has been silenced because of the daunting prospect of following Debbie and Eddie. "And when we're both demised, she will step out, as Liza did when Judy died."

She is sure that being the daughter of America's Sweetheart gave Carrie an identity problem when she was growing up, and is only thankful that with the success of the *Star Wars* films the focus has now shifted to Princess Leia. After *Star Wars*, Carrie bought Debbie (who was then in the financial doldrums) a Cadillac. A few years ago, Carrie received a windfall residual check and had to be dissuaded by Maxene from buying her mom a Rolls-Royce—the diminutive Debbie would have been positively dwarfed by it and unable to handle it. Instead, Carrie bought her a magnificent sable coat, which rumor has it, despite her loud protestations, Debbie took to bed with her that first night.

Debbie's unsurpassed maternal moment came at a party when Carrie, who was fourteen at the time, introduced her mother to her contemporaries thus: "I'd like you to meet my parents." "That was parents with an 's,' " Debbie reiterates, "and that was the ultimate compliment. I had to leave the party because I started to cry. It was too much. Parents with an 's.' I thought that was quite adroitly stated."

Reynolds does not expect a *Mommie Dearest* tome to be rammed between her shoulder blades, because both Carrie and her brother Todd are talented. Children who write such books, in her opinion, suffer from a paucity of talent and have no other means by which to express themselves.

Debbie raised her children with an eclectic approach to religion: they attended a Catholic church, a temple, and a Presbyterian church. Todd, who studied theology, is highly religious and intended to become a minister, but has turned instead to producing religious TV programs. He is very close to Carrie. "Fused," according to their mother, who says there is no rivalry. "It is like she has three arms, not two. And he has five and they are all for her."

Carrie's career began before she was seventeen, when Warren Beatty offered her a role in *Shampoo*. Debbie, who deemed unsuitable the role of a sexually experienced young woman who uttered "the F-word," put up a good fight. As did Mr. Charm. Could Warren not at least change the offending "F-word" to "screw"? No, he could not. Eventually Mom relented, but not without comparing the films in which she had appeared at Carrie's age—*Abbadabba* and *Singin' in the Rain*—with the blatant promiscuity of *Shampoo*.

If there is a ground wire in the Reynolds family it is Maxene, who is a recent convert to the mothers' groups but generally gives the glitter attached to her daughter and granddaughter's success as wide a berth as if it were something nasty and infectious. She did, however, put on her glad rags to attend a Thalian Ball with Debbie, and went along for the ride when Carrie taped Johnny Carson's "Tonight Show." "They're so . . . nothing, to go to," she says dismissively. Not impressed? Not likely.

"Honey, we all put our pants on the same way, we all got here the same way. It's as unglamorous as it might sound, and I don't think there's anything more unglamorous than conception. The only time I was ever impressed with meeting anybody—and I even met the Queen—was the first astronauts. Now, *those* guys impressed me, but movie stars? No." She herself would not be game for a trip into the stratosphere, however. "No Ma'am! I get seasick in the bathtub! Now that is really mental inefficiency." To her credit, she is as intolerant of her own weakness as she is of others'.

She lives in the San Fernando Valley, directly across the street from Debbie and her son Bill, who is a make-up man on "Knots Landing" and occupies a camper on Debbie's grounds. Maxene gives a guided tour of what was once a cocaine- and crack-selling establishment and is now her home. The kitchen walls were pitted with black spots from the explosions involved in the drug processing, she says knowledgeably. She is not happy with the drapes (she wanted frou-frou lace, "more of a whorehouse look"), or with the freshly painted bedroom, because she thinks it was the dope dealer's laboratory. Escorting her visitor from the premises, she points to little holes in the exterior wall of the house. "Bullet holes from the night they raided the house. The SWAT team was here," she says, seeming rather to enjoy the notoriety.

Maxene Reynolds is strong, feisty, and a survivor. The same might be said of Anna Cosby, for Anna is the epitome of rock-solid determination and strength—but all wrapped up in a deceptively diminutive, four-foot-eleven package with a faint, girlish voice.

"If you get into an argument with my mother, I suggest you go with her when she walks out the door . . . because when she closes it, the ceiling's going to come in." So says Bill Cosby's brother Bob of their mother. Her three sons read her with inbuilt radar, the efficiency of which has been honed over the years.

Her sons' advancing years (Bill is over fifty, Russell and Bob in their forties) has not in any way diminished her powerful influence. Put the Cosby brothers in a room, Bob says, and have their mother walk in, "if you want to see three men look as if they are ten years old. We're little boys again. 'Hey, mom just entered the room, everybody behave themselves!' "

The woman who commands all this respect lives in what used to be a hay-storage barn until Bill's wife, Camille, masterminded its conversion into a cozy minicottage with high, wood-beamed ceilings. Anna lives alone but is hardly lonely. Her cottage is literally a stone's throw from Bill's front door, sitting on the immense grounds of his Massachusetts estate. She also has her catfish, neon fish, and lovebirds for company.

A nursing diploma hangs on the wall amidst dozens of Bill's awards (some are for showing his Welsh Terriers: "Would you believe that little devil made me go and collect them?"). She has a very adventurous set of family photos since, courtesy of Bill's success, she is a well-traveled lady. There is a photo of the Great Wall of China, the certificate for crossing the date line in Tristan da Cunha, and a plaque Bob gave her which reads: *God couldn't be everywhere so He created mothers*.

Only rarely does she hanker after the old house in Philly (now occupied by her only remaining sibling, Bertha) where she raised the boys. Two days a week, Anna does auxiliary work in a hospital gift shop and x-ray department. Twice-weekly bridge sessions are a social highlight. Bill's "spies" keep an eye on his precious mom to make sure that she does not overdo things. She is indignant when asked if Bill's driver takes her to her job, however. She drives herself.

Anna Pearl Hite was born in Virginia. The youngest of six, she hero-worshiped her brother Bernard, who was fourteen years older. So desperately did she envy his boyhood freedoms of climbing trees, fishing, and riding that she wished she had been born a boy herself.

Father was a peanut- and dairy-farmer whose livestock included cows, pigs, chickens, turkeys, and ducks, so the Hites ate well. Until Anna was six, that is. Her beloved daddy died suddenly, forcing her mother to sell up and move the family to North Philadelphia, where she found work as a domestic and eventually remarried.

Anna was raised a strict Methodist, which meant no riding around in cars, no dancing, and endless Sundays spent with her nose pressed against the windowpane, wishing she were allowed out to jump rope or throw some jacks.

"Uh-uh. Mother would say, 'This is God's day, and you're to be still.' Oh boy. And she meant just that." She sighs dramatically, suddenly looking all of five years old. But in later years Anna would emulate her mother's strict tactics as head of her own household. She was barely more lenient with her sons.

When she was eight, she met her future husband, William Henry Cosby. He carried her books, but there chivalry ended— he also teased her and chased her home. When neighbors said, "Oh Anna, there goes your boyfriend," she remembers smiling and saying coyly, "Oh, no . . . I don't like him."

Love crept up on them nevertheless and they married soon after she turned twenty. Bill was their firstborn, followed by Jimmy eighteen months later. Russell is six years younger than Bill, Robert (a.k.a. Bob) nine years younger. Jimmy died of rheumatic fever at age six and Anna is not sure she ever really got over that. She had been married for forty-four years when William died in 1974 in Boston's disability hospital.

Her husband was a career man in the Navy. Originally, he planned to be an undertaker and Anna was to be his nurse. She giggles; she is glad it did not turn out that way. She and her boys grew used to Cosby Sr.'s prolonged absences at sea, some of which stretched to two or three years. Bill naturally fell into the role of father figure for his younger brothers while Anna worked grueling hours, often leaving home at six A.M. and not returning until late at night. Bill's help was invaluable: he was father, mother, sister, and brother all tied into one. She prepared dishes he could heat up after school, and when they had eaten, Bill commandeered his brothers into washing dishes and cleaning the kitchen.

"You definitely learned how to make a sandwich and cook," says Bob Cosby, recalling that his mother's influence loomed large even when she was out of the house. Her philosophies: no excuse for wearing something dirty or wearing the same thing twice, because no matter how hard times were, soap was cheap. The boys wore hand-me-downs, but by the time Anna had ironed and folded their shirts they looked as if they had emerged straight from the package.

Anna was the iron fist in a velvet glove. Presented with a poor report card, her response would be a soothing, "That's okay, darlin'. I'm quite sure when Mommy sees this again the grades will be up." According to Bob, who currently teaches in California, invariably they were.

Bill, Anna says, was always a funny little guy whose sense of humor she imagines came from her husband. He once so infuriated her that she threatened to cut him in half and Cosby Sr. said, without looking up from his newspaper or missing a beat, "Why would you want two of him?"

The Cosby boys had no run-ins with the police for teenage pranks or rowdiness. They were not raised to take part in that kind of foolishness, and they knew it. There was never any whiff of rebellion.

"Bill says I'm a crybaby," Anna explains. "He says, 'We'd do anything so we wouldn't hurt you and make you cry.' " But when Bill went into the service there were not enough buckets to hold all the tears she shed; every shoe of his she tripped over, every sock she picked up, set her off again. "I swear I don't know how I lived—and it was peacetime, so I had nothing to fear. But I was so miserable."

To this day, the Cosby sons do not get away with much, even though Russell is in Atlanta and Bob lives roughly twenty-five hundred miles away in Los Angeles. If his mother telephones and he is napping, Bob swears that somewhere in his somnolent state he knows it is her and answers immediately. Anyone else, and he sleeps right through the ringing. Bob's stories sound like material for one of Bill's routines, but they are just classic Anna:

"Mom would say, 'I don't want you fighting, do you hear me?' 'Yes, Ma'am!' Then she'd say, 'But don't let anybody push you around!' But no way in the world I would ever get myself suspended from high school, that would be like death. It was a respect type of thing. You kept yourself out of trouble."

The worst Anna had to contend with was a slew of tickets for traffic violations when Bill, in the first flush of success, treated himself to a little MG and could not resist speeding to and from New York.

Bill had an entourage when he was a tot. He would bring his friends home, sit them on the floor, and keep them spellbound with his tales. "Then he'd holler, 'Mom, can we have some cupcakes?' I'd say, 'Oh my goodness, I can't afford to make cupcakes.' Ooh, they did love them."

When he was little, Bill said he would never leave his mother, and he was almost as good as his word, living at home until he was twenty-six. That is when he met Camille, the woman he told Anna was "just like you, Mom!" "Well honey, I saw Camille, then I went upstairs to look at myself and I said, 'No *way* that child could look like me'—she was gorgeous. But he meant she was like me inside."

Bob believes that Bill's routines paint a clear picture of the mother who raised him: "You *know* there's a very strong woman there." She did not throw footballs or baseballs, however, nor did she feel the need to play father as well as mother. She ruled the roost in her quietly forceful way so effectively that when her husband did return, his large presence (he was six-foot-one and weighed 235 pounds) and booming voice were almost intrusive. An adjustment was required all around.

Anna admits that her husband's departures did not inspire the same tearful reaction as Bill's. She grimaces and giggles. This woman for whom motherhood was definitely a vocation says that Russell was particularly upset by the change in the status quo. Once or twice she was so worried by the way he shook, grunted, and groaned in his sleep that she took him to see a psychiatrist.

"If my husband just wouldn't try to correct the boys. Oooh, that used to burn me up. And he'd say, 'Poor dear, you know they're my boys too!' But I just didn't want him to holler at them." She intervened if he tried to discipline them with a spanking. "Yes, of course I won," she says, then adds impishly, "Maybe I was an evil little woman, I don't know."

Bob recalls that during his leaves, Cosby Sr. sometimes had a few drinks and came home rather the worse for wear; he is careful to point out that Bill, being nine years older, might have different memories. What impressed Bob was the way Anna took Cosby Sr.'s behavior in her stride, without once making his sons feel ashamed of him or lose respect for him. It was just made plain that they were different.

"Russell and I would always ask, 'Why did you marry him?' She said, 'Well, when I saw your father, I always believed he'd make some real strong boys, and he did that very well.' So she got what she wanted."

Bob believes the Cosbys were the only boys in the neighborhood who during the throes of adolescence did not once toy with the notion of taking on their father.

"We'd look at our dad and say, 'Hey, it's over, don't even try it!' Regardless of the way he was, you're talking about a good person. My physical toughness is my father and my mental toughness is my mother—and those two together!"

A tale handed down in Cosby lore is of Cosby Sr.'s reaction to seeing Bill in a cast after he broke his collarbone in a school football game. Not only was there no sympathy forthcoming, but the very idea that Bill could wear shoulder pads and still break his collarbone rendered him a truly pitiful specimen. It was the naval influence—hard medicine to swallow, but character-building.

It was of paramount importance to William Cosby that his sons not grow up to be sissies, and he accused Anna of tying them to her apron strings. Secretly, she worried that he might be right and prayed nightly that he was not. She heaved a sigh of relief as each married and had children and proved their father's prophecy wrong. "Then I felt better. I said, 'Sissies! They're not sissies!' "

All three sons' devotion is highly evident, and Anna does not hesitate when asked the real secret behind it. "Oh, love, honey— the thing that money can't buy. You have to love your children and show them that you really and truly love them. Some mothers say, 'Oooh, I love you,' but they don't show it."

She has a naughty gleam in her eye as she recounts this interchange with her daughter-in-law: "Camille said, 'Oh, Mrs. C., you did a good job on Bill, he really knows how to love, he's so tender and so sweet.' So I said, 'Yeah? Well give him back!' "

Cast in a very different mold from soft-spoken Anna is Berniece Janssen, mother of the late David Janssen (a.k.a. The Fugitive and Harry O), who died on February 13, 1980. Berniece is far more strident and overtly opinionated, but she too is a survivor. While she has never quite recovered from the shock of David's death, her dominant strength is unmistakable. "I said 'Jump' and expected my children to say 'How high?' " admits Berniece.

The eldest of eight, she grew up on an alfalfa farm in Naponee, Nebraska, where she played "foreman" to her siblings when her father went into town: "I'd get on my horse with a bull-snake whip and if they didn't get their work done, I'd knick them lightly in the back! They still remember that!"

That old farm, she has heard, recently changed hands for $400,000; during the Depression her father was forced to sell it to the banks for $1. In 1928, shortly before the crash, Berniece Janssen was crowned Miss Nebraska; she then tied for sixth place in Miss Universe and went on the road with Ziegfeld's *Rio Rita*. She still belongs to the Ziegfeld Club.

In 1930 she met David's father, Harold Meyer, a handsome young banker whom she married within three months. David was born eleven months later. Harold was a rather refined fellow, prone to appearing at breakfast in a red velvet smoking jacket.

When the banks collapsed, the Meyer family was "brought down a peg or two," Berniece says, explaining that Harold did not adjust well to the accompanying drop in living standards. He became surly, and David was not sorry when she left him. (He and his father remained estranged throughout David's life, despite Berniece's efforts to reunite them.)

When her marriage failed, Berniece had to find work. Finally, her mother's cousin offered her a job in her dress shop in Goodland, Kansas. Ironically, it sat above an empty bank in a building once owned by Harold Meyer. Berniece moved into the bank with her fifteen-year-old sister, Florence, and little David. The money vault, with its heavy door, became their wardrobe. Only now does she realize the chance she was taking—suppose the door had closed behind her?

Berniece fashioned a table out of a couple of orange crates. She and Florence slept on a couch that pulled out into a bed, and little David slept on a cot his mother was given. "He'd reach over and hold my hand. It was tough. Made eighteen dollars a week in commissions. There was no welfare, there was no food stamps, there was no unemployment [benefits]. There was nothing."

She brought her young son to Hollywood in '39 and got a job at Dolores' Drive-In Restaurant. A later marriage to Gene Janssen gave her two daughters, Terry and Jill, and gave David his name.

Looking back, Berniece is convinced that listening to radio

plays while she was pregnant with David influenced his life. "Doesn't it seem like it? A farm girl raising one of the greatest stars?" David played accordion on the radio, then started to work in films at fourteen. Since his debut, Berniece has appeared on screen in thousands of anonymous, unsung roles as an extra.

Despite the phenomenal success of first "The Fugitive" and later "Harry O," his mother is afraid the public might begin to forget David. Needless to say, she cannot. She does not care whether a son is eight or forty-eight, it is absolutely devastating to lose one. She can barely remember the funeral; she presumes she blocked it out of her mind.

Prior to his death, David was proud he had given up smoking. The same could not be said for drinking. Knowing her distaste for both, he did not allow his mother to witness either habit. She believes those who say David drank heavily, but takes comfort from hearing that he was just a sweet, happy drunk and not a mean one.

His last film was *Father Damian*, and something about that still haunts her. Why was he suddenly so curious to learn about the Catholic Church? Why did he want to play a priest? With hindsight she feels sure that he knew that his time was up.

To say there is not much love lost between Berniece and her son's two ex-wives, Ellie Goldfarb and Dani Janssen, would be to express Berniece's sentiments with considerable tact. She last set eyes on her son after a Christmas Eve party at David and Dani's home, when he walked her to the elevator. "He said, 'Mother, have a nice life.' Wasn't that kind of strange? And he kissed me and hugged me. I got downstairs and I said to myself, 'Have a nice life? There's going to be a wreck on the plane!' I went through agony waiting until the plane got back."

Now that David is gone, she considers it a glaring omission that he does not have a star on Hollywood Boulevard. Berniece is the kind of mother who will not rest until her son is appropriately honored. A powerful mother figure indeed.

Are women all intrinsically strong? Do those hidden reserves of strength simply come to the fore in the hour of need for those who have to raise their children single-handedly? A number of star mothers might have qualified for medals had they ever been handed out for battles well fought on the home front, Lana Turner's among them. According to Lana: "Looking back, I can only marvel at the strength that pulled her through the Depression years—a woman alone, with a child to support."

Lana was nine when her father died in 1930. Her mother told her he had died a war hero; only later did she learn that he had been murdered after winning a crap game, his head smashed in with a blackjack. Although Lana was boarded with a family for a time when her mother simply could not manage, she harbors no bitterness, only admiration.

In a similar vein, Lauren Bacall says of her mother, "Through her belief in me she convinced me that I could conquer the world." Lauren's father disappeared after he and his wife divorced, but Bacall's mother was uncomplaining. She simply turned her attention to supporting them both and even backed Lauren when she chose to go to the costly American Academy of Dramatic Arts rather than join the work force, although she surely could have used the extra income.

It was Jon Voight's late father, Elmer Voight, who was the heroic figure in the life of his three sons. A golf pro, at sixteen he became the youngest player to qualify for the U.S. Open, and thirteen years after his death, an annual Elmer Voight Pro Am tournament was established at the Sunningdale Country Club in New York, where clearly he was much loved by one and all. Yet it is impossible to meet Barbara Voight without immediately recognizing that she too is a force with which to be reckoned.

"What did Jon tell you? Did he tell you how nuts I am?" she asks in a fashion bordering on ferocity. No, he did not. He did, however, say that she was quite a character, and chuckled in a meaningful fashion. "That I'm sure of, because he knows me," she says, clearly pleased with this assessment. "Yeah, I do have a mind of my own, and I am a little bossy. But I speak my mind usually."

She is as good as her word. Cheerfully, she reprimands her visitor for not arriving in Florida equipped with a bikini ("You're a dumb broad!"), for refusing a glass of wine ("You're nuts!"), and for not being a carnivore. Putting the bacon that was headed for a quiche back into the refrigerator, she says with an air of finality, "Okay, that's it! You're nuts. I'm not going to worry about you!"

Her feisty words, however, are completely contradicted by the welcoming way in which she serves an unexpected lunch (Jon's mom makes a mean pumpkin pie), then hops in her car and voluntarily ferries her interviewer all the way from her winter home in Jupiter, Florida, back to West Palm Beach airport. Zipping along the highway in her Toyota, she issues a last-minute reminder to call her daughter-in-law Joanie in Scarsdale, New York: Joanie will show the holiday decorations Barbara concocted in her home there as further evidence of how nuts she really is.

Although the decorations remain unseen, against this backdrop it is not at all difficult to envision Jon Voight's silver-haired and delightfully steely mom making her maiden voyage down the Aspen ski slopes some time after waving good-bye to her seventieth birthday. "I absolutely loved it. I had the best time. Everyone said, 'Don't do it. You'll break a hip. You'll break a leg.' I said, 'So what? I'll break it.' "

She and Jon, an athletic fellow with superior natural ability, took their first lessons together. "I went to the top slopes the first day," Jon recalls. "Well, *she* went to the top slopes the first day! She was the only person in the world that, that particular day, did the same thing I did! Of course, her instructor would have been on the mad side, too, but I don't know if they could have stopped her! Quite an extraordinary gal."

One day, she lunched at the top of a mountain with the aforementioned young ski instructor, after which even Barbara was not prepared to ski her way down. Instead, her instructor organized a snowmobile. "I thought they'd see me in the back and say, 'Go easy on the old broad,' " she says, with a grin. "Not a bit of it. He went zooming over the bumps. I was laughing all the way down!"

From his teens, Elmer Voight was plagued with back problems, resulting from a car accident, which were sufficiently severe to mean the forfeit of a competitive golf career. He was, however, a pro golfer until his death in a car collision in 1973, just two weeks after the birth of Jon's first child. Elmer kept his chronic pain to himself and never complained, but Barbara, of course, was aware of it, and merely set about tackling tasks that might otherwise have fallen to the man of the house. She would literally turn her hand to anything, including painting exteriors.

Jon recalls the time she fell off a ladder and broke her arm. Unlike your average person—which she surely is not—she did not head for the hospital. Instead, she wrapped up her arm and proceeded to make dinner for Jon's father. Only when she was satisfied that he had been taken care of did she excuse herself and pop off to the emergency room to get it set.

Barbara is spunky, very positive, an organizer who combines what Jon calls "the most lovely, light, little bubbly attitude toward it all" and "the fierceness to fight in any way for something that she thinks is required. I think she's most loud in preparation when she doesn't quite know what to do. If she doesn't know what's going on, she'll say—" his voice suddenly booms out "—'Well, let's do it! Come on!' You know what I mean?"

Jon does not receive the star treatment from his family. Besides the fact that the star slot was and is reserved for Elmer, there are three Voight sons of whom Barbara is equally proud. Wes, the youngest, is a songwriter, and wrote "Angel of the Morning" and the Troggs' No. 1 hit "Wild Thing," under the name Chip Taylor. Barry, the eldest, is a professor in geology and engineering at Penn State. Barry was roundly accepted as the clever one, and it was his standards to which Jon aspired. In his capacity as an avalanche- and earthquake-expert, Barry was above Mount St. Helens in a helicopter during the second eruption, which predictably leads Barbara to opine, "He's a nut, too. We're all nuts, the whole family is nuts."

She and the extraordinarily handsome Elmer met while in high school—she rode on the handlebars of his bicycle. Barbara, a tailor's daughter, put her teaching qualifications aside in favor of raising a family. They had been married thirty-six years when he died.

"This gal," says Jon, "was his . . . I don't know, his true love and his best pal and whatever! I never knew them when they were not in that way, you know? They seemed to be matched quite well. He was always quite admiring of my mother's physical strength, her energy, and her drive. He depended on her enormously, and not only physically."

Barbara is the stoic sort for whom it is a big concession to admit that in every life a little rain must fall. To keep her children near their father she became a lifeguard at the country club. Whereas Elmer was the theatrical storyteller, the ham, the charismatic hero, Barbara was the positive-thinking powerhouse. She has, in Jon's eyes, the essence of the pioneer woman about her.

"She was always a character to us when we were growing. She was a general, she'd get everything in line, take care of everything."

She was so active that from time to time some culinary concoction would inevitably be cremated while her mind had moved on to the next thing. One day Jon and Chip smelled smoke wafting up the stairs and hurried down to investigate.

"You couldn't see ahead in front of your face, there was so much smoke in the room! And my mother was sitting there, reading a paper! She was just sitting there, reading the paper. And we said to her, 'Mother,' and she said, 'Yes?' And we said, 'Do you notice anything?' She looked up and went, 'Oh, my God, what *is* this?' Then of course it was, have to paint the whole place, do all the drapes, everything. She was very happily enmeshed into fixing and renovation after the disaster. She's a funny one."

On Mondays, Elmer's day off, the entire tight-knit family went regularly to a double- if not triple-feature movie marathon, armed with a couple of loaves of Italian bread which Barbara would cut into wedges for them to devour during the films. She thinks Jon had his sights set on stage design, rather than acting, until he got a taste for it in his senior year at Catholic University in Washington, D.C. In retrospect she can see that he was always acting.

Jon's celebrity barely affected her, Jon says. "It didn't calm her down any. She didn't pay more attention to me than she ever had. It was kind of just delightful to her. But then, of course, there were other things to concern herself with." Like the way Jon treated his fans and friends of the family. "She would say, 'I hope you were nice to this one?' and 'I hope you sent a nice little picture to this one.' She had her two cents about that too!"

5   *Stars in the Making*

It terrified Laura Hawn: the sight of her deceptively angelic-looking, flaxen-haired daughter, Goldie, frenetically flinging herself around the room as she acted out a favorite childhood skit, best summed up as "two friends fighting." A plot complicated considerably by the physical difficulties inherent in one small body simultaneously enacting both parts, and a highly impressionistic event, needless to say, but a feat nevertheless and portentous in light of Goldie's comedic future.

Skip a decade or so, and there was Laura Hawn, positively enthralled by Goldie's grace as the lovelorn Juliet. She was seventeen when she stretched her Shakespearean wings at Williamsburg's semipro theater. The outdoor stage provided a glorious setting, and Laura Hawn, eyes shining, says unhesitatingly that her Goldie was the most beautiful Juliet she had ever seen. The dark skies drizzled unkindly throughout the performance, yet no one stirred from their seat, nor even opted for a permissible getaway during intermission. Like Laura, they were damp but entranced. Laura, who admits to entertaining a dream or two of seeing Goldie dance in *Swan Lake*, says, "I think it was the only time in my entire life that I forgot Goldie was my daughter. It was the first time I ever felt that special magic."

Special magic indeed. None of us is impervious to being stirred by it, and star moms are privileged early observers of its most shining examples. The appeal of applause is universal, and as star moms and non–star moms will testify, there is a little of the ham in each of us, some of that appetite for attention—what varies is the length to which we are driven to achieve it and conversely the degree to which we are kept from it by fear of criticism, rejection, or purely pragmatic considerations like financial hardship. Dr. James Grotstein, who is struck by the prevalence of a hankering to be encouraged to perform despite vigorous protestations of terror, believes that if this were the Soviet Union and performing was rewarded commensurately with other tasks, vast numbers would flock to do so.

In Goldie Hawn's case the love of performing was constant. The variable? The delicate, ultrafeminine Goldie and the tomboy-ish, prankster, natural comedienne Goldie. (Later, Goldie Hawn the Star would embody both.) For Laura Hawn, Goldie's Juliet was the first real fruition of a dream that had taken root many years earlier when she determined her daughter's natural talent must be nurtured. Goldie Jeanne (named in honor of a favorite aunt) was three years old. She was introduced to tap and ballet at the Roberta Fera School of Dance in Takoma Park, Maryland (a suburb of Washington, D.C.), where you could say she had an "in" with the proprietors. Laura, a one-time government worker with a good business head she says Goldie has inherited, co-owned and ran the school. Her older daughter, Patti (eight years Goldie's senior), was off at school, and rather than hire a babysit-ter, Laura took Goldie with her to work.

As she blossomed into a superb little dancer, Goldie gravitated toward serious ballet (jazz and modern dance came later), and when she was ten she danced in Ballet Russe de Monte Carlo's production of *The Nutcracker Suite*. (She still has her fifty-dollar paycheck which was framed for posterity.) Laura remembers being reluctant to relinquish her usual role of dressing Goldie to Ballet Russe's wardrobe mistress, but thrilled all the same.

Appropriately enough, Goldie made a singular impression in her professional debut. Not having been instructed to the con-trary, she decided to take her bow right along with the prima ballerina. "It brought the house down," Laura recalls with a throaty chuckle, "so they just let her do it every night. She was just a funny little girl, really."

Laura was not a dancer herself, but music coursed through the Hawn branch of the family tree. Goldie and Patti's father ran a watch repair shop by day, but was primarily a musician and was equally at home with violin, saxophone, and clarinet. Edward Rutledge Hawn, whom Laura calls "Rut," was a descendant of Edward Rutledge, the youngest signer of the Declaration of Independence. Laura Steinhoff (as she was then called) met him in Washington; they both lived in Maryland boarding houses one block from the District of Columbia.

Goldie's dad performed at Washington's embassy events, at White House inaugurations, and for official visits by heads of state—most notably, before U.S.S.R. premier Khrushchev. Rut Hawn relished his inside view of the seat of power and regaled his family with irreverent tales of the guests he encountered, ranging from King Farouk to Franklin D. Roosevelt. Without doubt, Rut was a source of comedic inspiration for Goldie, who was a natural mimic even as a little girl. Arriving home from a performance in the early hours, Laura's husband took great delight in setting up pranks to greet his daughters when they awakened the next morning. Courtesy of Rut, an imposing stuffed pheasant Laura's father had given her made a surprise appearance all kitted out in her spectacles and babushka. Rut also built an accessorized Laura-look-alike snowman, which made Goldie and Patti howl with delight. "He would do *anything* to entertain those girls." Laura shakes her head in amazement at the extremes to which he sometimes went, recalling the time Goldie needed an excuse note for her junior high teacher and Daddy kindly wrote one which explained that his daughter would be absent from school because she had appointments with her parole officer in the morning and her psychiatrist in the afternoon. Only later did Goldie learn its contents. "She absolutely wanted to kill! Do you believe that?" her mother exclaims.

After her husband's death in 1982, Laura Hawn moved from Washington to California to be near Goldie and Patti. She lives in a spacious Brentwood condominium, the walls of which are lined with happy family photographs and a colorful, highly intricate collage depicting Goldie's career which was painstakingly executed by her proud mom.

Laura reports that while Goldie and Patti are close now, Goldie was "the proverbial little sister, awful to live with." Imitating

Patti, all dressed up in silk stockings, high heels, and make-up, Goldie was in her element. She was only too happy to keep her sister's punctual boyfriends company while Patti finished getting ready for her dates. "She did some beauties," Laura wryly recalls. "I heard her one time in the den with two young fellas, telling dirty jokes. She was seven, maybe six. Patti was mortified." On another occasion, Goldie ran off with the candy Patti's date brought her. Infuriated, Patti gave chase through the house, screaming at her little sister in a very unladylike fashion—all in front of her horrified date.

Laura's daughters were afforded equal opportunities and both took dance and piano lessons. Patti was tutored in fiddle too—a short-lived effort abandoned due to lack of motivation on the pupil's part. Patti "wanted everything NOW!" says Laura Hawn. What Goldie possessed was the drive and tenacity.

To hear Goldie tell it, her teenage years were a case of "Wherefore art thou, Romeo?" Yet she was a very pretty (and busy) teenager, according to her mom—it was just that she did not think so. "Goldie was a bit of a wallflower," Laura Hawn concedes in her distinctive, gravelly voice. "She thought everything was wrong with her. We had a bit of trouble with that."

Physically, Goldie was a late bloomer. "She was flat-chested and she almost gave up dancing because she thought that was what caused it," Laura says, allowing herself a smile. She soothed Goldie when she tearfully complained of her lack of "titties" and blithely promised she would soon be fighting off hordes of would-be suitors. Wearing falsies did not entirely stem the flow of jokes and rude remarks from her peers, which she has since described as devastating, marveling that she did not end up with an inferiority complex.

She may have been miserable about her looks, but she was never rebellious. "She honestly didn't have the time." Goldie learned to type and attended college for two years, but even her professor encouraged her to go out on the road. Whereas Patti, who spent twelve years working with the handicapped and now works in film publicity, thought she was headed for the unemployment lines with no secretarial skills, Laura knew performing was what would make Goldie happy. "We didn't push her. I would have been very happy to try to open a dancing school for her."

Even Laura Hawn, with her daughter's wholesome image, has felt pain at the hands of the press when reading about Goldie's early days. "There has been a lot printed about all the go-go dancing and the starving she did, and I got very upset," she admits, explaining that Goldie went to New York, danced at the World's Fair in the Texas Pavilion, then traveled on the tent circuit with Goober, Ford, and Gross. She danced in Puerto Rico, then Melodyland in Anaheim, and briefly in Las Vegas, which she did not like.

"She might have done a little go-go dancing and I didn't know about it," Laura concedes, but says, "I was sending money for lessons, so you don't have to do that for ten dollars. She could have. She did have one bad experience in New York. She went across the river to New Jersey and danced on a table, but it was for another girl Goldie was living with. She was sick, so Goldie went—it wasn't her job. It was a terrible experience. These drunks, it was the usual brawly kind of place. She did it once."

As Goldie told it to Celeste Fremon of *Playgirl*, she danced on tables to pay the rent. When money was tight, it did not occur to her to waitress, she was a dancer after all, so she found a go-go agent and danced in cages and on wobbly tables. It was a rough time, culminating with a bad experience in New Jersey when she realized that a man in the audience who she had noticed staring at her—she thought sympathetically—was masturbating. "Well, my knees buckled and I thought I was going to faint," she told Celeste Fremon. She was on the verge of going home to Mom and Dad when, in the nick of time, she was offered the chance to go to California.

Virtually the moment she set foot in Hollywood, Goldie was signed up for twenty-six weeks on "The Andy Griffith Show." She then appeared in a forgettable TV show, "Good Morning World," which rapidly sank into oblivion—but not before she had been spotted for "Rowan and Martin's Laugh-In." The 1968 show capitalized on a series of Goldie's natural faux pas. There she stood, making blunder upon blunder, giggling infectiously, and tickling a nation's funny bone.

"Goldie never aspired to what she got. She never even tried to get what she got . . . it was just like handed to her. Goldie's story is a fairy tale. It just doesn't happen, you know? And I knew that it would. I knew that it absolutely had to," says Laura.

In much the same way that Goldie tasted the heady thrill of applause by taking her bow with the prima ballerina in *The Nutcracker Suite*, so Elizabeth Taylor grabbed an early magical moment in the limelight. Her ballet classes began less than illustriously. She attended week after week, only to stand at the side of the class, rooted to the spot, shyly hiding her face in her Nannie's uniform although she was desperately keen to participate and even coerced her mom, Sara Taylor, into sewing ballet dresses for her and a friend for Christmas gifts.

Just as Sara was about to give up, her teacher invited the little girl to waltz with her. Grittily determined, she fought back her tears and rose to the occasion. After that, there was no stopping her, and very shortly thereafter, she donned a white net ballet dress and wings as a little ballet butterfly to dance in a hospital benefit. When all the fledgling ballerinas flew gracefully away, one remained. It was Elizabeth, still fluttering madly, face down. When she realized she was the sole butterfly left on stage she started to flutter off, but suddenly she had a change of heart—she was in the spotlight and she decided to play up the unexpected solo for all it was worth. She circled around the stage again and took another deep curtsy before exiting, to thunderous applause.

That day left no doubt in Sara's mind that Elizabeth was destined to follow in her footsteps on the stage. She herself had been an actress, under the name Sara Sothern—an improvement on her real name, Sara Warmbrodt, which she loathed. She worked in stock companies from the time of her premature departure from high school until in 1926, at age thirty, she married Francis Taylor. She had received a set of rave reviews while playing a crippled girl on the London stage in *The Fool*, but abandoned her otherwise unremarkable career with no regrets.

Elizabeth Taylor was born in February 1932, weighing a healthy eight and one half pounds and boasting an abundance of dark hair, but she bore little resemblance to the beauty she was to become. In fact, confounding doctors and frightening her mother, she kept her tiny eyes tightly shut for the first days of her life. Whenever the doctor attempted to pry them open, they rolled back in their sockets and all that was visible was the whites of the eyeballs. Sara Taylor could do little else but pray and cling to her faith that all would be well.

Sure enough, ten days later those dark-lashed eyelids separated to reveal the pair of heart-breaker violet irises which are now arguably the most famous in the world. Simultaneously little Elizabeth smiled—although the nurse insisted it was merely wind. The eyes were beautiful, but Elizabeth was not. Sara observed in *Ladies' Home Journal* in 1954 of her first meeting with her daughter:

"As the precious bundle was placed in my arms, my heart stood still. There inside the cashmere shawl was the *funniest*-looking little baby I have ever seen! Her hair was long and black. Her ears were covered with thick black fuzz, and inlaid into the sides of her head; her nose looked like a tip-tilted button, and her tiny face so tightly closed it looked as if it would never unfold."

Sara's mother's advice three years earlier, before the birth of Howard, Sara's first child, had been to fill her mind with beautiful thoughts, and indeed Howard was a beautiful baby, complete with golden ringlets. What, Sara wondered, could have been in her mind before Elizabeth arrived.

"From that day on I held her in my arms every day and silently asked God please *not* to let the hair grow in all the wrong places —*not* all over her ears, arms, and back!" Sara was forced to field comments from those who could not resist comparing Elizabeth unfavorably to her cherubic brother. She has since admitted that Elizabeth did little but gurgle and drool for the first year of her life; "it looked for a while as if she would have to have dentures." Then at sixteen months, suddenly, she was transformed into the beauty with the legendary double rows of black lashes.

Sara Taylor is not willing to reveal precisely how she felt at the moment that Elizabeth's eyes opened although she readily admits it was an intensely emotional experience. The reason for her reticence is one not unfamiliar to biographers: she is saving the story for the book she is writing. What is slightly unusual is that this would-be author is over ninety.

When asked about the moments she most treasures as a star mom, she is cannily evasive, letting little slip other than that Elizabeth is always buying her beautiful hand-made lingerie. "It's awfully hard to say anything, because I'm just going to work now on my story, and I'm trying to get it finished because I'm having problems with my eyes." She cannot work with a tape recorder, or a typewriter—too mechanical. So she is forced to labor away with pen and ink and a tablet of paper, she complains, sounding rather like the author of a Declaration of Independence.

According to Sara, she spends a lot of time fending off requests for interviews. She is very well aware that she is not Kitty Kelley and is fiercely protective of her genteel anecdotes, as though the roof over her head depended upon them. Which, of course, it does not. Elizabeth has been and is a very generous daughter. Her book, if it is published, will trace back to Elizabeth's grandparents and forward to the present. "It's her heritage, or her roots. I think I have about a thousand pages now and I'm trying to bring it to a close . . . but it doesn't want to quit."

Not only does she have her wits about her, she is thinking like a saleswoman who envisions clinching a deal. She is astute enough to fear that telling her interviewer too many little stories about Elizabeth would deplete her stockpile. "I'm saving them for my book, dear, because there's been so much published about her, that it's only what I know, and if I give that away, then what have I left?"

It is more than thirty years since she wrote her innocuous story called "Elizabeth, My Daughter," for *Ladies' Home Journal*. She had hopes then of turning that into a book, but admits no publisher would touch it, "because it didn't have any sex in it!" She laughs. "This book I'm writing—no one may want to publish it. I have a lot of publishers waiting to see it, but when they find out there's no sex in it, *it* may wind up in the *Ladies' Home Journal*!" If nothing else, her literary efforts will become a record for her grandchildren, a family tome.

Kansas-born Sara has frequently been accused of being a daunt-less stage mother and it is a matter of record that Elizabeth was screen-tested at age eight and put under her first studio contract. Yet, to hear Sara Taylor tell it, it was not so much a case of spotting star potential in Elizabeth as a case of weakening reluctantly under the weight of constant offers. "We fought it all along, we didn't want her to be in films at all." It was because Elizabeth was such a startlingly pretty child, she explains, that the subject would not disappear: "Wherever we went, they tried to get her in pictures." Eventually, the Taylors changed their minds because their refusal came to seem "like we were interfering with her future."

Originally, the thought was that Elizabeth would work in front of the cameras until World War II ended and the family made its intended return to England, where Sara's husband, Francis Taylor, ran an art gallery for his millionaire uncle, art dealer Howard Young. It was only the outbreak of war in 1939 that had forced them back to the States. Sara moved in exciting social circles and reveled in, for example, attending King George VI's coronation with a well-connected friend.

Elizabeth was a determined child and game to try anything. When she was really quite small, she was very keen to box with her brother Howard, so she too had boxing gloves and Howard used her as a sparring partner before his big matches. She threw punches with every ounce of strength she could muster and was enraged if he did not respond in kind.

Elizabeth's nanny discovered that the only punishment that was effective with Elizabeth was to ignore her completely. She so hated that, that it prompted little "sorry" notes on Sara's pillow. Sara still has a collection of those notes and as far as she is concerned they are priceless.

She does not give much thought to her daughter's superstar status, she says. "Well, it never occurs to me. I never think of it in that way. I mean, she's just Elizabeth to us; she's not anything else, just Elizabeth. She's a wonderful mother and a wonderful daughter. And it's just something that we're very grateful for. Am I proud of her? Oh, what do you think! I would say that I couldn't be more proud of her than I am. I know her for all her wonderful qualities—and I just can't go into all of it."

She would like to see more of her daughter, but Elizabeth lives in Los Angeles and Sara would not want to give up the desert oasis of Palm Springs. She loves her "very sweet" home there. She pedals around it on her tricycle and relishes its sweeping views of the golf course and nearby snow-capped mountains. She enjoys watching the oranges on the trees slowly turn gold, the roses coming into bloom.

"From the time I was a little girl, roses were a feature in my life. And we had a rose garden in England—oh, a beautiful rose garden," she says, casting her mind back to Heathwood, the London home they occupied when Elizabeth was small, with its formal rose garden and herbaceous flower garden.

Elizabeth was just three when she had her first serious illness, a fever of 103 degrees, abscessed ears that required repeated lancing, and a persistent sore throat. Her career has been plagued by health troubles, and yet she is always back on her feet when the seconds leave the ring. "I don't know where she gets her strength from," her mother admits. Perhaps it is from Sara, her interviewer suggests? "Well, I don't know. I like to think I am. Yes, I would say that I am, but I don't want to be bragging. . . . Elizabeth says we're indestructible, because we've been through such horrendous illnesses, you know. Because she's had a rough time healthwise. I've had so many operations for diverticulitis, it's been sort of a problem, but I'm on top of it. That's what counts."

No one would dispute that Sara Taylor is a strong lady encased in a sweet, ladylike persona. But should further proof be needed, witness her behavior in the devastating Bel Air brush fire of November 6, 1961, that swept across the hilly terrain, claiming five hundred homes.

Marion Lederer, who was throwing a surprise birthday party for her husband, Francis Lederer, reports that by noon that day, Bel Air looked like Dante's Inferno from her vantage point some miles away. She did not expect her guests to appear that night since many were Bel Air residents, but most did because, after hurriedly rescuing treasured paintings and wrapping silverware in pillowcases which they threw into their swimming pools for safe-keeping, they were among the thousands who had been evacuated.

Sara was not with them. Francis Taylor was ill, confined to his bed, and they did not want to vacate their home. So Sara clambered up onto the roof, from which lofty height she, with the aid of a garden hose, kept the roof wet and single-handedly fought back the flames that edged ever closer. The story goes that she saved not only her own abode but some of her neighbors' homes too.

Lesley-Anne Warren was another early starter in ballet shoes, appearing in her first tap-dancing recital at age three. At six, she began ballet classes with a vengeance, announcing to her mom her intention of becoming a prima ballerina. Margot took her to see Gertrude Lawrence's final matinee appearance in *The King and I*, and the next day, Lesley mimicked everyone in the show. As an ex-nightclub singer who earned the nickname "the white Billie Holiday," vivacious Margot Warren certainly has her quota of rhythm, but Margot claims she has two left feet.

Lesley-Anne, on the other hand, was accepted to study with ballet master Balanchine at twelve and seemed on her way to bringing her plan to fruition, until a couple of years later she decided the ballet life was too rigorous. Unbeknownst to Margot and her father, she slipped off to audition for *Bye, Bye, Birdie* on Broadway and landed a small dancing role with a couple of lines of speech.

"She came home all excited." Margot shakes her head, remembering Lesley-Anne's bitter disappointment: "My husband, bless him, said, 'No, you can't go. We don't want you in show business. When you get older, if you want to go into it, you can.' Well, she never gave up!"

Somewhat contradictorily, Lesley-Anne has referred to being uncomfortable with her parents' expectation that she would dance, saying she knew she was loved and appreciated—but in her mind it was more for what she did than who she was. But Margot insists that she, like her husband, was ambivalent about Lesley-Anne's early efforts, but for reasons different from his. Her own mother had pushed her hard (Margot was an only child) and she had no intention of repeating that with Lesley-Anne. She even refused to go on auditions with her.

British-born Margot and her Russian-born mom had moved to New York in 1939, whereupon Margot sang for six months with the Tommy Dorsey Orchestra, then moved on to the club circuit. They had fled the cry of war in Britain, and their move began a ten-year separation from Margot's father, who stayed in London doing civil defense work (as Margot puts it, "picking up the bodies with all the rubble after the bombs"). Today, her father, who is ninety-two and still boasts a Cockney accent, lives four blocks from her in Los Angeles, walks to the local supermarket daily, refuses to let her do his laundry, and still loves to sing the old English vaudeville songs.

Margot's parents were Jewish. When her mother was four the family fled persecution in Russia, escaping in a wagon. Margot's father was well-to-do. Her grandfather was the first to own a two-story haberdashery in London's East End, so when Margot became very ill with tuberculosis as a little girl, her parents could afford to send her to a costly sanitarium in Switzerland for two years' treatment until she made a full recovery.

She first got into the theater while living in Montreal, where she spent eight of her school years. She was not at all keen, but her aunt entered her photograph in a contest and that started the ball rolling. When she was fifteen, she was crowned Miss Montreal and went off to sing with Buddy Rogers at the now-defunct Roxy Theater in New York City. A couple of years later, living back in London, she appeared in a production of *Idiot's Delight* with Raymond Massey. Massey encouraged Margot, telling her to contact him if she ever came to New York. With his introduction she began singing in New York nightclubs. Unlike theater, she loved it.

Her tryout was at a nightclub in the Village, and nerves melted away when she heard the opening bars: "You walk out, the lights are dimmed and the spotlight is on you; you start singing and there's a hush. It's a wonderful feeling; it just seems to fill your entire body. Of course, if you get an audience that's cold, it's not pleasant at all—an audience that's rowdy, heavy drinking, the twelve o'clock show." Love songs were always Margot's specialty, but the blues influence hit her once she was in the States, and the English rose learned to sing rhythm. She became "the girl who sang center stage" at clubs like the glamorous Copacabana, to the delight of her housewife mother, with whom she shared a small apartment off Central Park West.

"Truthfully, Mother should have been the one in the business.

She was a gorgeous woman, beautiful lady, and had all the fire and all the appeal. Lesley is very much like her. But generations back, it was hard and my grandmother was concerned. Horrors! You didn't go into that business, not a bit respectable!" Ironically, when Margot began to make headway, it was grandmother who ran around showing off her newspaper clippings.

Margot and Bill Warren, Lesley-Anne's father, were brought together by a copy of William Shirer's book *The Last Train from Berlin*. Margot put the book down in the dressing room of the Copacabana to go onstage, and when she returned, a handsome lieutenant was reading it. A lively discussion ensued, and Bill teased Margot, saying that, being British, it was her fault he was in uniform. When she returned from singing her next number, he had disappeared.

Margot, who was widowed in 1986, smiles and recalls that at dinner that night, someone noted, "Methinks she doth protest too much about this young lieutenant." "I was constantly talking about him, apparently. So I made him pay and I married him!" Bill Warren was a lawyer (and one of a pair of identical twins) who was stationed in Paris and worked in Intelligence (he trained with Clark Gable). "We did most of our romancing on the telephone," Margot says wistfully.

They were married on a Friday, just months after meeting. Fridays have been significant in Margot's life: she also met Bill on a Friday, she received his first batch of post-wedding letters on a Friday, he was eventually discharged on a Friday, Lesley-Anne was born on a Friday, and two years later their son Richard was born . . . on a Friday. "Isn't that incredible?" she asks, adding with disbelief, "And now Bill's gone, after forty-two years."

Margot decided that performing in nightclubs was incongruous with her status as a married woman and promptly retired. "I honestly never regretted giving it up. I never had that drive. To me it was sort of a means to an end. It was my work, what I did best." By then, she had made a couple of what she describes as mediocre records, one of which Bill carried with him around Africa and Italy during the war, carefully keeping it in one piece until just before D-Day. When Bill was medically discharged from the service, they settled down to start their family, and "my star was born!" she exclaims. She swiftly points out that Lesley-Anne is not the only star in the family: son Richard scores the background music for TV shows like "Remington Steele" and "Dallas."

Raised in proximity to Broadway, Lesley-Anne's desire to dance was unwavering, and at sixteen, she was given the ingenue lead in *A Hundred and Ten in the Shade* with Inga Swenson, for which she earned rave reviews. She persuaded her mom and dad to let her participate by promising, "Give me a year, just a year, and if nothing happens I promise to go to college." "Well, she never went," Margot says with a smile and a shrug. When Lesley went to California for the TV special "Cinderella," she led the way for Margot and Bill, who flew in to visit her on alternate weekends and in 1968 made a permanent move.

Margot was particularly proud of Lesley-Anne's outrageous performance as the platinum-blonde exotic dancer and gangster's moll in Blake Edwards' film *Victor, Victoria*, and says that when she heard Lesley-Anne was being nominated for an Oscar, "I just went out of my mind, I was so thrilled." Margot knew Lesley had good comedic instincts (she herself is outgoing, with a good sense of humor), but was stunned by her daughter's daring, especially as Lesley-Anne was a very proper little girl. "She doesn't boast about herself or rave about herself, so that comic role came as a tremendous surprise," her mom admits.

Before the Oscar nomination announcements, Margot was lunching with her daughter-in-law, Margie, when she overheard a conversation the gist of which was: "Well, she's unbelievable. We're going to put it through for a nomination, we've *got* to, the work is unbelievable!" The unknown diner had not mentioned *Victor, Victoria*, the role, nor Lesley-Anne, yet Margot's ears involuntarily pricked up, and to Margie's intense embarrassment, Margot announced she was going over to find out who they were talking about.

"I said, 'Excuse me,' and they looked at me thinking, 'Who's this dizzy old broad?' And I said, 'Something is bothering me, making me feel very excited. Who are you talking about?' One man said, 'We just finished a picture with Blake Edwards. We're talking about the girl who played the part of the blonde dummy.'

This is the honest-to-God's truth, because I have Margie to prove it. I said, 'Lesley-Anne Warren?' He said, 'Yes, you know her?' I said, 'I'm her mother.' He said, 'My God. Well, she is going to get an Oscar for this role.' "

Margot and Lesley-Anne's teenage son, Chris, attended the *Victor, Victoria* premiere in Century City. "They had this big buffet and all the muckamucks, red carpets, limousine, Chris all dressed up in his tuxedo. She wouldn't let us see the film before that. I was so excited. I was sitting on the edge of my seat, saying, 'Oh, my God, that's my baby!' like an idiot."

Margot acknowledges that Lesley-Anne chose a very tough business, but says, "She keeps a lot to herself, she doesn't burden me. Lesley's been just a dream daughter, and she was the same way when she had her ups and downs." She refers to the tragic break-up of her daughter's marriage to hairdresser-turned-producer Jon Peters, which left Lesley to raise their baby son alone. Although it was a less-than-happy union and there had been various separations, it took her years to get back on track after their divorce, which was made all the more traumatic by headlines painting Barbra Streisand as the villain in the piece.

"Lesley was marvelous," her mom recalls. "It was living hell for her. But their break-up came before Barbra Streisand entered the picture—the press *put* her in the picture, naturally, because it made for good reading. She was not to blame. Barbra and Lesley are friends. That's Hollywood, but they are, they're friends. Barbra had always been somebody Lesley idolized. It was hard. Every photo magazine, every Hollywood magazine, and every paper filled with her personal life. She went down, she had lows, but she worked her way up slowly. She's a remarkable young woman —she has helped her mother survive."

The death of Margot's husband is still a raw issue, but she takes comfort from the belief that she will see Bill and her mother, who also died in 1986, again. Margot claims to be a little psychic and Lesley-Anne is very much involved in metaphysics. Shortly before his death, Bill encouraged Margot to visit the Greek Islands and Paris with Lesley, who was doing publicity for the film *Choose Me*. Margot often went along on these jaunts to keep Chris company while Lesley worked. Bill also urged her to spend an extra week in London to make the most of her long-awaited reunion with her family. Pleased, Margot changed her flight plans accordingly, but inexplicably had "the strangest feeling," and within twenty-four hours had switched them back. She telephoned Bill but just got their answering machine and left her new travel plans on it. Bill was not there to meet her at the airport. Instead she heard, "Paging Mrs. Warren, please," and her heart dropped to her feet.

"Bill had had a very bad heart attack, had called my daughter-in-law, Margie, and could hardly speak. (My son Ricky, a marathon runner, was out running at the time.) Bill said, 'I don't want the paramedics,' but Margie knew it would take her a good twenty minutes to get to him, so she called them immediately and said, 'He's there all alone, seventy years old, and I want you to get there fast,' which they did. They put him into intensive care, and that was the beginning of going downhill. Now I think that's psychic."

Margot and Lesley-Anne are frequent companions, enjoying theater, ballet, and sushi bars together. "Lesley's not a party-goer. She loves to be with her dear friends, loves to entertain, but she doesn't go out to all these star affairs. I'd get a thrill out of it, but in that respect she's more like Bill. Maybe I'm living all the excitement through the eyes of my daughter, or my son. It's wonderful. When I go to the theater with Lesley, I'll be sitting there and looking around and she'll say, 'Mom! Mom! The stage is up there. Don't do that!' I'll say, 'Honey, please.' She says, 'Don't do it, Mom, or I won't go to the theater with you,' so of course I stop immediately. I'm glad she's like that, it's brought her through, but I get such a kick out of people craning their necks to see. All the mothers do, they all feel the same way I do, it's wonderful."

A close friend of Margot's is Gena Rowlands' mom, Mary Allen Rowlands, a painter and sculptress, whose colorful character is like a flamboyant edition of the low-key Gena's. Margot and Mary Allen met while under neighboring hair driers and now regularly play bridge together. It was Mary Allen who introduced Margot to the Motion Picture Mothers group. For Mary Allen Rowlands, the realization that Gena had something special dawned early. But there was no prior history in the business. Mary Allen, a surgeon's daughter from Arkansas, was a great beauty, but had no interest whatsoever when a Ziegfeld scout offered her a chance to join the Ziegfeld Follies.

As a little girl, Gena was neither bold nor extroverted—in fact, she was happiest at home with her nose in a book—but when she was eight, Mary Allen noticed something curious. When Gena was involved in little school productions, she emerged from her shell: "I thought, 'She's so happy, she's so at home, she's so comfortable.' They get on that stage, and the sheep separate from the goats. There is one that is just shining out there—and that's the kind of child Gena was."

Doris Richards' son, Keith, thrilled her as a bright-eyed choirboy at Westminster Abbey long before he rose to fame as a decadent Rolling Stone. Keith, now roundly recognized as one of rock's virtuoso guitarists, first laid hands on his granddad's guitar. Doris's father, Theodore Augustus "Gus" Dupree, led a semiprofessional dance band during the '30s and played guitar, saxophone, and violin; so it was that Doris always did her housework to big band music.

Doris, who worked part-time in a bakery, spoiled Keith. When he started school and was nervous about walking there alone, she simply carried him. Most importantly, she facilitated the development of Keith's obvious musical talent by buying his first guitar for the then-princely sum of seven pounds, with the stipulation that he learn to play properly.

Sally Willson Cotten, Joseph Cotten's mother, was another mother who could not help but be aware of her son's flair. As a small boy he took to making grand entrances at dinner, arriving late for dramatic effect, then launching into an emotionally charged delivery of a nursery rhyme. Not that he was conceited—merely supremely confident, acccording to his mother, who envisioned Joseph Jr. might find his niche in either the pulpit or the theater: "At any rate, we knew that vanity would get him somewhere."

Georgia Holt will never forget the special glint she saw in Cher's eyes when she took her, as a young girl, to see Frankie Lane in Las Vegas. "She wore a beautiful royal blue velvet dress with a lovely lace collar and she was shining. When Frankie Lane sang 'Little Coquette' he sang it directly to her, so the spotlight kept flashing on her and she loved it. The audience loved it too, they wouldn't stop applauding when he finished the song. I've often wondered if something like that makes an indelible impression on a child's mind."

Cher had a hard row to hoe before she became a star. Her first professional appearance was with Sonny, opening for the Righteous Brothers at her uncle's Hollywood club, the Purple Onion. He paid them twenty-five dollars. Georgia bought Cher white silk crepe pants and an oyster beaded top for the occasion, and remembers feeling a shiver of excitement on hearing her daughter sing "The Battle Hymn of the Republic." It was a revelation:

"I could tell what was going to happen with Cher. I'd got everybody I knew to come that night and I told them all she was going to be a star, but they said, 'Sure, sure. We know! She's your daughter!' Nobody believed me! But when a person has that incredible presence, it's just a question of time. Sonny probably had one of the worst voices in life, but he sounded good with Cher and she would never have done it alone. If you look at early footage of them, she was always looking down at the floor, with her hair covering her face."

There was music in John Lennon's genes, too; his maternal grandfather was a musician. And during the spasmodically happy times in their marriage, John's father, Fred Lennon, serenaded his mom, Julia (who also liked to sing), with Italian love songs picked out on his ukulele. Fred also sang in crew concerts while away at sea as a ship's steward.

John grew up not with Julia, however, but under the strong wing of his Auntie Mimi, her older sister. An aura of destiny hovers over this Julia-Mimi-John triumvirate; there was a striking sense of fated acceptance between the sisters about the way John slipped from being Julia's to being Mimi's. Julia was a healthy, able-bodied woman, and although John's father was off at sea for long stretches of time, she was hardly helpless.

What was the strongest factor dictating the transfer? Did Julia feel unable to cope with John and a new relationship? He was two when she moved in with Fred Lennon's successor. More likely Mimi's urgent, maternal love for the boy, coupled with the stability of the home life she and her husband George could offer, simply tipped the scales.

Prophetically, Mimi was the first person to rush to the maternity hospital to visit Julia—and to see newborn John. Fred Lennon's work took him to far-away places like New York (a romantic-sounding life that initially had much to do with the appeal he held for Julia, who was employed as a cinema usherette before their 1938 marriage), and predictably, Fred was sailing on the high seas when John was born in October 1940. It was a night on which the skies were ablaze, courtesy of the Luftwaffe doing its worst to obliterate the seaport town of Liverpool.

"I was dodging in doorways—running as fast as my legs would carry me," said Mimi, who never had children of her own. She was insistent that John was not wrinkled like all the other new babies, but he was exactly like them in one respect; he too was placed beneath his mother's bed for safety during the air raids.

Tellingly, Mimi admitted to writer Hunter Davies in *The Beatles: The Authorized Biography*: "The minute I saw John, that was it. I was lost forever. A boy! I couldn't get over it. I went on and on about him, almost forgetting Julia. She said, 'All I've done is have him.' "

Julia, whom the family called Juliet, was born in 1914, the youngest of the five daughters of Annie (also an avant-garde character) and George Stanley. It was the job of George, an official with the Glasgow and Liverpool Salvage Company, to retrieve submarines, an important function which rendered the Stanley family privileged amidst Merseyside's chronic unemployment. Mimi (more formally, Mary Elizabeth Smith) provided the solid presence in John's life which, in conjunction with Julia's more ethereal one, had a truly profound effect. Mimi, who ruled with love, exhibited steely determination, although she conceded that her beloved John knew how to get around her.

Auburn-haired Julia was a free spirit, fun-loving, carefree, gay. Julia's predilection for eccentricity and humor foreshadowed John's. She would go for walks wearing a pair of knickers on her head like a hat, the legs hanging down the back. She feigned being oblivious to people's stares. Sometimes she added spectacles with no lenses to this attire. She would then stop someone in the street on the pretext of asking the way and, perfectly straightfaced, rub her eye through the empty glasses frames. John and his friends who witnessed these scenes would be beside themselves. Years later, when John amused himself during bus rides by tickling the bald patch of some poor unsuspecting fellow in front, then whisking his hand away in the nick of time to avoid detection, the prank had the ring of Julia about it.

The evident instability of Julia and Fred Lennon's marriage was brought into the open via a missive from Fred in which he implied that since his return date was so uncertain, his wife might just as well go out and have a good time. Julia being Julia, she duly did. Eventually, considering herself a deserted wife, she moved in with the hotel waiter whom John derisively named Twitchy.

The words "Mimi" and "Mummy" became inextricably linked in John's mind, although his names for Mimi and George were "Mater" and "Pater." Mimi, as John's full-time custodian, kept the whys and wherefores of John's parents' situation to herself, leading John to believe that Julia was far away, instead of merely a bus-ride. Her reasoning, she told Hunter Davies, was, "I just wanted to protect him from all that. Perhaps I was overanxious. I don't know. I just wanted him to be happy." Years later, John said that Julia never left his thoughts. John questioned Mimi after a couple of Julia's visits, but she was evasive; she did not want to say that his father was no good and his mother had found someone else.

When John was five and Julia was living with Twitchy, Fred Lennon reappeared unexpectedly to reclaim his wife and son. Perhaps they could start anew in New Zealand? There was no love lost between Mimi and Fred (class-conscious Mimi considered Fred beneath her sister), but Mimi felt unable to deny him when he asked to take John for a little holiday. Fred, however, did not return when expected and Julia had to track down her ex-husband and son in the nearby seaside resort of Blackpool. There was a confrontation, during which Fred cruelly gave little John the task of deciding his own future. In his confusion and panic, John initially chose his dad, but as soon as the door closed on Julia he ran after her crying uncontrollably. Neither John nor Mimi heard from Fred after that incident—not so much as a simple inquiry about his son's welfare—until 1964, by which time John was a Beatle and Fred was a hotel dishwasher outside London.

It was Mimi's husband, George, who ran a dairy farm near the house, who was the father figure in John's life, bathing him and, with the aid of the *Liverpool Echo*, teaching him to read and write when he was four. The two passed secret notes, plotting to out-maneuver Mimi and go to the cinema, for instance. George provided a refuge from Mimi's discipline and was doubtless behind John's lifelong passion for books: Richmal Crompton's *Just William* series, *Alice in Wonderland*, and *The Wind in the Willows* were special favorites. When John finished a book, he would relive it all over again in his mind; he had devoured most of the classics by the time he was ten, not to mention encyclopedias, and Aunt Mimi's twenty volumes of *The World's Best Stories* and Balzac. (Mimi thought Balzac's influence was visible in John's song-writing.) He always had a pencil in his hand and over the years craftily developed secret handwriting that Mimi was unable to decipher.

John listened to Radio Luxembourg under the bedcovers, and his TV favorites, during which Mimi and George were shushed into silence, were "Dick Barton, Special Agent" (his face went deathly white when Dick was in trouble, Mimi said), and "The Goon Show," whose characters' voices he imitated.

George's sudden death of cirrhosis of the liver, when John was twelve, devastated him. Red-faced, he retreated to his room while Mimi was openly heartbroken, but in what was to become a pattern, John was simply burying the hurt inside him.

Aunt Mimi did not resort to physical violence during John's adolescence, but must have been sorely tempted. Aside from their (literally) countless arguments, John was in constant trouble at Quarry Bank High School, where he was labeled a disruptive influence and indolent. He mocked teachers and often ended up on the wrong end of a teacher's cane. Once, filling in a space for parents' comments on John's school report, it was Mimi's suggestion that her wayward charge receive the traditional British punishment of half a dozen cane strokes. "Six of the best," wrote Mimi, presumably with feeling.

John would not be deterred from wearing his skintight drainpipes to art school, but Mimi's influence remained such that he took the trouble to conceal them under his "normal" trousers until he was out of her sight, then slipped them off (often while waiting at the bus stop) so he could make his entrance teddy-boy style. He hated needing glasses and rejected the mass-produced, wire-rimmed, National Health style completely—the very utilitarian specs he would later make fashionable—persuading Mimi to buy him a black, horn-rimmed design.

John was treasured but not spoiled, and Mimi insisted that he regularly mow the lawn, paying him five shillings for the task. She recollects that he would do a barely passable job, then come in, hand outstretched, demanding his money. Evidently Mimi's efforts to teach him the value of a pound paid off, for she told biographer Ray Coleman that John took great pride during the Quarrymen's early days of success in handing her a few banknotes and saying, "There's the money for my keep."

Contrary to his working-class hero image (and just like his nemesis, Mick Jagger), John Lennon grew up in a genteel, middle-class neighborhood. "Mendips," Mimi's house, was semi-detached, and Woolton one of Liverpool's nicer suburbs.

In the age-old manner, John refused piano or violin lessons when they were offered, but the guitar—now that was something else entirely. His guitar-playing, with which Mimi was so convinced John could never make his living, was confined outside, to the house's glass front porch. (John was awarded the M.B.E. by Queen Elizabeth II, and before he handed it back as a political protest, he presented it to Mimi along with a custom-made plaque on which he had had engraved: "The guitar's alright, but you'll never earn your living with it.") To Mimi, having the boys rehearse rock 'n' roll at Mendips was unthinkable. She did not approve of George Harrison, with his pink shirt and extremely pointed winklepicker shoes, any more than she approved of Elvis Presley, whose records blared all day and whose poster hung in John's bedroom, from which she was suddenly banished.

"One of these days, I'm going to be famous, and then you'll be sorry you were like this to me," John chided his aunt, when her voice boomed up the stairs: "There's going to be a change in this house. We're going to have law and order." John was never able to resist parroting Mimi's pet chastisements back to her once he became a star, but typically she was unmoved. She simply repeated another oft-heard observation: it was not that she thought he would not become famous, just that she worried he was more likely to be infamous—on which count she was not entirely wrong.

During John's second year at Quarry Bank, Julia began to play a larger role in his life. John's mom was rated "a groove" by his schoolmates because she joined in making fun of teachers and the other mothers, just like one of the kids. Julia could pluck a few chords on the banjo, a skill she passed on to John, who pleaded with both the women in his life to buy him a guitar. Unwilling to undermine Mimi's authority on this, Julia would not comply, so he was forced to order a cheap model via a newspaper ad, and canny enough to have it mailed to Julia's address and not Mendips.

Mimi's first sight of John in musical action was with the Quarrymen at an outdoor fair and in fact she found him mesmerizing. She did note that his grin disappeared as he spotted her approaching: "I don't know why—I was pleased as punch to see him up there." In fact his aunt's reprimands about his clothing were ringing in his ears, but John, never lost for words, began to sing the improvised refrain: "And Mimi's coming down the path, oh, oh."

John lost Julia soon after rediscovering her and just as their friendship was deepening. It was 1958, seven months before the death of his beloved Buddy Holly. John was waiting for Julia at her home in Spring Wood the afternoon she died. Leaving Mimi's after a cup of tea and a chat, while crossing the road to the bus stop, Julia was sent hurtling into the air by a car and died instantly. (The driver of the car that killed her was an off-duty policeman. There was a court case and he stood trial, but was acquitted.) She was forty-four, John was eighteen. She had had three illegitimate children outside her marriage to Fred Lennon, one of whom was reportedly adopted at birth and is apparently living in Sweden. "Julia was a carefree person. She used to enjoy herself," explained a source who knew the family.

"When she went with the new man," Mimi told Ray Coleman, "I said that to think of another man providing for him shoes, clothes, and food and perhaps grudging it later on—it's not fair. Nobody was going to have the chance to look sideways at one of ours. And Julia agreed. So as John got older, he naturally got to know his mother better. He was broken-hearted for weeks. He just went to his room, into a shell."

Mimi knew that she had been losing John back to Julia at that rebellious stage in his life, but there was no bitterness; the sisters, although so different, had always been close and they never quarreled about John. The build-up of emotional scarring from the losses of his father, Uncle George, and Julia was later articulated in songs he wrote like "My Mummy's Dead," "Mother," and "Julia." It also led to John's trademark veneer of aggressive belligerence and caustic, sometimes downright vicious, wit. Yet John was soft enough to rescue a stray cat from the snow (Tim, a half Persian) and to telephone Mimi (the reluctant custodian) for progress reports on his three cats when he was on the road.

Cynthia Lennon, John's first wife and the mother of his son Julian, remembers John wearing Uncle George's old jackets and saying that he missed George terribly, but clamping down if Fred's name was brought up. Julia's death was even more of a taboo subject. "He didn't talk about his Mum to anybody but me," Cynthia told Ray Coleman; she remembers John being prone to sudden rages. "It shattered his life. It was obviously too painful for him to open up very much."

When John and the Beatles moved to the bright lights of London, Mimi was typically stoic, hiding how much she missed him. "I was determined that there would be no clinging vine stuff." Socially and class-aware, she was irked enormously by the broad Scouse accent (typical of Liverpool's working class) that John cultivated. She viewed it as a direct reflection on the way in which she had raised him. His excuse (that it went over well in Brooklyn and was what fans expected to hear) cut no ice with Mimi. "You know how to speak properly," she reprimanded.

Mimi remained resolutely unintimidated by John's fame and told him in no uncertain terms exactly what she thought of the Beatles' endorsement of the 1960s drug culture. Lennon cheekily reminded his Aunt that she herself took aspirin, then explained more seriously that she did not understand the tension they lived under, and reassured her that he could handle drugs. Mimi was unmoved, saying, "Well, don't have me to come over to your house while all this is happening."

As John matured, the old tensions between them dissipated and his respect increased for the woman who had lovingly raised him. He wrote to her regularly and telephoned her, confiding his problems. She was perhaps the only real constant in his life, the one person who did not disappoint him by disappearing. In 1964, John even took his Auntie along on the Beatles' tour of Australia and New Zealand. The following year he bought Mimi a luxury seaside bungalow in Bournemouth, on the south coast of England, far (he hoped) from the madness of fans sleeping in her driveway. Nowhere in the British Isles would have been far enough, and Bournemouth certainly was not. Much like in Woolton, Mimi was swiftly treated to boatloads of holiday-makers cruising past, pointing fingers as megaphone-carrying tour guides broadcast her identity.

Mimi tried to dissuade the young girls from waiting outside the house, hoping for a glimpse of John, but if they would not budge, she took pity on those who had hitchhiked across the country, inviting them in for tea and sandwiches. They begged to be allowed to drink from John's cup and squealed when Mimi said he had used them all. Fans even telephoned from America and Australia. She changed her number so often that eventually the telephone company's well of new numbers ran dry.

Mendips, which John persuaded her to sell when she moved south, has since become a big tourist attraction. Her sister Harriet looks after Mimi, who is now ailing, in her eighties, and living back in her old hometown. Believe it or not, Mimi still has occasion to deflect camera crews and reporters from her property all these years after John's death, and does so adeptly.

Mimi lives surrounded by mementos of John (like his early artwork) that would now fetch a fortune. "She's nobody's fool. Money does not matter one iota to her," one friend observed. She has turned down huge sums offered for her memoirs, and with almost no exceptions, her lips have remained sealed, even since John's death. She has been horrified by much of what has been written about John and is enormously suspicious. John's deep respect for taciturn Mimi was based greatly on such qualities. One of the few reporters ever permitted a rare view of her home and its contents rapidly had the privilege revoked when he observed that it was nice of John to buy everything for her. Mimi Smith's pride had been underestimated.

Winston Churchill, after whom John Winston Lennon was named, had a mother other than his own in his life—in his case, a loving nanny. His mother was entirely absorbed with her society life. In his novel *Savrola*, Churchill wrote of his hero's redoubtable nanny:

"It is a strange thing, the love of these women. Perhaps it is the only disinterested affection in the world. The mother loves her child; that is maternal nature. The youth loves his sweetheart; that too may be explained. The dog loves his master; he feeds him; a man loves his friend; he has stood by him perhaps at doubtful moments. In all there are reasons; but the love of a foster-mother for her charge appears absolutely irrational. It is one of the few proofs, not to be explained even by the association of ideas, that the nature of mankind is superior to mere utilitarianism and that his destinies are high."

It is an observation which, molded into a slightly different shape, is equally applicable to John Lennon's relationship with Auntie Mimi.

6 When Pain Leads to Fame

The irony of it. There they sit on their pedestals—adored, desired, lusted after, dreamed of, not to mention emulated, admired, and revered. And yet these objects of a million fantasies are as riddled with insecurities as we life-sized mortals. Correction: perhaps more so.

Jessica Lange could not see herself as pretty, any more than could Joan Collins, Cybill Shepherd, Cher, Meryl Streep, Britt Ekland, and Carly Simon, all of whom perceived themselves as plain, if not downright ugly, at least once upon a time. Lesley-Anne Warren would have us believe that at thirteen she was the most unpopular girl in school, overweight, unattractive, and awkward. Elton John's mom, Sheila Farebrother, never quite understood it, but knew that deep down her son (then called Reggie Dwight) truly believed he was "the ugliest thing that ever walked. I don't know why, he's a bit short but not bad-looking." Saturnina Schipani's daughter, Pia Zadora, might never have become a star but for her excruciating shyness. At Catholic school, her papers earned double gold stars, but little Pia went to pieces the moment a nun entered the classroom, her mother recalls. "She put her head down and the tears would flow on her bosom, and she cried and cried. She was so shy, oh, tch, tch, tch!"

Tally up the stars of stage, screen, and song who grew up believing they were anywhere from unattractive to the proverbial ugly duckling. Add in loners and those who fell somewhere between tongue-tied and cripplingly shy. Toss in those with a pervasive sense of low self-esteem, and for good measure, throw in

111

stars who were chronically ill or physically handicapped in some way. The total might well populate the crowd scenes for a remake of *Ben Hur*.

It is possible that there is a greater preponderance of those so afflicted in this field than in any other: show business is frequently an irresistible magnet to men and women who in their hearts do not hold very high opinions of themselves. Their horrible dark secret is often effectively camouflaged behind tremendous bravado, but nevertheless, there it lurks in their lives, like a closely tracking thundercloud.

Very often a star's damning self-assessment is not grounded in reality. The public faces we see on Jessica Lange, Cybill Shepherd, and Meryl Streep, for instance, bear no evidence of those feared and imagined adolescent imperfections. Yet the mud of youth sticks to the psyche, be it flung there by tactless teasing at home from siblings or cruel schoolyard taunts, and the deepest scarring is invariably that which stems from parental blows. A mother might not be able to literally transform an ugly duckling into a swan, but she can surely help build in her child the inner belief that he or she is attractive, likable, and worthy of others' attentions.

Dudley Moore is undeniably staccato in stature, added to which he was born with a club foot, but he is extremely attractive to women; his far-from-diminutive charms are considerably enhanced, of course, by his sparkling wit. Yet to hear Moore tell how ashamed he was made to feel of his handicap (largely by his mother's embarrassment about it), it is a wonder he ever mustered the confidence to step outside his front door.

Dustin Hoffman and Sammy Davis Jr. were not dramatically unrealistic in their physical self-appraisals; no one would argue that they are hunks or pin-up material. But surely we cannot seriously be expected to see Laurence Olivier—the ultimate Heathcliff, for heaven's sake—as the ugly, weedy weakling he saw himself to be?

Billy Dee Williams' mom, Loretta, says her son is now a svelte shadow of his ten-year-old self—he was then a veritable butterball at 150 lbs—but such indisputable, tangible physical change is the exception rather than the rule. Many stars had no idea that they were pretty or attractive or handsome, irrespective of the "truth" reflected back at them in the mirror—that "truth" being only as true as their ability to believe it. Knowing it intellectually is meaningless unless one accepts it emotionally, so beauty (or its lack) remains firmly in the eye of its owner and these feelings are cemented very early on. And mother is the first mirror we peer into for a view of ourselves. The same applies to self-confidence and sense of self-worth. If these anxiety-ridden adolescents did not have it in their hearts, they did not have it—and quite possibly still do not have it, despite appearances to the contrary.

Yet all these so-called handicaps and drawbacks are below-the-belt blows that can ultimately carry a kiss of kindness with them. A poor self-image can be one of the most crucial of the factors which drive someone to succeed, to achieve, to crash through all obstacles that dare to block their path to being desired, admired, and wanted.

The sharpest example of this syndrome in action is perhaps Barbra Streisand. Barbra was on the receiving end of a double-whammy of negative input, without which she herself concedes she might not be where she is today. She was blessed with a well-meaning if pessimistically inclined mother, Diana, who told her she was too thin, too unattractive, and too peculiar-looking to act. "She said I wasn't pretty enough, not talented enough," Barbra has admitted. Enter Louis Kind, who married her mother when Barbra was six, and fathered Barbra's half-sister, Roslyn. Mr. Kind was anything but. With staggering cruelty, he described the two girls as "The beauty and the beast." As witnessed by her older brother, Sheldon, "He was really mean to Barbra. He taunted her continually, telling her how plain she was compared to Roslyn." With maturity, Barbra came to terms with her looks, saying, "I think from certain angles I am beautiful. And from certain angles I am really awful-looking."

She is not the sole "ugly sister" to have become a superstar. Georgia Holt always told her older daughter that her darkly exotic look was special, but as a child Cher could not help but envy her sister Georganne's more traditional fairy princess appeal—the blonde hair, the blue eyes. When she was small, Cher was enormously self-conscious, a state of affairs compounded by her reading and learning disability, dyslexia, which was not diagnosed until she was thirty. To this day, she is less inhibited in front of fifty thousand people ("it's real impersonal") than in front of five, and claims it still does not take much to shake her fragile confidence to the bone.

"I was a shy, ugly kid who led a big fantasy life," Cher admits. Only in her thirties did it strike her that she is actively glad she looks the way she does.

Lorna Luft's finer features are, in the accepted sense, more attractive than half-sister Liza Minnelli's. Yet Barbra, Cher, and Liza have each outstripped their younger siblings immeasurably in career success. Did they simply get there first? Or did they try harder?

Carly Simon stuttered in family plays as a youngster and saw herself as the proverbial ugly duckling in a nest of swans. Her mother was unable to negate this impression, particularly as it was compounded by Carly's late father, Richard Simon, cofounder of Simon & Schuster, who seemed always to compliment those swan siblings and dismiss the ugly duckling. When young Carly, swept away by the romance of *Gone With the Wind* and Clark Gable, asked her father if he had any handsome friends he could invite to the house, he said that indeed he had—one who looked just like Clark Gable. Excitedly, Carly put on makeup, fixed her hair, and went out of her way to look her prettiest to greet the much-anticipated gentleman. She told Timothy White of *Rolling Stone*:

"When the dinner guest showed up, I came down the stairs, Scarlett O'Hara–style, and he was just a little old man with glasses. I saw my father laughing at me, and I was crushed."

The ultimate blow was struck by writer Sloan Wilson, a frequent guest of the Simons, who mentioned in his memoirs the striking good looks of the family—and noted the exception of Carly: "There it was, the horrible truth, finally confirmed," said Carly.

It is hardly surprising that such feelings would leave an indelible impression and create a greater-than-usual desire to fight for Mommy or Daddy's approval, a need to right the unrightable wrong. In reality, the wrong is not only rightable, it is a blessing, albeit in heavy disguise. Physical beauty's advantages are, in the long haul, outweighed by its liabilities. Like being born with a silver spoon in one's mouth, being born beautiful removes the need for effort, instilling instead a sense of complacency.

A true beauty who does not feel attractive, or a handsome man who still feels inside like a tongue-tied, awkward schoolboy, will fare better because they have never lived off their physical attributes and so are less dependent upon them for survival. That kind of dependence unavoidably leads to pain as the years take their toll. Those who are not "special" by birthright quickly learn to adjust, to adapt, to try harder. They are forced to find out who they are. They become richer for their efforts.

Carol Burnett's mother, Ina Louise, was pretty, funny, sexy, and everything that Carol—who pulls no punches in saying she would have killed to be beautiful—was not. Rather, Carol described herself as gangly, skinny, all bones and no meat—and that was just her body. Facially, she saw buckteeth, what she calls the Burnett lower lip, and an accompanying lack of chin. Her pleasure in getting taller was quickly eroded as Carol realized that she had left behind the boys she fancied and that the shorter girls were growing curvier—a fact of life not erased by her influential grandmother's claim that they acquired those "titties" by fooling around.

Ina Louise would make the hurtful assertion that it was wonderful Carol had drawing talent, because you could become an artist no matter what you looked like. The slight was undoubtedly felt more acutely when her mother voiced the opinion that Chrissy, Carol's illegitimate half-sister (born when she was eleven), was the most beautiful baby she had ever seen. Crushing news for a teenager who prayed nightly that a different face would greet her in the mirror the next morning, who slept in pincurls and pressed her finger against the tip of her nose for extended periods of time in a futile attempt to upturn it.

Ina Louise, an alcoholic, was estranged from her husband, Jody Burnett (also an alcoholic), by the time Carol was four. Carol's father was handsome but ineffectual, spasmodically employed, and largely absent from her life—he was, however, kind. When her mother drank, she was often verbally abusive to Carol, who at age seven moved into her grandmother's cramped and cluttered room down the hallway and slept on the couch. Ina Louise's manipulative, hypochondriac mother, Mae, lived on welfare, but she was devoted to Carol and proved a strong force in Carol's life. It was she who waved her on her way to New York with the warning, "Well, if you're not a star by Christmas, come home."

From this chaotic backdrop, Ina Louise's daughter emerged as ferociously tidy. Carol grew up amidst turbulent and loud domestic discord, with constant squabbling, yet she herself repressed anger and had difficulty expressing her emotions. She had two strong factors in her favor, however: she loved her far-from-perfect family and never doubted her own ability to survive.

As a child performer, Julie Andrews' physical shortcomings were under the glare of the spotlight and thus under the close scrutiny of the parental magnifying glass held by her mother, Barbara Morris, and stepfather, Ted Andrews. Barbara entertained the troops in World War II through ENSA (Entertainments National Services Association) with Andrews, a Canadian who had emigrated to England as a relatively successful vaudeville entertainer.

Julie took an instant dislike to her mother's flamboyant, extroverted new husband, whom she has described as having "thundered" across her childhood. Barbara had separated amicably from Julie's father, Ted Wells, when Julie was four. Wells, a woodwork and metalcraft teacher of whom Julie was enormously fond, was given custody of Julie, but he allowed Barbara to keep her, believing a growing girl needed a mother's influence. (Julie's younger brother John continued to live with his dad, however.) To this day, Julie maintains a close, affectionate relationship with her father and her long-time stepmother, Winifred (better known as "Win"), who is a hairdresser.

The fledgling Julie was by her own admission, according to an interview in Britain's *Woman* magazine, "an ugly child with buckteeth and a squint," and bow-legged, to boot. Not for her the luxury of outgrowing the aforementioned gracefully. Barbara and Ted Andrews subjected sensitive Julie to the rigors of fast improvement: wearing braces on her teeth, drinking gelatine-enriched mixtures for her nails, and having highly painful massage for her one wayward eye.

Julie was coached simultaneously in dance, deportment, and elocution, and her budding bosoms were constrained in clothes that Barbara and Ted hoped would minimize the evidence that their child star was blossoming into womanhood.

Barbara Andrews played the piano at an evening dance school run by her sister Joan, and from the beginning had an agenda of aspirations on Julie's behalf. She had herself hoped to be a concert pianist, a dream she could not fulfill for purely practical reasons. Her parents died when she was eighteen, and from that moment on she was forced to support both herself and her younger sister. It was at Joan's dance school, at age two, that Julie was given her first stage part, as a fairy.

Julie hated singing initially, a reaction which doubtless stemmed from feelings of resentment she harbored for her pushy stepfather. She was, you might say, a reluctant child prodigy. At age eight, during World War II, she took her share of neighborhood shifts peering through binoculars scouting for German airplanes and lethal "doodlebug" bombs. During the long hours spent waiting in air-raid shelters for the all-clear signal, there were often sing-alongs to revive flagging spirits and alleviate the tedium. Julie's five-octave voice span, once noticed in these echo-chamber confines, turned her into an object of curiosity. Her remarkable range was capitalized upon by Ted Andrews, who incorporated her into the family act. Julie's talented presence became its increasingly crucial mainstay, and as Barbara and Ted Wells' career ebbed toward eventual retirement, so Julie's rose until she took over entirely as the family's breadwinner by age thirteen.

Without Barbara and Ted's drive, Julie's life would doubtless have progressed quite differently. She was just twelve when Ted Andrews convinced fellow golfer Val Parnell, whose booking firm owned the London Palladium and Hippodrome, that he should hear Julie sing. Parnell gave her a break and a show-stopping solo in *Starlight Roof* for which she received fifty pounds a week. At thirteen, Julie became the youngest soloist to perform before Queen Elizabeth (now the Queen Mother) and Princess Margaret.

To her intense embarrassment, until she was eighteen Julie appeared in pantomimes and shows in short dresses and ankle socks. She kept her angry feelings bottled up, ever the trooper, but many years later her father said, "All the pent-up unhappiness of that period suddenly caught up with her—so she sought the advice of a psychoanalyst." It was an exercise her mother dismissed as "bloody nonsense," a view not unusual in Britain then or now.

Ted and Barbara Andrews would have to be described as stage parents, yet for all Julie's apparent earlier unhappiness, she does not point the finger of blame at her mother. She told writer Lynn Barber of the London *Sunday Express Magazine:* "She wasn't the grasping, greedy sort of hackneyed stage mum, but to a degree, yes, she had ambitions and she was very happy when she saw them come true for me."

For Barbara Andrews, her daughter's success was a dream realized and its highlight came in 1956 when she first saw Julie's Eliza Doolittle. "Opening night of *My Fair Lady* in New York was the greatest night of my life," she said, reveling in the thundering, appreciative ovations earned by her daughter.

For all Julie Andrews' early success and apparent advantages, at twenty she remained a confused young woman, very shy, and had a low sense of self-esteem, rather like Neil Diamond. Diamond's physical shortcomings—a gangly build, oversized ears and nose —contributed in no small way to his poor self-image, but unlike Julie he always saw singing as his salvation.

Mrs. Diamond was a working mother and Neil was a latchkey kid who regularly left a school where he had few friends to go home to an empty house. His father was a dry-goods merchant whose business difficulties precipitated nine school changes for Neil before high school; this in turn played havoc with his friendships, and Neil ran away from home at thirteen. Neil Diamond's songs about loneliness and insecurity were born of that pain. The solitary child who grew up and wrote the hit song "Solitary Man" says, "I was always an outsider," and, "I was a lonely, withdrawn kid."

Musically, however, the parental influence was strong. His mother and father loved to go ballroom dancing and were natural performers, although strictly amateur. Seeing his father theatrically lip-sync to operatic records undoubtedly inspired Neil. In any event, he was singing on sidewalks by the time he was ten, giving vent to his frustration as his "cry in the night."

Diamond is still riddled with self-doubt, but has finally forgiven himself for not being Beethoven, and acknowledges his purposeful choice of a profession where uncertainty was the name of the game. Fear, he has said, is the high that keeps him going—that element of risk. Sheila Farebrother's Jekyll-and-Hyde son, Elton John, also seemed drawn to put himself on the line. In sheer flamboyance, Elton became Britain's cross between a rhinestone cowboy and Liberace, but he grew up "a bundle of nerves." He told reporter Brian Glanville of the London *Sunday Express Magazine*:

"The clothes I wear have always been to conceal the fact I'm horribly shy. Look at me; I'm plump, I'm hairy, I've never been part of what they call The Bare Chest Brigade."

His grandmother let him pound on her piano from the age of three and his mother spotted definite musical promise, which she nurtured. At school, however, Elton was nicknamed Fat Reg and derided by the other kids for carrying a violin case. As an adult, fending off scrutiny with the very same oversized specs that defiantly invite it, he has contended in a dignified fashion with football crowds chanting nasty ditties about his sexual proclivities from the stands.

Sheila stood staunchly behind Elton when he went public with his bisexuality, more concerned with her son's happiness than with the gender of his companion. In the seventies, stalwart Sheila aided Elton through another rough patch: a suicide attempt, albeit Woody Allenesque, with windows opened before the gas was turned on.

Reg became bitter as his parents' tumultuous marriage ended in divorce when he was fourteen. He was angered as he heard his mother's infidelity blamed, knowing full well that his father's was swept conveniently under the carpet. He watched hardworking Sheila, whom he has described as "the most wonderful woman I've ever met," struggle to keep them afloat financially. She was employed in a grocer's shop until she married Reggie's kindly stepfather, interior decorator Fred Farebrother.

Elton/Reggie was never close to his real dad, Stanley Dwight.

Stanley was the strict type who worried that a rebounding football might damage his precious rosebushes and forbade his teenage son to wear trendy suede Hush Puppies. At one point, however, Stanley was a trumpeter with a radio show-band— which had more impact on Elton than his subsequent post as an RAF squadron leader.

To add insult to Reggie's injury, within six months of leaving his family Stanley Dwight remarried. Within four years he had four more sons, and his firstborn wondered, had he been a mistake? (Sheila admits Stanley had wanted a daughter.) Stanley Dwight was driven to write to Sheila upon learning that Reggie was foolhardily planning to leave school just weeks before his long-awaited A-level examinations to go to work for a music publisher. *Reg should never go into Rock and Roll, over my dead body,* wrote Stanley, who envisioned a career for his son in the aircraft industry, or at the very least in classical music. As Elton has stayed close to his staunchest supporter, his mom, so his relationship with his father has remained distant and strained.

As a small boy, Sammy Davis Jr. had a poor self-image. He was tormented by a group of neighborhood children. Once, when he caught them drawing him, they tore up the portrait, stifled their laughter, and ran off. Laboriously, Sammy pieced together the fragments of paper they had left behind and discovered a picture that bore a vague resemblance to his face, but with the nose flattened right across its width, the head as large as the body, and the arms hanging gorilla-style down to the shoes. Beneath the distorted figure was the word *ugly.* Shredding the drawing so that it would evermore be beyond repair, he tossed it down the toilet, flushing three times for good measure.

Later he scrutinized himself in the mirror, hating what he saw. When he noticed his paternal grandmother, Rosa B. Davis, watching him, little Sammy (who was at the time more familiar with her than with his mother, Elvera, and addressed her accordingly) said, "Mama, what d'ya think of how this suit fits me?" She stroked his head and said, "The suit's nice, but I like what's in it. That's really something good to look at," Sammy recalls. "I fell into her arms and cried."

Sammy Davis Jr. first performed at three years old and learned early that applause could dull those feelings of inadequacy. Sammy saw little of Elvera while he was growing up (he was raised primarily by his vaudevillian father), yet they have since made up for lost time and he takes good care of her.

Elvera's mother, who turned 104 on Valentine's Day 1988, had been a dresser to show people, yet it was by a quirk of fate that Elvera joined a chorus line in 1925. She was seventeen and had had no training whatsoever when Will Masters and his stage partner, Sammy Davis Sr., spotted her—working as a coat check girl in her native New York. They needed a chorus girl for their act, and Elvera went on the road with them as Baby Sanchez, the new stage name her mother dreamed up.

Elvera and Sammy Sr. wed in 1925, and when their daughter Ramona was born, two years after Sammy Jr., logistics dictated that Elvera leave the show—with, in her opinion, a not uncommon result: "The break-up of the relationship . . . he goes one way and you go another." Elvera had no choice but to be pragmatic about the separation from her son—she had Ramona to support and was already forced to leave her with her mother when she went on tour. But when Sammy stayed with his father, it was *not* by mutual agreement: "No, he just had him and took him." The separation was painful for Elvera, who had no idea what Sammy had been told. She was concerned that he might think she had abandoned him, and worried whether he understood.

In his 1965 autobiography, *Yes I Can,* Sammy wrote of his mother's visits to the theaters where he was performing with his father's act, and of being too young to understand quite who this lady was and why he cried and hurt so badly when she left. Elvera worked in the Lafayette Theatre in uptown New York and toured Baltimore, Philadelphia, and Washington, and Sammy Sr.'s beat was primarily the Boston-Canada route, so these reunions with her son were only spasmodic.

"Oh, he knew me," Elvera says emphatically. "I was in a show one time in Detroit and he was working in Detroit, and I used to go in the hotel where he lived and read the comic books to him. And he'd want me to read them over and over and over again. It was heartbreaking to me . . . I used to cry, cry, cry all the time." For all her suffering, at the same time she felt her small son had been blessed, had been selected for something special. And in her heart, she believed, however reluctantly, that he was better off with his father than he would have been with her:

"It was bad enough for me to be making eighteen dollars a week, to support a daughter *and* send money to my mother, Louisa Sanchez."

Elvera worked once with Bojangles, and more frequently with Duke Ellington, Cab Calloway, Tommy Dorsey, Charlie Barnett, and all the big bands. "Glamorous? Not when I was in it, honey. When I made $22.50 a week, that was big." Elvera steadfastly avoided the club circuit after childbirth "because most of the costumes are naked," and she believed her body was no longer good enough to reveal to the world.

Her dancing years spanned 1925 to 1941, and after that she moved into the only job she believes surpasses show business as an education in the ways of the world—a barmaid: "You gotta be a 'mother confessor,' a psychiatrist, a marriage guidance counselor, everything. I didn't have any education, darling; I did not have the booklearning, I did not graduate from grammar school, but between those two—really, it's a school in itself."

When Elvera later learned that Sammy Sr. was not sending Sammy Jr. to school, she asked the social services department to help her get her son back or, because of his travels, to at least help her force the school issue. She got no satisfaction. Sammy Jr.'s father's rights equaled her own, she was told.

She shakes her head. "So anyway I say this, I tried and I couldn't. But then God works in a mysterious way, because you don't know what Sammy might have been. He might *never* have been the person he is today. But then sometimes I wish he was a truck driver," she says wistfully.

"Oh yes, darling. If he wasn't as popular, everybody wouldn't be around him and over him. If he was a truck driver, they wouldn't be noticing him . . . and then maybe I'd have a little more of that love. But then, if he had been a truck driver, I wouldn't have been living the way I'm living today, God bless him!" she adds, waving her arms around her comfortable, compact, but by no means palatial apartment in a well-situated highrise on Manhattan's Upper East Side.

Overall, Sammy's stardom had little effect on Elvera's life because it was never a shock to her. "I knew he was going to be a star, I knew God looked down on him and blessed him. That's the way I feel. Everything happens through Him. He knows what's going to happen to you when it happens."

Atlantic City is like Elvera's second home and one proud moment stands out in her mind. Years ago, on Sammy's closing night in the Club Harlem where she was working, she witnessed what to her was an unprecedented gesture—all the waitresses and club staff threw red roses at her son. "Oh boy, that was wonderful."

She and Sammy are now "pretty close" and she has met all of his friends who habituate the inner sanctum of star-studded circles: "I've met Sinatra; I've met Dean; I met, God bless him, Peter Lawford."

She is in no doubt as to how her son got to the top: "He had talent, for one thing. He will tell you that Sinatra helped him, but if he didn't have something to show for it, I don't care who would help him, it wouldn't do no good."

Elvera only divorced Sammy's father a few years ago. Meanwhile, Sammy Sr. had a thirty-year relationship with a woman named Pee Wee, who Elvera liked a great deal. She saw staying married as a protection against another marital blunder, but eventually, "I knew that I had a mind of my own and that I wouldn't be crazy to marry nobody. So we got a divorce and Sammy's father and me, we're good friends. Poor Pee Wee, she died."

The late Lillian Hoffman was unable to rescue her son Dustin from the pain of his adolescence, a period of time when in his picturesque view he was shy, vulnerable, anxiety-ridden, lonely, girlfriend-less, had "one of the worst cases of acne in Southern California," and felt "immensely ugly." In case the point has not been made sufficiently forcefully, he hated the way he looked and to this day has a propensity for smiling with his lips sealed, as though still trying to conceal the dreaded braces behind which his teeth were clamped for eight long years.

It is an old story but remains poignant. In the middle of delivering a school book report on Jimmy Durante's autobiography, *Schnozzola,* and speaking of the pain the comedian suffered because of his prominent nose, young Dustin ran from the room with tears streaming down his face.

Lillian once said that her son's disruptive, jokey classroom behavior was "probably compensating for being the smallest kid in the room." She described Dustin, who was unhappy with his mediocre performance in school, as a perfectionist; like his father, Harry Hoffman, Dustin was never satisfied. It was a situation exacerbated by Dustin's brother, Ron, who went from straight-A student to economist, then to assistant to the Secretary of the Treasury. (Harry Hoffman has since admitted that they underestimated their younger son's intelligence.)

Dustin, who subscribes to Bette Davis's theory that no one who likes himself goes into acting, believes that had he been tall and handsome, he might have become a doctor; he would not have become an actor, of that much he is certain. As it was, he launched into acting to meet his driving need for affection and love, and most especially to eliminate depression. Miraculously, acting could do those things for him.

Like her son, Lillian Hoffman once dreamed of a turn in the spotlight. As a young girl she danced in the aisles of a cinema; it made her feel joyously alive. She once even auditioned as a dancer, but her mother would not hear of her pursuing a career as a hoofer. Vibrant and lively, Lillian was fashion conscious and loved to play with her makeup, her hair, her jewelry. It was her spirit and warmth which later provided Dustin with the inspiration he used to shape *Tootsie*'s Dorothy Michaels.

There was a darker side to Lillian's life. Her marriage was stormy. As a boy, Dustin took it upon himself to try to defuse the tension at home. He minimized his own anxiety about the tumult by mimicking his angry father and mother, by tempering the atmosphere with a joke. Dustin also had his own frictional relationship with his tough father.

Harry Hoffman had envisioned himself as a Hollywood movie producer, and while he once supervised props for Columbia, he ended up as a considerably less glamorous furniture salesman— not the fairy-tale ending he had hoped for when he drove his family west from Chicago. He worked long hours, occasionally ran afoul of creditors, and was too busy with his own problems to worry much about the turmoil his son was enduring.

Harry's mother died when he was nine, and being unappreciated himself, it came naturally to him to give his son neither approval nor attention. Dustin became desperate to be noticed, relishing even the laughter he garnered when he deliberately danced with the largest, least-attractive girl in school. There were happy times. Although Jewish, the family celebrated Christmas and to Lillian's delight Dustin once decorated the tree with bagels.

Lillian first came close to death in 1980, paralyzed by a stroke, but Dustin engineered a show of familial unity to spur her into clinging to life. He arrived by helicopter and managed to communicate with her as no one else had been able to, learning that her legs were numb—which led doctors to realize that blood clots were forming. As she was being readied for emergency surgery, Dustin kissed first his father and then his brother in a rare show of affection for his mother's benefit, then he kissed her, willing her to live. She did, for sixteen more months, before finally succumbing to cancer in the fall of 1981.

Fame was no magical cure for what ailed Dustin; once he could afford it, he went into heavy psychoanalysis. He believes friends who tell him he looks better with age—but then, in his estimation, there was only one direction in which to move.

Meryl Streep is the daughter of a commercial-artist mother (Mary Louise Streep, Meryl's namesake) and a pharmaceutical-company-executive father, both of whom gave her every encouragement. Yet Meryl, not sparing her own feelings, admits she was bossy, prim, big-mouthed, and so frumpy she was more like teacher than pupil. She was "an obnoxious show-off," not to mention ugly and overweight, with—here it comes again—braces; spectacles; frizzy, dull hair; and a large mouth. Should this description be a little negatively biased, even one of Meryl's two older brothers, Harry, described her as "a pretty ghastly" tyrant.

She wanted desperately to be accepted and popular. She also wanted her interest in boys to be reciprocated. The main asset she had in her favor was a coloratura voice, the beauty of which sent chills down the spines of those assembled at her high school when she sang a solo, "O Holy Night." Meryl's parents afforded her every opportunity to capitalize on this natural advantage and she studied in New York with Estelle Liebling, Beverly Sills' tutor, but Meryl had more serious business afoot.

Her plan was to transform herself from a plain mouse into the kind of glossy swan who stared out at her from magazines. She bleached her hair, abandoned the specs and the braces, and within a year had blossomed into a high school cheerleader. In addition, she became a member of the Honor Society, starred in a school musical, and was voted Homecoming Queen. This staggering transformation has been described as her first successful characterization. It did not, however, have the desired effect on her popularity or happiness. Boys were no longer Meryl's problem. She had emerged as such a notable beauty that, to her dismay, the other girls at school were jealous.

When Meryl landed the role of the mother who leaves her child to go off and "find herself" in the film *Kramer vs. Kramer,* she discussed the character with her own career-woman mother. Mary Louise stunned her daughter by admitting that all of her friends had contemplated, at one time or another, leaving their families and living different lives. Presumably, she would understand Gregory Peck's mom, Bernice.

Bernice Peck picked her baby son's name out of the telephone book. Eldred (as Gregory Peck was then known) was born in La Jolla, California, in 1916. He was a shy boy and very sensitive. Bernice (nicknamed Bunny) was a beautiful woman who loved the bright lights, but her Irish husband, Gregory, a druggist, was the quiet, stay-at-home type. Almost inevitably, this incompatible pair split up in 1922, when their son was six. In practical terms, that meant that Eldred was left with his father and grandparents. He was shuttled back and forth for a couple of years, but he remained in touch with his mom, and at eight, went to live with his maternal grandmother. At ten he was packed off to a Roman Catholic military academy where he remained for three years, then it was back to his father, who was by then living in San Diego.

Between the ages of thirteen and sixteen, he sprouted over a foot to his present six-foot-three and says, "I was lonely, withdrawn, full of self-doubt." His very first time on a stage, he realized that for all his fear, he had stumbled upon an avenue to approval, a way to express himself. He took off for New York to try his luck and Gregory Peck the star was born.

Bernice Peck remarried and worked with her husband, check

writer Joe Maysuch. They were a lively couple, dressed beauti- fully, and loved a day at the races. Joe died a few years ago, and Bernice, who is now over ninety, lives in an antique-filled apart- ment on San Francisco's Nob Hill, with an ex-secretary of Greg- ory's as her companion. Mother and son are close and good pals.

Bunny is, the star says, as lovely and spirited as ever. She has not lost her fondness for the races, where she does rather well, betting on colors, names, and birthdays. Each month she flies from San Francisco to the room still reserved for her in Peck's Holmby Hills mansion. "She's the one who brings us all to- gether," Gregory Peck explains.

Bob Hope was born in a modest flat in Eltham, South London, to Avis Townes and William Henry Hope. Avis, the daughter of a Welsh sea captain, had sung in concerts in Wales before marry- ing. She was petite, dark-haired, shy, and fragile-looking, an ap- parently gentle soul who had seven sons and one daughter, her namesake, who died as an infant. Since her husband found solace in drinking to escape his business difficulties, it fell to Avis to run the family affairs, which she did adroitly. (Her sons respectfully called her "Ma'am.")

Young Leslie Hope (a.k.a Bob) was apparently rather accident- prone and had two brushes with drowning—once as a baby and once in his early teens—from which his older brothers saved him. As a young man, his face was smashed so badly by a near-fatal encounter with a falling tree trunk that he was not allowed a mirror for three weeks. Enter the legendary ski-jump nose. Les Hope had also to contend with his anagramatic nickname, "Hopeless." Understandably, he adopted another pre-Bob name, Lester.

Avis's husband, William, was a rather distant father. Like his own father before him, he was a stonemason and something of a workaholic. An amateur comic, he did the rounds of the English pubs. Two of William's brothers transplanted themselves to Cleveland in 1907, and soon after, William went out to join them, followed by the rest of his family. Leslie/Bob was four.

Under financial pressure, Avis took in ever-increasing numbers of boarders. Confiding in her sons, she encouraged each of them to help ease the burden by earning money in a myriad of ways.

Bob caddied, delivered newspapers, worked in a butcher's shop and a shoe shop. By age seven, his voice—a cross between high tenor and soprano—earned a warm enough response on streetcar rides to warrant passing around a hat to fellow passengers.

Avis was more than just an efficient manager, she was a good mother, much loved by her boys, and every inch as hardworking as she encouraged them to be. Her faith in all her sons was so unshakable that she did not panic even when Bob, at age twelve, reportedly developed a worrying fascination with the pool hall. (He was a great billiard player.)

His brother Fred has described the young Bob as "a big show-off," and his mother definitely boosted that confidence. She took him to vaudeville shows and never missed an opportunity to encourage his obvious talent. By his junior year in high school, he had decided to drop out and dance at the local Bandbox Theater. His career was on its way.

Bob's staunchest supporter, Avis succumbed to cancer in 1934, just a couple of years before his father died, and losing her was the saddest time in Bob Hope's life. Fred called him a show-off, but in fact he has a need to make people laugh that is unrelenting. His friends have learned not to be surprised by his late-night phone calls; as they answer, he launches into a joke or two and on hearing the expected laughter, promptly hangs up without another word. Need met, mission accomplished.

While it might seem a contradiction in terms, shy people often seek out for themselves the very terror-inducing limelight they so fear. A self-doubter like Neil Diamond is compelled to repeatedly put himself right on the edge of his inner fear that each concert might be the last at which an audience will applaud. Diamond and all the others like him are drawn to precisely the kind of extroverted activities that their inhibited, introverted selves fear most.

Why do it? To beat the demons that plague them into submission; to conquer their fears, master their weaknesses, and lay to rest their insecurities. Freud first raised the concept of the repetition compulsion, where people again and again put themselves in situations where they have experienced difficulties, as if in an attempt (not always successful) to master them. The experience is anxiety-provoking, but the confrontation is an optimistic step, a cry for life, an act of aggression rather than a whimper of submission.

For a counterphobic personality, the action is more of a defense mechanism. On some level those people are telling themselves, "I am scared but I refuse to let it show. I am just going to act as though it's as easy as pie and plunge straight into it."

The nuances of individual circumstances aside, it is no great accident that the performing arts are densely populated with the shy and the insecure, acting out their extroverted side behind the mask of a character, a role, or a rock star persona. Of course, shyness is not uncommon. It afflicts over 40 percent of the population, and speaking before a group is reportedly the most common human fear.

It is difficult to imagine the effervescent exhibitionist Pia Zadora being as crippled by it as her mother insists that she was, less so to imagine Linda Evans in her shell at Hollywood High School, where she was so shy she barely spoke to anyone.

Henry Fonda told Ross Benson of the London *Daily Express,* "I was a painfully self-conscious, shy young man and had very little to say." Fonda's father was a master printer who raised his son as a Christian Scientist, and Henry learned to deplore crying and to suppress his feelings. When Henry Fonda's son, Peter, was small, his dad berated him for his skinny arms, a scenario which Peter has recently been able to put into perspective. As he told Michael Leahy of *TV Guide*:

"He wanted me to be what he was not. I found out, after he died, that he was always embarrassed to go around in short sleeves because he thought his arms were too skinny." Fonda felt for his son the same fear that plagued him as a youngster—fear of the critical evaluation of others, fear of the possibility of humiliation or embarrassment. Such preoccupation with the way others will judge is often accompanied by a tendency to be judgmental or critical. It frequently passes from mother to child. The mother so identifies with her child that she feels their rejections as if they were her own.

Michael J. Fox is another shy star who, like Dudley Moore, found humor to be his saving grace. "Girls think you're cute and bullies want to thump you, so you've got to be pretty damned funny or you'll get thumped," he says by way of an explanation for having developed these coping skills. The five-foot-four actor found a way to turn his diminutive stature ("There's not a hell of a lot you can do about being short") to his advantage as an attention-getter. Accepting his Emmy for "Family Ties," all smiles, he quipped, "I feel four feet tall," and there is no shadow of a chip on his shoulder.

Few adolescents would be willing, as Fox was, at fifteen to swallow hard and pass himself off as a ten-year-old for the Canadian TV series "Leo and Me"—the sign of an enterprising streak shining through, but also of a self-confidence and inner security for which the multimillionaire's mom, Phyllis, must take some credit. Phyllis Fox infused him with the positive outlook that would stand him in good stead. He learned to say to himself: "I might be getting negative attention right now, but I'll figure out how to turn it into positive attention. Right now, I'm the New Short Kid, but in a couple of weeks I can be Funny Mike or Smart Mike." But not *too* smart. "If I went home and started that, there would be a lawn mower in front of me before I could blink."

Phyllis and Bill Fox neither encouraged nor discouraged their son's acting pursuits, but they did not fuss when he dropped out of high school and set off for Hollywood. When Fox, in his dark days, was thirty thousand dollars in debt and about to throw in the towel, his folks showed touching faith in him, emphasizing what he had achieved rather than what he had not. Michael J. is the fourth of their five children. As the son of a Canadian Army career officer, he learned to be adaptable during frequent moves, although he spent much of his childhood in Burnaby, a suburb of Vancouver. Even though Fox now lives in Los Angeles, he remains close to his parents. When he bought a convertible black Ferrari equipped with a phone, he chose to christen it with one of his thrice-weekly calls to Mom.

Even heartthrob Mel Gibson, an American-Australian hybrid whose first twelve years were spent in small towns such as Peekskill, New York, had his troubles. He was both drawn to the adventure of moving to Australia and afflicted by the adjustments inherent in leaving behind friends and finding acceptance in a new world. "The kids made fun of me and called me 'Yank,' and I had a fairly rough time of it."

It was Saturnina Schipani's doctor's idea that she enroll her daughter Pia Zadora at the American Academy of Dramatic Arts. While there, Pia performed to order, but once the classroom door closed behind them, Pia was just as solemn, quiet, and withdrawn as before.

Saturnina herself had started singing professionally with her sister, Longina, when she was six years old. They were sponsored by Breyer's Ice Cream in Philadelphia on the radio station WIP, and appeared Andrews Sisters–style in vaudeville shows at theaters and clubs around Philadelphia and New Jersey, even singing with Frank Sinatra. Their mother sang with the Philadelphia Opera Company and played piano during theater intervals. Longina went on to sing with the New York City Opera and the Polish Opera Company, until a stroke ended her career at thirty.

Saturnina, who had studied opera and piano, was invited to perform in *Guiseppe* with the Chicago Opera Company, but the invitation held no allure. Although she married into the business (Pia's father, Alphonse, was a conductor), she shuddered at the thought of performing, preferring to work behind the scenes with costumes. While at high school, she had taken evening design classes in clothing and draping at Pratt Institute and as a little girl had sewn dolls' clothes on her mother's sewing machine.

Sometimes Saturnina still wakes up from dreaming of the thunderous applause she received as a child performer. The dreams do not haunt her, but neither are they appealing.

In her six or seven years with the New York City Opera's wardrobe department, she felt privileged to dress divas like Joan Sutherland, but was so determined to keep her promise to herself never again to tread the boards that she leaned forward at the most perilous angles to fix the singers' costumes rather than step on the stage. When treated to this strange spectacle, Joan Sutherland asked, "Saturnina, can't you get a little closer?" and she was forced to explain. Eventually a couple of her coworkers broke the spell by forcibly dragging her across the stage.

Never, ever did Saturnina regret not pursuing a career, and she was enormously ambivalent when, after Pia had spent three weeks in her Saturday classes, Burgess Meredith said that he would like to use her in a Broadway show.

Pia had been a blue baby, born with a severe systolic murmur and one chamber of her heart depressed. When she was fourteen months old, however, Saturnina decided to ignore her doctor's advice. Instead of keeping her baby tucked up in bed as suggested, she took Pia's recovery into her own hands, instigating an exercise program which, her tender age notwithstanding, had Pia on roller skates daily for four-hour stints in the park. Come rain, come snow, come freezing temperatures, Saturnina piled Pia's bicycle and scooter onto the baby carriage and made these outings. The effort paid off. Before she was two, Pia was ice-skating; she rode horseback at two and a half, and her legs were growing steadily stronger.

When it seemed her little wunderkind was headed for show business, Saturnina was thrown into a quandary. She had promised herself she would work her fingers to the bone rather than have her daughter a child performer. In her view, that kind of money was blood money. Besides, she wanted her to go to college. "Then, all of a sudden, voomp, she's under contract and she's working." Immediately, Pia was hooked. Attempting to unhook her would, Saturnina knew, have been fighting a losing battle.

"Want this? Did I! I knew I wouldn't have to go to school!" said Pia, acknowledging that her mother devoted herself to her career. "She traveled, she gave up her life entirely, spending weeks away from Dad." Every cent Pia earned (save for money spent on pictures and the occasional special dress Pia needed) remained untouched until she married. With the many commercials she made, the nest egg became massive, Saturnina says proudly, her perspective doubtless shaped by her family history.

Saturnina's maternal grandfather was a well-to-do miller from Lublin County outside Warsaw. His entire (and ever increasing) family made about eight sea voyages carrying grain between Poland and Philadelphia or Detroit. Four of his twelve children were born on those turnarounds in the States, and Saturnina's mother, the tenth child, was one of them. This enterprising man died soon before Hitler marched through Poland, wiping out much of his extended family and snatching his land and grain. Saturnina's equally imaginative grandmother, a spritely woman in her eighties, took two of her grandchildren into the woods, hid them in an underground trench, and schooled them there until the war was over.

Saturnina's mother was more fortunate. By World War II she was safely ensconced in Philadelphia, which is where she met her husband, a fellow immigrant, but from Russian cossack stock.

Saturnina met her husband via Longina, who had married a well-known violinist. Despite her mixed feelings about Pia working, there were moments of glowing pride. She will never forget hearing her voice, pure and crystal clear, ringing out from a classroom while she played "Greensleeves" on the piano. Saturnina also found exciting and gratifying the encouragement Pia received from stars like Tallulah Bankhead (with whom she made her Broadway debut in 1961 in *Midgie Purvis*), Hal Prince, and Gene Kelly.

Pia has described her mother as the original Polish sergeant, saying she wore the trousers in their house. When she took summer breaks from her job in the wardrobe department and accompanied Pia touring in shows, she made very sure her daughter did every scrap of her homework by mail and she herself learned the latest math form so that she could give Pia extra tutelage.

It was during an out-of-town matinee of *Applause,* with Alexis Smith, that Meshulam Riklis sat in the audience. Pia, who was just seventeen, popped out of the cake onstage and fizzed "like a piece of dynamite," dazzling him immediately.

After the performance, Pia informed her mom that an "old man" had invited her to dinner. How old? her mother asked, "Oh, very old and decrepit, but he has this great big car," replied unsophisticated Pia, who had only seen limousines at funerals and weddings. Saturnina encouraged Pia to accept the invitation, but envisioned the dinner taking place at the plush, revolving supper room atop their hotel in Dayton, Ohio. Smiling, she recalls:

"This codger, he had a different idea. He hired the biggest stretch limousine there was, it was probably used for the president when he was in town. He had also switched to a larger hotel suite and made reservations at a riverboat restaurant." Saturnina did not doubt that these preparations were made lecherously. "His tongue was hanging out at this nice young girl." She laughs. Little did he suspect that Pia was only allowed to date if chaperoned. Sometimes Saturnina kept a watchful eye from another table across a crowded restaurant.

This mother hen effectively thwarted Mr. Riklis's plans for a quick conquest. First, Pia insisted he meet her mom, which definitely was not on his agenda. Saturnina did not see the expected old codger, but rather a gorgeous fellow, "all perfumed up" and dashingly attired in a nautical-style, gold-buttoned, double-breasted blazer, with a white shirt and red tie. The formalities over, Pia went up to the restaurant on his arm. This was a man known to take "five broads" with him on a business trip to Paris, stashing each in a separate hotel suite, his mother-in-law says gleefully. What did Pia do? She insisted on taking her life-sized rag doll right into the restaurant with them and sat it beside her. Saturnina, with undisguised mirth, says Pia gave him the whole treatment to send him running.

As star-watchers well know, he did not run far. They wed four years later and have been happy for more than a decade. The first morning of their marriage, Meshulam Riklis telephoned his new mom-in-law and complained, "Your daughter doesn't even know how to cook eggs, she doesn't know how to make breakfast!" Saturnina was unsympathetic. "I said, 'Mr. Riklis, son, I'm sorry. No refunds, no exchanges.' And I hung up."

It was a nice family twist to Pia's career that before his death her dad, Alphonse Schipani, became her concert master when she performed at the Beverly Theatre in Beverly Hills. Alphonse was Italian, and was brought to America when he was nine. He already played ukulele and guitar, and soon after taking up the violin, he made his Carnegie Hall debut. Saturnina proudly describes *New York Times* reviews declaring him a potential prodigious talent. He was with *La Cage Aux Folles* as concertmaster before his death in 1986. He also shared the limelight at his daughter's much-heralded Carnegie Hall debut, a night that is one of Saturnina's most treasured memories: "It was a pleasure for me to see my two dearly beloveds up on that stage. She introduced her daddy and he stood up and threw a kiss to her, and that got almost as big a hand as she got for her number."

Clearly, Pia has outgrown and shaken free of her crippling shyness. Of course, shyness seems but a minor obstacle when measured against more serious handicaps like Stevie Wonder's blindness. Born four weeks ahead of schedule, Stevie spent the first fifty-six days of his life in an incubator. He developed retrolental fibroplasia, which rendered him permanently blind, because too much oxygen was pumped into the incubator. Looking on the bright side, he could have died.

Lula Mae Hardaway primarily raised her son alone, moving from Saginaw, Michigan, to the projects in Detroit while he was still a baby. (A fortuitous choice, since Detroit became the home of Motown.) Stevie claims he vaguely remembers what his mother looks like, but admits he could be dreaming. More concretely, he knows how fortunate he is to have a mom who is both strong and soft: "My mother was a pioneer. She took a lot of steps with me that a lot of other mothers wouldn't have."

Lula Mae encouraged Stevie's adventurous spirit to such an extent that he became a fearless child. He once fell in a river while playing cowboys and Indians with his brothers, because he did not heed their shouted warning; he thought they were trying to trick him. Wonder sees no reason why he should not be able to drive, and Lula Mae still believes her Stevie will be able to see one day. She would give her own life to make it happen.

Little Stevie was never a guilt-inducing child, spiritedly telling Lula Mae, when he was just five, that she should not worry about his blindness because he was happy. Stevie attended Whitestone Baptist Church, and at age eight, the talented little chap was playing soulful harmonica, bongos, drums, and piano. He was eleven when in 1961 he met Motown's Berry Gordy Jr. Gordy thought he was cute but was in no rush to sign him up; he had no idea he had on his hands a fledgling musical genius.

Lula Mae Hardaway lives in Los Angeles in a house bought for her by her loving son. Stevie not only takes good care of his mother, but also of his sister Renee and four brothers. After all, it is them Wonder has to thank for his I-can-do-anything approach to life.

Alan Alda was a polio victim, and but for the swift action of his mother, he might never have made the recovery he did. She suspected the dreaded disease when her seven-year-old son vomited and had headaches, his knees buckled, and he was so stiff he could not bend his head to drink orange juice. Alan's father dismissed it as probably just a cold, but she was insistent upon calling the doctor and Alan was whisked off to the hospital, where he was subjected to eight months of painful treatment. Squares of woolen blanket were folded into triangles like oversized diapers, he recalls, saying that they were boiled until they were "so stinging hot the person who applies them can't even hold them. I remember them being *dropped* on me. And then they're wrapped tightly around every muscle and pinned on. *Every hour.*"

The smell of the wool still haunts him. But he thinks it was harder on his parents. He felt only the physical pain; they had to contend with hearing his screams. Along with his mother, Alda also feels he owes his life to the hospital nurse who invented the treatment and insisted on using it. She did not buckle in the face of an overwhelmingly derisive reaction from all the male doctors. No wonder Alda loves women.

Ex-Beatle Ringo Starr, who had the most poverty-stricken of the Beatle childhoods in the Liverpool slum of Dingle, was also a sickly child. Elsie Starkey, his mother, was told three times that her only son would not live until the following morning. Another gross underestimation of the will to survive, although Ringo did spend long periods of his early life in a hospital bed. Roy Scheider would sympathize. He was stricken with rheumatic fever again and again until at fifteen he was forced to stay in bed for a year. His weight ballooned up to almost two hundred pounds from boredom and inertia, which explains Scheider's preoccupation with staying slim. "To this day, when I look in the mirror, I see this fat, miserable fifteen-year-old kid," he says.

Like Cher, Richard Chamberlain and Tom Cruise grappled with their schooling under the handicap of dyslexia. Chamberlain's case was mild, but his slow reading no doubt contributed to his hatred of school. "It's very important for me to be successful, because I had a relatively low self-esteem as a kid," Chamberlain, who is normally taciturn on personal topics, has admitted. "I need some kind of worldly approval."

Tom Cruise was lucky. His mother, who along with Tom's three sisters is also dyslexic, recognized her son's difficulties immediately and arranged for him to have remedial reading classes. Prior to his parents' divorce, Cruise's family moved constantly due to Tom's father's job as an electrical engineer and that disrupted his schooling. "When you're a new kid, all you want to do is blend in with everything and make friends. It was a drag. It separated you and singled you out." Once again, it is that sense of not belonging, of being different, that is the most painful of fates for any adolescent.

7 *Mom's Misfits*

Jacqueline Stallone's bathroom boasts a decades-old photograph of her displaying a fair amount of flesh as a feathered and spangled Billy Rose showgirl at the Diamond Horseshoe club. Not that she is recognizable in the picture; in her mid-sixties, the blonde has given way to dark brunette and the diamonds are those worn liberally about her person.

In the 1960s, the feisty, eccentric Jackie owned Barbella's, a women's weight lifting gym with a traffic-stopping picture of a large-breasted woman over its door—and this was long before pumping iron was considered an acceptable female pastime. The raucous, outrageously flamboyant Jacqueline was never a run-of-the-mill mom, and Sylvester, even before he turned Stallone into a household name, was never an ordinary son.

Sly was one of the stars who grew up more than just the odd man out, more than a bit of a loner. Rather, he was a downright misfit. He traces some of his troubles back to the way he came into the world, claiming he was born in a charity ward where a doctor squeezed his face too hard during delivery, giving rise to his partial facial paralysis. Jackie, despite being in the throes of five-minute-interval labor pains, had refused to take a taxi to the hospital. With typically defiant aplomb, she went by bus—polishing off a loaf of bread en route.

Sylvester, so the story goes, was a baby so hyperactive that he had to be kept in a crib with a lid on it, so rebellious that he made his first bid for freedom when he was three and tried to run away from home. He spent those early years on this planet causing havoc in a railroad walk-up in New York's rough Hell's Kitchen district, while his parents worked to get the family out of the slums. Jackie's life and fortunes have been nothing if not varied.

Sylvester thinks his mom should slow down a little and put her feet up, but that is asking a tigress to shed her stripes. Jacqueline's bloodline has a built-in competitive streak. Both parents were of French descent. Her mother—daughter of the mayor of Brest, France—swam the English Channel. "Would *you* put your toe in the Channel? Now that takes guts! And my father was a child-prodigy violinist before he became a lawyer, and his father invented the typewriter ribbon. So it was a family of everyone trying to outdo one another. And I guess I passed it on to my children." Her father was also a fitness fanatic; it was he who pushed her into wrestling when she was a young woman, although female wrestlers were considered highly outlandish.

Jacqueline's first burst of independence came when she ran off to New York to join the circus. Unfortunately, she was allotted a snake charmer for a roommate, which did not sit well with a woman who was scared of worms. She rapidly moved on to a job as a cigarette girl at the Stork Club and then spent five years at the Diamond Horseshoe club, until she met Frank Stallone, a Sicilian immigrant, and fell madly in love. Sylvester and Frank were its products, but it was, she says, a disastrous marriage; she is the first to admit she was hardly the traditional wifely type.

Frank Stallone Sr. had been in the army before switching, rather incongruously, to hairdressing. He could have been another Perry Como, according to Sly, but crippling stage fright thwarted his prospects and kept him singing out from behind the curtains of burlesque houses. Nevertheless, as part of the package from Mom and Dad, Sly Stallone obviously received a double dose of unfulfilled performer.

When Sylvester was five, the family moved to a suburb of Washington, D.C., where Frank moved into the lucrative field of real estate after launching a chain of beauty salons with Jackie's help—she had gone on to study cosmetology. Jackie's parenting was a touch unorthodox. She stood over Sly with a stick to force him to practice piano and paid him to read books. She claims that Errol Flynn's autobiography inspired him to start fencing, and that a book about a prostitute fired his ambition to write and made a lifelong reader out of him.

Sylvester used to say he felt unwanted and abused as a child, a claim he tempered as he began to learn of the real abuse to which some children are subjected. Stallone Sr. was not given to praising him; in fact he was highly critical. Sylvester, who inherited his mother's stubborn streak as well as her wild one, became hell-bent on impressing and pleasing his father, a man he says exuded a Stanley Kowalski kind of Neanderthal charm. Jacqueline and Frank Stallone divorced in 1956, when Sly was eleven, but Jackie soon remarried, choosing another Italian husband, a pizza king from Philadelphia.

He was a strict stepfather to Sly and Frank and father to Toni-An, but his requirements that his children be squeaky clean and well-behaved were not met by the boys, who were problematic students to say the least. Jacqueline was asked to remove them from an inordinate number of schools, and by the time Sylvester was fifteen, his turbulent childhood had left this permanent blot on his school record—he had been ejected from twelve schools for, among other things, hacking a model Santa Claus to pieces.

One divorce later, Jacqueline opened a cosmetology clinic of her own in Florida, where she effectively knocked out her competition by marrying the owner of a rival clinic. Divorced for a third time, she is now happily single. A born entertainer and committed workaholic, she still retains a professional outlet for herself, busily managing a women's wrestling team. (As her children can attest, she knows all the right moves. Jackie once wrestled Sylvester's aunt to the floor and sent her flying unceremoniously down the hallway.)

Ms. Stallone flings herself wholeheartedly into everything and lives for a challenge: from daily tap dancing lessons to astrology to linguistics, to making *Silver Foxes*, her exercise video for older folk, for which she corraled Farrah Fawcett's mom, Pauline; Dustin Hoffman's pop, Harry; and Al Pacino's dad, Sal. Lining up other star moms and pops was a trial, she told writer Mary Fletcher:

"Some of them were drunks, some were physically unfit, irresponsible, had bad backs, were afraid of flying, had phobias, or boyfriends they couldn't leave. Oh, it was discouraging! But I badgered the ones I wanted until they said yes."

Jackie's extroverted, domineering personality and penchant for hogging the limelight doubtless contributed to Sylvester's thirst for his own helping of airtime. The flip side to all that character is that Jackie is precisely the kind of star mom who could be (and indeed has been) something of an embarrassment—although her derogatory remarks about Sylvester's second wife, Brigitte Nielsen (she claimed she was a gold digger), came to seem less incendiary after the couple's brief marriage collapsed than they did at the time she uttered them, dampening Sly's prenuptial bliss. Jackie, the protective mama, was vindicated somewhat when it came to light just how hard Brigitte had hit her son in the financial jugular.

The repercussions from her indiscretions have not tamed her tactlessness. Nor did they stop her from claiming that Sly's long-suffering first wife, Sasha, who took him back after his affairs with tall blondes and is the mother of his two sons, "would still be a waitress if Sylvester hadn't met her. He never wanted to marry her." Nor did they stop her from revealing that during Sly and Sasha's marriage, he dated other women with his wife's consent.

Expecting Jacqueline Stallone to keep her energetic mouth zippered while she is frenetically pursued by the ravenous world press is as fanciful as expecting a chocaholic to escape unscathed after being locked in a candy shop. Jackie likens it to keeping a lid on her head. Low-profile is not in her nature; rather she owns up to a fondness for gossip and to dabbling in her sons' affairs. She is very much the proud mama. "Sure I'm proud of them; what mother wouldn't be?" she says. "But whether they're proud of me is a good question. Some days I'm sure they think I should stay home, shut up, and bake apples."

Jacqueline boasts that she has all her own teeth, but has not been heard claiming that her eyesight is twenty-twenty. While Brigitte Nielsen was still married to Sylvester, one of mom's less contentious remarks was, "I like Brigitte. I know it's a vain thing to say, but she looks a lot like me."

Writer Mary Fletcher observes, "Jacqueline has the eyes and

coloring of Sylvester, talks with the drawl of Mae West and has decorated her house in a style of which Liberace would be proud: huge glass chandelier over the grand piano, walls of mirrors and Sly's Oscar on a ledge in the entrance hall. She is a real character and she is not going to fade into the background until she is lying in her grave. She wants to be out there in the spotlight, she wants to be somebody very special . . . and she *has* had a very interesting life, she is a wonderful p.r. for herself."

In this particular star mom's opinion, there is only one answer to the question "Where does the talent come from?" and that is, "It comes from us!" She drinks in the power that her son's immense success affords her, saying, "I can pick up a phone and call anyone—even the President of the United States will speak to me because of Sylvester—otherwise they'd tell me to go to hell, I know that."

If there is an archetypal misfit, however, it is Woody Allen who represents him. Nettie and Martin Konigsberg's son was, like Sly Stallone, always a problematic student, a rebel in unlikely physical disguise. His early writings were labeled dirty by his teachers, whose wayward charge in turn labeled them ignorant, stupid, mean, and anti-Semitic. Allen attended Midwood High public school and spent eight years in Hebrew School, a double bill of horror for the boy who considered it "a spectacular treat to be sick." Nettie, whom Woody has called a female Groucho Marx, was a familiar face at school, called in often because of her son's truancy, bad marks, and general disruptive behavior.

The man who eats in restaurants 360 nights of the year went into training in his Flatbush, Brooklyn, home, where he chose to dine alone rather than with the family. He also spurned after-school activities. "I would go in at nine and come back at three and would never participate in God squad or whatever; then I'd go right into my bedroom and shut the door—immediately."

The reportedly agnostic Allen Stewart Konigsberg (a.k.a. Woody) comes from a family of Orthodox Jews with—according to the man himself—no cultural background whatsoever. He has described his childhood in this noisy ethnic family as perfectly average, with the basic values of God and carpeting. Nettie was one of nine sisters (Woody had no shortage of female influence via his aunts and many cousins) and worked as a bookkeeper in a flower shop. Martin Konigsberg hopped around between "a million little jobs." Nettie and Martin are now in their eighties. They and Woody's younger sister, Leddy, are near neighbors in Manhattan.

The man who loathes the countryside was a good athlete (basketball, baseball, track, swimming) and did not go short of friends, nor girlfriends for that matter. Even so, he was primarily a loner who, if he is to be believed, was frequently yelled at and hit by his parents. He played hooky from school, drawn by the charms of the Automat and 42nd Street cinemas, and was sufficiently assured of his future as a writer that he had no qualms about throwing his books into a bush and taking days off. Later, he did a short stint at City College to please his parents, who were appalled when their son did not follow his friends into college and medicine.

While it is no easy task to discern plain fact from creative embroidery among Woody's lore, it appears the Konigsbergs raised the kind of man who is umbilically tied to New York for reasons such as, "I know where to duck in and go to the bathroom if I have to." He turned his pen to comedy at sixteen. In fact he simply began to write and the results were funny. In another belated attempt to appease his mother and father, he attended New York University, but his marks were so poor, the school dropped him. He majored in film and even in that he somehow contrived to be a dismal failure. Worse, he failed the limited program which consisted of just three subjects. He could not have cared less, and why should he have? By seventeen he was earning a princely fifteen hundred dollars a week writing the jokes for comics.

Donald Sutherland went through his childhood terrified of how people saw him; afraid they might literally recoil and say, "Ugh." While it is possible to *perceive* in him the sickly *Dumbo* kid, it is also true that his much-heralded sex-appeal owes a great deal to precisely those gangly, quirky, off-beat looks.

He was two when he suffered the bout with polio which left one leg longer than the other. The list of ailments he endured included a year-long bout with rheumatic fever at age ten (pre-penicillin, so treatment involved a gas mask and enemas), two tonsillectomies, hepatitis, and a mastoidectomy. At the hospital he received plenty of attention—of the unpleasant variety. Not surprisingly, he was preoccupied with death.

His mother was a minister's daughter and rather straitlaced. Donald thought his first erection was venereal disease and was beside himself with worry about how to break this news to her. When he once asked her if he was good-looking, Donald's mom did not shrink from the task of telling him that he was not. She softened the blow by adding that he had character.

Theirs was a close, loving family. He grew up on a farm in New Brunswick, Nova Scotia, one of five children. Yet he was the perennial loner and all-round misfit; nothing felt right. He was too tall. By age eleven he was a head above his peers, and by thirteen he measured six feet four inches and was a veritable giant. "The local freak," says the star, of the boy he once was. His face was long and thin, his ears stuck out, and the nicknames that rang in them were ego-smashers like Goofus and Dumbo.

"I *knew* I was a homely kid. They don't call you Goofus and Dumbo for nothing. It was because of my big eyes and ears and teeth, and my mother used to shave off my hair in summer. With the shape of *my* head, that didn't help."

He recounted an extraordinary childhood incident to Claudia Dreifus of *Playboy* magazine, relating the time he walked beneath a tree and the giggling children concealed in its branches urinated on his head. His mother's reaction was hardly reassuring: "Well, Donnie, what did you expect?"

He desperately wanted to feel normal; instead he felt unlovable. The prescription seemed written for failure, and the merest sign of judgment fed into his raging self-doubts: "If anybody criticized me, I would automatically think they were right."

Donald's father was a Goodyear tire salesman with a penchant for gambling and a live-for-today philosophy which could be painful for his mother. After one gambling loss, Donald remembers his dad ordering an extravagant meal, while his mom was in tears.

Donald's father wanted him to become an engineer, but he had talent as an artist and wanted to act from the age of eleven. At fourteen, the oddball adolescent moved a step closer to his goal by becoming Canada's youngest disc jockey. For all his stardom, Sutherland's childhood legacy is an appetite for love and appreciation that remains gargantuan. An autograph-signing session is to him a mere snack.

Dudley Moore's view of himself as a misfit also had its roots in childhood illness. He was born with a club foot and for the first seven years of his life spent stretches of time in hospitals and convalescent homes having surgery to attempt to correct this inward-turned, misshapen left foot, the first operation taking place when he was two weeks old. Dudley, who felt scared, isolated, and abandoned when he was away, did not return to a home environment conducive to the releasing of his pent-up emotions. Father, a railway electrician, was religious, and his secretary mom, the daughter of a faith-healer, did not show her son physical affection. As if that were not bad enough, she passed on to Dudley her own troublesome feelings of guilt and shame about his handicap. His inheritance was a limp (one leg was shorter than the other), much repressed rage, and a ravenous craving for love.

Nevertheless, the Moores were musical, and Dudley was encouraged to sit and practice piano when he was six. He sang in the choir, and when he was eleven, his parents finally bought him the violin he had longed for. It was a hard realization that his talents did not lie in that direction after all, but he returned to the ivories and so excelled at organ-playing that he was awarded a scholarship to Oxford University—a rare honor for a working-class boy from Dagenham, Essex.

Pint-sized Dudley reached out to humor in a manner not entirely unfamiliar to those of his stature; it became his way of saving himself from school bully boys and earning the acceptance of his peers. Cyndi Lauper and Dudley Moore would have a lot to talk about, because she was sure that the laurels were hers for being the ultimate misfit. Her mom, Catrine Domenique, was well aware that Cyndi was desperately unhappy at school and suspects it was her pain which gave her the determination and the strength to make it to the top. Cyndi, who felt she was an odd-looking little girl and wore crimson corsets, petticoats, fishnets, veils, and gypsy gear at eleven, was always an original, an innovator. But those very traits which would turn to her advantage later in life were first the cause of much suffering.

Catrine and Cyndi's father divorced when Cyndi was five. Their separation was civilized, a mutual decision, yet Catrine knows that her pain transmitted itself to her children who also felt their own loss of their dad, a shipping clerk who played xylophone in his spare time and loved archaeology. The saving grace was Catrine's warm, loving, and close relationship with her daughters, Cyndi and Ellen, and her son, Butch.

There was also an outside dynamic to contend with: divorce was greatly frowned upon in the 1950s and Cyndi's Catholic school ejected her from its ranks, which naturally added to her sense of alienation. Then, Cyndi had to watch her loving mom, who certainly deserved better than to be treated like a sinner, work hard, fourteen-hour shifts as a waitress in diners to support her family. Cyndi noted, "She looked like she was killing herself," explaining that as a consequence, she was not attracted to women's traditional lot in life.

Although Catrine knew about Cyndi's unhappiness, she never understood it. She was truly perplexed by the isolation of her warm, giving, and talented daughter. Desperately, Catrine shifted Cyndi from school to school in the hope that she would find a niche for herself. At one, Cyndi made her First Confession; horrified by the experience, she decided nuns and God could not possibly be connected and thought she had been sent to a torture chamber for kids by mistake. Cyndi just became more shy and withdrawn.

She was also sensitive, and cruel schoolyard taunts about her off-beat clothes hurt her badly. "As a teenager Cyndi was one of the originals as far as wearing antique clothing," her mom recalls. "She loved it. I didn't; I couldn't understand what she saw in it. If you're in Manhattan, people are more into things, but in rural areas at that time, especially in Queens, people aren't accustomed to such drastic changes. Sometimes when the kids saw her dressed like that they used to throw rocks at her. It happens to anybody that's original. It's a funny thing about human nature. What you don't understand, you fear. And what you fear, you ridicule." She was more a left-out kid than a voluntary loner, but she managed to survive her childhood with her originality intact.

Always, singing was Cyndi's escape valve. Her mom believes it was the only time her shyness abated and she felt secure, confident, and happy. "There are a lot of scars, and that's one of the things that makes her so sensitive to other people's needs and feelings. Cyndi really relates to people and I think they sense that."

A music-lover herself, Catrine sang in the church choir and exposed her children to the strains of Louis Armstrong's "All That Meat and No Potatoes" and, at the other end of the spectrum, Eileen Farrell singing the role of Madame Butterfly. Catrine always sang along, Cyndi and Ellen strummed guitars, and until the Beatles came and ousted all but rock 'n' roll, their Queens home was constantly alive with jazz, popular music, classical music, and Catrine's much-loved albums of Broadway musicals. One favorite was *The King and I*, which Cyndi played repeatedly, but Catrine and Cyndi were both partial to Barbra Streisand and Catrine loved to hear her little daughter mimic the Brooklyn Songbird. She remembers Cyndi selecting "Rat-A-Tat-Tat," a song from *Funny Girl*, to sing at the end-of-term school talent show.

"You've got to hear the song, then picture Cyndi at ten, a little blonde, hazel-eyed, petite cherub singing that song on stage with the Jewish accent, the whole thing. She was fantastic! The kids were rolling on the floor, the teachers were hysterical, when at that moment, who appears at the doorway but the principal?

"He was a very staunch man, very strict. Well, he came marching down the aisle, up on the stage, and grabbed Cyndi by the scruff of her neck. He took her off the stage and out of the auditorium. He turned beet red, I thought he was going to have a stroke—the words are a little sophisticated for a ten-year-old. I just died.

"I was going over this recently with the teacher and she said to me, 'Wouldn't you know it? Cyndi never missed a note, she sang all the way to the door!' To this day, the teachers are still talking about it. Cyndi was a very lovable child, you couldn't help but love her. She wasn't spoiled. She was obedient, but like all kids in the sixties she was rebellious against the establishment, established ideas.

"She wasn't one to wear make-up as a teenager, but for Halloween she'd put all kinds of crazy colors together and was very creative. She had a pretty little face. I didn't think she needed any make-up. It was only later on when she went into the entertainment field that she really started with the make-up and this look that she's got."

Cyndi's hair has now been almost every color of the rainbow, but she was just eleven when she first horrified her mother by putting green food dye in her hair and green make-up on her face. Catrine, who was afraid it would never wash out, screamed. She still cannot find the words to express quite how she felt when, years later, she first saw Cyndi's freshly shaved hairdo and half-bald head.

"I said, 'Is it ever going to look normal again?' She said, 'What do you mean? This is very special!' It took a little getting used to, but once I did I thought it was cute, too. Of course, I wouldn't do it myself," she adds, somewhat unnecessarily. She is so fiercely protective of her daughter that if she hears a word said against her, Catrine has to restrain herself from beating up Cyndi's critic.

Cyndi had a rocky ride to the top. After getting her high school equivalency diploma, she went to Canada with friends, then enrolled in college in Vermont to study art—her mom says she draws and paints beautifully. When she was around twenty-one, she returned to New York and got into a group. Those were difficult, discouraging years. She had nodules on her vocal chords and lost her voice. While Cyndi whispered to heal it, she was informed by a specialist that she would never sing again.

"She'd been singing like Janis Joplin, whom she admired a great deal," her mom recalls. "Everybody used to say that if they closed their eyes they thought she was Janis and she got a very eerie feeling from that. I don't think she liked it. Anyway, she really was very discouraged, but she found this fantastic voice coach who helped her come back and taught her how to exercise her throat so that she would be in complete control and wouldn't damage it. She was with her for years and they are still friends.

"In my heart I always felt Cyndi should be a star. I'd say to myself, 'Well, is it because I'm her mother?' But I used to admire her singing. I could sit there and listen to her sing all day. Unfortunately you also have to have the right connections, to know the right people. When she went with Polydor she almost made it, but there were problems later so that ended that. There were problems with her manager too . . . until she met David Wolff. Thank God, he knew how to handle the situation and was able to show the world her talent."

Cyndi and Catrine have always shared a special love of all animals. Once, they almost bought a monkey in a pet shop. Catrine came to her senses just in time. She now lives with a mutt called Sparkle who was found by Cyndi and Ellen and adopted by Catrine after the dog had surgery and could no longer negotiate the five flights of stairs up to Cyndi's apartment. "She's about eighteen now and I love her. I say, 'This is the granddaughter I've never had.' "

When Cyndi was little more than two, a neighbor took her to a chicken farm and asked her to pick out a chicken. Cyndi, believing it was going to be her pet, complied—and watched in horror while its throat was slit and it was hung for the blood to drip out. Catrine, who never could understand why Cyndi wouldn't eat chicken, only recently found out about this traumatic event. As she got older, Cyndi started keeping fish.

"One night she got so involved in her homework, she didn't realize that the little heater had gotten too hot. When she finally found them, the fish were floating on top of the water and she was very, very heartbroken about that. It didn't matter how small an animal, she would always bury them and be very sensitive about them." Before she became a star, she took odd jobs working in stables and kennels—she could never have fit into a dull old office routine.

Catrine herself is so fond of Siamese fighter fish that she once studied books on them so she could perform surgery to cut away a tumor on a favorite female. When the fish healed, naturally she felt a strong bond with it. At mating time, she was extra careful to keep the vicious male from the female with a netted separator until the female was ready to mate, her belly was full of eggs, and the male had built the necessary bubble nest with his mouth.

Finally, satisfied that all was well, she took the separator out and went up to bed.

"When I got up the next morning, I found the female all chewed up, floating on the top. I was so angry that according to Cyndi, I picked out the fish with the netting and yelled at him. Then—and this was raw emotion—I took a pencil and hit him with it, somehow chopping his tail off! I was so furious, I'd wanted the female fish to live so badly." She groans at the memory of what made it even worse: "I just wanted to dig a hole and bury myself when I heard Cyndi tell this story on a TV talk show!"

8 *Rough Roads, Rich Rewards*

Sporting a trademark hat and his notoriously wicked smile, which is familiar to three billion people in eighty-six countries, the star spurned the yellow Rolls-Royce in the garage and climbed aboard the motor scooter parked outside his multimillion dollar, Malibu beachfront property. His elderly companion, also a star, looked suitably jaunty in a white pantsuit, and without blanching at the mode of transport, she clambered onto the scooter behind him. She clutched her yellow purse, attempted to anchor her hurriedly grabbed hat, and wrapped her arms tightly around his waist. Off they sped down the Pacific Coast Highway, just like a couple of teenagers.

Larry Hagman and his mom, Mary Martin, otherwise known as J. R. Ewing and Peter Pan, come from different galaxies. He is a TV king, she a queen of the stage. And although trim, vivacious Mary is a septuagenarian, her derring-do on the scooter comes as no real surprise from one long accustomed to flying around on wires.

Hagman and Martin's companionable sortie in search of a sandwich lunch bore witness to the triumphant and happy resolution of what was not always the most tranquil or harmonious mother-son relationship. Now that Larry Hagman's mark has been made—etched might be a more appropriate word—and he is the bigger, brighter star, the internal jealousy has inevitably eased. From the current warmth between them, it is clear that the tension and estrangements have not only dissipated, they have given way to a kind of mutual encouragement and admiration

151

society. Mother and son have grown comfortably into a friendship between peers who share a common interest, as befitting two people who are divided by a mere seventeen years in age.

Their relationship was not so tranquil when twelve-year-old Larry refused to be adopted by his stepfather or to change his name when his mom remarried producer Richard Halliday. "Larry had it rough as a little boy, much rougher than I realized until much later," the usually reticent Mary now admits.

"For the next few years, Larry, Richard, and I had a checkered career. There were moments of great joy and utter sorrow, tensions, times when we didn't speak, misunderstandings, anger, reconciliation, tears, everything. The love and comprehension Larry and I now have belong to another moment, another chapter . . . ," she wrote in her 1977 autobiography, *My Heart Belongs*.

As a Broadway star, Mary gave her love to her audiences. On the positive side, her decision not to martyr herself to motherhood, but to pursue the career of her dreams (for which she was infinitely better suited), negated the potential for guilt on Larry's part. There was no question of "what she had sacrificed for him," but he considered himself lucky, not rejected. And was it so selfish? Surely it was better that his mother pursued the career she hungered for than to have forced herself into a life that did not suit her?

Larry long ago grew tired of telling reporters he did not resent his mother's success or absences. What was the point? They persistently wrote the opposite. Personally, he put those youthful rifts, which sometimes spanned two or three years, down to immaturity on both their parts. He resented the focus on their stormy periods, which he considered no worse than those endured by many families.

Larry Martin Hagman, a second-generation star-to-be, was born in 1931 weighing eight and a half pounds. Seventeen-year-old Mary, a petite ninety-pound bantamweight, found giving birth traumatic. Still a child herself, she was frankly scared of the baby and felt more fraternal than maternal. Her parents were Preston "Pet" Martin, a lawyer, and Juanita Presley. Mary's musically talented mother was a violin teacher at what is now Weatherford College, Texas; consequently, Mary was a fledgling (although reluctant) violin student at age five.

Juanita had hoped for a son, but Mary could take considerable consolation from knowing that her mother had risked her life to have her after being warned it would be dangerous to give birth to another child. She had the joyous, stable childhood that son Larry did not.

Mary was fourteen when she met Larry's father, Benjamin Jackson Hagman, the nineteen-year-old grandson of Swedish immigrants. Her tender age was a contributory factor in Mary's parents' decision to pack her off to finishing school in Nashville, Tennessee, when she turned sixteen. But Mary immediately became incredibly homesick for Mother, and presumably even more so for Ben, and only stuck it out for a couple of months before Juanita either took pity on her or was scared of the repercussions of ignoring such a situation, and chauffeured the young couple to Hopkinsville, Kentucky, where they wed. After the ceremony, she chauffeured her straight back to the finishing school, from which Mary was swiftly ejected as soon as her new marital status came to light.

After Larry's birth, Mary initially managed to cover her ambivalence about motherhood well, hiding behind something for which she was rather better qualified—playing the role. There were novelty props to divert her, like a house, a car, and furniture from Daddy, but the first formal picture of Mary with baby Larry showed her in her graduation dress—a poignant reminder of her immaturity. When Ben, inspired by Mary's father, decided to become an attorney and the little family moved back to Weatherford to live with her parents, the game was over. Juanita stepped in and took charge of her grandson, while Mary turned her attention to opening a dancing school in her uncle's grain-storage loft.

For the girl who had prophetically whiled away many school hours experimenting with different styles of signature, it was the first step toward her new life. To better qualify her to teach, Mary took a trip to Hollywood for some training, and by the time she returned, her indulgent parents had built her a new dance studio just for a little "welcome home" surprise. The ever-inventive Juanita had tie-dyed vast lengths of cheesecloth to fashion its blue sky.

The cracks in Mary and Ben Hagman's immature marriage rapidly became evident under Mary's parents' wing, and Juanita became physically ill every time the possibility of their departure (little Larry's departure, to be specific) came up for discussion. Mary and Ben were divorced by proxy in 1935, and Ben did not resist her request for custody of their son. Once she had her freedom, without more ado twenty-one-year-old Mary left Larry in the tender care of his devoted substitute mom and headed for Broadway.

Sadly, her so-proud father had a cerebral stroke during Mary's first year in New York. Ironically, she was playing Dolly, the dumb blonde in *Leave It to Me*, the musical which gave her the chance to sing the Cole Porter classic "My Heart Belongs to Daddy." Mary gave two performances on the Saturday she heard her father had been taken ill, then flew home to see him. He emerged from his coma during her brief visit, but she was not to see him alive again. A born trooper, she did not miss a performance and was back on stage for the Monday night curtain up. That evening, she sensed something strange about the audience . . . and she was right. Those who had paid to see her knew what Mary did not. Only when the curtain fell did Sophie Tucker break the news of her father's death. She was devastated by both his death and the inevitable headlines: DADDY'S GIRL SINGS ABOUT DADDY AS DADDY DIES.

Within three years, Mary Martin achieved the stardom she somehow instinctively knew would be hers, with the Broadway shows *Peter Pan* and *South Pacific*. When Hollywood beckoned, Juanita and Larry moved in with Mary for a time, but she barely saw them. She left the house before dawn (a schedule with which Larry has become only too familiar from his years on "Dallas"), and scraped back just in time to see Larry being bathed before bedtime. Juanita was the dominant presence and force during the first twelve years of Larry's life. When she died, everything changed.

Mary and her son finally had to adjust to being together, which required infinitely more effort on Larry's part. In his new life with

Mary and Richard Halliday, he felt a terrific shift in focus. From being the center of his grandma's universe, suddenly there he was, thrown into a world which revolved entirely around Mary Martin, The Star. Of paramount importance were Mary's sleep, which had to run undisturbed until noon each day, and the conservation of her energy and voice for that night's performance. Not much fun for a young boy.

Mary enlisted her unhappy son in a stream of first-rate private schools, which did nothing to alleviate the situation, and a military academy which he abhorred. At fourteen, he attended a progressive school in Vermont—evidently not progressive enough, since he was asked to leave. As an adolescent, Larry opted to move in with his father in Texas rather than take a role which Mary pushed his way, touring with her in *Annie Get Your Gun*. Father and son enjoyed their own companionable cowboy period of hunting, fishing, drinking beer, and smoking, and Larry's rebellion against Mary's world was in full flight.

Between 1949 and 1952 his mom was once again the toast of the theater world in a revival of *South Pacific*, and Larry and his roommate stood through a performance, too proud to ask for tickets. It was almost inevitable that Larry's natural talent as a second-generation ham would find expression in school plays, and by the time he was seventeen he decided that he liked theater after all. Looking back on his start in show business, Larry has said he rode on his mom's coattails. Mary's proud view is that her son did it alone.

Mary and Larry's relationship was peaceful by the time Larry and his wife Maj's children, Preston and Heidi, were young, and the brood regularly visited Grandma in Palm Springs, arriving in a converted United Parcels vehicle, kitted out with a king-size divan, hi-fi system—and Larry's favorite champagne on ice.

(Phyllis Quinn's son Teddy worked on Larry's old TV series "I Dream of Jeannie," where he was somewhat stunned to see the star arrive on the set dressed in railroad cap and overalls topped with a regal cape, which he periodically flung open, revealing that it was lined with champagne bottles. Teddy was also invited into the inner sanctum of Hagman's black-light dressing room—pretty heady stuff for an eight-year-old.)

Larry Hagman was just in the throes of pouring a glass of the bubbly stuff for Australian writer Mary Fletcher, who interviewed him at his Malibu home in 1987, when the phone rang. He answered it, saying, "Okay, put her through," cupped his hand over the receiver to tell Fletcher it was his mom's old pal Nancy Reagan, then said, "Hi, Nancy, it's Larry Hagman here. How are you doing, honey?" Later, Mary Martin (whom he calls "Mommy") bounced in on Fletcher's interview with Hagman. Fletcher describes her as one of those chatty, bubbly people who does not come into a room quietly and who clearly likes the spotlight angled on her. Her son merely sat back, content to let her have the floor.

Larry Hagman grew up accustomed to liberated women, and he was certainly not alone in being the product of a broken home. Divorce also marked the early lives of Julie Andrews, Carol Burnett, Jamie Lee Curtis, Sally Field, Michael Douglas, George Hamilton, the Gabor sisters, Cher, Lauren Bacall, Billy Joel, Brooke Shields, Nastassia Kinski, Liberace, Rob Lowe, Colleen Dewhurst, Olivia Newton-John, Liza Minnelli, Al Pacino, Stefanie Powers, Tina Turner, the Carradines, Ally Sheedy, David Cassidy, Robert De Niro, Chevy Chase, Tatum O'Neal, Prince, Rock Hudson, and William Hurt. To name but a few.

The increase in frequency of divorce has done nothing to lessen the devastation it inflicts on children who suddenly find themselves deprived of one parent's daily presence. Of the 75 percent of the stars scrutinized whose childhoods fell short of the apple-pie ideal, a high 38 percent of those emerged from families wrenched apart by divorce. Which does not mean to say that they were unloved or desperately unhappy. Divorce is a minor upheaval, compared, say, to the death of a parent, particularly if a divorced Mom's ties to her children are strong, as were Janet Leigh's to Jamie Lee Curtis, Maryline Poole Adams' to Timothy Hutton, Catrine Domenique's to Cyndi Lauper, and Julie Powers' to Stefanie, for instance.

For many stars, there was not even the privilege of sampling united family life. For those like Alec Guinness, who was never made privy to his father's true identity, there was no family to break up; they were deprived of mother, father, or both, raised by relatives, or shuttled back and forth amidst family turmoil. If, as psychiatry claims, we each are burdened with the unfinished business of our childhoods, then the 75 percent whose rough roads led them to rich rewards were doubtless driven by some need to rewrite their personal history. Via the spotlight, they tried to plug up that feeling of emptiness left by a missing parent, to capture the approval of a parent who had seen fit to abandon them, to bask in the warmth of a missed love.

Mickey Rourke's parents divorced when he was seven. Rourke's father ran a bar in the U.S. after emigrating from Cork, Ireland. After the divorce, Mickey's mother took her son to Miami, where she tried to cope with a restless, undisciplined child. "If you aren't real happy as a kid," Rourke explained to Lesley Thornton of *Cosmopolitan*, "you lose yourself in your head. That gave me something as an actor."

It is Kate Hepburn's belief that love and pain are two of an actress's greatest assets: "A great actress, even a good actress, must have plenty of both." Dr. Grotstein, while bowing to her first-hand expertise, suspects that the "must," the essential ingredient and common denominator among actors and actresses, is not pain so much as it is drive. Stars are driven.

Sylvester Stallone typifies the phenomenon. Glued to the typewriter writing his success-vehicle *Rocky*, doggedly refusing to sell it unless he could play the leading role, pushing himself beyond the brink of sanity, he described himself to Sue Russell as "blazing. At times I singe my nails, I melt a Bic pen. I really can get possessed by it until finally I pass out on my inkwell, nose down."

The show business life is generally so tough and unrewarding, the black hole between "making it" and "not making it," where the vast majority fall, so abysslike, that those who persistently strive to earn a living in the performing arts often do so not from choice but because they feel compelled to do so.

Looking at the sheer number of stars who are possessed, tunnel-visioned, and single-minded, who nothing short of cataclysm will deflect from their course, it is obvious that the development of such focus is not hampered by the rough roads of childhood experience. There are few more apt examples of drive in full flight than Bob Geldof, whose role as a rock star was edged out while the Irishman brought the world's attention to the plight of the starving in Africa, and who earned himself a knighthood in the process.

Geldof was six when his mother was snatched from him without warning. She was a warm and likable cinema manageress with a good sense of humor. Young Bob sat happily on Ma's lap one evening; the next morning she was dead, struck down by a brain hemorrhage at forty-four.

At the end of the year in which Ma died, Bob's eighteen-year-old sister Cleo, his substitute mother, was diagnosed with leukemia. The family doctor informed their already-distraught father that she had three months to live. The doctor was wrong; she did not die. But the burden borne by Bob Geldof Sr., who chose to keep the news a secret, was enormous. During the week, his work took him traveling around Ireland, and he compensated for those absences by becoming a weekend disciplinarian. Bob, of course, was unaware of his father's pain and difficulties and had his own view of the tension between them, but he does believe his mother's death had much to do with his development as a reluctant schoolboy and self-confessed "awkward bugger." He treasures memories of her still, in her party finery—"lipstick, gloves, and sequins. Not a bad memory of your mother."

Who is to say which scars more deeply? To have loved and lost a parent? Or never to have had the parent at all? It probably depends upon the resilience of the person, but many stars were forced to confront death during their childhoods or adolescent years.

When their fathers died, George Burns was seven, Charles Bronson was ten, Judy Garland was twelve, Ingrid Bergman was thirteen (her mother had died when she was three), Greta Garbo was fourteen, Teri Garr was eleven, George Hamilton was seventeen, Paul Newman had just graduated high school. Laurence Olivier was thirteen when he lost his mother. Paul McCartney was fifteen and Madonna was six when their mothers died of breast cancer.

There is no easy age at which to lose a parent. Virginia-born actor George C. Scott was eight when his mother died, and he felt her loss so acutely that his home life did not regain its balance before he left to join the Marines at age eighteen. For Linda Evans, the loss of her father when she was fifteen was the most testing time of her life. "It was just horrifying to me that he wouldn't be there forever, my dad." Losing her mother, after Linda was married, was less of a shock. Clark Gable had no conscious memories of his mother Adeline to cling to—she died when he was seven months old. His grandparents cared for him for two years until his father, William H. Gable, a farmer and oil driller, remarried. Clark Gable was fortunate—he worshiped his new stepmother. Gable's early marital preference was for older women—a reflection of his missing mama.

Richard Burton's mother, Edith, died at age forty-four, before he reached his second birthday. Just a few days earlier, she had given birth to her thirteenth child, Richard's brother Graham. (Four of her children died as babies.) Edith Thomas was born in Swansea, Wales, where her birth certificate erroneously certified her as a male child; the registry office has since offered the explanation that perhaps the registrar was drunk. She was employed as a barmaid in the Miners Arms pub when on Christmas Eve 1900, she married twenty-four-year-old Richard "Dic" Jenkins against the wishes of her worried parents. In their eyes, Edith was still a baby, yet the pretty, fair-haired seventeen-year-old was not only considerably taller than Dic Jenkins, she rapidly revealed herself to be the power behind the throne.

One of Richard's four doting older sisters, Hilda Owen, still lives in Pontrhydyfen, the Welsh mining village that was the family's home. Hilda was only nine when Edith died, but vividly remembers the way her mother took her considerable responsibilities in her stride. "She was a very strong character, a very *capable* woman, she could turn her hand to anything. She went out wallpapering. She was a wonderful woman, anyone would tell you that."

Besides papering neighbors' parlors, Edith took in laundry to supplement the family income; no mean feat in view of her own wash-load. Perennially industrious, Edith also made candies for sale in the village. Then, for sale and for family consumption, she brewed "small beer" from hops and nettles. (Small beer, Hilda points out, is not the alcoholic variety, but a soft drink traditionally served along with Sunday lunch.) On Sundays, the family ritual was for Edith to escort her brood to chapel and Sunday school. She had a lovely voice and sang in the choir, as did her eldest daughter, Cissie, who sang soprano and was a staunch chapel-goer.

Cissie, who raised Richard, is now in her eighties, hard of hearing, and living near London. She was just twenty and newly married when she and her husband, Elfed, took her little brother into her spotless Port Talbot home, five miles away from Pontrhydyfen. Tom Jenkins, Edith and Dic's oldest son, took the new baby to live with him. Widowed Dic Jenkins worked long hours down in the coal mines, so it was tacitly understood by his family that Father could not possibly have coped with his two under-twos.

Cissie took her responsibilities seriously. Besides caring for Richard, she visited the family once or twice weekly, divvying up cooking chores with an assortment of aunties. Hilda and Cissie still have nothing but praise for their father and make light of his spasmodic drinking episodes. More important to them, their father was first-generation literate, a rather quiet fellow who was very partial to a good book. "Father was a good provider," says Hilda, "and mother always believed in having the best of foods, butter, and other little luxuries. She was a terrific cook. We were all upset when she died, but my sister Cissie was terrible, and oh, my father didn't know really where to turn. Because, you see, my mother was the one to do everything. She was *responsible* for everything. He only went and earned the money then, really."

It was a curious thing, but Richard, who had been at that stage of bursting into tears whenever his mother left his sight, did not ask for Edith once she was gone. There was no way of measuring how acutely a two-year-old felt the loss—but if he did miss her it was not evident at the time. Hilda is sure, however, that it was hard for Richard to leave his home, his father, and his siblings when he moved to the comparative quiet of Cissie's. Cissie eventually had two children of her own, but held a lifelong soft spot for her young brother. "Of course, she adored him . . . Richard was like a second son to her," says Hilda. "He was very loved and he had everything that we did. He could never have had better, even if my mother was alive."

Richard Burton's lifelong affinity for women was no doubt rooted in the fact that he had four older sisters, each of whom spoiled him. Years later, when he saw Elizabeth Taylor, it struck a chord and hit him that it was Cissie for whom he had been searching all his life. Cissie was his protector, his surrogate mother, and the one to whom he was deeply bonded. In his autobiographically based piece of fiction "A Christmas Story," Richard Burton wrote of her as a green-eyed, black-haired, gypsy beauty who was innocent, guileless, and "infinitely protectable," and had "become my mother, and more mother to me than any mother could ever have been."

As Richard moved toward adolescence, however, his relationship with Elfed grew increasingly tense. The hardships of wartime were bearing down on the family and Richard was urged out of school and into a job at the local Co-op shop, which he positively loathed. The lucky lad was rescued from what he considered to be a fearful fate by schoolmaster Philip Burton, who took him under his wing and his roof, ensuring his return to school, his path to his theatrical niche in life, and giving him the name which would end up in lights.

Whether or not there was any offense taken at this seeming defection, none of the Jenkins family was remotely surprised by Richard's success. He had always been rather theatrical, prone to grandstanding—he would climb up on a stool and pretend to give a sermon, for instance. "We all thought he would have been a minister," Hilda admits, "because he had 'a voice' and he was always acting the preacher type, you know? Oh, yes, when he was little. He was really a star. Oh, Mother would've been over the moon with Richard!" Hilda sighs.

Paul McCartney's bond with John Lennon ran deeper than their mutual love of music. Paul was fourteen when his mother, Mary Patricia, died in October 1956, just months before the two boys met. Mary had been having breast pains, but when her son Michael found her crying after a visit to the doctor, he did not ask why. The reason became all too clear when, despite surgery, the boys' mom died of breast cancer within a month.

Mary and Jim McCartney wed in 1941, when she was thirty-two and he was thirty-nine, late by the standards of the times. Paul McCartney arrived in style. He was treated royally in the maternity ward. Mary had been in charge of it prior to her marriage, after which she had become a health visitor. Paul's later charms were well hidden, according to his father, who, in Hunter Davies' *The Beatles: The Authorized Biography,* remembers Paul's birth quite vividly.

"He looked awful, I couldn't get over it. Horrible. He had one eye open and he just squawked all the time. They held him up and he looked like a horrible piece of red meat. When I got home I cried, the first time for years and years."

Mary, a conscientious worker, was called away from her home on a nightly basis to tend to women in labor, and held down two jobs as a domiciliary midwife. She was ambitious for both sons and tried to tame Paul's Scouse accent, which, judging by the lower-class neighborhood in which Paul was raised, was doubtless considerably more acute than Lennon's. Her greatest legacy to Paul was perhaps her capacity for hard work and dedication, although Jim McCartney was a positive force in that way too.

When his wife died, Jim McCartney was bereft. He was fifty-three and financially stretched to the limit. Despite the aid of his two sisters, who rallied round to help, it can not have been easy to raise two adolescents. The McCartneys devoured the traditional British Sunday roast in their Allerton home on Mondays, thanks to Jinny or Millie.

Jim McCartney's wife's salary exceeded his own as a salesman in the cotton industry, as Paul heartlessly pointed out to him immediately after her death. "The first thing I said was, 'What are we going to do without her money?' " he bashfully admitted in Hunter Davies' book. Shock, doubtless. That night both boys cried into their pillows, and Paul remembers praying for her to come back, promising that he would be good forever. Those prayers going unanswered shook his faith in religion. As his brother told Davies, Paul's musical obsession began right after their mother's death.

"It took over his whole life. You lose a mother—and you find a guitar? I don't know. Perhaps it just came along at that time and became an escape. But an escape from what?"

Jim McCartney was a skilled pianist who once had his own traditional jazz band, so the McCartney boys grew up around jazz, musicals, and music of all kinds, and were actively encouraged to participate. Jim McCartney was not fond of John Lennon, fearing that his influence might sway his son from a safe career in teaching or accounting. His fears were realized, but Jim was never again in financial need once Paul became a star.

A number of stars grew up fatherless. Charlie Chaplin's dad left when he was a year old and Marilyn Monroe never met her father. Rock Hudson's pop deserted him when he was five.

Rock Hudson was born Roy Harold Sherer Jr., in 1925, in Illinois. He weighed just five and a half pounds but measured an astounding twenty-seven inches from head to toe, and the painful labor sealed his position as the sole child of Katherine Wood, who was not remotely anxious to repeat the experience—a fact of which she frequently reminded her young son.

Roy's father, Roy Sr., was an auto mechanic. Hit by the rampant unemployment during the Depression, he was particularly devastated by the loss of his job. In desperation, he left for California, purportedly to start anew and later send for his family. Roy, who was vacationing on his grandparents' farm, was not even privy to his father's departure. With it came a dramatic change in circumstances. Kay (as Katherine was known) and her son were forced to move into her parents' cramped quarters, along with her brother, his wife, and four children. Inevitably, the atmosphere was tense. The saving grace was the hope Kay instilled in her son (and harbored herself) that Roy Sr. would soon send for them.

Two years later, tired of waiting, Kay and Roy made the bus trip out to California and managed to track him down. But the long-anticipated reunion ended on a sour note when he refused to return home with them. Kay was beside herself, and Roy was in shock. His father's rejection all but guaranteed the adult Rock's confusion, his sense of inadequacy and powerlessness. Roy did then what Rock did later; he concealed his pain and inner turmoil behind the oh-so-calm exterior with which the world became familiar. Only those who saw him up close could testify to his telltale lifelong habit: badly bitten nails.

Kay remarried, and Wallace Fitzgerald adopted her son, but

was an abusive drinker who beat them both. In a strange way, Kay and Roy were bonded by their common need for refuge from his behavior, yet Kay's apparent willingness to repeatedly forgive this man was hard for her wounded son to comprehend. But then, as always, he concealed his most private thoughts.

Kay cannot have been unaware that her bond with Roy was loosened by this marriage. He continually chose to escape the miserable home life and spent less and less time around the house. So it remained, until Kay divorced his stepfather eight years later.

Kay's marital patterns might not lend her the appearance of strength, yet her personality and sheer energy were considerable. When Roy emerged from a stint in the Navy at age twenty-one, it was Kay who saw him slipping into inertia in his subsequent job as a mailman and took the initiative, sweeping them off to the new and infinitely more promising horizons of Hollywood.

Rock Hudson's birth certificate designates Roy Harold Sherer as the father of Roy Harold Jr. There would be no reason to question this part of his history were it not for a curious conversation that Rock's one-time personal secretary Mark Miller had with Kay and later reported to Sara Davidson, the official biographer who Rock Hudson appointed shortly before his death.

Miller's conversation with Kay, which cast a small shadow of doubt over her son's paternity, seems slightly out of character for a woman generally as reticent on personal matters as she was. It took place after Kay and Miller had flown to St. Louis, where Rock was performing at the Muni and a reunion with the Sherers was planned. Despite the sweltering heat, Kay could not resist shouting her new station in life by appearing resplendent in a mink coat which she set off with expensive jewelry.

Later, Kay dropped her usual guard, riding on the crest of her fury at a relative's remark made at the reunion. Someone commented on how fortuitous it had been that the Sherers had relinquished her son to her, instead of keeping him. The compliment about the way Rock had turned out was dwarfed by the inherent implication that Kay might not have been allowed to keep him had the Sherers not permitted her to. According to Miller she was enraged, and driving home in a haphazard manner, she did not turn to look him in the eye but said, in a manner loaded with meaning: "Did you notice that Roy doesn't look like *any* of the Sherers?" Mark Miller asked her if she meant what he thought she did.

"Mmmmm," was Kay's enigmatic reply. Miller admits that Kay neither confirmed nor denied that at which she hinted. The truth will never be known—Kay died in 1977 after a stroke—but the paternity question could account for Sherer's ungallant desertion of his family, had he known of it.

Kay remained close to Rock throughout her life; indeed the death of his mother, his only blood relative, his ally during his childhood, devastated him. The prospect of it was so terrifying that he could not face seeing her when she was ailing during the last six months of her life. A selfish decision, but he did not regret it, according to his longtime friend Tom Clark, because, he said, "I remember her as she was—a real goin' Jessie, driving, speeding, a whirlwind." Christmas, a joyous holiday they had always spent together, would never be the same again—Rock made sure of that. There was no Christmas tree at the Hudson residence from that year on; no Rock either. He left town rather than face the painful prospect of missing Mother's presence.

Rock Hudson cannot have been unaware of the enormous amount of love lavished upon him by his multitudinous fans, yet that love was never able to warm the cold spot inside him.

The taint of illegitimacy had lost much of its sting by the mid-sixties, at least in progressive circles. In any era, in any moral clime, the term "illegitimate" has a far more distasteful ring to it than does "love child." The charismatic young Roman whom Romilda Villani met near the Trevi Fountain fathered both Sophia Loren and her sister Maria. But he would never marry Romilda, a lingering source of bitterness for the woman who struggled to raise her daughters alone. "Every time I think of the past, I am destroyed. The memories are all ugly." From the vantage point of the eighties, it takes a leap of imagination to begin to sense the effect of the stigma of illegitimacy on the life of Alec Guinness, who was born in 1914.

Alec Guinness's early life is the personification of tumult and confusion. While his birth certificate named him Alec Guinness de Cuffe, it was more an unnecessary confirmation of the identity of his mother, Agnes Cuffe, than it was a clue to his paternity. His father's identity remained a mystery (to Alec, at least) which would meander through his mind for more than fifty years, in a not particularly pressing fashion. Young Alec had more immediate matters with which to concern himself.

When Alec was five, Agnes married Alec Stivens, thereby presenting her son with an intolerable stepfather. Their three-year marriage was violently unhappy, Guinness reveals in his autobiography, *Blessings in Disguise:*

"He once held me upside down from a bridge, threatening to drop me in the river below; and another time he held a loaded revolver at my head, threatening to kill me and himself to get whatever it was he wanted out of my mother; he made life a terrifying hell for three years."

Agnes was hardly a model of stability. Aside from a brief respite when, at age six, his mother sent him to boarding school, his life was a chaotic reflection of his mother's, bearing the ramifications of financial stress and her unorthodox methods of dealing with it.

At fourteen he was nonchalantly informed, without explanation, that his real name was Guinness. By then, he and Agnes had inhabited around thirty temporary accommodations in London, ranging from hotels and lodgings to flats, most of which were vacated at short notice, "leaving behind, like a paper-chase, a wake of unpaid bills."

In fact, Guinness's short idyllic stay at Normandale boarding school was marred by Agnes's solitary visit; she arrived by taxi but minus her purse, so it fell to the Maths master to lend Agnes five pounds. This was not an isolated embarrassment. His fellow thespian, the late Jack Hawkins, was persuaded to part with ten pounds when he ran into Guinness's mother in a Brighton pub. Once more, she was without her wayward purse.

When Guinness became a working actor, touring in repertory, Agnes somehow gained access to his Notting Hill Gate bedsit. Upon his return, he found that she had replaced various articles of his clothes and possessions with pawn tickets. While turning his energy to evading the discomfort of her behavior, Guinness seems to have borne no serious grudge against the woman who took the definitive identity of his father with her to her grave.

A recognition and acceptance of Mother's weaknesses and failings, her human imperfections, is a recurring theme among those who managed to transcend less-than-idyllic circumstances.

Eric Clapton, whose virtuosity on guitar earned him the uninvited nickname "God," began to suspect something was amiss when he was six. It dawned on him that there was a discrepancy between his name of Clapton, and that of his "parents," Rose and Jack Clapp. "My feeling of a lack of identity started to rear its head then," says Clapton, a recovered heroin addict, who blames that void with much of his behavior in later life.

Eric's mother, Patricia Molly Clapton, was more schoolgirl than mother when she gave birth to the son she knew she would not be able to raise: "I shall never get over it, and never lose the guilt, but I suppose that's the penalty I have to live with for having an illegitimate child when I was only sixteen." Eric's father was a Canadian soldier stationed in England. Into the breach stepped Eric's devoted grandparents, Patricia's mother, Rose, and her second husband, Jack Clapp.

Jack Nicholson's story is remarkably similar, except he was deluded for longer. As a boy, he never did know he was illegitimate. Nor did he learn that his "parents" were in fact his grandparents or that his "sister" was in fact his mother. Only when he was in his thirties and all of the principal players had passed away did an aunt and uncle reveal the truth.

Jack was born in April 1937 to seventeen-year-old June Nicholson. For propriety's sake, Jack was raised by June's mother, Ethel May Nicholson. A strong, feisty woman, she supported Jack (who called her "Mud") and his so-called sisters, June and Lorraine, by running a beauty parlor in her Neptune, New Jersey, living room.

Ethel May's marriage broke up while Jack was still a baby, so the alcoholic sign-painter and window-dresser Jack believed to be his father lived in another part of town and they had only intermittent contact. A more dominant male force in his life was his "sister" Lorraine's husband, Shorty Smith, who helped raise Jack. Jack has described Shorty, whom he loved and whose penchant for lounging shirtless in gin mills he admired, as "as good a father as anybody's ever going to get or need."

If Nicholson was deprived of the truth, that is the only thing of which he was deprived. He enjoyed what he called an idyllic childhood as the cheeky, freckle-faced object of the affections of three women whom he has described as Irish-German backyard intellectuals. Jack was given to stubborn behavior and explosive tantrums, the volume of which drove the ladies under the hair driers to drop their magazines in fright. Mud rationed out a few stinging slaps in retaliation, but Jack's infectious grin was already in place, defusing tension rapidly.

Only in his teens, when his chubbiness naturally became more burdensome, did his emerging insecurities give rise to his wise-cracking-rebel persona.

The true story which has since unraveled throws an interesting light on Jack's feelings for his "sister" June, expressed when he had not the slightest clue that she was in fact his mother. To Jack, June personified glamour. He was little more than a tot when she landed a job as a show dancer in Earl Carroll's stylish Vanities review in Miami, but he was duly impressed. When June married a roguish test pilot who was on the team that broke the sound barrier, the lively, charismatic couple's lives clearly ignited a spark in young Jack: "My sister June was another story. She was a symbol of excitement, thrilling and beautiful to me."

June divorced the test pilot and returned home with what Jack believed to be his niece and nephew, but her fire was far from extinguished, and she was soon off again to California with her two young children. She encouraged Jack to pay her a summer visit when he finished high school. Inspired by June's lead, Jack stayed on, finding work at MGM as a mail clerk.

Ethel May also moved to California, but she was in poor health. June was busy nursing her, when, with shocking speed, cancer claimed her own life. Jack visited June in the hospital near the end and was horrified to find her in constant pain and to see that she had lost over forty pounds in a matter of months. He was devastated by the loss of his special confidante and inspiration.

When Nicholson learned of the true roles of the women in his life, he said, "I didn't feel angry or resentful, not in the least. I felt tremendous gratitude, clear and simple."

Like Mary Martin and Larry Hagman, Janet Leigh and Jamie Lee Curtis are another two-generational minidynasty. While Janet Leigh appears to have had the stability Jamie Lee did not, when you scratch the surface you see things are more complex.

Janet Leigh's parents stayed together until the death of her father, Fred Morrison, in 1961. Jamie Lee's parents, Janet and Tony Curtis, divorced that same year, when Jamie was just three years old. Yet the Morrisons enduring marriage was in truth tumultuous, with drinking and fights that scared their daughter. Jamie Lee's broken home, on the other hand, was rapidly stabilized. (One more reason not to judge the family book by its cover.) By 1962, Janet Leigh had married stockbroker Bob Brandt, who was to prove a steady, loving, fatherly presence in the lives of Jamie and her older sister, Kelly, minimizing the effects of the absence of their father, of whom they saw very little when they were growing up.

Janet Leigh (in those days, Jeanette Helen Morrison) got her start in the film business when she was discovered by Norma Shearer, who spotted her picture in the lobby of the Sugar Bowl Ski Lodge, where her father worked as a desk clerk. Shearer passed on the picture, and in true fairy-tale fashion, Janet Leigh was put under a seven-year contract to MGM. Her first appearance on film was in 1947, in *The Romance of Rosy Ridge*. Not so fairy-tale was the fact that Janet had two marriages behind her before she was seventeen.

Despite their marital discord and money worries, Fred and Helen Morrison were loving parents. Nevertheless, Janet was openly miserable when they moved from Merced to Stockton, California, when she was fourteen; it meant she was forced to leave behind her first love, Kenny. Brimming with enthusiasm, a group of friends and Kenny's parents helped Janet plot a way to keep her in Merced. She and Kenny married in Reno—they lied about her age, of course.

The marriage had been consummated by the time her horrified parents rushed onto the scene, whisking her away, arranging an annulment, and telling her to forget that it had ever happened. The bitterness and recriminations that followed left scars that mark her to this day. What had seemed so pure and beautiful, was made to seem dirty. Compounding that feeling, the annulled marriage was kept a deep, dark family secret. Her second marriage to sailor (and aspiring musician) Stanley Reames was also short-lived, and she married Tony Curtis in 1951.

Daughter Kelly arrived first; then in 1958, Jamie Lee was born. From the start, the writing was on the wall: Jamie Lee was definitely a survivor. She had two near-misses before she even came into the world, and a hernia operation when she was just two weeks old.

When Janet was six or seven months pregnant with Jamie, there was an accident on the way back from a poker game at Peter Lawford's house. Tony was driving one car, with Janet beside him, and Jeannie and Dean Martin and Gloria and Sammy Kahn in the back. Frank Sinatra and his lady companion were following them when an erratic driver hit them broadside. Janet was not hurt, only shaken. In her eighth month, while driving in the rain she was rear-ended and her car went into a spin. Once again, she escaped unharmed.

"Jamie was not always the easiest child to rear, to reach, to understand," says Janet. "I've wondered about that, and I'm sure it's also because of what's brought into the lives of the mother and father at that time. And when Jamie came, it was a troubled time. Tony's father had just died, and the seeds, or little sprouts, of discontent had started between us. So maybe she reflected that, picked a little bit of that up in the atmosphere and gave it off. It wasn't that she was bad or rebellious, just a little more difficult to get through to, to penetrate."

Tony's father died at the end of Janet's pregnancy and was, in fact, buried the day Jamie was due. "It was difficult, because you want your second baby to have all the same kind of focus that your first baby had; you don't want your husband's attention diluted. Those thoughts do come into your head, you can't help it. But it all worked out okay."

In August 1961 (the year she was nominated for an Oscar for *Psycho*), Janet went to Cap d'Antibes with Jeannie Martin (then married to Dean) and Pat Lawford, for Princess Grace of Monaco's International Red Cross Ball. While she was mingling with the beautiful people, Tony Curtis called to tell her that her father had committed suicide. He left no notes, no messages.

Her parents had visited Janet the day before her departure for Cap d'Antibes. Her father was in financial difficulty and needed a loan, but her mother did not want him to ask Janet and Tony to lend them money. Besides, Tony, who was irked at having been urged by his wife to be less extravagant, did not want to give it. It was a nasty encounter all around and the Morrisons left on a bad note. Over twenty years later that still hurts Janet, although her father's death is no longer a mystery.

"He wasn't prone to depression, no, but he was volatile, and I think it was just sheer frustration with life with my mother. It just seemed such a waste. It's still painful, I miss him. It took a long time to get over, it really did. But also, you can't succumb to it either. You can think about questions and harbor the guilt, or whatever, for years. You can do it so much it destroys you. You can't let that happen. One thing I learned—try not to go away from someone without resolving a problem."

No strangers to film sets, Jamie Lee and Kelly were virtually born to the business. "What's the norm for some people isn't the norm for others," Janet explains. "I took the girls to film sets so they knew where Mommy went and what she was doing when she said good-bye in the mornings, so that it wasn't a mystery. Not to expose them to the film industry, but just so that they understood this was Mommy's work. I've got a picture of them on the set of *Wives and Lovers,* the film their father and I made with Van Johnson. It's so cute, they're really very intent on what was going on, it was almost like they were evaluating whether we were good or not. I got a big kick out of that."

Looking back on her childhood, Jamie believes Janet did a good job of implementing normalcy into her childhood, but Janet suspects that although she put "wife and mother" before "actress," because she was a professional, and a very visible one at that, it cannot always have been easy for the girls.

"You're not the same, no matter how much I tried to be a normal mother. I drove car pool, did things with the P.T.A., I was on mothers' committees, she wore hand-me-downs, but still, I'm sure it was difficult for her. I really tried to keep my children's heads straight and values straight. On the other hand I wasn't the kind that believed they should be deprived of certain niceties just to teach them a lesson. As long as they hopefully realized they were lucky, and that it wasn't just expected. There were famous people around the house, but they could have been butchers for all she knew."

In fact, Janet and Bob's Beverly Hills residence is decidedly down-to-earth, any formality having been swiftly nipped in the bud by the unruly and hairy presence of dogs and cats. Janet says, "Jamie came out of the womb tap-dancing, she did anything to get attention." Rather naively, however, she gave little thought to the shadow into which her aspiring-actress daughter would be stepping. Although, she certainly remembers Jamie always joking that she had the longest middle name in town—Jamie Lee "Daughter of Janet Leigh and Tony Curtis" Curtis.

"The lay public might think that she got her start because she was the daughter of two people in show business, but it was on the contrary. That's really, really not true. Being the offspring of two visible parents might open a door, but once she's inside the door, it's actually more difficult, because then they sit back and say, 'Okay, kid, show me!' I truly believe the children of known parents have to be better than Mary Smith coming in off the street, so that's a hurdle."

Jamie did go through an identity crisis of sorts in 1977 when she was eighteen. She dropped out of college after just six months and landed a role in TV's short-lived series "Operation Petticoat," but admits, "Shadow-wise, it was tough, and I didn't realize how tough it was until now. I look back on it and I realize how much pressure there was. They worked very hard to try to relieve that pressure, but . . . you always have that shadow, so therefore getting an identity together, a feeling of self-worth, is very hard."

Throughout those times, mother and daughter remained close, which Jamie explains rather simply: "When somebody has held your head in the bathroom while you're being sick and let you share everything with her from losing your virginity to losing a job, then she's your friend."

The success of *Halloween* was a terrific break for Jamie Lee, who then, of course, had to make a conscious effort to break away from the horror mold. Mother could certainly sympathize: "After *Psycho*, if I was offered one, I was offered five hundred roles like that," she says with a wry smile. The decision to act was Jamie's, just as the decision to become a stockbroker was Kelly's—although Kelly, at the last count, was studying acting in New York.

"I wouldn't urge someone to go into it, or prod," Janet says firmly. "You have to want to do it. I would never urge or push someone into any business. But I'd certainly never have said, '*Don't* do it,' that would be ridiculous. It's given me a wonderful life, and any business is a tough business. The hardest thing is the rejection. That's difficult for anyone. If shirts are your business, it's an inanimate object; but when 'you' are your business, or your commodity, it becomes a very personal product."

Very much the pragmatist, Jamie likens herself to a marketable commodity, saying, "I'm a turbo Porsche. I've got to keep my tires blown up, my chassis tight and all that stuff, and my engine in good condition. It's real hard work because you're constantly thinking about yourself."

"Jamie's strong," Janet says proudly. "But I think, also, that strength has come from *having* to be strong, and there's a lot of little girl in there, and vulnerability. But that's a very intriguing combination for an actress, to be vulnerable and then also exude strength."

Geographical instability caused its own problems and heartaches in the early lives of many stars. Mel Gibson, George Hamilton, Sylvester Stallone, Kathleen Turner, Sammy Davis Jr., William Hurt, Michael J. Fox, Victoria Principal, Robert Duvall, Neil Diamond, John Wayne, and Clint Eastwood—all moved either repeatedly or in a major fashion.

For some, it was a toughening experience; for others, like John Lithgow, it was painful. Theater was in his blood, but with that legacy came disruption. His mother was an actress and his father a producer whose responsibility it was to establish Shakespeare festivals and theatrical companies around Ohio, prior to heading Princeton's McCarter Theater. All of which led to nine moves before John was seventeen . . . and he loathed each and every one of them. Seventh grade was an all-time low, with two moves in one year. "I'd go to school praying I could get through the day without bursting into tears," he admits.

Tyne Daly attended nine different schools before sixth grade because of the career of her late father, James Daly, the actor who costarred in "Medical Center" for seven years. Jerry Lewis's parents were show folk. When he was with them, he was constantly flung into new school environments where he did not even linger long enough for teachers to learn his name. It is hard to imagine how a child could walk into thirty different schools in the space of two years, but Lewis did. At other times he lived with his grandmother, whom he loved dearly. It was her death, when he was eleven, that seemed to catalyze a huge appetite for attention, the precursor to his role as a clown. His instability and pain, like that of so many of his peers, did not stop his stardom.

9 Rich Mom, Poor Mom

Necessity being its mother, invention is endemic to Tennessee's Smoky Mountain folk. Avie Lee Parton, needing a toy to give her fourth child, Dolly (whose delivery had been paid for with a sack of meal), fashioned a doll from a stripped corncob. Painstakingly she reattached the fine strands of corn silk to resemble a head of hair, then sewed a miniature outfit from scraps of fabric.

Frances Bergen's privileged princess of a daughter, Candice, who was born in Hollywood Presbyterian Hospital, might have laughed herself silly had she seen that corncob doll; but then again, perhaps not. She also grew up with a rather unusual companion—Charlie McCarthy, her father Edgar Bergen's alter-ego.

And just as the corncob doll had little in common with Charlie McCarthy, so also Avie Lee Parton's and Frances Bergen's worlds were as foreign to each other as if they were divided by a continent and a language. Yet each had a daughter who became a world-class star.

Poverty and wealth. It is obvious which is the more attractive, harder to say unequivocally which state is the richest. The complacent ease of existence which blesses the "haves" would seem a less fertile breeding ground for ambition than the urgent state of need, hunger, and deprivation which confronts the "have-nots." It is easy to envision penury nurturing a longing for whatever grows so much greener on the other side. It is less easy to imagine contentment, luxury, and abundance giving rise to the ache for stardom—or the ache for anything very much at all.

To reduce the picture, even briefly, to one that is purely mon-

175

etary is of course to overlook many ultimately more pertinent factors. Nevertheless, it is interesting to peer into the checks and balances of the family backgrounds of stars like Candy Bergen and Dolly Parton and Charles Bronson, to see the role that money —or the lack thereof—played in their formative years.

Kirk Douglas and his now equally famous son, Michael, exemplify the two polarities all wrapped up under the one Douglas name. Kirk Douglas's mother, Bryna, was abandoned by her Russian immigrant, junk-dealer husband, Herschel Danielovitch, who left her their son, Issur (who would become Kirk Douglas), and his six sisters. Kirk, who was fourteen, can remember being so poor he had to bake a potato in the gutter. By contrast, Michael's memories are of jetting across the country for summer vacations at his movie star father's Hollywood mansion. Diana Douglas divorced Kirk when Michael was five and raised him and his brother Joel on the East Coast in a somewhat formal fashion that would doubtless have seemed alien to Avie Lee Parton.

Avie Lee was just fifteen when she married Dolly's father, Lee. Together, they raised their twelve children in a cramped, two-room shack—without running water—set on their spartan farm on the Little Pigeon River, way back in the foothills of Tennessee's Smoky Mountains. In the Parton household, hardship and material shortcomings were amply compensated for by the warmth of the familial embrace.

Dark, angular-featured, and slender, Avie Lee Parton does not much resemble Dolly, who took after Daddy's side of the family. She is a deeply religious woman who passed a powerful spiritual legacy to each of her children. She taught them humility, and that through God all things are possible. Dolly grew up with that belief as much a part of her as her porcelain skin and her crystal-clear voice. Dolly's heroes and heroines were a reflection not of television or of films, but of the fairy-tale characters populating the few, well-thumbed books she shared with her brothers and sisters; she dreamed of kings, queens, and royalty, and the characters she came to know and love through the Parton clan's homemade music. Which is why Dolly's desire for stardom attached itself to a glamorous but more pantomime-style persona "*like* a movie star. With the jewelry and the fancy clothes and the loud, gaudy colors, and, you know, just flashy, showy. And with the big hair-dos," says Dolly.

Avie Lee's folk all could hold a tune. Her Daddy was a preacher, so inevitably her children grew up steeped in both gospel music and old-time mountain songs. Dolly was *born* singing, could sing before she could talk, so the story goes. She was given a very special gift of music, and from an early age the determined little girl set her sights high, way above and beyond her beloved mountaintops: "I wanted to be something special to the world." Avie Lee always bet that Dolly would be a star someday. Those lessons she taught her cropped up repeatedly in Dolly's songwriting, which began when she was "a little itty-bitty kid." She had a knack for rhyme and loved to write about dolls, butterflies, flowers, pretty things. Until she could write her lyrics down herself, Avie Lee committed them to paper for her.

Instinctively, Dolly knew that her music was her passport to another world, "a way that I wouldn't have to spend my life being poor." Dolly did not resent being poor. The nearest town in Sevier County was Sevierville, population 5009, hardly New York City, so she was barely conscious of the degree of her family's deprivation. The yardstick by which she measured did not reach to the excesses of Beverly Hills; it spanned only her immediate environment. Besides, without her humble beginning, how could being rich and successful mean so much?

Neither Avie Lee, nor anyone else in the family, really comprehended that it was possible to become rich and successful through something as simple as singing. She certainly did not imagine Dolly building a four-hundred-acre amusement park called Dollywood in tribute to her beloved mountain home and its people; or creating a Dr. Robert F. Thomas Foundation in memory of the Methodist minister who rode miles on horseback to care for folk like the Partons who lived in inaccessible places, and was willing to practice medicine for sacks of meal. And how could Avie Lee have envisioned that one day her husband's checks would be inscribed, *Lee Parton, Sevier Company Bank, Dolly Parton Parkway?*

Avie Lee Parton's brood was always close-knit and contented. She instilled in her children the importance of being respectful of nature, of the land, of their parents, and of plain, decent folk.

Dolly credits her courage to be different to the inner stability and security and confidence she learned at her Mama's knee.

There is also a light side to Avie Lee, who is now in her early sixties and is, Dolly says, the source of much of her effervescence: "My mom has a bright personality, my dad has a great sense of humor. Just open, big-mouthed, big-hearted people."

Avie Lee inspired one of Dolly's biggest hit records, "The Coat of Many Colors"—Avie Lee and what Dolly calls "that background of parents that care enough and know enough to teach you that money is not the only thing in life that makes you rich."

The song's lesson was one she wanted to pass on to other children whose folks were not cash-rich: "Mother made a little coat for me because I didn't have anything to wear. And to make me proud of it, knowing probably that I would get ridiculed with it, she told me the story of Joseph in the Bible. She set me up in such a way that no matter what anybody said, *I* was the one who had a special deal." Avie Lee's ploy worked. If the coat was good enough for "somebody famous" like Joseph, it was certainly good enough for Dolly. Her memory of that patched-together coat becomes more cherished through the years, as she knows the lengths to which her mother went first to make it, then to make her feel privileged to wear it.

When Avie Lee's eldest daughter, Willadeene, married, Dolly was ten, and it fell to her to take over the role of Mama's helper. Since Avie Lee was frequently in one stage or another of pregnancy or nursing a baby, she depended on Dolly's help bottle-feeding, weaning, and caring for the other little ones. Dolly loved her siblings dearly, but it seemed to her that she had not slept a single night in her entire life uninterrupted by the crying of a child who needed a bottle.

In 1964, when she was eighteen, she graduated from Sevier County High School and the very next morning left for Nashville to start her new life, certain that at last she would get that longed-for night without that "commotion." Wouldn't you know it? She missed her Mama and Daddy and those noisy kid brothers and sisters so badly, she was sure she would die from homesickness. But she was too stubborn to give up and run home to the family she was growing to appreciate more by the minute and her old

Tennessee mountain home, a near-perfect replica of which now sits at the Dollywood theme park as the Parton Family Back Porch Theater.

Avie Lee Parton is proud of Dolly, but no more than of Rachel, Stella, Freida, Floyd, or any of the others. Dolly readily admits, "I've probably been a pain in the neck too." She knows that having a famous daughter has definitely cramped her publicity-shy mother's style. "Mama says, 'I wish you'd never become a star. I can't even go to the store in my hair rollers, dipping my snuff.' She dipped snuff for years and years, now she smokes cigarettes. She says, 'I have to clean up and dress up.'

"My Daddy, he says, 'I can't even go to the feed store without somebody saying, 'I want a job up at that Dollywood now. Dolly'd want you to give me a job.' And Daddy says, 'Dolly didn't get where she is by listening to me." Avie Lee and the Parton clan (many of whom do work at Dollywood) have grown used to hearing variations on remarks like "You're Dolly Parton's uncle and you're driving that old trap!" It is assumed, because she has hit the big time, it is within her power to make her entire family rich. Clearly, the spirited woman under the wigs has changed very little. She would even have us believe she retains a fondness for quaint country customs—such as peeing off the back porch. As she told a reporter from *People* magazine, "There's nothing like peeing on those snobs in Beverly Hills."

One somehow suspects that Charles Bronson would empathize with Dolly's adherence to plainspokenness, although her childhood hardships pale against his. Bronson was one of the fifteen children of an American mother and an illiterate Lithuanian mineworker. The family was forced to sleep in shifts, so small was their cold-water shack in Pennsylvania. To complain about hand-me-downs would indeed seem churlish on hearing that Bronson sometimes inherited his older sisters' clothes and remembers going to school in a dress, and having to share a pair of socks with his brother.

Candice Bergen was exquisite-looking from the moment she first batted her long eyelashes at this world. She arrived with so much in her favor—looks, talent, wealth, top schools, an international education, the entree that being Edgar Bergen's daughter gave her—it was virtually inevitable there would dawn a time when she would ask "Why me?" when the guilt and the belief that she had done nothing to earn or deserve what she had would seriously overwhelm her.

Frances Bergen is a strikingly handsome, honey-haired woman now in her mid-sixties, who was born in Birmingham, Alabama, and whose voice once dripped magnolia blossoms. She positively glows when speaking of the daughter to whom she has never felt closer. Yet, looking back, she readily admits, "She went through a terrible period, she really had tremendous guilt. And that makes her a better person consequently, because she is enormously sensitive . . . and sensitive to the needs of others."

It was not always so. Neither Frances nor Candice would deny that. Before Candice came to feel uncomfortable with her good fortune, she first lost sight of just how many riches the world had laid at her feet. And Frances, whose own youth had been infinitely less ideal, grew impatient with her pampered daughter's myopic transgressions. There followed some "encounters," as Frances so delicately describes them. (In Candice's blunter language, mother and daughter fought furiously.)

Candy's earliest childhood impressions of her mother were of Frances like a beautiful fairy princess, with her ice-blue, taffeta-draped dressing room aglitter with antique silver and miniature enameled boxes. As she now well knows, there is far more to her mother than that.

Frances Westerman was a self-confessed "daddy's girl" whose life was turned upside down when tall, handsome William Westerman, the center of her universe, died of tuberculosis after three months in a sanatorium. Frances was just ten. Her distraught mother, Lillie Mae, to whom she was less close, wrenched her young daughter from all that was familiar, her friends, *and* a leading role in a musical at Robert E. Lee Junior High, and moved West to a fresh start in California.

Lillie and Leo, flame-haired twin sisters born in 1898, whom Frances describes as a couple of Southern belles Tennessee Williams would have loved, have shifted very little from the mid-Victorian attitudes they held when Frances grew up. In the company of a man, Lillie Mae still dimples, grows coy and kittenish;

her sense of propriety was dreadfully offended when recently Frances casually referred to herself as a saloon singer.

Frances was coddled by her widowed mother and learned to fear the unknown. Although she was a very lonely only child after her father's death, her life did not become happier when her mother took another husband. Parry Boyd was a handsome, likable man from a fine Bostonian family. His credentials notwithstanding, it was a bad match that ended within three years and marked the onslaught of real financial hardship.

Not atypically for a Southern belle, Lillie Mae knew nothing of business. Frances's father, a vice-president of an interior decorating firm who had gone on to work for the Dr. Pepper company at its inception, had left them very well provided for, but in the hands of Lillie Mae—who concerned herself more with etiquette than such practicalities as which end of a check to endorse—the money did not last. With Parry Boyd's assistance (his job as an iceman was no more than a token gesture of a willingness to work, soon abandoned once Lillie Mae began to support him), this nest egg was rapidly eroded. With it evaporated the money set aside for Frances's education and her hopes for private singing lessons. Frances did not blame her mother for her ineptness; William Westerman was the kind of man who had not encouraged his wife to be self-sufficient.

When Parry departed suddenly, Lillie Mae was quite unable to cope. Forced to work, she plunged into depression, and Frances, as her sole companion, bore the brunt of this. She soon dreaded coming home from school to spend yet another interminable evening sitting across the table from her mother in pained silence.

"She was just totally devastated. Come to think of it, I didn't have the greatest childhood," Frances adds wryly.

When she graduated from Los Angeles High School, Frances worked first as a filing clerk, then as a catwalk model for the I. Magnin department store. She was torn between desires to sing and to become a John Robert Powers model, but decided to try her luck in New York as soon as she had saved enough money.

Frances met Candy's father, Edgar Bergen, a dyed-in-the-wool bachelor more than twenty years her senior, the day after her nineteenth birthday—she had been taken to a live broadcast of his show at NBC, by the wife of his then head writer. To the fatherless Frances, Bergen's paternal appeal was enormous. Bergen, too, was interested and wanted to know, who was the girl with the long legs? They were introduced, but he went off to dinner with a good-looking blonde.

The very next day, however, he telephoned Frances to invite her flying in his private aeroplane. She was terrified. She had not flown before, period, let alone in a "little bitty" single-engined model, but she was unwilling to reveal this lest it make her seem unsophisticated. Dutifully, she acquired her mother's permission before making the flight with great trepidation—and more than a little nausea.

Years later, in a triumph of will, Frances took secret flying lessons. She even managed to fly solo—only to emerge from the cockpit and collapse on the runway in a faint. Edgar Bergen doubtless came close to that reaction when she sprang on him her prized pilot's license. (A gutsy lady, she also managed to submerge her fear of water and, with Edgar's help, learn to swim.) She had rather hoped that Bergen would stop her from leaving for New York, but at that stage the confirmed bachelor was still clinging to his bachelorhood, so off she went as planned.

She was rapidly signed to John Robert Powers. Coincidentally, another svelte blonde, Trudy Marshall (mother of actress Deborah Raffin) was in the throes of leaving the agency to try her luck in Hollywood. Frances had set her heart on high-fashion work, but her healthy, suntanned, California look did not go down well with *Vogue* and *Harper's* beauty editors who were in those days mightily obsessed with haughty, sunken cheeks.

She was successful, nonetheless, in the commercial field. Her long legs not only caught Edgar Bergen's eagle eyes but landed her a hosiery advertisement. Her main claim to fame was becoming the Chesterfield cigarette girl on billboards. The Chesterfield girl's perk was to receive a couple of free cartons of cigarettes a month, which, since cigarettes were still hard to come by postwar, made her enormously popular. She still has "that rotten smoking habit."

At fifteen, Frances had been given a Charlie McCarthy doll as a cheer-up gift while recuperating from a skull fracture she sustained in a car accident. She was a rabid fan of Charlie from the radio show and, despite her years, even took the doll to bed with her upon occasion. Little did she imagine then that in June 1945, just four years later, she would marry Charlie's creator in Mexico.

"I don't know frankly if I ever even split the two in my mind," she says. "Of course Charlie was his alter ego, no question about it, and the man had such wonderful wit as well as humor."

Their marriage was far from popular. Besides Edgar's own misgivings about the age difference, his lawyers warned him that Frances was after him for his money and fame. In fact, their highly successful union lasted over thirty years, confounding critics.

It was not, however, without its surprises. While outgoing in his work—via the uninhibited Charlie—Edgar Bergen was a formal, undemonstrative man (his own dummy called him an "emotional hermit") even, or perhaps especially, around those to whom he was closest. Although he was utterly devoted to his wife, telling Candy before his death that he did not feel complete without her, Edgar rebuffed young Frances's earnest attentions and was uncomfortable with her declarations of love.

This pattern would repeat itself with his children. Candice, who admits that her desire to please her father remained unabated right up to his funeral in 1978, wrote this of her mother as a newlywed in her book, *Knock Wood:* "So Frances learned some of those lessons it takes a life-time to unlearn again. She learned not to curl up in her husband's lap and to hang back from hugging him and to swallow 'I love you's.' And that is how loneliness grows."

"It was impossible for him to convey his feelings," Frances concedes when reminded of this. "He did it in writing a couple of times, but it was just not there physically. I felt shut out."

Both she and Candy strove constantly for Edgar's approval. A treasured memento which Frances keeps in her dressing room is a photograph inscribed by her husband while they were separated prior to their marriage.

"I used to tease him. I said, 'You must have been a little drunk when you wrote this.' It says, "To the music and the beauty of my world, to my love, Frances.' Now, that's just about as poetic and romantic as you can get, and yet that was never verbalized until the last couple of years, when he was not well at all."

She still looks dazed by the memory of how Edgar ended one of his very last appearances in Las Vegas, which she was watching from the front row with friends.

"He just totally knocked me out. He wanted to introduce the person in his life who meant more than anything to him in the world, and to thank them for their love and support and whatever. I really didn't even know who he was talking about, I give you my word! Then he said, 'My wife, Frances.'"

As the spotlight swept onto this woman who had grown accustomed to staying in the shadows, she was dumbfounded. "I could hardly get out of the chair, because he had acknowledged me to the world, so to speak. It was very touching."

After her marriage, she worked periodically alongside Bergen when he appeared in nightclubs, and performed for troops in Berlin during World War II and later in Vietnam. She calls that "a very dramatic and fulfilling experience." But on the fringes of war, she was struck by a sense of unreality—she might almost have been on a backlot at MGM, making a movie. The full impact of the Vietnam experience hit her later, when she watched news footage on television, knowing how close she had been to the carnage she saw.

As her husband's onstage helper, Frances donned a short, white satin uniform with a rather low neckline to play the nurse in Bergen's old vaudeville skit, "The Operation," which remained a favorite of audiences and which he performed until the end of his career.

There was a time, she will admit, when she rather cherished the idea of basking in a few watts of her own limelight. Candy was eleven, her son Kris not yet born, when Frances polished up her nightclub act, with its repertoire of standards and ballads. Overcoming her terror, she performed in New Orleans, Montreal, and the St. Regis in New York, where Edgar played backstage husband.

She then received an offer to appear at London's now-defunct Colony Club, but Edgar balked, fearful that if she were successful, he might lose her. In the face of his objections, Frances "meekly gave in." Oh, she teased him later about it, particularly as women's liberation gathered momentum, saying, "Boy, if that was the case today, I'd say, 'You stay home and take care of the baby, because Mama's going to go do her job.' "

She has fantasized about what might have been and believes she might have made the big leagues had she put her heart and soul into it. But she quickly qualifies her self-confidence: she could be wrong, perhaps she was lucky it worked out as it did.

"I know there was some frustration through the years," she admits pensively, revealing that on only one of Edgar Bergen's radio shows was she given the chance to sing, although her voice was a match for that of the singer he hired. "And that was a little selfish on his part, God rest his beloved soul."

All of this is said without a trace of bitterness; she clearly harbors no regrets. She was thirty-nine, Edgar sixty, and Candy fifteen, when Kris Edgar Bergen was born in October 1961. For Edgar especially, his son represented a new lease on life. For Candy, very temporarily, this beautiful baby boy was an unwelcome competitor for her father's attention and she was struck with jealousy so intense that she stooped to making choking sounds in the nursery which she knew would scare her parents via the dining-room intercom.

Frances had been twenty-four when Candy was born and "Charlie's room" was redecorated in pink and blue and renamed "the nursery." "I rather miss seeing his shorts, with the initials, hanging over the chair," Frances told a journalist wistfully at the time. An adept player in the Charlie game herself, she admits to wondering how she and Edgar would explain to a little human being why Charlie, a piece of wood, was so idolized and important.

"But Candy never once questioned it. It was the darnedest thing. Never a question about it. She accepted it, and of course at a very early age, her father was always fooling around throwing his voice. You don't really throw the voice, but throwing voices through stuffed animals. So she got to the point where, 'Daddy, make the teddy bear talk.' But she never questioned, 'How can you make them talk?' Other people don't do that, but Daddy does."

In retrospect, Frances can see that the Edgar/Charlie figure and Candy's unique variety of sibling rivalry did indeed present problems and she feels rather remiss for not having perceived them at the time. "Of course I should have known. She was very conscious of being Charlie McCarthy's sister. And of course he had Daddy's attention and Daddy's approval."

How do you raise a child in privilege and affluence, and yet instill in them a proper appreciation for what they have, a strong sense of values? The Bergens were not the first to grapple with that problem, nor the first to see no virtue in withholding that which they could afford. And so it was that Candice Bergen attended the costly and prestigious Westlake School in Los Angeles, where she was May Queen in her senior class, and then flew off to Montesano, an exclusive Swiss finishing school.

Her pleas to go there had beaten down parental reservations, which returned with renewed vigor when Frances and Edgar visited her in Switzerland. Out of reach, their daughter and her compatriots were having themselves a merry old rebellious time, sampling afternoon cocktails in bars, often to excess.

She greeted her horrified parents with bleached hair, some shameless name-dropping, and a staggeringly nonchalant suggestion that they go down for a drink at the bar, where she promptly ordered "un Bloody Mary" and lit up a Salem.

Emerging from this spoiled brat era, Candy moved on to hurting, angering, and offending in print, courtesy of interviews she gave as a fledgling actress. What Frances Bergen calls the "smart-ass period" was essentially a time during which she seemed bent on criticizing all that her parents held dear:

"She was really knocking the background she had had, Beverly Hills, home, meals, where we moved, and whatever. And that teed me off as much as anything!" Frances recalls. "I said, 'I wonder if you really would have liked better being born in a ghetto? Or living where your mother lived?' Because, at a point when finances were so bad, I had to watch my mother wait on tables in a boarding house."

From the vantage point of calmer waters, Frances knows all too well that Candice was striking out, reacting to her intense embarrassment at the unfashionably affluent background with which she was burdened in the socially conscious 1960s. There was no longer any trace of the precocious finishing school pupil; she transformed from socialite to socialist and did so wholeheartedly, taking food and clothing to the Salvation Army on Skid Row. She also waxed poetic on the plight of the American Indian, expounded the evils of militarism, and condemned her father's hobby of duck shooting, none of which encouraged peace and harmony on the home front.

"It's understandable now, but it was damned difficult then," Frances says with considerable understatement. She found her daughter's ungracious attitude "unforgivable" when lucky Candy was not required to screen-test for her first film, which was in any case handed to her on a platter at a time when her sights were not even set on acting. Frances's reaction was exacerbated by her intimate knowledge of how hard others worked without achieving anything like her daughter's opportunities. "She was pretty arrogant about it—which she admits and has had some regret about since."

Candy had eleven films behind her by the time she was twenty-five, without so much as a single acting lesson. At nineteen, she shocked her parents with her decision to play Lakey, a lesbian, in the film of Mary McCarthy's book *The Group*. At twenty-one she did it again. For her birthday party, which boasted an extravagant smorgasbord planned by Frances and devoured by the likes of Julie Christie, Rosalind Russell, and Cary Grant, she issued incongruous black-edged invitations to mourn the passing of her youth.

Doris Day's son, Terry Melcher, was Candy's first high school sweetheart. When they met again in 1967 he was a record producer who had the Byrds' hit record "Tambourine Man" to his credit. Candy was convinced that their "living together," and Terry's politics and life-style, would be totally unacceptable to her father. And so an elaborate pretense was born. She kept this new arrangement from her parents by convincing them that she was living in New York. Phone calls to her mother (who worried about Candy's bill) were made with radio static piped into the receiver of an extension, which produced a passable imitation of a long-distance connection.

In fact, Candy and Terry were ensconced in his house on Cielo Drive off Benedict Canyon, uncomfortably close by. Driving to Beverly Hills she would slouch down in the car, and after a few close calls too many, Candy was prompted to confide in her mother, who was of course livid.

But instant complicity sprang up on this issue: there would be a code of silence about Terry. Edgar Bergen would not have been thrilled by the seriousness of his young daughter's romance. The relationship did indeed run its course, as Frances had imagined it would.

Near the end of their time together, Candy and Terry moved to Doris Day's Malibu home, where one morning the telescope mysteriously disappeared from the deck. Word reached them that Terry's acquaintance Charles Manson had been looking for him. A week later, Sharon Tate and her friends were slain in Terry's old home on Cielo Drive. Months passed before Charles Manson was arrested and Frances and Candy learned what Edgar never did—how close Candy had come to the possibility of encountering Manson's murderous clan.

Emerging intact from the "trying periods that Candy and I had" was what Frances believes forged the beginning of the true closeness that now exists between her and her daughter.

It was not an instant or miraculous transformation. When Bergen was seventy-five and ailing, both of his children were arrested —Candy for obstructing a hallway in the Senate, her fifteen-year-old brother for having pot in his possession.

Charlie McCarthy's heyday had ended with a sad time of uncomplaining descent for Edgar Bergen, made especially poignant (at least to Candy) by his daughter's passing wave as her career ascended. By then she was acutely aware of the extra blow her fame inevitably dealt to her mother's already shadowy identity. When would Frances have her day in the sun? No wonder her mother was triumphant when a telegram inviting her to take part in a celebrity tennis tournament came addressed to her personally, and to her alone. Candy was sensitive to the fact that she, Dad, and Charlie hogged the limelight while mother's talents were hidden, Frances explains. "She's always been enormously supportive of anything I've done."

Edgar Bergen's retirement was inevitable. Three days into his farewell run in Las Vegas, when his tearfully smiling family had joined the smilingly tearful audiences in toasting his and Charlie's sixty-year partnership with standing ovations, Edgar Bergen died peacefully in his sleep. It was September 30, 1978. He was eulogized by Ronald Reagan, Johnny Carson, and Muppet-creator Jim Henson, who took from Bergen his inspiration for Kermit the Frog. Charlie McCarthy took up residence at the Smithsonian Museum in Washington. Nothing was the same.

Within two months of her husband's death, Frances received what she felt was a horribly tactless phone call. A casting agent invited her to read for a part in *American Gigolo,* in which John Travolta was due to star. Working against the clock to clean out Edgar's nine-room office suite, which was chockablock full of magic books and manuals, wands, scrapbooks, and trunkfuls of dummies' clothing, she was still reeling from the shock of her husband's death, and admits to wondering if the ignorant man did not read the newspapers. Tactfully, however, she suggested that while his offer was flattering, she was in the midst of a difficult time. Quietly, he informed her that that was precisely why he had called. Perhaps this would take her mind off things? She loved him for that.

American Gigolo was shelved temporarily, but when it did go in front of the cameras with Richard Gere as its star, Frances had a part. She has since appeared in *Hollywood Wives* with Candice, and admits to feeling somewhat defensive about the natural assumption that her daughter helped her get that part—which she did not. Among other things, she had a small role in Jane Fonda's film *The Morning After,* and joined the national touring company of *On Your Toes* when Leslie Caron was aboard.

After her father's death, Candice seemed somehow freed to put her full weight into her acting work, and in 1979 she won a Best Supporting Actor Academy Award nomination for *Starting Over.* The golden girl still has it all, says her mother, telling proudly of granddaughter Chloe; her husband, director Louis Malle ("a special human being"); the apartments in Paris and New York.

Candice was married in "Le Coual," Malle's country home in southwest France, her perfect day made superlative by the presence of her mother and her brother, who was on a leave of absence from college in San Diego. (Now in his mid-twenties, Kris works as a film editor.) Frances gave Candice a handkerchief embroidered by Edgar's mother, a blue satin garter, and the loan of her own diamond engagement ring. It seems fitting to give Candice the last word on Frances. In *Knock Wood*, she wrote:

"My mother has become my biggest booster; I, hers. I marvel at the capability with which she has assumed her place as head of the family. Will you look at my mother? I think. What a beautiful woman. What a knockout."

10 Troubled Waters

"I agree with the English writer, whoever he was, who said that a miserable childhood is the ideal launching pad for success. I was sure as hell not going to repeat my mother's miserable life. No way." So said Joan Crawford, the world-famous star.

For Joan, the institution of marriage was inextricably linked in her mind with quarreling. After her own experiences as a child, she felt "afraid for my children to hear angry voices in the dark." Later, that fear and ability to identify with the pain of a child, all those good intentions, would be subjugated to Joan's own maternal aggression when, as is often the case, the abused child became the next generation's abuser. But such patterns do not have to be repeated and sometimes the child becomes fiercely determined to live her life differently.

When it is Mom or Dad rather than circumstances that disrupts a child's life—through alcohol or drug abuse, physical, verbal, or mental abuse—or when the occasional healthy release provided by a marital argument is carried into constant bickering or full-blown fighting, the disturbance goes deeper. Robert Blake, James Garner, Marvin Gaye, the Wilson-brother members of the Beach Boys—all were physically abused as children (James Garner by his stepmother; his mom died when he was four). Rock Hudson's "boozer" stepfather beat him. Cary Grant's father drank, as did Marlon Brando's mother, Pete Townshend's mother, and Warren Beatty and Shirley MacLaine's father.

Exposure to tumult and chaos, providing it is not too extreme, has its advantages. Children who have been exposed to it are perhaps better equipped to fight for what they want in life, and less likely to be sideswiped by rejection and obstacles.

Joan Crawford was certainly survivor material. Her mother, Anna Belle Johnson Cassin, came from genteel Southern stock and stood a petite five feet in stature. Joan Crawford (then Lucille Cassin, later Lucille LeSueur, more commonly known as Billie) tellingly once described herself as a homesick girl who had no home to be sick for. She recognized the void inside her but was enough of a pragmatist not to harbor the illusion that her family could fill it.

Anna Cassin's firstborn died at age two, so in all likelihood Anna resented Billie, the second daughter, who came along and survived. At any rate, Anna focused her affections on her third child, Hal. It seemed to Billie that she carried the blame for everything: if a switch was being flicked, her legs were its target and Hal silently acquiesced as his sister took medicine that should have been his. Every undeserved, unjust punishment simply edged Billie further down the road to rebellion.

Her world revolved around her daddy, Henry Cassin, who was short and solidly built, and dark like her, although infinitely more passive and easy-going in disposition. He was not outwardly affectionate either, but from him, Billie did feel love. Henry also unwittingly became the source of comfort and escape in Billie's life via his job as the manager of Lawton, Oklahoma's, two prime theaters.

When she was let loose amongst the myriad props, scenery, and costumes stored for his vaudeville house, she was transported into another world, a refuge from the hurts of real life. Molding herself on the dancers who so entranced her, to Anna Cassin's displeasure Billie took to running, skipping, dancing, tree-climbing tomboy-style, but never walking in a sedate, ladylike fashion.

At eight, the already-wayward Billie slipped out of her skirt and climbed a water tower, all to meet a dare. Her attention-getting antics brought her as much negative feedback as positive, but the disdain, disapproval, rejection, and stares somehow seemed to please her.

When she was eleven she stepped on a razor-edged chunk of broken milk bottle, cutting her foot so badly that she severed muscles and tendons, prompting her unsympathetic mother to remark, "Maybe this will make a lady out of her."

It was an episode that left Billie with pain and a limp but also, for the first time, some glimmer of belief that Anna perhaps loved her. Her mother spoon-fed her, cried and laughed with her, and generally drew closer to her during that convalescence (which Billie/Joan would at various times in her life claim took "weeks," "several months," and "a year and a half"), a reaction which only cemented the idea that suffering brought its own rewards.

That same year, Billie's world fell apart when she stumbled across a canvas bag of gold coins in the house, an obviously unwelcome discovery which precipitated fighting between Anna and Henry, both of whom immediately swore her to secrecy. From that day on, their marriage deteriorated drastically.

Hal and Billie were packed off to Anna's folks' farm near Phoenix, Arizona, while this mysterious business about the money was resolved. While they were away, Hal broke the shocking news that Billie's beloved Henry was not her father at all. Their real father, he asserted, was Thomas LeSueur, a French-Canadian whose bold features were indeed far more like Billie's. She flatly refused to dwell on this unpleasant thought and her love for Henry remained undiminished—although she did later adopt the more romantic-sounding LeSueur name, as did Anna and Hal.

On their return from Phoenix, Billie and Hal found their house in disarray and a move to Kansas City imminent. Apparently, the gold coins were bail bond money, given to Henry for safekeeping by a woman criminal. Henry had reportedly succumbed to the temptation to hang on to them in the mistaken belief that no one would dispute his word against hers. As it was, the family left Lawton under a cloud of suspicion and disgrace. Anna and Henry enlisted Billie at St. Agnes Academy in Kansas City, where, Henry explained, she would learn, live, and work. Sneaking out at the first opportunity, she walked back to the dilapidated hotel where the Cassins were living (Henry worked on the desk), only to learn that he had moved out. Mortified at the loss of her ally, she of course blamed her mother for driving him away.

When Anna married Harry Hough, Harry found Billie a post at Rockingham Academy like that she had held at St. Agnes, and she did not resist. Although Billie later claimed she was beaten there almost daily, the punishment meted out was evidently not sufficiently severe to send her running home to Anna's unwelcoming arms. The taunts she endured from socially superior girls served a purpose; they made her depression and fear give way to ambition and cast-iron determination.

Billie got her first break as a Charleston champion called Lucille LeSueur, then danced in Chicago strip-joints before taking on Hollywood as Joan Crawford. Anna initially disapproved, but those feelings soon dissipated in the face of her daughter's success. The more Billie/Joan achieved, she would later complain, the more she was burdened by the financial responsibility for her dependents. Anna freely indulged her love of department stores at her daughter's expense, hiding the bills, allowing them to pile up until Joan Crawford became aware of their existence in a considerably less pleasant fashion, via lawsuit notifications from various stores. Curiously, Joan indulged her mother's latter-day childishness and simply set to paying the bills off by installments.

She rented Anna and Hal a bungalow and retrieved her freedom, saying, "They deserved each other. If I sound unkind— well, for over 30 years I supported those two freeloaders, and I can count the number of times either of them said 'thank-you' on one hand." When Anna died, Joan felt guilt pangs. Should she have done more for her? She did not deny her own "lousy childhood," nor did she delude herself that her mother had loved her, but she was surprisingly forgiving and understanding of the trap Anna had fallen into: too many marriages too young . . . and too many men in between.

Jane and Peter Fonda were no strangers to feelings of guilt. They were entirely misplaced, but inevitable once they learned their mother, Frances Seymour Brokaw, had not died of a heart attack as they had been told, but had cut her throat in an asylum when they were twelve and ten years old respectively.

Henry Fonda married the beautiful socialite in 1936 within two months of meeting her. They were drawn from entirely different worlds. Frances was the widow of a New York congressman, but wealthy and well-connected in her own right, claiming direct descendancy from the first Duke of Somerset, whose sister,

Lady Jane Seymour, was Henry VIII's third wife. She was haughty, distant, and given to dramatic mood changes. She had a five-year-old daughter, Pamela, when they wed but was nevertheless anxious to start a family immediately. Henry, on the other hand, thought it prudent to wait a while. But Frances had her way and Jane Seymour Fonda was born in December 1937.

Frances had no intention of deserting her East Coast ways; Jane would be brought up as she herself had been, with an emphasis on manners, self-discipline, and organization. She was strict, with little tolerance for normal childish behavior or for Henry's casual untidiness and her reprimands irked him. Frances took care of the garden and kept her eagle eye on all household details, but their initial social whirl rapidly died down and their Brentwood home, with its pool house—tailor-made for parties— was oddly quiet. Henry's show business friends held little attraction for Frances.

Henry Fonda joined the Navy in 1942, and his departure threw his children into their mother's world for three whole years. By the time he returned, he seemed to have lost all tolerance for her regimens. The marriage was in trouble and Frances's depression accelerated accordingly. She was also despondent about the prospect of growing older. With hindsight, Jane says she could feel her father's affection for Frances ebbing away, and sensed her helpless mother's resulting panic. The marriage broke up in 1949, and Frances was dead the following year.

The truth about Frances's suicide did not reach Peter until he was fifteen; Jane learned of it sooner, but then conspired in the cover-up perpetuated by the family. Their eventual discovery of the truth affected Frances's children in drastically different ways, although both harbored the question that inevitably haunts the loved ones of someone who takes their own life. Did their mother kill herself because of something they had done?

Peter was particularly troubled. He had missed Frances badly when she was in the hospital, and during that time, he dreamed that she had died and that Henry had married his schoolteacher. The disloyalty of the dream compounded his guilt. He was frustrated by his father's resolute silence (Mother's death was a taboo subject at home), and worried, if she was crazy, perhaps he was too? The cruelty of schoolchildren took its toll. Thoughtless taunts, like "Your mother jumped out of a window," once drove Peter to cut another child quite badly by ramming a glass into his face.

The effects on Jane were, she suspected, so profound that she might never identify them, although her battle with bulimia might well have been a reflection. "Sometimes," she has since admitted, "I have to pretend I'm not moody and depressed in order for people to like me."

Similarly to children of abuse, the children of suicides tend to tread one of two paths. They can follow the same road to destruction (in this case self-destruction), or veer completely away from the person they come to see as a loser or victim. Young Jane Fonda's fantasy role models were all male, save for the super-strong Sheena, queen of the jungle. She looked up to men, admiring them and envying their exciting lives, and looked down on Frances's old role of homemaker. With her mother gone, she idolized Henry and craved his love . . . and since her needs were not met, she craved it all the more.

When Cher brought Sonny Bono home to meet her mother, it struck Georgia Holt immediately: "Except for the nose, Sonny looks exactly like Cher's father!" Father-substitute or no, she did not approve of her sixteen-year-old daughter's twenty-eight-year-old beau, whom she describes as "the funniest-looking thing I'd ever seen in my life. He had a Prince Valiant-type haircut—before long hair was in fashion—squaw boots, and buckskin pants that kind of hung down in the back. When he left the room I said, 'What was *that?*' Not tactful, I admit, but I was in shock. Cher said, 'That *happens* to be the man I am going to marry.' I think Sonny expected me to disapprove of him, and I did. There was a power battle. *I* had been the power figure in Cher's life until then."

Georgia tried hard to deter Cher from the liaison, spurred on by her own marital track record. She herself had been married three times by the time she was twenty-one, and despite brief marriages to six husbands, she had struggled as predominantly the sole provider for her two daughters. "I realize that my emotional instability cannot have been easy for Cher or Georganne," she admits. All the more reason for them to do things differently.

Georgia was born Jackie Jean Crouch in Kensett, Arkansas, in June 1927. Her mother, Lynda Inez Gully, was thirteen years old, and Lynda's maternal shortcomings doubtless had much to do with her own rough path in life. Lynda's father had been blown up in a dynamite accident while working on the railroad when she was five and she was subsequently farmed out to different relatives.

Lynda met Cher's grandfather, Roy Crouch, in the bakery where he was apprenticed. He was a farm boy, the youngest in his family's Hillbilly Crouch Brothers Band, and a funny, charismatic character. He was also an alcoholic who beat her mother severely, and little Jackie Jean did not blame her mother for walking out on them when she was five. Jackie Jean's voice became the key to their income in those Depression days.

"I would stand, barefoot, smoke in my eyes, fighting sleep, and sing to farmers and salesmen in the local tavern. Then Daddy would pass the hat around and collect a few coins until we had enough to eat. I could hold a tune and Daddy had faith in me even then. By the time I was nine I'd sung in just about every gin mill and honky-tonk bar clear across the south Midwest. That film *Paper Moon* was my life, only my daddy didn't sell Bibles like Ryan O'Neal, he sold me."

The sour, stale smell of those bars, a cocktail of cigarette smoke, spilled whiskey, and beer, will stay with her forever. Nevertheless, that early taste of the limelight, coupled with her favorite Saturday matinees (she collected empties for the price of admission), left Jackie Jean in no doubt whatsoever that she wanted to be a movie star.

She was not alone in her dreams. Roy Crouch was convinced that if he could only get her to Hollywood, her voice would lead him to the pot of gold at the end of the rainbow, and everybody in Searcy, Arkansas, who had heard her sing egged him on, as did the legendary Bob Wills and his Texas Playboys in Oklahoma City.

Georgia started singing on the radio in Oklahoma City at age seven and won the State Championship of Arkansas when she was eleven. "I was very proud of that because my background was so bizarre, for me to do anything was a big deal."

They hitchhiked cross-country to make their dreams come true, but when no magic struck them instantly upon their arrival at Hollywood and Vine, Roy Crouch fell back on his trusty old friend the whiskey bottle for comfort, and stayed in a stupor for days. Until that is, the auditions for *Meglin's Kiddies* (where Shirley Temple got her break), whereupon Jackie Jean was offered a scholarship. But faced with the daunting problem of providing her with the required dancing shoes, Daddy again sought refuge in the bottle; once again he had been stumped by the establishment.

Throughout her childhood, Georgia/Jackie Jean was shunted back and forth between her parents, attending seventeen different schools in all. She spent time in Salvation Army hostels and on welfare. Everything she owned was hand-me-down or handouts: "I'd wear the underwear and the things you couldn't see, but I just refused to wear those green corduroy jackets, because everyone knew they came from Welfare. Cher doesn't understand those times, she doesn't know what it's like to go hungry. I had to stand on street corners with my brother, selling Christmas seals.

"We lived in some terrible places, everything that crawls and could eat you, we had. Lice, bedbugs, roaches, ants, you name it. One night I lay on my cot, looking out the window, feeling so desperate and deciding, 'I will not live this way, I will *not!*' "

When Roy Crouch was sober, he worked nights as a baker's assistant and Jackie Jean kept her brother out of the reach of neighborhood perverts and gangs. "When I was eleven, my father tried to gas me and Mickey because my mother had gotten custody of us. It's something I blocked right out of my mind for years, until it all came out in therapy. I guess he just didn't know how to cope any more." Her quick action and good sense of smell saved them both. At thirteen, she crammed a job as a mother's helper alongside her schoolwork and got her first tantalizing glimpse of another, more affluent life-style, one with clean sheets and pretty things.

She was eighteen when she married Cher's father, Johnny Sarkisian, whom she did not love or even really like. She was drawn by his magnetic, powerfully persuasive quality. "When Sonny and Cher became famous, Cher said, 'He's going to get in touch, I know he is.' Sonny said Johnny would never set foot in their

Left to right: Cher's grandmother Lynda Walker; Cher; [1]
Chastity; Cher's mom, Georgia Holt; Cher's sister,
Georganne La Piere; Georganne's grandmother
Betty Stricker.

When Georgia learned she was pregnant, her mother insisted
she have an abortion or return to her husband: "But once there
at the doctor's office, I knew I couldn't go through with it. Can
you believe that I came that close to not having Cher?"
GEORGIA HOLT, *mother of Cher.*

Georgia and Cher.

Debbie Reynolds and Carrie Fisher.

Debbie Reynolds's unsurpassed matriarchal moment came at a party when Carrie, who was fourteen at the time, introduced her mother to her contemporaries thus: "I'd like you to meet my parents." "That was parents with an 's,'" Debbie reiterates, "and that was the ultimate compliment. I had to leave the party because I started to cry." **DEBBIE REYNOLDS,** *mother of Carrie Fisher.*

4

Martha Selleck with son Bob and baby Tom.

Anna Cosby with son Robert.

5

Anne Hamilton (seated center front) with, from left to right, son George; George's ex-wife, Alana; son Bill; son David's wife, Heller; and David.

6

Berniece Janssen with son David.

Barbara Voight with sons Chip,
Barry and Jon.

Laurie Williams with son Robin.

Robin Williams credits his mom, Laurie—along with being dropped on his head as a baby—as major influences on his life. "Well, I'm sorry he fell on his head. He bounced, but I caught him."   **LAURIE WILLIAMS,** *mother of Robin.*

Sara Taylor with daughter, Elizabeth.

Laura Hawn with daughter Goldie.

Mary Martin with son Larry Hagman.

Margot Warren with daughter Lesley-Anne.

14

Catrine Domenique with daughter Cyndi Lauper.

"As a teenager Cyndi was one of the originals as far as wearing antique clothing. She loved it. I didn't. Sometimes when the kids saw her dressed like that, they used to throw rocks at her." **CATRINE DOMENIQUE,** *mother of Cyndi Lauper.*

15

Janet Leigh with daughter Jamie Lee Curtis.

16

Cybill Shepherd and mother, Patty Micci.

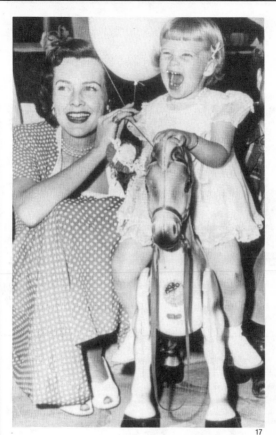

Frances Bergen with daughter Candice.

"She was really knocking the background she had had, Beverly Hills, home, meals, where we moved and whatever. And that teed me off as much as anything! I said, 'I wonder if you really would have liked better being born in a ghetto?'"
FRANCES BERGEN, *mother of Candice.*

Dolly Parton, top left, with (clockwise from top left) her sisters and brothers, Willadeene, Denver, Floyd, Bobby, Freida, David, Cassie, dad Lee, mom Avie Lee, baby Rachel, Stella and Randy.

19

Eva Jagger with son Mick.

"He's still your son. He's still your little kid. You brought him up. I don't grasp it. It isn't that I'm not proud of him, I think it's marvelous."   **EVA JAGGER,** *mother*

Diana Kind with daughters Roslyn Kind and Barbra Streisand. 20

Natalie Wood with daughter Natasha and her mother,[21]
Maria Gurdin.

Maria Gurdin is adamant about one thing: "I didn't want her
money. I was too proud... We were never pushy. It was her own
will to act."   **MARIA GURDIN,** *mother of Natalie Wood.*

The Howard family. From left to right: Rance, Clint,
Jean and Ron.

Betty White with her mother, Tess.

"Values, that's what she gave me. She said, 'You can lie to me, you can lie to the world, you can lie to yourself, until you are on your own and you look in the mirror.'"   **BETTY WHITE,** *daughter of Tess.*

24

Tippi Hedren and daughter Melanie Griffith.

"I don't know that she was any wilder than anyone else, except that she happened to be in a situation of being a Hollywood brat." **TIPPI HEDREN,** *mother of Melanie Griffith.*

25

Julie Powers with son Jeff and daughter Stefanie.

26

Doris G. Tate with daughter Sharon.

"Until you have lost a child, you don't know what it is. Parents are supposed to die first," says Doris G. Tate, mother of Manson family victim Sharon Tate, and now an activist and campaigner for victim's rights. "I have to do what I feel is in my heart. If not, Sharon's died in vain." **DORIS G. TATE,** *mother of Sharon.*

Loretta Williams with son 27
Billy Dee.

28
Charlotte Sheedy with, from left to right, Ally, Patrick, and
Meghan.

29

Tatum O'Neal and her mother, Joanna Moore.

30

Diahann Carroll with, clockwise from left, sister Lydia, daughter Suzanne and Diahann's mother, Mabel Johnson.

31

Gerry Dreyfuss and son Richard.

"It was *impossible* not to treat Richard differently, because he was in Hollywood. What were we?" says Gerry Dreyfuss of her son Richard's difficulty in handling fame. "It was *his* problem. Nobody asked him for money, nobody asked him for favors. If your relative was Robert Redford, could you talk to him the same way you talked to your cousin who was working in Vons market?"
GERRY DREYFUSS, *mother of Richard.*

Diana Douglas and son Michael.

33

Zelma Bullock with daughter Tina Turner.

34

John Lennon with his Auntie Mimi.

35

Annette Funicello with her mother, Virginia.

"It was a nightmare. Her wedding was ruined," says Virginia Funicello, of death threats leveled against her daughter Annette. "We were scared. We were afraid."   **VIRGINIA FUNICELLO,** *mother of Annette.*

Brandy Foster and daughter Jodie.

Pia Zadora with her mother, Saturnina Schipani.

Some of the Motion Picture Mothers at the group's annual birthday party at the Motion Picture and TV Country House and Hospital. Left to right: Ron Howard's mom, Jean; Dennis Dugan's mom, Marion; Barbra Streisand's mom, Diana Kind; Tina Turner's mom, Zelma Bullock; Tom Selleck's mom, Martha; Natalie Wood's mom, Maria Gurdin; John Ritter's mom, Dorothy; Billy Dee Williams's mom, Loretta; Diahann Carroll's mom, Mabel Johnson; Cher's mom, Georgia Holt; David Janssen's mom, Berniece; Annette Funicello's mom, Virginia. Seated at center front, author Phyllis Quinn.

38

house, but within three months, he was their road manager and living with them, that's the kind of man he was," she says by way of explanation for her strange attraction to him.

Johnny and Jackie Jean had already separated when she learned she was pregnant, and her mother insisted she have an abortion or return to her husband: "I remember sitting in that office, waiting, on an old-fashioned chrome chair. The chrome was cold, yet the sweat was running off me, I was so scared. But once they got me up on that table, I knew I couldn't go through with it. Can you believe that I came that close to not having Cher?"

Instead, she returned to Sarkisian, but hard times followed. She walked around New York with baby Cher wrapped in a man's overcoat. "I didn't do well as a mother, I was hysterical all the time. She cried a lot and my milk was no good, I think it was the turmoil I was in." Desperate, she put Cher in a Catholic home for nine dollars a week so she could toil in an all-night diner for one dollar a night and tips. "But because I sang in a bar, the Mother Superior thought I shouldn't be allowed to keep her and tried to stop me taking her back," Georgia recalls.

When she left Johnny, she and her mother went to Reno together (each to get a divorce) and she won her first beauty contest. "I had no concept of what I looked like; I had gorgeous legs and didn't know it," says Georgia, who changed her name from Jackie Jean in 1949 to sound more glamorous. She subsequently worked in the film and TV industry and even lost a role in *The Asphalt Jungle* to Marilyn Monroe: "I always set out to be a star. I just never arrived."

When Cher was five, Georgia gave birth to her second child, Georganne. Georganne's father, actor John Southall, became a surrogate father to Cher. (Her father died in 1985.) John Southall adored Cher, but he was no paragon of virtue either and finally his alcoholic rages forced Georgia to leave him. In 1954 she was alone with her two young children, homeless, penniless, jobless, and her furniture had been repossessed. "There were times when the anxiety attacks were so severe I couldn't function." Just as things were looking rosier, John returned, begging her to give their marriage another chance—not the romantic gesture it might sound.

"One day he broke down the front door and stood there brandishing a butcher's knife. I felt sure he was going to kill us. He ran through the house looking for the boyfriend he was convinced I had hidden away, but we rushed out back and I threw Cher and Georganne over a six-foot cyclone fence, then we ran off and hid. I marvel at what you can do when your life depends on it. Throughout all this, I was just so proud to be able to hang on to my kids. That might sound strange to most people, but coming from my background, it was no small feat."

To make ends meet, she worked as an actress and a model. She appeared regularly on "Ozzie and Harriet," "I Love Lucy," and "The Lucy Show." It frequently fell to Cher to look after Georganne, and Georgia admits, "I relied on her way too much, but I had no choice. But at least I didn't go running down the street chasing Cher and Georganne with a butcher knife, so in my eyes their childhood was a day at the beach compared to my life with my father.

"Halloween was always Cher's favorite holiday, next to Christmas. She loved to dress up in my peasant skirts and dangly earrings and have me set her hair and put makeup on her. If it was warm, we sat on quilts on the front lawn and told ghost stories. One time their grandmother appeared draped in a sheet and moaning like a ghost. They ran away, scared to death, until she took off the sheet, and we laughed until our sides hurt."

At one point Roy Crouch stayed with them, prompting Georgia's sweet Southern landlady to calmly say, "Georgia, we love you and the children, but we just *cannot* have your father running nude down the street chasing your stepmother." Also nude, by the way. "Daddy was fun when he was a little drunk, but when he crossed the line he was mean and dangerous. Yet I hold such a fondness for him in my heart because he had this wonderful sense of humor."

Cher was eleven when she had her first date—a little fat boy with pimples bought her a corsage. "She didn't know it, but from the time she was twelve, Cher had a magnetism, a sensuality, a power to attract men to her. When she was fifteen, she dated Warren Beatty, though I didn't know."

As a teenager, Cher was downright rebellious. "She talked back constantly. She wouldn't back off, she'd just stand right up in my face and dare me to whatever. When she was thirteen, I was called to the police station at 3:30 A.M. one morning. She had been arrested for car theft! It was a false alarm (it turned out she had driven off in a friend's car) but scary nevertheless." After being in therapy, I realize that all that bad behavior was a desperate cry for my attention. She does the same thing now, but she does it with conversation. She gets my attention now because she is so smart, intuitively and instinctively.

Soon after meeting Sonny, Cher pretended to move into an apartment with an airline stewardess friend, an explanation which satisfied Georgia until she dropped by unannounced. "Cher called through the intercom: 'You'll have to wait a minute, Mom! The house is ridiculous! I've got to straighten up before you come in.' She was stalling while she frantically tried to remove all signs of Sonny's presence. She literally grabbed all his clothes and threw them out of the back window into the street. Not suspecting, I went into the kitchen to get a Coke and I was looking for a can opener when Cher suddenly ran in shouting, 'Will you stop going through my cupboards! There's nothing to find! You don't have to be sneaky!' That's when I knew there was something to hide."

Georgia was working as a model on "The Lucy Show" when Sonny and Cher's first hit record climbed the charts. She had been telling Lucy about Cher for months, but Lucy's reaction was disappointingly underwhelming. "Finally, in exasperation, I said, 'Lucy! My kid's record is at the top of the charts! They have knocked the Beatles out of first place!' She said, 'Who? What? You mean your daughter's *Cher* of Sonny and Cher? You tell her to get herself over to this stage!' Cher came over and had her picture taken with Lucy, Desi, and Lucie Arnaz. They were all big fans."

Georgia long ago grew used to dramatic swings in fortune. She caressed the wheel of a white Rolls Royce during one of her brief but more financially stable marriages. Then again, she also drove cross-country in a two-and-a-half-ton truck with a lover twenty-one years her junior. When the Rolls Royce marriage ended, Georgia was forced to sell her car, her piano, and even the diamond earrings that Cher (who was by then rich and famous) had bought her for a birthday gift.

"More than anything else in the world I've survived because I have a sense of humor. My shrink told me I should be alcoholic, a drug addict, or dead, and the fact that I am in one piece is a miracle." She has often wondered how different Cher and Georganne might be had they grown up in a stable environment with a lawyer or an accountant for a father. Not that she is complaining. "I think coming from such a bizarre family makes you unique. And God knows we've earned our great sense of humor. One of my greatest joys is being around Cher and my youngest, Georganne, when they get going. They are so funny, so bright, and so outrageous, they make me laugh till I cry. I look at them both and I'm so proud we survived. They're beautiful and funny and charming, and coming from their childhood, that's almost a miracle."

Shirley MacLaine and Warren Beatty's two-star parents, Ira Owens Beaty and Kathlyn MacLean Beaty, were married until Ira's death in 1986. Their relationship was always tumultuous, sometimes entertainingly so and sometimes disturbingly, a dynamic which had a not-inconsiderable effect on their children. Kathlyn MacLean grew up in Canada, where her mother was a university dean of women. She met Shirley and Warren's father at Maryland College, where she taught drama and Ira was a professor of psychology and education.

The Beatys (Warren added the extra *t*) were a Baptist, middle-class family from Richmond, Virginia, who later moved to Arlington, a suburb of Washington, D.C. "In many ways everything Warren and I are, everything we represent, is anti-establishment because we are products of the establishment itself," Shirley has observed.

Kathlyn (who Ira nicknamed Scotch) is now in her eighties and something of an enigma, considering that her two children have been superstars for many years. Shirley concedes that she and Warren always very jealously guarded the privacy of their parents, but she readily reveals that they made a colorful couple for whom she and Warren were, as children, a captive (and often captivated) audience.

"My dad was sort of a country storyteller. He'd rattle on for hours and hours, and mother would drop some apple pie in his lap or bump into the furniture just to get some attention, and then it would be on her for a while. It was like watching two vaudevillians. In many ways, I think Warren and I had as theatrical an upbringing as the Redgraves and the Barrymores, except that they weren't professional. There was no way we could not have been actors in that family."

It was a scenario where she and Warren were, according to Shirley, "bit players" to the two stars. (Ira Beaty had enormous potential as a solo violinist, but chose not to pursue a career, at least in part because of his fear of competition.) Ira and Kathlyn's banter reflected their roles, with curmudgeonly Father goading, and Mother unable to resist being goaded. "Mother played the tyranny of the fragile and Daddy the insecurity of the tyrant," wrote Shirley, in her book *Dancing in the Light.* Shirley revealed the downside to this competitive power play, admitting that there were times when the parental bickering and sniping reached war-like proportions, her father's not-so-secret secret drinking being the most frequent bone of contention between them.

Shirley MacLaine began taking dance classes at age three; her parents hoped they would strengthen her very weak ankles. Dance immediately became Shirley's great passion, and at twelve they enrolled her in ballet school. It was Kathlyn, who also directed amateur stage productions, who first pointed the expressive Shirley away from pure ballet and toward acting, where she could fully utilize her talents.

The exposure to Mom and Dad's vaudevillian act had rendered both Shirley and Warren shy, Warren especially. He was also a lonely boy and spent hours shut in his own private world—luckily, the large closet in his room had its own window. In turn, the shyness propelled them both toward finding their own outlet for self-expression.

Whereas Kathlyn was a sacrificing homemaker, it did not occur to Shirley to give up her career after she gave birth to her daughter, Sachi. Most important, she has never felt guilty about her need to express her creativity, "and I think the reason for that is that my mother didn't explore any of her talents, and I saw her frustrated as a result of that. And it affected me as a woman, seeing her repress her own creative aspirations to become a mother and a housewife." Not, she hastens to add, that her mother is remotely bitter. "She is living through my success and is so proud, and, by the way, not at all surprised at either one of us."

11 *The White Picket Fence*

Patty Micci is resplendent in jewel colors—a purple, royal blue, and fuchsia silk suit. The honey-blonde's long talons are pearlized silvery beige, her wrists and fingers are set off with sparkling gold bangles, gold and diamond rings. The features are familiar, just one generation on. But Patty, who badly wants a facelift, is glamour personified, and her TV-star daughter Cybill Shepherd (who is justifiably adamant that she does not need one) is perennially tomboyish.

"Cybill, sometimes you have to suffer to be beautiful," Patty Micci recalls telling her, long before Cybill carved a niche of notoriety for herself by becoming the first star ever to team an evening gown with Reebok jogging shoes.

Cybill Shepherd, who sang in the Episcopalian church choir, is one of the 25 percent of stars who had what you could describe as an apple-pie upbringing. She evidently does not cling to every morsel of Mom's advice, however, and has put the aforementioned Reeboks in her mouth on more than one occasion, trotting out remarks that have had Patty Micci blushing to the core. First she told Jimmy Carter that she loved his peanuts. Then came her shocking public sexual appraisals of a line-up of famous men, including an assertion that she had heard that Mickey Rourke, although sexy, does not bathe. An ungallant remark, it seemed the veritable height of discretion compared to her revelation of the intimate act she would *not* like to undertake on Teddy Kennedy. (She later claimed that her comment to an *US* magazine reporter was off the record.)

"Oh, I just die!" Patty Micci rolls her eyes heavenward in apparent dismay, yet manages to look indefatigably cheerful as she says in her dulcet Southern tones, "I just think sometimes if she *just* would shut up. But that's Cybill. I'll say again, I wish a lot of times she would hush." Irrespective of her admonishments, Patty's smile never falters. Patty's seventy-eight-year-old mother (nicknamed Sweet Mama) also lets Cybill's verbal violations wash right over her, although both reportedly paled when Cybill went topless as Jacy in the 1971 film *The Last Picture Show*—until critical acclaim softened the blow.

Such mildly scandalous controversy notwithstanding, Cybill Shepherd is the product of what Patty Micci apologetically describes as an idyllic childhood, and theirs was the perfect mother-daughter relationship: "That's what's so bad. I can't tell you very many bad things about Cybill," she says, grinning broadly with unconcealed pride.

Eva Jagger, casting her mind back to Mick's pre–Rolling Stone years, might almost claim the same thing. Michael Philip, while admittedly a touch hirsute for the taste of Dartford Grammar School, basically conformed to the confines of the traditional maroon, gold-trimmed uniform—cap included. He was not "goody-goody," but neither was he overtly rebellious. He always completed his homework quota. "Oh yes, his father saw to that," Eva confirms. But as Mick's tresses were among the vanguard of those creeping down over ear-tops both sides of the Atlantic (a shockingly anarchistic length in the far-off 1960s), trouble brewed. "That caused an absolute furor," Eva Jagger says wryly, "especially with us. We were horrified, absolutely horrified."

Since the demon barber was persona non grata, Eva went to great lengths to persuade Mick to sit still for her scissors. Mick's father, Joe Jagger, was relentless on the issue, much to Eva's frustration. His constant refrain was, "Get him to have his hair cut!" "I used to get so fed up with it," she recalls with a large sigh. "I'd say, 'Look, I can't *make* him.' Well, we did in the end." No sooner had Eva started clipping than Mick was crying, "Don't take too much off! That's enough!"

Living, as they did, in a rather refined and sedate suburb—the British equivalent of a white picket fence neighborhood—Eva was a mite concerned about what people might think as Mick rose first to national then international status as a figure of controversy, but says of her renegade rocker, "You just had to give in and try to understand. Some families almost turned their children out. We would never do a thing like that, we never got to that stage. It was just a bit of a worry."

Twenty years on, even she finds it exceedingly difficult to remember quite why all the fuss over a few straggly heads of hair. Positively tame in light of the shocking multicolored confections and mohawks that followed, as Mick's infamous dress worn at the 1969 Hyde Park Concert soon after Brian Jones' death now seems veritably macho compared to the androgynous likes of Boy George. "When I pass these orange- and green-haired youngsters I think, 'Oh my God, I couldn't sit across the kitchen table looking at *that,* they're ten times worse," Eva says, with obvious sympathy for their long-suffering moms.

Cybill Shepherd and Mick Jagger are far from being the only superstars who had stable childhoods, and evidence that stability does not preclude rebellion. Superstars like Tom Selleck, Peter O'Toole, Goldie Hawn, Jon Voight, Richard Gere, Robert Redford, Jeff and Beau Bridges, along with musical mutineers like David Bowie and Bob Dylan, were raised in environments which might fairly be described as happy, stable, calm, and constant. Proof positive that creative souls can lurk unmolested in suburbia and that childhood equilibrium can indeed be a launching pad for stardom. If the term "normal" had not been virtually relegated to the psychological trash can, it would seem that "normal" has its role in spurring success.

The recipe for family health has its roots in three structures, according to Dr. R. Barkley Clark. First and foremost is a solid marital relationship that is mutually satisfying and supportive and that operates independently of the children. "When the kids leave the household, there is a stong glue that still holds those people together: they enjoy being together, they share pains and expectations. That is the backbone of a healthy family." Ideally, that kind of marital success is coupled with an environment where children are an important, integral part of the family but do not rule it entirely, where they know their parents enjoy their company, but life does not revolve around them.

Katharine Hepburn was the product of a marriage between a

surgeon involved in the social-hygiene movement and an idealistic, philosophic, humanitarian mother. Hepburn's liberal mother did not hold a job in the traditional sense, but was committed to a set of beliefs (she was an early proponent of birth control) and traveled making energetic suffragette speeches. One of six children, Hepburn, who was also spanked regularly and dunked in cold showers, recalls this lesson most clearly: "I was never allowed to be a bore or dominate the conversation at our house."

Ultimately, the recipe for family health has virtually nothing to do with the building in which it is concocted. As Dolly Parton's mother Avie Lee can testify, it no more requires the New England white picket fence than it does two stories, or a Volvo in the driveway. Which is why the white picket fence is meaningless in and of itself. It is merely strips of painted wood, the book cover without the pages.

Why did the Jaggers and Bowies and Dylans of the world, with one swift blow, reject all that the previous generation had strived for, all its hard-won accomplishments? They rejected boredom, if you will. They balked at the bourgeois life-style just as their successors would come to reject yuppiedom. To them, being classless, working-class, or any other class was preferable to the mundanity of being middle-class. Mick Jagger donned the persona of a working-class hero by dropping Mike in favor of the more plebian Mick, and by trading in his middle-class accent. Instead, like a badge of honor, he wore a brasher Cockney identity, courtesy of speech inflections which were more akin to those emanating from the residents, fellow Rolling Stone Keith Richards among them, of the local council flats (a newer relative of the projects).

Despite being rather nicely brought-up and well-educated, Jagger maintained a curious mix of street-fighting, rough talking, a mocking manner, and a transient Cockney accent which he could, and did, pick up or drop at will. Despite his Aunt Mimi's protestations, John Lennon underwent a similar fashionable, voluntary class-downgrade from middle-class Mersey tones to a more pronounced Scouse (Liverpool) accent. There is more at work than just the influence of family, then.

"It's the Zeitgeist, the spirit of the times, the current mythology of record," says Dr. Grotstein, explaining that the era in which we are born has much to say about the way in which we turn out. Even for leaders like Jagger and Lennon this holds true: "We are the creatures of the times as well as creator of them." There is also the influence of the dominant mythological heroic figure to be considered, be it the proletariat protestor, or—as in the 1930s—the dissipated, overindulged member of the upper-class.

The inevitable (and desirable) separation between Mom and child begins with the first, "No!" the first step away from her, and builds to a crescendo of self-sufficiency and autonomy at around age eighteen. A sense of rejection is an intrinsic part of that separation; the child is spurning what the family is offering, which is not without pain for either side. If the apple does not fall very far from the tree, at this stage it seems to.

Robert Redford, always an active daydreamer, was plagued by guilt caused by the discrepancy between what he *felt* (he was prone to black, gloomy depressions, insomnia and nightmares) and his angelic, wholesome good looks. He felt alienated because he did not fit the mold in which his family, and later his fans, sought to cast him, and he rebelled by hanging out with a gang of boys. Yet Redford's mother, Martha Hunt Redford, sacrificed for her children, and Robert's background fit the supposedly desirable parameters of the nuclear family. Stefanie Powers' did not. Her childhood deviated from the textbook ideal in that she came from a broken home, but it was nonetheless idyllic.

Julie Powers divorced the father of her children when Stefanie was seven and Jeff ten, at which time Julie allowed them to choose with whom they wished to live. Stefanie's verdict? "Well, I miss having a father," she told her mom, "but to have a father like that, this is better." Julie's claim that they were inseparable, like "three buddies," is borne out by their closeness today; Julie lives in Stefanie's house in Los Angeles and is her frequent companion. Divorce was doubtless a happier option than a four-person household rife with tension.

Having knocked down the white picket fence, it is nonetheless interesting to look at those who grew up behind it. Take Cybill Shepherd. For all her verbal transgressions, Patty Micci holds fast to the belief that Cybill is inhibited by the idea of "What will mother say?" "Now this sounds ridiculous and sugar and cream and all that, but so help me I never heard a cussword in my home, my parents' home, or in our home." She laughs, remembering the time she chastised Cybill's secretary for uttering an unladylike word, only to discover the source of this unattractive expression: Cybill.

"Cybill, you could at least say spit!" Patty reprimanded her daughter, the one time she caught her cussing. Mrs. Micci gasps dramatically and launches into an imitation of Cybill's reaction. "She said, 'Oh mother, I'm sorry! Excuse me!' She knows. She's a mess. Messpot, I used to call her when she was little. That's kind of a love name, to me," she explains, puffing on a cigarette, then stubbing it out. (With her daughter a spokesperson for the National Lung Association, Patty arranged to see a hypnotist in an attempt to give up smoking.)

This mother of three was an only child herself. Patty's Missouri-born father, Cy Shobe, served in the Navy during World War II. An affluent man who owned and flew his own airplane, he was a whiz at building radios and was responsible for bringing the first talking box into his home state. Folk flocked from miles around by horse and buggy, just to hear it. Cy could take Patty's mother's broken watch apart, then reassemble the minuscule pieces in working order; he just had that magic touch. As electronics grew more sophisticated, Shobe developed an electronics distribution business in Memphis which, still owned by Patty and her mother, wholesales into six states. Patty's mother's folks had a treasure trove of a general store in Arkansas, stocked with everything from cloth to groceries.

Patty's parents met at a young men's club dance. They wed when her mother was sixteen and her father eighteen, which is why Patty claims she raised them as much as they raised her.

Nevertheless, Patty Micci is an unabashed modern-day Southern belle who has never worked a day in her life (save for one summer, cashiering at the Naval air base) and is proud of it. She does not pretend to understand how career women do what they do and readily admits that their lives would scare her to death. That does not mean she was spoiled. Her parents were too busy to overindulge her, she says, although in her mother's case it was a whirl of bridge parties and volleyball and basketball games that kept her busy.

What Patty *is* bashful about is having "collected movie stars" as a youngster—buying fan magazines, then rushing home, cutting out all the pictures of her favorites and pasting them in a book . . . a page for Norma Shearer, a page for Loretta Young. Sometimes she and her friends spent the entire day bartering movie stars. Patty's crowd's weekend ritual was to stroll down to the local movie theater and pay ten cents for a ticket. They put on backyard shows, hanging sheets from washing lines. Yet for all these signals of interest in the movies, Patty grew up with thoughts of falling in love and having children, nothing more. The movie star books have been long since thrown away. She does not remember telling anyone about them before, and seriously doubts her interest influenced Cybill. Her tenacity in nudging Cybill into entering beauty pageants, on the other hand, most certainly did.

The source of Cybill's controversial outspokenness and general assertiveness is likely Micci's powerhouse mother, to whom Patty speaks daily, often from the freeway on their camper's telephone. Sweet Mama, at almost eighty, is "still going full blast" and, on her frequent vacations in Florida, hates to miss a single party. Cybill and Sweet Mama are two of a kind. If either takes a sudden dislike to, say, a rug or a garden fountain, no matter how costly, it must be removed from sight immediately. Often the offending object is just thrown into the trash, sent to "rug heaven" or "fountain heaven," Patty says, rolling her eyes.

Patty Shobe was three weeks into her studies at the University of Mississippi when she brought her education to an abrupt halt by deciding to marry Cybill's father. William Jennings Shepherd —a handsome fellow of six-foot-three whom she had known for just over a year—was about to be drafted overseas. Patty was eighteen and already engaged to a prisoner-of-war, so initially she felt honor-bound to reject Bill's repeated proposals. At the eleventh hour, she had a sudden change of heart and in a whirlwind three days, Patty selected a china pattern, silverware, flowers, and an off-the-peg dress. The all-naval wedding was a fine affair held at Cybill's godparents' house, which boasted a wide, sweeping staircase down which the bride made a suitably impressive entrance. (Patty still sees her old fiancé in Memphis. He has forgiven her for deserting him, but she is not so sure his family has.)

Cybill (named for grandfather Cy and father Bill) was born in February 1950. She, sister Terry (who is a nurse and four years older), and younger brother Bill (who works in the commercials business in Memphis) were brought up in a religious atmosphere. Mr. and Mrs. Shepherd were much involved with church work—Patty coached the girls' basketball and softball teams. Cybill progressed from singing in the Episcopalian church choir to folk groups, and then, like any loyal Memphis girl, became an Elvis devotee. She still warbles to herself around the house constantly, which is Patty's clue that she is home.

Cybill's was reportedly a trouble-free adolescence; aside from the famous time the fraternity sweetheart dated an unsuitable Mick Jagger look-alike. Patty and Bill erroneously thought they had put a stop to the friendship, but it transpired that the harmless frat boys who came to pick up Cybill were a collective "beard" for her persona non grata suitor. When Patty and Bill eventually learned that their daughter was taking late-night excursions, exiting surreptitiously via a window, "my husband went in and got big, long nails and nailed the windows down," Patty says, laughing merrily.

That infraction aside, at sixteen Cybill was very much the wholesome girl-next-door, president of her sorority, voted "Most Attractive" during her senior year at East High School. Always outdoorsy and athletic, she was a tomboy even as a little girl and only ladylike if Patty purposefully dressed her up for Sunday School with little white gloves. Cybill is a good shot but contrary to reports does not pack a gun when she jogs. Her mother shakes her head at that, which she says was Cybill's idea of a joke, and says, "She's been a comic all her life—and I've always wondered why they gave her such serious parts—so she's hit her niche with 'Moonlighting.' "

Patty's daughter was a typically insecure adolescent who, despite the accolades awarded her looks in school, was convinced that she was awkward and drab-looking. (She now says the Southern society in which she was raised did not encourage confidence in women.) In Patty's eyes, however, Cybill was always pretty, and her cousin agreed apparently, since, to the bookish Cybill's dismay, he took it upon himself to enter her in the Miss Teenage Memphis pageant. Patty persuaded her to go through with it and Cybill won, albeit somewhat reluctantly. She did not go on to win the national pageant (losing to a girl who danced the hula) but, to her embarrassment, won the Miss Congeniality Award instead. Then she put the business of contests behind her —or so she thought.

As a graduation gift, Patty's parents sent their granddaughter to Europe where Cybill was keen to study history of art. She was registered at Louisiana State University for her return, but in the interim was invited to enter a local heat for the CBS Fashion Model of the Year contest. Consistent in her reluctance, Cybill had once again to be cajoled by Patty into entering.

In that bygone era of the late sixties, young girls rolled up their hair as a nightly masochistic ritual. Cybill had foregone the rollers on this occasion and Patty remembers that her hair hung as straight as string the day she persuaded her to at least go and *meet* the contest organizers. After what seemed like an eternity, Cybill returned with a winner's bouquet of yellow roses attached to her side.

"She kept saying, 'Mother, I am *not* going to New York.' And we kept telling her, 'Cybill, it's just a free trip. Go, enjoy yourself!' " Patty smiles. She was "sent for" as soon as her lonely, homesick daughter arrived in Manhattan. Privately, she wondered quite what her daughter was doing amongst the most beautiful young women she had ever seen. But when she saw Cybill up on stage in all her finery, those reservations were swiftly replaced by pure pride. She was "numb" as Cybill was declared the 1968 CBS Fashion Model of the Year on national television. (She won twenty-five thousand dollars guaranteed minimum for her first year with the Stewart Models Corporation.) Cybill was barely eighteen. She was a naive country girl cast loose in New York, so Patty stayed on and smoothed her highly ambivalent daughter's transition into the now-legendary Barbizon Hotel for Women.

"For two cents, Cybill would have thrown in the towel and gone home to Memphis and on with her studies," admits Patty, who steadfastly encouraged her to fulfill the prize's one-year obligation. To her surprise, by the end of this "sentence," Cybill chose voluntarily to stay in New York, modeling part-time and attending night classes at NYU. In 1970, she earned more than eighty thousand dollars in front of cameras, making commercials for Coca-Cola, Breck Shampoo, Ultra-Brite toothpaste, and Cover Girl makeup, to name but a few.

While Cybill was becoming established in New York, her parents' twenty-seven-year marriage fell apart into divorce. Bill Shepherd was a handsome fellow at "that" stage in life, Patty says. There was another woman. Patty made the transition surprisingly well, enjoying her newfound single status and freedom to travel at will—until she met Mondo Micci. Cybill's party-loving stepfather owns formal-wear rental shops in Memphis and would willingly spend eight nights a week twirling on the dance floor. The traditional Italian patriarch with whom Patty seems to have found something rather splendid, is very jovial. The couple have coexisted in a state of bliss for nine years now. Even so, when Mondo sequesters himself behind a newspaper across the coffee shop from us, they cannot resist making eyes at one another, Patty giggling like a young girl.

Mondo is a father of five, and between them, they share thirteen grandchildren. With Cybill's daughter, Clementine, and twins, Ariel and Zachariah, head counts at family gatherings now total around thirty-three. This extended family is a leveling influence on Cybill, as is her sense of roots, according to her mother. When ABC gave their prize star her free choice of activities to lure her into filming a promotional segment, Patty says Cybill chose to go to the Miccis' Alabama summer house and have Mondo cook ribs: "They sent their whole film crew to Alabama and we just had a big family barbecue!"

Earnest socializers, the Miccis live in Memphis, and keep an oceanside condominium in Fort Lauderdale and their summer home on the Tennessee River in Florence, Alabama. To visit Cybill in California, they zip across the States in their luxury motor home (equipped with microwave and color TV), Patty retreating to the couch and covering her eyes when they hit the Los Angeles freeway traffic. During these jaunts, daughter Terry cares for their aquarium, their seven pairs of cardinals, and a squirrel called Lucky ("Lucky he's not in the pot cooking," according to Mondo).

Once Cybill's film career became entwined with director Peter Bogdanovich's, hits were followed by flops, and in a notoriously unforgiving business, she was rapidly branded talentless. Then, in 1978, she sang with a jazz band at the Cookery in Greenwich Village, which she calls the most horrifying experience of her life. At Patty's suggestion, she headed home to lick her wounds. For Cybill, Memphis is a healing, soothing, peaceful place, far removed from Hollywood's "burnout element" and it is where she wants to be buried one day in a plot near her grandfather.

Unflinchingly honest, Cybill has described what came next as a dip into oblivion. With no more magazine covers, she was soon able to go unrecognized at the grocery store. Four years of anonymity later, a less-than-tactful Hollywood agent informed her that she might as well be dead.

Patty, however, does not recall this rough period in her daughter's career. She will admit it irritated and hurt Cybill to be judged a dumb blonde, and she is proud that her daughter did not take those jibes lying down. Certainly, it was a fruitful time in one respect—Patty's granddaughter Clementine was born there in 1980. (Myrtle, who helped Patty with her children when they were young, now works for Cybill.)

These days, when Patty collects Cybill at Memphis airport, she confronts her daughter's fame head-on via a host of ever-present autograph hunters. Yet, she says, Cybill's life has not changed, any more than her own has. "She goes to the grocery store and does about anything she wants to do," says Patty. "I don't put her in the same category with Candice Bergen or Cher or any of those, but I guess she is. It's hard for me to believe."

She is hard-pressed to isolate a special highlight since her daughter became a star. "It's all been a highlight, I'm just very proud of her. I wish I wouldn't sound so sweet. I say what I think, but I just can't say anything else!"

Patty does not subscribe to the theory that it is uncool to react to seeing stars—when she spotted George Burns in a Beverly Hills restaurant, she could not wait to telephone everyone back in

Memphis. She is still unashamedly star struck; she imagines she always will be.

The same cannot be said of Eva Jagger, who managed to sit alongside Faye Dunaway at one celebrity event without even recognizing her world-famous face. "I just treat them like everybody else. I like meeting them, but I don't kneel at their feet," she explains.

Eva Scutts was born in Australia in 1913. She spent the first four years of her life in the suburbs of Sydney—her father was employed as a boat-builder in the Harbor. Eva was part of a six-generational run of Scuttses who had left England for Australia. There are still Scuttses and their kin scattered between the antipodes and the English suburb of Dartford, Kent. Eva's mother (one of thirteen children) initiated the return to England; she was homesick and the excessive heat of Australia's clime did not suit her.

Eva's entire family loved music and possessed fine, if amateur, voices. She herself was partial to Bing Crosby, and savored the dance music she heard on the radio and the jazz she found by tuning in to the more avant-garde Radio Luxembourg. Eva's eldest brother had an extensive record collection encompassing light music and musicals, and bought a second-hand piano. Eva took lessons, but grew bored after four years. She did better than Mick, who was not remotely interested in lessons when they were offered. This did not stop him from chastising his mother later. "He said, 'Why didn't you make me learn the piano?' And I think, God—I did *try!*" Eva clearly remembers Mick and his younger brother Chris gathered around the piano with the family, thoroughly enjoying their Christmas sing-alongs.

As a small girl, Eva and her brothers were often taken by train up to London, forty minutes away, to a show at the Palladium or a performance of *Cinderella* at the London Coliseum. Eva's mother sang Gilbert and Sullivan (word-perfectly) around the house. Eva lined up to see the films of the day and was especially partial to Tom Mix. "I never wanted to be a film star, but I suppose we all had a yen for that sort of thing. We had our idols in the films, just as the kids have their idols in pop stars. *I* did. Clark Gable—I could go on forever." She danced in school displays, took part in country dancing in the Vicarage garden, and at a very early age mastered ballroom dancing, which she loves to this day. "I still go, but not often, because I haven't got the energy I used to have."

Eva bought Mick a record player for one birthday and remembers him bringing a guitar home from a holiday in Spain. He loved Latin American rhythms and, undeterred by the fact that he did not speak the lingo, accompanied the songs on the radio on his guitar, adding his improvised Spanish-inflected noises. Little did the Jaggers know that their son's burgeoning vocalizing would soon have the bulk of their generation groaning and up in arms.

With the possible exception of its volume (which as she sensibly points out, is easily regulated by the turn of a knob), Eva is a staunch supporter of pop and defended the Stones' music to those who decried it. After all, her own youthful tastes had been derided. When she was a twenty-one-year-old hairdresser, her middle-aged employer said of her beloved Bing Crosby: "That's not music! You don't call that singing!" "You see? The same thing!" she exclaims.

Eva soon witnessed firsthand the excitement the Stones could generate—she was in the audience at their first concert. Not so thrilling was the bombshell Mick dropped immediately afterward. After two years of working toward a degree in business, he was leaving the London School of Economics.

"I was, well, not shattered . . . but I was a bit worried. I knew that my husband would be upset. He'd worry whether you could make a living. Nobody in their wildest dreams could anticipate or foresee what would happen, but as it happened Mick had the right idea," she says with masterful understatement. "We had confidence in him, we were just concerned. We knew he was levelheaded and it was his life anyway. You take it as it comes, don't you? You don't think, 'Oh, he's going to be a star.' You're only too pleased that they're making a go of it."

The father Mick once described as "bloody awful, he was so disciplinarian" gave Mick his first sampling of the limelight. Joe was considered the foremost British authority on American basketball. He published a book on the subject in 1962, lectured in

American universities, and lectured teachers in physical education at Strawberry Hill College, Twickenham, which is just outside London. Joe Jagger also imbued Mick with his competitive edge and brought him up to be success- and goal-oriented—atypical for a British boy.

Mick was something of an elitist at Dartford Grammar School as the only pupil to sport real basketball shoes. When Joe worked as an advisor for the British TV program "Seeing Sport," he took Mick along to demonstrate some of the activities for the benefit of the cameras. Perhaps the seeds were sown? In any event, Eva believes her husband definitely was a tremendous influence on Mick (who runs about five miles on stage during the average concert) in the arena of fitness. Like his father, Mick enjoys American football, soccer, and cricket, and together they have an interest in a gymnastics club.

Mick and Chris's relationship, while good now, came under typical adolescent strain when the Stones were starting out. Mick did not want to be bothered with his considerably younger brother who was aching to be included, and the playful Chris teased Mick relentlessly. The four-year age gap was at its widest. "They'd go into their bedrooms and Chris would keep on going in when he [Mick] was getting dressed. They used to have little fights. A lot of it was in fun."

Chris spent four years tucked away in the seclusion of boarding school while the Rolling Stones were off taking the world by storm. Mick was having all the fun, and then some. It was a time of trial for Chris, whose strong personality was inevitably overshadowed by "MICK." All Chris's schoolmates succumbed to their overwhelming curiosity about his infamous brother, which Eva concedes was natural. "It was exciting for them, I suppose, to know Mick Jagger's brother." On one hand, Chris was very proud and loved all the fuss. On the other, as a talented singer and musician who plays guitar and flute, he needed to be known for himself too.

"He didn't want them to keep on about it *all* the time," Eva explains. "I suppose they didn't realize that they were perhaps overdoing it a bit. It's a pity really, you see? And it's nobody's fault. It's not Mick's fault, it's not Chris's fault, but you just live in the shadows of somebody like that. I wish Chris had wanted to do something entirely different. He's not unhappy. But it hasn't been easy for him, we all realize that."

According to his mom, Mick has not fallen prey to the danger he views as inherent in success. "He's himself really. He doesn't try to be what he isn't, does he? I don't think so. He puts on a front, or he used to. In the early days he had to. He hid, not so much behind a facade, but he had to get a bit of rhino skin. He was so vulnerable, and you had to put on this hard front because people were so rude."

She does not think it would have been normal had it not gone to his head a touch in the earliest pioneer days, but insists he was never a big-head. "Not in my eyes. He's coped very well. He's level-headed, he's got a good business head. L.S.E. stood him in good stead anyway. He's not just playing music, he loves the business side of it."

Eva Jagger is a veteran of the press wars, but she had rather let her guard down when in 1986 Britain's less-than-reliable tabloids printed that a neighbor of Eva's said Eva was angry with Mick for not marrying Jerry Hall, the mother of his two children.

"It was such utter rubbish. It was on the radio that I was disgusted with him, they used such strong words. I joked about it afterwards; you either have to laugh or you would cry, let's face it. To say he should marry her because she's given me two lovely grandchildren? Well, blimey, I've got seven! I'm not going to jump over the moon. They're all lovely. I would never say a thing like that. I'm not the type, I don't express myself in that manner." Her anger was not because she was concerned about what Mick would think. "No, no, Mick would treat it as rubbish. If I thought he believed that! I was more upset because it cast a slur on my neighbors and they were all very irate. If people believe it, they immediately think, 'What a mother he's got!' People do believe a lot of rubbish."

For all her complaints of constant phone calls when any snippet of news about Mick breaks, one senses she rather enjoys it all and fields the queries like a local p.r. office, adroitly pulling the legs of journalists whenever possible.

Eva believes that the less she knows about Mick's activities, the better. At least until the last minute. Then, if she is quizzed about a christening, for instance, "at least I don't have to tell any fibs. I say, 'Well, even if I did know, do you think I'd tell you?' All these people ring up wanting to know every little detail, and I think, gosh, can't they have a private life for once? Well, this is fame, you see. You're not allowed a private life."

She remembers the notorious WOULD YOU LET YOUR DAUGHTER MARRY A ROLLING STONE? headline only too clearly. "Who cares whether they wanted their daughters to marry a Rolling Stone?" she laughs. "I don't suppose he'd ask any of those mothers for their daughters!" Then more seriously she admits, "That was very upsetting. You felt very vulnerable then, because it was the very early days and they got so much flak from the press. Mind you, this was Andrew Oldham (their manager). He built them up as images. They didn't do half the things they were supposed to have done, but it was good for business and the Stones played up to it. But when you're on the other side, you pick up a paper, you read all these things, it's pretty upsetting sometimes when it's aimed at you.

"You're a little bit on the defensive, because you don't quite know what people are thinking of you. It isn't that you're ashamed of your son. You think people might believe that about him; it's hurtful, really." Whenever there was a barrage of negative publicity, she just wanted to keep a low profile. Not that anyone ran Mick down to Eva. All her old friends, the people she had known all her life, seemed only happy that Mick had made it.

She prefers to cooperate with photographers if asked; the results are better. "I think, 'Well, they've got a job to do.' I'd rather have a decent photograph in the paper than a terrible one. Then you see it in the paper and you think, 'Oh, my God, why didn't I smile?' As you get older, you hate it."

She was less happy all those years ago when photographers hounded her and her husband after Mick and Bianca had left their little daughter, Jade, in their care at his country house, "Stargroves." At those moments Eva was actually afraid of cameras, the threat of a kidnap attempt always a fear to be reckoned with. "We didn't want any photographs taken for obvious reasons, we were sort of bobbing down trying not to be seen. I don't know how these people found us; I think so-called friends sold the information—nobody should have known that I had Jade there. It was really awful, watching [us] in the house, that wasn't very nice." Nor did she look kindly upon a critical headline during Mick's absence that labeled Jade POOR LITTLE RICH GIRL, as if she were being neglected.

Eva is far more philosophical now, but in the Mick-and-Bianca days, one columnist so incensed her that she says, "I've never wanted to punch anybody on the nose, but if ever I'd met that woman, I don't think I could have stopped myself. She really was so bitchy. I really was upset. I've never really forgotten it."

12 Negative Reinforcement: Weathering Its Storm

"Tell a Cockney he's no good, and he'll dedicate his life to proving otherwise." The observation by Michael Caine, who experienced the phenomenon firsthand with his father, might be overly narrow geographically, but the sentiment is pertinent. While Mother and Father's influence is monumental, it is not always positive input which propels stars forward—negativity, obstruction, or just plain old discouragement can also fire the determination to succeed. An angry child can possess a fierce drive to overcome even seemingly overwhelming odds.

Debra Winger made it to the top with these words from her Hungarian-Jewish parents, Ruth and Robert Winger, ringing in her ears: "You can't be a movie star. Movie stars are beautiful." Their damning verdict was confirmed by director George Cukor, a customer of Daddy's burglar-alarm business. With her walk and her looks, an actress? Never. Ruth Winger chose to name her daughter Mary Debra, with a nod to 1950s star Debra Padget, but she provided no overt encouragement for the career Debra set her heart on when she was six years old and the Wingers shuttled from Cleveland and the family's kosher meat-packing business to the palm tree—lined home of the movie-making industry.

A lesser spirit than Debra's might have been castrated by those preprofessional reviews, but a seemingly undaunted Debra went on to corner the market in screen sensuality—her nonglamorous look finally crashing through the parameters traditionally defining screen sex symbols, and making them seem ridiculously superficial.

None of the steam went out of her dream, any more than Barbra Streisand was deterred by the double-dose of negative input she received on the homefront. Barbra simply rose phoenix-like above both mother Diana's opinion that she was not pretty enough to make it as an actress, and stepfather Louis Kind's crushingly cruel assessment of her and her pretty half-sister Roslyn as "The Beauty and The Beast."

Barbra always possessed a sense that she was "chosen"—but juxtaposed with a conflicting view of herself as a lonely misfit with slightly crossed eyes, a long nose, and a mild case of acne. She was a target for childish cruelty by the time she was nine, and for reasons she never quite understood, neighborhood girls ganged up on her, poking fun until she ran off in tears.

Realistically, Diana Kind—who is anyway a cautious woman by nature—was justified in her reservations. The screen was full of young beauties and protective Mama did not think Barbra stood a chance, so she tried hard to sway her into the more practical and secure world of clerical work, with its pension prospects and paid vacations.

Clearly Barbra's reservoir of strength and determination was enormous. She was able to capitalize on devastating negative input and literally transform it into positive drive. If she once was bitter about her mother, she is not now willing to bite the hand that inadvertently fed her ambition, although she admits that she used to resent her for not encouraging her acting. But she told Lawrence Grobel of *Playboy* that she loves her mother, saying, "In a sense, she's probably responsible for my success. Because I was always trying to prove to her that I was worthwhile, that I wasn't just a skinny little marink."

Throughout her career, Barbra has received plenty of similarly negative input from other quarters to keep her ambition pumping, like suggestions that she should fix her nose or change her name. In later years, as Barbra wrestled with her decision to make the film *Yentl*, she told a *People* magazine reporter, "I needed a direct challenge. Somebody like my mother to tell me I couldn't do it. Then I'd get mad and do it." In the case of *Yentl*, her then-lover Jon Peters got her fired up by telling her she would never make the film.

The I'll-show-you! syndrome is, according to Dr. R. Barkley

Clark, the most adaptive outcome for which one could hope in this kind of situation, a positive release for the deep resentment and anger which is inevitably harbored by any child exposed to destructive criticism.

Why should one child be resilient enough to bounce back from all this negativity and even gain momentum on the rebound, while another, equally gifted, caves in under the weight of negative input? Other key figures in their lives might be the key to why they prevail. A close, positive, and reinforcing relationship with a grandparent, aunt, uncle, sibling, neighbor, or teacher can bolster a child's internal strength, become a psychological lifeline, and effectively compensate. And even children who have grown up in very pathologic situations can be extremely astute when it comes to identifying someone healthy and latching onto them, says Dr. Clark. Carol Burnett had her grandmother to spur her on. For Tina Turner, it was her cousin Margaret, only three years her senior; to Tina she was "God-sent," her only real friend and her first teacher.

Intelligence is another factor which sorts the sinkers from the swimmers. Genetic heredity, biological differences between similarly situated children, also affects their ability to surmount obstacles and to emerge from traumatic environments, if not unscathed, then functioning. Psychiatry is barely scratching the surface of understanding such internal constitutional traits, but Dr. Clark believes, "Intelligence is certainly a good prognostic sign. People can better conceptualize the life that they have been through, and separate themselves more easily from the experiences that they have had, if they have a higher level of abstracting ability."

Barbra Streisand's intellectual legacy is impressive. Diana Kind, herself one of four children of a cantor, describes Barbra's late father as "that beautiful, educated man, Emmanuel Streisand." He died in August 1943 at the tragically early age of thirty-five, when Barbra was just fifteen months old. Mr. Streisand (as Diana often formally refers to him) had a master's degree in education from Columbia University, and a Ph.D.; taught English and psychology; and wrote two doctoral dissertations. The son of an immigrant fishmonger who owned a store in Brooklyn, Streisand was a teacher respected for his ability to coerce reluctant pupils into school. During the Depression he also spent two and a half years as superintendent of schools at Elmira Reformatory, where he taught English to prisoners.

Emmanuel, Diana, their nine-year-old son, Sheldon, and baby Barbra were all vacationing in the Catskill Mountains resort town of Fleischmann, New York, when he died. Diana was initially reluctant to make the trip, but her country-loving husband was an executive helper for a children's summer camp. She was daunted by the prospect of the long train ride, and besides, she preferred her own home cooking. "I don't know, something within me was nervous," she says. She is not suggesting she had a premonition; rather she admits to being high-strung, a habitual worrier. That summer was particularly hot, and one afternoon Emmanuel Streisand, who was prone to migraines, felt unwell, lay down to rest, and fell into a deep sleep. Diana paced nervously in their room, holding Barbra in her arms: "It was a frightening situation being so far away from home."

Her beloved husband of thirteen years died within twenty-four hours of being admitted to the local hospital, without regaining consciousness. Diana went into deep shock, so stunned and un-comprehending that she could not scream, cry, or even speak and felt as if her throat were physically blocked. "And such a healthy, strapping man, an athlete . . . had everything to look forward to, a bright future," she says now, shaking her head, her face still registering disbelief.

The cause of death was apparently respiratory failure, probably precipitated by an adverse reaction to morphine, with which a doctor had injected him to halt an epileptic seizure. Diana was and is evasively foggy on this issue, probably more from embarrassment than confusion, and an understandable but now redundant residue from the unenlightened times when epilepsy carried a stigma. Diana discouraged her children from quizzing her on their father's death, which Barbra and Sheldon for years believed was caused by a cerebral hemorrhage brought on by overwork. The truth, when it finally came out, relieved their profound fears that they might meet the same end should they work too hard.

Emmanuel Streisand was an observant Jew who would walk

miles rather than ride on the Sabbath. He was a scholar, but was also, his devoted wife says, charming, handsome, humorous, sporty, and strong. He worked as a lifeguard to support his studies, dreamed of going to California, and thought longingly of becoming a writer. Diana did not tell Barbra any of that, or that she had inherited his solid build . . . and his interest in drama. Diana rarely spoke of him to Barbra at all, or told her how much he had loved her. She kept her fond memories to herself, fearful that sharing them with Barbra would stir up too many emotions and just make her miss him more. Intimate communication was minimal.

"Emotionally my mother left me at the same time—she was in her own trauma," Barbra told *People* magazine in 1981. Diana did indeed take the loss of her husband desperately hard and was only pulled from her tearful misery by the inescapable reality of caring for her children. She faced serious practical problems: her young husband had left her only with a minimal pension, and Diana had been out of the work force throughout the thirteen years of her marriage.

Distraught and desperate, she squeezed into her parents' three-room apartment with Barbra and Sheldon, where she had to share a bed with her baby. Seen through Sheldon's eyes, his grandparents were good, hardworking folk, but their home lacked love and discipline was stringent. Understandably, Diana, who was frequently exhausted when she came home from work, viewed the situation rather differently. Her parents were her salvation; how could she have managed without their help? And of course, some generational tensions were inevitable. Diana remembers Sheldon's youthful interest in Indian lore and speaks proudly of his skill in fashioning moccasins, chieftain headdresses, and breast-plates from feathers, beads, leather, claws, and bones—but the feathers aggravated Diana's mother's asthma.

Diana was a perennially anxious parent, and in little Barbra she had an active, curious, and adventurous handful. One day, en route to work, something compelled Diana to pop back to the house, where she discovered her mother engrossed in the kitchen, oblivious to the fact that her two-year-old charge was perched very precariously on a chair she had somehow dragged alongside a dresser, and was busily smearing her grandmother's lipstick all over her face with her favorite piece of blanket.

At age five, an already imaginative Barbra dressed up in her brother's knickers and suspenders and hid beneath the big dining room table, playing at being George Washington. Around the same time, she began singing in the hallways of her apartment building; discerningly, she opined that she liked the resonance it gave her voice. Concerned that Barbra did not eat enough, Diana switched to a job nearer the school just so she could check up on her daughter's lunch consumption. Dancing lessons inspired more anxiety. "I was afraid that this would hurt her legs. And was I happy when this instructor moved away after six months! She wanted everything: she had a high hat, a stick, was trying toe dancing. I did not like to see all this."

Barbra's determination was evident from the time she was very young. She once insisted upon singing in an evening performance at an auditorium, never mind the fact that she had spent the day in bed, suffering with a raging sore throat: "I couldn't believe this kid!" says Diana, with obvious pride. She withheld comparable praise from her children, clinging stalwartly to the belief it might make them develop "blown-up egos."

Barbra's relationship with her stepfather, Louis Kind, seemed destined for trouble from the beginning, when he and her mother visited her at Hebrew summer camp prior to their wedding and Barbra then refused to let them leave without her, a whiny stance that can hardly have endeared her to him. While admitting she might well have been obnoxious, she also claims her stepfather hated her—even Diana described him as allergic to kids. In 1953, Louis Kind abandoned Diana, Sheldon, Barbra, and his own daughter, Roslyn, disappearing after going to get the proverbial pack of cigarettes. His departure was no great loss to Barbra, whom he hardly championed, any more than his presence had lessened her perception of herself as a victim because her daddy died when she was fifteen months old. She was angry both at having been "abandoned" by her father and at not having a daddy to call her own—a combination which led to her refusal to become friendly with any child luckier than she.

By the time she was nine, Barbra was harmonizing with neighbors on the stoop of her Brooklyn home. Diana, who always discouraged the acting ideas, saw potential in Barbra's voice and at various times took her to audition at MGM and the Steve Allen Studios, where her singing earned raves but, to Diana's annoyance, no rewards. "When they said, 'No pay,' I said, 'No child.' "

Barbra has described her mother as being a beautiful light soprano, and believes that underneath, she wanted to be a singer herself but was too shy to pursue it. Diana insists she did not hanker after show business and has no regrets. She has intimated she had a few dreams of her own, but unlike Barbra, she never had any intention of turning them into reality. Her aim in life was to have a husband she could revere, and in Emmanuel Streisand, she found fulfillment and did just that.

At fifty, however, Diana did take one uncustomarily competitive step, going back to college to prepare for a test she had to take for a job she wanted as school secretary. Despite delays caused by her various irksome health troubles, Diana became one of eleven hundred to pass, out of four thousand students. "Was I happy! Was I nervous!" she says, obviously thrilled with her accomplishment.

Barbra had been a cute "Gerber-picture baby" who friends even suggested Diana put in commercials—an idea of which she did not approve. But her beautiful baby seemed headed for a troubled adolescence.

"She was not happy, she was not a good-looking girl," Diana Kind recalls. "I guess she thought that it meant so much, you know? It might mean so much sometimes when you meet a guy, until they get to know who you are. But in show business at that time, there were very pretty girls around. And I thought, really, she is taking a big chance." Barbra hankered after looking like Catherine Deneuve, but even once she could afford it, she did not indulge in the cosmetic surgery fad that had been prevalent among the Jewish girls at Erasmus Hall High School. "She would not do her nose. She was afraid to. They said it would change her voice," her mother explains.

For years, Barbra was driven to unhappy distraction by noises in her ears, but she kept her problem to herself, preferring to withdraw into her own world than to share her troubles with her mom. Barbra, at various times, suffered chest pains, feared she had cancer, and had a morbid preoccupation with death. Her secretiveness had much to do with the fact that in her heart, she did not want to be any more abnormal than she already believed herself to be.

Since Diana was poor and it was impossible for Barbra to emulate the more privileged Long Island girls she so envied, she defiantly intensified her misfit status, painting her face with her mother's violet lipstick, bleaching the top of her hair blonde (with tinges of blue and green), and clothing her skinny body in long, droopy dresses purchased from thrift shops. Diana went to great lengths to select department store dresses for her daughter, but Barbra rejected her choices outright. She always felt out of place, and success did not change that.

On a country vacation, thirteen-year-old Barbra was invited to sing one night to entertain the hotel guests. For the first time, Diana, who would tell Barbra her voice was too weak, watched her captivate total strangers and bask in their applause. Yet Barbra's ambitions remained firmly focused on acting, not singing, and her mother was reluctant, to put it mildly, when at fifteen, Barbra begged to be allowed to attend a summer workshop at the Malden Bridge Playhouse in the Adirondacks.

Not for the first time, Barbra managed to wear down Diana's resolve. "Oh, she couldn't stand me saying no to her. But I had to sometimes," says Diana who, in exasperation, paid the three-hundred-dollar fee. (Cunningly, Barbra pretended to be seventeen to gain admittance.) Diana attributes much of her poor health that summer to her worrying about Barbra, particularly after she received a letter informing her that the camp's cook had left.

"Can you imagine how I felt hearing such news, when what she needed most was good food and rest to go on with her studies in the fall?" Diana exclaims, her horrified reaction seeming more fitting to a national disaster. "Well, she finally got home and I thought she was cured of her acting ideas, but no way."

Barbra graduated high school in 1959 and, while she was still eighteen, won a monumental fifty dollars warbling her way through an "amateur night" contest at The Lion in Greenwich

Village. Still, Diana hammered at her burgeoning confidence. According to Shaun Considine's book, *Barbra Streisand: The Woman, The Myth, The Music,* Barbra had her mother attend a 1960 workshop, hoping at least for some praise or reinforcement. Instead, Diana informed her that she was kidding herself. Barbra did not break down, but stood her ground and told her mother she was wrong.

Once liberated from school, Barbra moved swiftly to a shared apartment in Manhattan. It was a wrench for Diana, although she now admires her for tenaciously following her dreams. The move saved Barbra the tiresome train commute to Greenwich Village (where she was singing regularly), and Diana the anxious waits for her safe return to Brooklyn each night.

A new set of worries replaced Diana's old ones: where was Barbra, who was she with, what was she doing? Diana and Roslyn visited Barbra in her new home and they had family sing-alongs. Diana (who in 1974 moved to California to be near Barbra and Roslyn) observed then, as she would observe again years later, on seeing Barbra perform in concert: "Many songs that I sang in my earlier years as a single girl were now chosen by Barbra for her to sing. I wondered about the fact how our genes must have crossed."

Barbra's triumphant Broadway run in *Funny Girl* did little to alleviate Diana's concern for her welfare; no one could accuse her of not caring. She was determined Barbra would get enough nourishment to sustain her through her grueling schedule and regularly left her job in Brooklyn in midafternoon and rode the train to Manhattan, clutching a packed lunch for Barbra (typically chicken soup with chicken and dessert), climbing the back theater stairs and delivering it to her dressing room.

"*I* was even embarrassed," Diana admits. "Finally, Barbra really got embarrassed and told me not to do that anymore, because she would send out for Chinese food, which she loved."

Funny Girl was a highlight for Mom, who sat in the audience many times, chuckling to herself at her secret: little did all those people sitting around her, lavishing praise on Barbra, dream that they were sitting beside her mother! It was her proudest time in all of Barbra's success, because she was right there in the thick of the excitement and still involved in her life.

"That was really—I could never announce it as I could feel it—as though my chest was hurting," she says, somehow making joy, too, sound like a health worry. She agrees she would have probably felt much better had she yelled and screamed like Georgia Holt who, in a similarly overwhelmed state watching Cher in Las Vegas, let rip with a loud rebel cry.

Seeing how driven Barbra was to succeed in show business, her mother eventually concluded that it was in her blood, heredity. Barbra's preoccupation with her lack of a father did not diminish with the years, she even fantasized about converting to Catholicism because a father was part of the package, and eventually that compelling need drove her to make *Yentl*. "Also an obsession," admits Diana, who will turn eighty in 1988, noting, "She never really talked about it till she was ready to film. And I didn't even know that it was bothering her that much."

For Barbra, Emmanuel Streisand was an enigma. For Diana, he was the source of a wealth of happy memories, from their first meeting ("Love at first sight, oh boy"), at the home of a girlfriend, onwards. Their budding romance ended abruptly after twelve months. Somehow they missed a rendezvous and neither telephoned the other. Diana's philosophy was, "If he likes me enough, he'll call me." In fact, she waited a year for that phone call, which came, blessedly, while she was otherwise engaged at a Sunday afternoon movie. She was excited to get the message, but sore enough not to call him back. Lo and behold, who should she bump into at the trolley car station? "It was Manny. I was dumbfounded. If that wasn't an act of God, nothing else was," she says with a smile. He had been preoccupied with his studies, but promised to contact Diana after his exams. They married a year later, when she was twenty-one.

Diana was very proud of Barbra's mammoth personal achievement with *Yentl* but envisioned a different ending. Barbra told Wayne Warga of *McCall's* magazine, "She said, 'When you dedicate the film to your father, you should also dedicate the film to your mother!' She was in there pitching right to the end. I said, 'Ma, I'll do another movie about mothers. I'll dedicate that to you.'"

Casting back to the notes she had prepared for the interview, Diana reads, "To sum all this up, she did not go to college, but pursued her career working very hard. But I did my duty and remained a typical Jewish mother, following her dreams all the way. I still do it with Roslyn."

Diana Kind was certainly not alone in discouraging her daughter. Mabel and John Johnson did all they could to discourage Diahann Carroll from going into show business, envisioning a more academic life for her, to capitalize on her above-average intelligence and educational opportunities. Charlotte Sheedy tried hard to discourage Ally; she readily admits it was a blow learning that her firstborn had set her sights on acting.

Charlotte is a literary agent who operates out of her home, so Ally grew up steeped in a literary atmosphere. Charlotte had been convinced Ally would follow her into the field, and with good reason. Ally wrote impressive poetry from the age of seven (at school she was once falsely accused of plagiarism, her imagery was so sophisticated), and at twelve she had a foothold in the publishing world with her first book, *She Was Nice to Mice*. When Ally was offered an acting management contract, Charlotte refused to sign it. Hadn't Charlotte always said you should love what you do, Ally asked? Why did she imagine Ally's values would be corrupted by acting? Weren't they already formed, and weren't they Charlotte's? The steam effectively taken out of her arguments, Charlotte agreed.

But she resisted again when Ally choose to go to USC, urging her to opt for an academic program on the East Coast instead. Charlotte confesses she still clung to the belief that Ally would become a writer once she had the acting foolishness out of her system. Ally pointed out that failure was not inevitable. "I said, 'I know, but a million kids go to Hollywood, Ally. It's so hard. Nobody makes it. And anyway, even if you get a few jobs, it's a dreadfully difficult life.' She looked at me and she said, 'Why is being an actor more difficult than being a writer? I see your writers in here all the time. They're despondent, they've been rejected, they have no money. It's a terrible life. So why do you think that is better than doing what I want to do?' And I didn't feel that I could argue against it."

A writer friend quizzed Charlotte on her motives for pushing Ally so hard toward writing. "I said, 'You're right, I know I've been wrong.' She said, 'Let her be. Let her find her own way.' It was an epiphany for me, because I didn't realize that I was trying to direct her life in a kind of way. Maybe it's that I wanted to be a writer, and I have great respect for writers."

Some stars' parents were not so much negative in their input as cold, distant, or elusive. If Mom or Dad withholds approval, warmth, and even just the occasional pat on the head, the battle to change that can become the prime driving force in a child's life. Even if Mom is positive and encouraging, if Dad is cold and undemonstrative, as was often the case in our research, Mom's input seems overshadowed by Dad's. Or vice versa—but cold, withholding mothers are a much rarer commodity.

Cold or undemonstrative dads influenced Candy Bergen, Jane Fonda, Bing Crosby, Burt Reynolds, Bette Midler, and the Wilson brothers of the Beach Boys. Paul Newman never found the approval he sought from his father; Robert Blake had cold parents and felt unloved. Discouraged in their endeavors by at least one parent were Woody Allen, Richard Pryor, Joan Crawford, Margot Kidder, Liberace, Ed Asner, and Katharine Hepburn. Humphrey Bogart's parents were also cold and critical.

Paul Newman's decision not to enter the family sporting goods business after graduation met with a lukewarm reception at home; even less popular was his wish to go into theater, a move his father felt would lead nowhere, in a field for which he had no respect. Paul felt no attraction to the retail business, however. He was desperately keen to play football (which would no doubt have pleased Dad) but in the ninth grade he was a weedy five-foot-three and a featherweight ninety-eight pounds, which left him with the intolerable option of playing amidst sixth-graders.

When pressed by writer Aaron Latham, the chronically reticent Newman admitted, "I guess I'm my father's boy." His father's death in 1950 at age fifty-seven came amidst this dispute over Paul's future. After his father had gone, Paul did make a valiant effort to step into his shoes in their business, but was rapidly disenchanted and reverted to his original plan.

"That's one of my great sadnesses, actually," Newman told Latham of his father's untimely death. How much more gratifying it would have been if he had stuck around long enough to see that his son did okay as an actor. It is also interesting to note that in later years Newman's passion for acting subsided, shunted aside to permit him expression of his jock ambitions behind the wheel of a racing car. Even more telling, Newman Sr. would surely have been delighted to find the prodigal son come home to retailing, with his highly successful salad dressing and spaghetti sauce operations. Still trying to please Daddy? Still hoping to find that approval?

13 Stage Mothers: An Extinct Species?

There are no Stage Mothers. By contrast, there is an ample supply of those who have heroically survived encounters with Stage Mothers, heard monstrous tales about Stage Mothers, determined never to become Stage Mothers, or taken a mighty, sneering dislike to Stage Mothers.

Hedda Hopper, the legendary gossip columnist, expressed her less-than-complimentary sentiments in this fashion: "I used to wonder if there wasn't a sub-human species of womankind that bred children for the sole purpose of dragging them to Hollywood."

Don Schwartz, a Hollywood agent and acting coach, once encouraged his young charges to air their complaints, listened carefully, then urged them to kick their mothers in the shins and caution them against ever again behaving like Stage Mothers. That his suggestion was made in jest did not stop a little optimistic fantasizing afterwards: "Maybe some of them really *did* kick their mothers. So what? Why shouldn't they? Stage mothers are the worst animals alive. If they kick them, more power to them."

There it is. Image-wise, the Stage Mother falls somewhere in the abyss with the Wicked Stepmother. As a consequence of that connotation it comes as no great shock to learn that there is a dearth—make that an absence—of candidates willing to step forward and own up to being Stage Mothers.

Elizabeth Taylor's mother, Sara, says: "I had a horror of being thought a Stage Mother. I don't approve of Stage Mothers. I don't approve of drilling children like you would a racehorse."

So, the definition of a Stage Mother used here requires that the slate be wiped clean. Inclusion in this category is not a criticism or judgment—innocent until proven guilty, remember? The definition of a Stage Mother is simply this: a mother who actively pursued work on behalf of her underage offspring, or a mother who chose not to refuse a bite at the juicy apple when it presented itself, all rosy and ripe. A Stage Mother is merely a stage mother.

It would be unfair to discount the fact that some of these women were deserted, divorced, or widowed and literally struggling single-handedly to fill the lunchboxes. Necessity forced Lillian Gish's mother into the Hollywood arena. Who in all honesty could blame her or the many others like her? What more could a mother do for her child's future than to secure it financially? And if, in the process, she fulfilled some unresolved desire or realized a dream of her own, placated a dissatisfied ego, then so be it. It is not entry into the field of stage motherhood which should draw fire, but how individual members conduct themselves once admitted.

Naturally, not all stage mothers' motives are selflessly pure. Greed and gross manipulation did flourish, especially in Hollywood's early "golden" days. It is precisely because some of the brightest stars of yesterday were exploited dreadfully and did indeed possess those monstrous mothers—Judy Garland, Betty Grable, Shirley Temple—that the stigma exists. But let us not forget that some stage mothers were merely determined, enterprising, and ambitious.

One would have to say that the mothers of Bing Crosby, Bette Davis, Fay Wray, and a whole host of others chased stardom for their children quite unabashedly. Fred Astaire was performing in vaudeville at age five, his and his sister Adele's talent already sufficiently striking to have prompted their mother to take them from Nebraska to New York for training.

Bette Davis's mother, Ruthie, and Ginger Rogers' mother, Lela, have frequently been labeled stage mothers in the derogatory sense. They were indeed strong women, but stage mothers? Not according to Bette and Ginger. Both stars dreamed of success just as fiercely as their mothers did and neither began working until they were old enough to say no.

Divorced from Ginger's father when her daughter was tiny, Lela Rogers was engrossed in her own work as a reporter, and during World War I she worked for the Marines. But once it became apparent that her teenage daughter was not to be dissuaded from dancing, Lela flung herself into helping her and then became a motivating force in Ginger's career.

Ginger was infuriated by an article in *Parade* magazine which quoted none other than Bette Davis as saying: "Well, *I* didn't have a stage mother like Ginger Rogers had! Ginger Rogers, Greer Garson, Anita Louise—they had *wild* stage mothers." Indignantly, Ginger has defended Lela (who died in 1977) by saying, "She was wonderful, and it drives me up the wall when they call her a stage mother!"

As with strong mothers, if the measure of the ingredients is right, the stage mother recipe can lead to extraordinary success and no less happiness than usual. But it is interesting to speculate: without their motherly push, their firm guiding hand and tenacity, how different might be the lives of their star children? How many would have chased the pot of gold for themselves?

Natalie Wood's mother, Maria Gurdin, is a petite five feet, a vivacious woman whose physical fragility belies a definite tenacity and strength. Her geometrically shaped cap of dark hair; her bright, hazel eyes; her entire aura would somehow be unmistakably Russian even if her accent were not still heavily laced with the inflections of her native tongue. In fact it has been barely tempered by fifty years in the United States.

Natalie Wood's career was cut tragically short by her death in 1981; nevertheless she appeared in more than fifty films between the ages of five and forty-three—a glorious record in which Maria Gurdin's role cannot be underestimated. Her canny determination surfaced immediately when her five-year-old daughter was spotted on the street in Santa Rosa, California, by director Irving Pichel; given a small part in his film *Happy Land,* starring Don Ameche; and subsequently invited to Hollywood for a screen test.

Maria chose not to tell her husband. Why invite trouble? Instinctively, she knew that conservative Nicholas Gurdin would never give the adventure his blessing; he viewed acting and dancing as occupations for females barely a step above prostitution.

Maria knew better. She sensed a chance in a lifetime and, concocting an alibi for their absence, whisked her daughter to Hollywood in secret. Could Maria at that moment conceivably have envisioned quite where that trip would lead them?

Proudly, Maria recalls that despite Natalie's dull, everyday clothes and the elaborate attire of the other aspirants, Natalie shone out from the crowd of hopefuls and won a seven-year studio contract and a part in *Tomorrow Is Forever*, starring Orson Welles. By the time Maria and Natalie returned to Santa Rosa, their future was sealed—one parental signature being sufficient to execute the Universal International contract.

Maria did not hesitate to bear this responsibility alone, although she was a little fearful of the reaction from Nicholas, who was given to spasmodic bouts of drinking, with accompanying rages, and who was already irked to have learned from neighbors that Natalie had appeared as an extra in *Happy Land*.

"Oh boy, did he hit the roof, he didn't want her to be an actress!" recalls Maria, whose ace in the hole was the indisputable financial strain they were facing. Presented with such a potentially beneficial fait accompli, and the pleadings of his adored first daughter, who cried that she *wanted* to be an actress, she *wanted* to be like Sonja Henie and Mary Pickford, how could Nicholas possibly justify resisting? "He loved her so much he couldn't say no to her," Maria explains, with the sure smile of one who had known that all along.

Natalie played piano at age four and was a born entertainer who begged to be allowed to sing and dance for her parents' guests. Making her screen debut, Natalie Wood precociously asked the director, "With tears or without tears?" and had no difficulty whatsoever in conjuring them up as requested to spill over a dropped ice cream.

Hollywood novice or not, Maria Gurdin rapidly revealed herself as an astute businesswoman. Armed with bookkeeping experience acquired while living in China, where her father was a businessman, she was adept at comprehending the zeros on Natalie's contracts. Maria was not remotely intimidated by the idea of Natalie signing a seven-year contract, a commitment to which she knew a young child could not be reasonably held.

When the time was right, she went into action. A casting director planted this seed: since Natalie was so in demand, why not leave the studio and come back later with a higher price on her head? Not an especially sophisticated negotiation strategy, but one Maria embraced with alacrity. She informed the studio: Natalie was tired of acting, Natalie had decided to retire. Her request that the agreement be terminated without animosity was doubtless met because she was expected to run straight back with a change of heart. When the executive she met with casually suggested that they simply tear up the contract, she sweetly demurred: "I said, 'Oh no, that's not businesslike.' He thought I knew nothing about law or anything."

Nor, of course, did he realize that she had deliberately armed herself with both a witness (a friend who purportedly had driven her to the meeting) and a lawyer. He was even less aware that far from retiring Natalie from films, Maria was secretly negotiating a much rosier deal with Twentieth Century–Fox which would be worth roughly double the current contract.

"That was bad of me," Maria says, now fleetingly sheepish about her blatant maneuvering but nevertheless clearly proud of her tactical skill. She did make her peace with the folks at Universal International, who naturally were soon aware of her ploy, because her conscience pricked her somewhat: "I call up, because I thought it was a dirty trick, but we need the money!" All was duly forgiven. Natalie worked for the studio again, on loan from Twentieth Century–Fox.

The reason that Maria felt she had justice on her side was that Natalie Wood, Child Star, aged eight, had become a family industry of sorts by the time her sister Lana was born in 1946. This was inevitable given the logistics of having a child in films. Maria was forced to be Natalie's constant companion at the studios (at one point when Natalie earned $1,000 a week, Maria earned an additional $250 for her duties). Maria was so enmeshed in the demands of Natalie's career that Nicholas was forced to leave his job in the studio special-effects department to care for Lana full-time. They were first-generation immigrants, there were no doting grandparents on hand to help out. A nanny seemed a viable option, until one "almost killed Lana" by feeding her a banana whole instead of mashed, causing the child to choke and turn blue. After that, Nicholas refused to entrust Lana to strangers.

Maria Gurdin is that rare bird who when described as a Stage Mother does not blanch; on the contrary she is proud of her feisty behavior while protecting Natalie's interests, and of once even tackling the mighty Jack Warner head-on to ensure that Natalie got what she wanted.

Maria is adamant about one thing: "I didn't want her money. I was too proud. I came from family with money, and I didn't want it." This was an annual ritual: the Gurdins, who received a small percentage of Natalie's earnings while the rest was saved for her coming of age, sat Natalie down for a talk. "Her father said, 'Natalie, you want to quit acting? There is enough money made for your future. If you want to stop we will be glad.' But she said, 'No, I don't want to quit.' We were never pushy. It was her own will to act."

In 1952, Natalie filmed *The Star* with Bette Davis and was required to plunge into dark, forbidding waters in San Pedro, California. For a young girl who had only recently learned to swim, this was a terrifying prospect; she was convinced that sharks lurked below the surface. If Maria was unaware of it before, she soon realized how scared of water Natalie truly was. She promptly sent her back to her cabin and briefed her to leave the rest to Mom: "Just keep on saying that you were planning to do it, but that your crazy mother won't let you."

Maria duly informed the director, who protested that Natalie had said she *would* jump in. "Only because she was too scared to refuse," Maria countered, ignoring his complaints about rescheduling and lost money, and briskly reminding him that Natalie's contract provided for her to have a body double. (Maria felt completely vindicated when later the champion swimmer who was hired was scared by something in those waters touching her legs.)

To understand Maria Gurdin's apparently fierce, stage motherly ambition, one needs to look back to Tomsk, Siberia, where Maria was born on February 8, 1912, weighing a precariously tiny two pounds, and at what she had endured en route to Hollywood. One needs to consider the suffering and hardships that had befallen her once-wealthy family. They had been forced to leave their homes, possessions, and native land while fleeing the Bolsheviks and the Russian Revolution. Those losses doubtless bore on the hunger with which Maria would view Natalie's opportunities.

Maria's parents had four children apiece from previous marriages and four together: Maria's memories of her spacious home in Siberia are limited, but some images pierce through the mists of time with clarity. Like the large grounds, with an area cordoned off for chickens and turkeys, another for hunting dogs—hunting was her father's passion. Like the three governesses in her parents' employ, the plentiful servants, a nanny assigned to each child. Her respected industrialist father (he owned factories which manufactured ink, candles, and soap) evidently could afford such luxury—then. Maria's mother, also named Maria, hailed from aristocracy and was well acquainted with the royal family (Maria worships their memory to this day).

Maria was around four when warning bells were sounded—their lives were in jeopardy. Immediately, the family and two governesses dressed unobtrusively in peasant ensemble and fled toward China. They left with heavy hearts. One of Maria's half-brothers had been absent, forcing them to leave without him.

Just a few days later they emerged from hiding and returned home, confident that their flight had been premature. They were greeted by a sight which has haunted Maria for over seven decades. Her half-brother was dead, hanged by the neck, right in front of her home. "I was so little and I just loved him so much," she says, wincing. "He always help me out. I saw him hanging there, I started to have convulsions."

To escape the bloodbath that followed the unceremonious deposing of the Czar and Czarina, Nicholas and Alexandra, Maria's family fled once again. They took their servants and minimal possessions—jewelry which could be easily concealed and sold later to raise money. Maria's father steadfastly refused to believe that Communism would take hold of his homeland and in preparation for their eventual return loaded a waterproof metal box with the family valuables—gold, jewelry, their fortune—and buried it, issuing each family member (except Maria, who was too young) a map indicating its location. Maria often wonders what happened to that treasure trove.

When they first arrived in Qiqihar, China, the family stayed in a stylish hotel. Maria remembers sitting on the wooden window seat, dressing two newly unpacked dolls, then gazing out at a sight she recognized. "Oh, my house!" she cried, and began screaming. Fearful that she would have another convulsion, her nanny and governess tried to calm her. But the more she was told that it could not possibly be "her house," the more agitated Maria became. Finally, to pacify her, her mother was given permission by the inhabitant of the house to take Maria upstairs to see "her" room, which she "knew" had angels on the ceiling.

"I run there and there *was* angels on the ceiling," she says excitedly. "How can you explain that? And in our Russian Orthodox religion you're not supposed to believe in reincarnation." This is not the only preternatural experience she describes.

Maria spent the remainder of her childhood in an almost exclusively Russian neighborhood in Harbin, China. There she learned English, French, and Latin, but her mastery of English was hampered by her teacher's thick Russian accent. When she was sixteen, Maria met her first husband, Alexander, and certain that her parents would not allow her to marry this "unsuitable" Armenian, she ran off to marry him and soon became pregnant. Olga, Natalie's little-known half-sister, was born in 1928.

It was Maria and Alexander's dream to emigrate to the United States with their baby daughter, yet when Alexander set sail, it was without Maria, whom the American consulate had determined unhealthily underweight at seventy-five pounds. She was told she would have been denied admission at Ellis Island.

A year later, somewhat fleshed out, Maria was permitted to follow. Out from under the protective wing of family and her Japanese nanny, she felt very much alone, nursing her baby to pacify her on the grueling journey. It began with a convoluted train ride to Korea, she went by boat to Tokyo, another boat to Hawaii (like all passengers, she and Olga slept on mats), then finally on to the land of opportunity.

It was hardly paradise gained, however. Not at first. Alexander met his family, but while en route to the boarding house in San Francisco delivered unpleasant news: "He told me, 'I have a mistress. We Armenians are very passionate, we can't stay whole year without . . . but I still love you.' He was very nice man. And I was like a child, I wouldn't let him touch me! But that was the end. I wouldn't have it."

America did not match up to her romantically dreamy expectations any more than did Alexander. She was aghast that there were no servants, and doubly so when she learned that the three of them would be cloistered in one small room within an already crowded household. To her mind, that was such a disgraceful state of affairs. She concedes that she was terribly spoiled: "They bring me Coca-Cola. I sip, and I spit it out! I said what kind of soft drink is that! It's horrid! Like medication! Oh, the things that I did . . . poor man."

Her rash claim that she would immediately leave her errant husband proved unrealistic. Not only was she unable to cook and ignorant of wifely "duties," she was penniless, barely spoke the language, and possessed no job skills with which she could assert her independence. The inevitable teething problems in this new land were compounded by the crumbling state of her marriage and the pain of losing contact with her family. Unable to write (they had moved to Shanghai and changed names), she could only wait and hope for word from them. She never did learn the fate of one sister.

Maria also had what can only be described as an extraordinary experience, albeit tinged with her own exotic touch of what is clearly a family strain of theatrical flair. Alexander was away at sea when she was admitted to the hospital, hemorrhaging from a tubal pregnancy. Despite emergency surgery and a blood transfusion, her condition worsened, confounding the doctors. Her legs and hands were paralyzed, she was unable to speak, dark circles formed beneath her eyes, and her tongue turned dark blue. Upon his return, Alexander was informed that his wife was deathly ill and would not last the night. "They tell him to pick up the body in the morning!" Maria says dramatically.

Later Maria learned that shortly before she was taken ill, her mother had gone to a service in a Shanghai cathedral; midway through the service, a woman pointed to icons of Jesus and Mary set high on the walls and blackened with age—suddenly, the black had begun to give way to shiny gold. Watching this phenomenon, the entire congregation knelt in reverence. Maria is insistent upon the story's veracity. The icons were then brought down and surrounded with flowers, a few of which were put in little bags and given to each worshiper. Maria's mother mailed her daughter the flowers, and the package arrived the day Alexander was told she was dying.

That night he visited her and, bending over her lifeless body, read out her mother's letter and slipped the flower bag around her neck. Unable to acknowledge it, Maria heard every word.

The next morning, the doctor pronounced Maria dead. Trapped in her paralyzed body, she was ill equipped to argue. Her eyes widen. "They wheeled me into that room where they freeze the dead until the relations come and pick you up, and there was not one box empty so they wheeled me out again. I remember thinking, 'Oh my gosh, I'm glad there's no box, I don't want to go in a box.' Then suddenly I felt warm, right in there—" she pauses to clutch at her throat "—so I start to pray. I say, 'Thank you, God, that I'm dying with these flowers.'" More pragmatically, she bargained, "'If I only can live for Olga, I promise I change.' Because, before I used to go to church to look at the boys, you know? And to look at the girls and think, 'Is my dress better than theirs?'

"Then suddenly I could move my hands, my legs too. Warmth came to my face first. I open my eyes, and I look at an old lady, a nurse, and I start to scream. She fainted! I have a newspaper that says that, but I won't show it to anybody—I look so horrid in the picture. She run out and said, 'She's alive! She's alive!' Imagine, they would have buried me, huh? It was just a miracle."

From that day to this, only the shower has come between Maria and her precious flowers, which she wears along with her cross. Maria gave a fragment of the flowers to Natalie, who put them in a locket she wore constantly. She was not wearing it the day she died.

Maria eventually separated from Alexander and met Natalie and Lana's handsome father, Nicholas Gurdin (then Nicholai Zacharenko), in 1937. Olga's father introduced them; Nicholas, who came from Vladivostok, was a fellow worker on the sugar cane boats.

Natalie was born on July 20, 1938, and Nicholas, who believed he was unable to father children, felt so protective of his newborn daughter that he insisted all visitors to the house wear masks to avoid breathing on her. It was a special, magical time for Maria. Olga's first years, with the trauma of leaving China and Alexander's infidelity, had not been the same. Natalie was special. Special then, special always.

Natalie's fame outlasted her lifetime, but child stars, however kindly treated, can face problems later in life if that fame disappears. In extremis their legacy (besides financial and experiential) is an underdeveloped sense of self. Adult stars are in the driver's seat. Children rarely are; child actors even less so. They inhabit an adult world, and those under contract to a studio, working consistently, are exposed to a less flexible framework.

The power of success is open to abuse not by the child in this instance, but by its guardian. So used do some of these children become to being appendages of their all-important, all-powerful mothers, that they have difficulty later in acting independently, in finding their solo place in the world, their very own identity.

Betty Grable's mother, known as Billie, focused her dreams on becoming an opera singer or actress, until at fifteen she fell in love. She met the man who would become Betty's father, Conn "Bud" Grable, at the St. Louis World's Fair, and three years later, in 1907, she married the twenty-one-year-old ticket taker. He would be her passport to freedom from her loving but confining Quaker family, or so she thought. The reality proved drastically different. Bud's family atmosphere exceeded even the repressive, claustrophobic one of her own.

Against that backdrop, her feelings for her firstborn, Marjorie, were, putting it charitably, unloving. A baby boy followed but died before he was two, a victim of bronchial pneumonia, and little Marjorie could then sense that her family was falling apart.

Billie's third pregnancy was spent in bed due to the recurrence of a mysterious painfully inflamed hip which bothered her periodically. This time the doctor encased her in a leather contraption. She whiled away the long hours absorbed in the escapist fodder of Hollywood fan magazines and scandal sheets. And so, a dream was born. The glamour of Hollywood was far more her style, Billie decided, and that was where she belonged.

Her dream attached itself to her third child. Elizabeth Ruth, otherwise known as Betty Grable. Betty was born December 18, 1916, and as she blossomed into a beauty whose potential was evident, she became increasingly important to Billie Grable.

Discipline was the keynote to Betty Grable's childhood, and Mother's authority absolute. Manipulatively, she twisted the circumstances of her hip ailment, making it seem the result of an accident during her difficult pregnancy, instilling in poor Betty the lasting impression that it was all her fault.

Billie relentlessly pursued show business leads, accosting performers who visited the St. Louis hotel where they lived, insisting that anyone potentially influential watch patiently while Betty demonstrated her routine. It was an excruciating experience for Betty which haunted her always.

The family spent a summer vacation in Hollywood, with the adolescent Betty enrolled in a dance school while Mother surveyed the film studio world. One step closer to her dream, Billie grew more determined and did not hesitate to leave her husband and Marjorie behind when she and Betty returned for an all-out onslaught on Hollywood in 1929.

Before her death, Marjorie told author Spero Pastos, who wrote *Pin-Up: The Tragedy of Betty Grable*: "I get more bitter as the years go by. . . . Take, don't give. And she didn't just leave Conn. She walked out on me, too. She was stagestruck, for cryin' out loud—absolutely stagestruck."

Marjorie already knew that her mother did not love her, but was devastated when she left her behind physically. She entirely concurred with her father's perception of Billie as a woman unable to love: Betty Grable was no more loved than Marjorie. She had become a piece of property, an investment, and her education ceased. Thanks to Betty's natural attributes, her "million-dollar legs," Billie's prayers were answered—for Hollywood success was the god at whose altar she worshiped.

By the time Betty was sixteen she had eleven films tucked under her belt, and circumstances improving accordingly, she and Billie resided at the elite Knickerbocker Hotel. Betty longed for her father and sister and began to see through her mother's false promises of a reunion, but Billie would not be budged from her course. Faced with Betty's increasingly tempestuous behavior, she would simply lock her in her bedroom.

The scene for parents who saw their talented offspring as an easy meal ticket was changed dramatically by Jackie Coogan, who married Betty Grable in 1937. The two had much in common. Coogan, the child star of 1920s films like *Peck's Bad Boy* and *The Kid*, filed suit against his mother, Lillian, and his stepfather/business manager, Arthur Bernstein, for the estimated $4 million fortune he had earned before he came of age—and expected to claim when his father died. Even though in 1923 he had been the recipient of a $500,000 check, a fifty-percent advance of his fee for a film and a staggering amount for the 1920s, while under age, Coogan received a paltry $6.50 a week allowance.

Shockingly, his father's will left everything to Lillian and included no trust fund for Jackie whatsoever, only the provision that the money would revert to Jackie upon his mother's death. Bernstein named Lillian president of Jackie Coogan Productions, Inc., ensuring she had full control of the estate and removing any remaining entitlement Jackie had to the money, even if he lived longer than Lillian.

"No promises were ever made to give him anything," his mother said in her court deposition. By 1935, Coogan's heyday was over; he had no work and no money. The result of the ensuing interfamilial court wrangle was the 1939 Coogan Act, which from that day forward protected child performers by giving courts the power to set aside a percentage of their earnings (often 25 percent to 30 percent) in trust for when they turn eighteen. The fate of the remainder was for the family to decide, but was intended to cover expenses and to compensate for loss of parental income, hiring babysitters for siblings, etc., all of which could prove quite costly, as noted by Maria Gurdin. (For Coogan, it was a hollow victory. He was able to retrieve just $126,000 from Lillian and had to pay five years' legal bills.)

Betty Grable's new status as Mrs. Jackie Coogan did not dent Billie's stage mother persona. Legend had it that Billie was so incensed by the way Paramount Studios later treated Betty that she requested a release from her contract. When it was not immediately forthcoming, she supposedly raised not only her voice but a cane, with which she lashed the desks of the powers-that-be.

Despite acknowledging that she had been tormented and locked up as a child, Betty went on to repeat her mother's treatment on her own two daughters. Betty did not overtly punish her mother—she bought her a house in Beverly Hills and treated her generously monetarily for the rest of her life.

Tellingly, after Betty's death, her daughter Jessie found a note at the bottom of her safety deposit box: *Sorry there's nothing more,* wrote the girl of whom so much had been expected and demanded.

Shirley Temple's career was also propelled by a determined and ambitious mother who did not allow her young daughter a voice in her·life. On Shirley's eighth birthday the enormously bankable curly-head was showered with 135,000 gifts from fans all over the globe. But she was so busy on Hollywood film sets that her massive doll collection remained untouched by little fingers; museumlike, it was eerily preserved in rows on shelves behind glass. Each night the unrelenting Gertrude would make Shirley run through her lines with her. "I soon learned not to let my affections make me too lenient," she said.

Gertrude even tried to ossify her money-making daughter in her preadolescent prime, chopping an offending year off her age. She finally announced to Shirley on her twelfth birthday that she was not twelve at all, but thirteen. Confused by this news, Shirley burst into tears, believing she had lost a year in time.

A similar struggle to extend youth befell Julie Andrews, whose blossoming body was constrained in restrictive costumes that minimized the impression that the child star was no longer a child. Julie, however, was apprised of her real age. Patty Duke was instructed to lie about her age by her managers and was also put through the embarrassment of wearing babyish clothes.

Gertrude Temple was reluctantly forced to accept Shirley's retirement when her daughter reached her early twenties, due to an inescapable dearth of scripts. Shirley has since referred to her childhood as a magical time, proving that a stage mother is very much in the eye of the beholder.

Gertrude Temple was doubtless so driven because her own

ambition to become a ballerina had never been fulfilled. So it was a bitter twist of irony indeed when, after a 1974 car accident, Gertrude faced the prospect of having her "ballet legs" amputated. Rather than undergo such radical surgery, she lived in enormous pain and was unable to walk. She died three years later.

Judy Garland's fiercely ambitious mother, Ethel Gumm, was a second-generation stage mother. As a young girl, Ethel had been encouraged to sing and play piano by her own mother, Evelyn Milne. Ethel was pretty and feminine, but her pathetic talents hardly matched her looks. Yet she and her mother were seemingly unaware of this fatal flaw in her potential and Ethel's unswerving desire for stardom was cemented.

She was playing piano in a local theater when she met Judy's father, an attractive Irishman named Frank Avent Gumm. They married when Ethel was twenty and together formed a highly unsuccessful vaudeville act. Deflated, the couple bought a small theater, but Ethel was so desperate to carve some kind of niche for herself in show business that she took to playing piano while her daughters performed what was by all accounts an excruciatingly poor stage act.

Frances Ethel Gumm—later Judy Garland—changed all that. She was born in 1922, the third daughter and Daddy's favorite. When she was just two and a half, she cried to join in the fun her sisters were having and forced her way onstage, whereupon she gave a tuneful rendition of "Jingle Bells." Previously hostile audiences loved it. This glimpse of her obviously superior potential was all Ethel needed. She persuaded her husband to move the family west and they settled in Lancaster (where Frank bought a theater), three hours drive from Los Angeles. Before long, Ethel left her other daughters at home while she and Judy went out on the road; Ethel was not going to give up her search for stardom.

It was a grueling life for a lonely child, sequestered in hotels, but if Judy complained, Ethel swiftly retaliated. She terrified Judy into submission by ignoring Judy's tearful pleadings and packing her bags and pretending to depart. Leaving her petrified daughter locked in the hotel room was Ethel's way of thwarting any assertiveness. Yet when Ethel eventually condescended to return, it was Judy who was cast in the role of begging for forgiveness.

Ethel became estranged from Judy Garland after her daughter married Sid Luft—Sid and Mother disliked one another intensely and Mother used the press to vent her anger at finding herself cast aside. Hurt by this betrayal, Judy would not see her mother. Ethel took a job on the assembly line at Douglas Aircraft for sixty dollars a week, sharing that news with the press, too, creating the impression that Judy had abandoned her.

The mother whom Judy had always supported died in 1953 after suffering a heart seizure in the parking lot outside the aircraft company. Judy Garland harbored a deep hatred of Ethel and was haunted by her memories of her mother for the rest of her life. She said this to Barbara Walters:

"My mother was the stage mother of all time. She really was a witch. If I had a stomach ache and didn't want to go on, she'd say, 'Get out on that stage or I'll wrap you around a bedpost.' "

Actor/director Ron Howard is a child performer who remained close to his mother. Sweet-faced, silver-haired Jean Howard was hired incongruously, but effectively, to play a witch in Dolly Parton's 1986 Christmas TV special. With or without broomstick, she could not look less like the stereotypic stage mother. Yet Ron was a veritable backstage baby. His parents' 1949 wedding ceremony was accompanied by six of Snow White's seven dwarfs tapdancing furiously to "Here Comes the Bride," and both he and his brother Clint, who is five years younger, acted professionally as young children.

Jean and Rance Howard are fellow Oklahomans who met originally in the drama department at the University of Oklahoma, and became further acquainted at the American Academy of Dramatic Art in New York. Their romance blossomed as they crossed the country in a children's theater company performing *Snow White* and *Cinderella*, culminating in their unique wedding in Winchester, Kentucky.

Both had set their sights on acting careers while in junior high —a "first" for their families. Jean's parents ran a grocery store in Duncan, where Jean was born, and later ran the sole hotel; her sister taught mathematics. Rance's brother kept up the family ranching tradition, his sister became a librarian.

Once they were married, Rance's career quickly took precedence. He landed a road tour of *Mr. Roberts* with Henry Fonda, and Jean disliked the separations. She continued to dabble in summer stock theater, however. After Ron was born on March 1, 1954, she took him along to rehearsals and he often sat and watched his dad direct plays. He was never bored. He earned his own first review in the *Baltimore Sun* before he was two: Jean carried him onstage in *The Seven Year Itch* and in less than sixty seconds, "he stole the show." So glowing a review, Jean says, feigning jealousy, "it almost ended his career!"

The Howards do not consider Ron's career something that they overtly chased; it was more a matter of circumstances clicking together, all perfectly natural. On Ron's fourth birthday, they signed a contract for him to travel to Vienna to make what turned out to be a highly forgettable Anatole Litvak film for MGM called *The Journey.* However, their young son shared the screen with Deborah Kerr, Yul Brynner, Jason Robards Jr., Anne Jackson, and Eli Wallach. An impressive debut.

A four-year-old is no judge of whether or not he wants to act or will enjoy it, and Jean candidly admits that the experiment was to appease their curiosity rather than Ron's. For the Howards, *The Journey* was a one-time experiment that need never be repeated and they could set aside Ron's earnings for his future. It was also an offer made considerably more attractive when Rance was cast to play a Russian soldier.

There was never any doubt in their minds that had Ron been reluctant or voiced any distaste for it, they would have called a halt immediately.

The film offer came out of an attempt to find work for Howard Senior, not Ron. Jean worked in the typing pool at CBS in New York, where she regularly scoured the bulletin board and on this occasion spied a note requesting horseback riders for a birthday party Mike Todd was throwing for Elizabeth Taylor at Madison Square Garden.

Rance took Ron along to the casting call. An agent who was impressed with his son told Rance of the search for an eight-year-old for an MGM film. Ron was not quite four . . . but of course had an audition piece ready, the *Mister Roberts* speech, the lines he had been throwing to his father since he was two years old.

Any brief hesitation the Howards felt about Ron doing a screen test was dissolved by the carrot dangled—Rance earned two days' pay for reading with all the children.

Ron's fledgling career, combined with his father's, gave the family ample reason to move to Burbank in 1958. Ron proceeded to appear in three "Playhouse 90" episodes—live—without a trace of nerves. By the time he joined "The Andy Griffith Show" as Opie, a year or so later, he had an impressive string of credits. Jean and Rance decided Ron would only work if one of them could be with him at all times. "The only problems that we saw arise were from children that didn't have supervision," Jean explains. "They are children working in an adult world and they need some buffers."

She is certain that child actors whose parents are in the business stand a better chance of success—and of survival. There are fewer illusions to shatter. "It's not for a lifetime, you take it with a grain of salt because you never know, this business is so fleeting." Ron and Clint inhabited a world in which they frequently saw the faces of their father, friends, and acquaintances pop up on the television or cinema screen, and it was "no big deal." In a similar vein, seeing themselves became "no big deal."

Yet with the best parental will in the world, a child actor is often the only child among adults and is treated as "special." There is a danger that those children will become, if not spoiled and out of control, at least somewhat isolated from their peers. Jean Howard concedes that a cute, small child is often fussed over by crews. The trouble begins when the crew goes back to work and that attention is suddenly withdrawn, which confuses the child.

"So then they start telling jokes or playing tricks, being absolute monsters, trying to get the attention that was showered on them so and was suddenly withdrawn."

Rance was determined not to allow his son to become an unspeakable brat. He drove home the point that while he hoped crew members would be friends with Ron, he wanted them still to like his son when he was twelve.

Jean Howard never had to contend with criticism for pushing Ron or accusations that she and Rance had cashed in on him for their own ends. She brushes aside the whole notion of pushy, desperately ambitious stage mothers. She did not see any when she was on the circuit. "Not as much as I did in Little League, that's where you see that!" In her experience, "pushy" did not pay: "The only people that I saw that I felt were pushy, it ended up being very detrimental to their child's career."

Southern California's Department of Industrial Relations then enabled child actors (and still does) to attend public school when not working. When they work they take their assignments and books to the studio school, where the teacher is versed in their curriculum and endeavors to keep them abreast of their peers with minimum disruption. Jean Howard found this system worked well for Ron and Clint. Ron, who was on "The Andy Griffith Show" from first grade through eighth grade, also joined his classmates in after-school activities to keep him in the flow. Ron did not miss a practice or game in five years of Little League. Each summer, his close friends were invited to spend a day with him on the "Andy Griffith" set to keep him company, but also to see what Ron was up to when he was absent from school.

In Burbank, where the largest industries are Lockheed and motion pictures and television, child actors abound. Ron's mother believes there was no jealousy, likening his job to another child's paper route. Children are unaware of the vast financial discrepancies.

There were a few adjustments to be made as Ron spun into the national limelight. He did not enjoy the attention he received outside Burbank. The Howards learned rapidly where they could and could not go. Disneyland, surprisingly, was a haven—especially if Ron wore a hat. He was no match for Mickey Mouse.

Ron's interest in acting waned briefly when his aspirations toward professional basketball gathered momentum. When "The Andy Griffith Show" was canceled, Ron took his junior year off from acting, a decision undoubtedly prompted by another factor which Jean does not address but Ron has revealed: the downside of fame. As Opie, Ron had become a household name, and that, coupled with his extreme shyness, rendered the experience of starting junior high "absolutely traumatic." It was a state of affairs exacerbated by cruel teenage jokes. Howard learned that a lot of stupid names rhyme with Opie, and has since admitted, "I didn't know whether I could cope with it. There was a tremendous amount of making fun of me."

He was subjected to further intimidation by his basketball teammates. His every shot was preceded by much merriment and an unnerving chorus of "C'mon Opie, shoot!" Not surprisingly, invariably he missed. Ron made the "B" team, but realized that at five-foot-eleven he was lacking height and by the end of the year was ready to return to work. Directing, rather than acting, had crystallized in his mind as where his future lay.

Ron was a wealthy young man by the time he graduated, and looking back, the Howards feel their family succeeded in retaining the status quo. "We never lived in Ron's house, Ron always lived in our house," Jean says emphatically. "The one thing that Rance was very, very firm about was that Ron's money went into the bank and that we supported Ron. He did not support us." They might have made more of his nest egg had they speculated, but his father was not concerned with whether or not Ron became wealthy, only that his money was waiting for him when he turned twenty-one.

Ron Howard, who majored in history at USC, was one of the lucky ones. For him there was not only life after being a child star, but a happy and a successful life. Jean doubts he will ever give up acting, but takes particular pleasure in his directing since that was *his* choice. *Splash* became a blockbuster, but for Jean it was while watching her son direct legendary talents like Don Ameche, Maureen Stapleton, Jessica Tandy, and Hume Cronyn in *Cocoon* that she found herself thinking, "He's got it!"

Clint Howard, who is best known for "Gentle Ben" and who debuted on "The Andy Griffith Show" at age two, works steadily as a character actor and has appeared in each of his brother's films. So nepotism flourishes in Burbank? Well, connections or no connections, Rance did not get the role in *Splash* for which he auditioned. And Jean, who had a speaking part in Dolly Parton's TV special (directed by Henry Winkler), was relegated by her son to the ranks of extras in *Cocoon*. Probably the only extra ever to be flown first-class and given the best room in the entire hotel. She leaped in and out of the *Cocoon* pool for two whole days (its magical youth-giving powers eluded her), and she got a cold for her trouble. If you blinked, you missed her onscreen.

Jean has coordinated extras on a few of Ron's projects and for five Gary Coleman films. She likes to draw on her large pool of old PTA friends, with whom she is most comfortable. Her acting appetite has once again been whetted and she is now aching for a great challenge. She is putting her picture in the Academy Players Directory (which is scanned by casting directors) and keeping her fingers crossed.

Jean's proudest moment as mother of Ron Howard, child star, actor, and acclaimed director? "Oh, well, when Cheryl had Bryce," Grandma says unhesitatingly. When Ron and her daughter-in-law asked her if she would look after her grandson one day a week, "it was the nicest thing that ever happened to me."

14 *Dearest Mommie*

Mae West dedicated her aptly entitled autobiography, *Goodness Had Nothing to Do with It*, to the loving memory of her mother. It was Bavarian-born Matilda Doelger West whom she credited with her career success and her powers of endurance. And, she noted in masterful understatement, "without whom I might have been somebody else."

The ties that bind mother to child are inestimable, but sometimes they are drawn so tightly even in adulthood that they are there for the whole world to see. As the butt of humor, the moms in these relationships are infamous. Walter Matthau told columnist Liz Smith that when he telephones his mother, Rose (an ex-seamstress), every other day, she lays into him as if he were twelve years old. "I guess you could say we have a sadomasochistic relationship without the sex," quipped Matthau.

Ginger Rogers, Elvis Presley, Glenn Ford, Lucille Ball, Peter Sellers, Loretta Young, Betty White—they all were tied especially closely to their mothers, as, of course, was Liberace. Liberace had a cold relationship with his father, Salvatore, an Italian immigrant, but mother Frances Liberace was the center of his universe.

Liberace loathed the fact that his love and devotion to Frances (who died in 1980) was often denigrated. He was unceasingly proud of her and always gave her credit for possessing not just class, but a positively regal aura. Presumably, he was right, since on the night he entertained Queen Juliana and Prince Bernhard of the Netherlands at a command performance held at the Coconut Grove in Los Angeles, when mother descended the steps with him, wearing white gown, fur wrap, and jewels, she was treated to a standing ovation by all those who wrongly concluded that she was Queen Juliana. Frances happily believed the ovation to be for her darling son . . . and he did nothing to shatter her illusion.

It was a source of enormous pleasure to the bejeweled pianist that wherever he traveled in the world, word of his mother preceded him. Even Queen Elizabeth, the Queen Mother, knew about Frances and enquired about her when they met.

When Gladys Presley died, Elvis was bereft. Gladys was the one person on whom he could count through thick and thin, the tireless friend who did not mind being awakened by his middle-of-the-night phone calls, and who offered solace, help, advice, and love. She was his best girl, his everything: "There will never be anyone in the whole world to me like my mother."

Before he was three years old, Elvis Presley became aware that his father fell short of perfection. In 1937, Vernon Presley, Gladys's brother, and a third man were charged with forgery. Vernon, so the story goes, had sold Orville Bean a hog, and greatly dissatisfied with what Bean had paid for the beast, the inept trio naively took the law into their own hands and amended Bean's check to what they felt was a more suitable sum. And so it was that due to this seemingly paltry offense, and despite Gladys's direct pleas to Mr. Bean, Vernon was sent to Parchman prison plantation for three years, where he labored daily in the fields until his release after serving nine months.

Although most of the locals stood firmly by Vernon, it is not hard to envision the jailbird stigma undermining Gladys's fragile confidence, or her embarrassment and shame transmitting itself to her impressionable son. Elvis took the early separation from his father hard, and the genesis of a duality took root. While Elvis clearly still needed physical mothering and caring himself, in his infantile way he promptly adopted the protective stance toward Gladys which he would maintain until her death on August 14, 1958. (Elvis died August 16, 1977.) He fell naturally into a role (that of Gladys's provider) which would gather momentum over the years and be fully realized via his fame and wealth as a star.

Interestingly, Father did not become the bad boy in his son's eyes. Elvis, whose boyhood hero was Captain Marvel, enveloped Vernon in his caring too. He was still in his teens when he assumed financial responsibility for his parents, to whom he referred as "my babies."

Psychologists label it the "savior complex." It is common for a child, Dr. Grotstein says, "out of a sense of loyalty to a fallen parent, to live out their ambition, rewrite their history, to become the messiah to the family. The child takes on a protective, parental role in Mother's life; it is as if he takes up a familial cause."

Bill Cosby's Navy career-man father was physically absent for long periods of time at sea and Bill developed a similarly protective attitude toward his mother, who raised her children to all intents and purposes single-handedly. Bill, as the eldest son, made childhood promises to give Anna everything that his father had failed to, and he went on to do precisely that when he became a superwealthy star.

While Elvis Presley and Bill Cosby were being lovingly mothered, they were also becoming prematurely parental. In Bill's case, of necessity, he took on the role in a practical fashion too, while Anna was at work. This kind of switch is a particularly common scenario to those in the psychiatric field who work with separations and divorces involving male children. It also crops up when, as in Gladys Presley's case, one parent is left to cope alone, either literally or practically, because of alcoholism in the family, for instance. Close bonds are formed in the hour of need.

The situation is not without its hazards for the male child (particularly those between the ages of five and ten) who is left behind with Mom. When mothers are lonely, vulnerable, and have been deprived of their prime adult companion, "without realizing, they gravitate to their children to get their needs met for companionship, and little boys quickly fall prey to being the man of the household," explains Dr. R. Barkley Clark.

The inherent danger in such a situation is that a small boy cannot possibly meet Mom's needs, he cannot take the place of an adult male. It can be frightening to see Mom lonely and needy, pushing him to take upon himself the responsibility to keep her from feeling miserable or depressed. The other potential peril in the overly close attachment is that it is that much harder to break at the appropriate time for separation.

Maria Gurdin claims that the omnipresent Gladys was a deterrent in the much-publicized romance between Elvis and her daughter Natalie Wood: "Natalie was so crazy about Elvis and we went on the set and visited him. His mommy, Gladys, was always there. He would say, 'Mother, give me a sugar.' That was when she had to kiss him before he started his scene."

"Natalie was a little bit disappointed in Elvis," Maria recalls. "I don't think he was very bright, he was a very good singer. They had matching shirts; Natalie bought them and she bought him presents. But it was boring for Natalie, Mommy being there all the time."

Gurdin is not the only person to assert that Elvis's connection to his mother remained umbilical. It has been reported a thousand times that Gladys took Elvis to school, then accompanied him home each day, the implication being that he was a mama's boy, a wimp. He was hardly the only child to bristle at the sight of a concerned mother dogging his footsteps, but according to an exhaustively researched biography by Elaine Dundy, *Elvis and Gladys,* there was more to it. Those walks to and from school were not so much evidence of a maternal stranglehold as they were ceremonial, a ritual confirming that Elvis was receiving the education that Gladys herself had not.

Indeed, Gladys was surprisingly lenient in other matters. Elvis drove at age ten, he chauffeured Gladys and Vernon in the family car at age twelve. But more significantly, from the time he was eight years old, he could be spotted at the local courthouse where WELO broadcast its amateur program. He would listen to the music, soaking up the wizardry of his first musical mentor, Mississippi Slim, and get up and sing. These Saturday afternoons were solo jaunts, Gladys was not clucking at his heels, and yet he went with Mom's permission.

Gladys Love Smith was a chubby, moon-faced brunette when she eloped with Vernon Elvis Presley within two months of meeting him. She was twenty-one, he was barely seventeen; she shed a couple of years and he added a few for the benefit of their marriage license. Elvis Aaron Presley was born January 8, 1935, on Old Saltillo Road, Tupelo, thirty minutes after his twin, Jesse Garon, who died at birth.

Elvis's maternal great-great-great-grandmother was a full-blooded Cherokee Indian called Morning Dove White. Gladys, who was born in April 1912, was the fourth of Doll Mansell's nine children and her fourth girl. Doll's husband, Bob Smith, was a moonshiner, a sharecropper, a jack of all trades, but a hard worker. But it was Doll, who spent most of her adult life confined to bed, enjoying ill health, who ruled the roost.

In *Elvis and Gladys*, Elaine Dundy paints a fascinating portrait of Gladys's development, with Doll its passively aggressive catalyst. While she was in fact spoiled, manipulative, and attention-grabbing, Doll continued to appear weak, helpless, and sad. Gladys's legacy from this familial state of affairs was inner conflict. She had a nervous, anxious disposition which she kept well hidden for the bulk of her life behind her sweet but determined exterior. She learned to put a brave face on it, and learned the lesson well.

Like Gladys, Elvis carried an inner ambivalence with him. There was guilt because his twin had died, but strength to be drawn from the knowledge that he had made it, survived and prevailed. He was a hero. Gladys veered from fear and neurosis to optimism and strength, and back, a dichotomy that she carried into her mothering—the sunny cheer she so often exhibited . . . and the dark fears that haunted her whenever Elvis was physically removed from her presence, which were doubtless compounded by the vulnerability of having lost one son. To please her, Elvis avoided airplane travel.

Gladys, like her peers, was not an educated woman. School-work had occupied a paltry four months of the year; farm work, physical labor in the fields, the remainder. She picked cotton, pulled corn, and did laundry and child-minding for a neighbor, at whose home she was first introduced to that magic machine, the Victrola. Elvis's mother was enthralled to discover that she could captivate a roomful of people when she danced, so mesmerizing was her uninhibited natural rhythm. She tasted the very applause and admiration, albeit on a considerably smaller scale, that her son would spend his life pursuing. And as Dundy observes, for a young girl who knows that she and her family have been the target of pity, it is hard to overestimate the dizzying effect of the power Gladys felt when she found that her dancing could make people cry and laugh and applaud and call for more.

She watched the films of Ginger Rogers (who at fourteen was Charleston champion of Texas) and Joan Crawford (who as seventeen-year-old Lucille LeSueur had Charlestoned her way to Hollywood from Missouri), and like so many other star moms, Gladys Presley explored her own unfulfilled potential in her day-dreams.

Despite Doll Smith's ailments, it was Gladys's hardworking father who died first. Bob went shockingly suddenly, struck down by pneumonia, leaving Doll in a predicament. The close family was not broken up in spirit, but was forced to leave Burk's farm, and in practical terms, splintered in different directions.

By the time she was nineteen, Gladys, who operated a sewing machine at the garment center, suffered what nowadays would be called spells of agoraphobia. She sought comfort in the Church of God and its caring congregation. Most importantly, the church exposed her to its rhythmical preachers, who strummed guitars, jumping and stepping and gesturing in front of the faithful in a foreshadowing of some of Elvis's famous guitar moves. From the time Elvis was a tot, Gladys took him to church. He was just two when he first felt moved to showcase his natural talents and leaped up to join the congregation in gospel singing.

In 1954, Elvis's career was ascending and his savior complex began to manifest itself in material ways. He bought his parents a pink Ford, a forerunner of Gladys's dream car, a pink Cadillac. He purchased two Mixmasters for her kitchen, one for each side of the counter to save her from walking around. He first elevated his folks' standard of living in 1955, moving them to a better neighborhood. Then, in 1957, he bought Graceland, the thirteen-room mansion that was once a church and is today a major tourist attraction.

Suddenly, Gladys and Vernon's world was one akin to a luxury hotel—freshly laundered sheets daily, someone to run the bath-water, someone to concoct meals in the middle of the night—and Graceland boasted the rose garden Elvis had always promised his mom. Daddy retired before he was forty, and the Presleys, whose beginnings were so poor, could put money worries behind them for the rest of their lives. Not that Gladys could forget what had gone on before.

When Elvis Presley, Superstar, was the honored homecoming

guest on Elvis Presley Day at the Mississippi-Alabama Fair, Gladys remembered her old friends. She sent tickets to those who had helped quiet the growling hole in her stomach when she could not afford to buy a meal.

To Gladys, Elvis's success rapidly manifested itself to be a double-edged sword. The thrill and the pride she felt were soon overshadowed by more practical concerns. Her son was gone. He was always busy, touring, performing, recording, working, anywhere but with her. Despondent, she began to long for the old days and their old way of life. She drowned her sorrows by drinking with increasing regularity. Her death was attributed to a possible heart attack brought on by cirrhosis or liver failure, but the specifics were inevitably overshadowed by Elvis's grief. He cried at her funeral, "Oh, God! Everything I have is gone!"

Betty White's mother, Tess, had reached the grand old age of eighty-seven when she died in November 1985. Not only did they remain closely bonded until the last, but Betty considers herself the happiest only child ever to have walked the earth. ("My mother and dad were very much in love, which helped.") In fact, Betty and Tess went beyond close to well-nigh inseparable, yet not in a dependent, clinging fashion; it was because they relished one another's company.

"Every once in a while," Betty admits, "they'd try to make me the 'poor little mother's girl,' under her mother's thumb and stuff like that—until they'd meet Tess and realize how that was not working. The week before she went to the hospital for the last time, she creamed me at Trivial Pursuit, and I was trying. And she was so sick; oh God, she was sick. But the humor never left her. For such a silly, funny lady, there was an iron butterfly underneath." Betty imagines she has an iron butterfly in her, although, she suspects, a less wise variety.

"Values, that's what she gave me. She always mitigated everything by saying how corny it sounded, so it never sounded preachy." A pertinent lesson from Tess was that ultimately we each are answerable to ourselves for what we do in life and how we behave. "She said, 'You can lie to me, you can lie to the world, you can lie to yourself, until you are on your own and you look in the mirror.' So the mirror to me has always been like another entity. There have been times when I've wanted to comb my hair in the reflection in a store window rather than in that mirror! But it's been a lovely rule of thumb."

Horace and Tess White met and married in Chicago in 1921 when both were twenty-one and madly in love. Horace worked in the electrical business for Cross Haines, rising from office boy and neophyte salesman to vice president. "Horatio Alger," says Betty. Tess worked in accounting. She was one of nine children, and was virtually raised by her Grandma Hobbs, a shirt-maker from Glamorganshire, Wales. Betty describes herself as "the stub end of the railroad—no brothers, no sisters or offspring, so it all ends with me." She was born in Oak Park, Illinois, in 1922 and when she was eighteen months old, the family moved to Los Angeles.

Periodically, Betty's grandmother lived with them to help out, but when she was around eight, Tess became a full-time mom. "We were buddies," Betty says of their conspiratorial bond that harked back to when she was a schoolgirl. "I never ditched a class in my life, but I would ditch them for a day with my mother. She'd drive me to school, and I'd do this selling job all the way, 'Now, I don't have any tests, I've got straight A's, and there's nothing going on today except dumb gym class.' And she'd say, 'No, you've got to go to school.' So maybe one day in seven we'd get in front of school and we'd look at each other, and she'd just keep pulling on, and we'd drive up the coast and we'd go on a picnic. And I think I got more out of those picnic days than I did out of school."

Nevertheless, Betty says she grew up in a house where "no" meant "no." She fully intended to be a writer, and at twelve penned a deadly serious grammar school graduation play, promptly wrote herself into the lead, and the course of White history changed. She began her career in theater with much parental encouragement, then moved to radio, then into the golden beginning of the television era.

When World War II came along, Betty segued neatly from Beverly Hills High into the Volunteer Services with Tess. "I'd been driving about twenty minutes, and found myself driving a Jeep in the blackout up in the hills. It was on-the-job training. And we sewed and did a lot of that."

Both Tess and Horace loved Betty's career and attended every one of her shows. "My mother, till she couldn't do it anymore, was at every single broadcast. To this day, I go out, a crew that I haven't seen for a while asks, 'How's Tess?' Then I have to explain that we don't have her anymore. She got to see 'Golden Girls' start, she got to watch it on the air, but she never got to a broadcast. I missed her in that first row, boy, and I still do."

Betty's sense of humor came straight from her mother and father's knees. When she was growing up, as her father added new jokes to his repertoire, he would award the clean bill of health to those suitable for repetition at school. "So that's where the bawdy sense of humor started. But the rule was a joke had to be funny, it couldn't be just dirty. They were both so fast that it was just incredible. Mom was the fastest one. She just thought funny, but never to be 'on' for funny's sake. She taught me that jokes are for yourself, they're not for 'Look everybody, I'm show-ing off, laugh at me.' You just keep your skin clear."

When Betty married Allen Ludden, she moved to the East Coast for six years, but the separation from Tess proved to be a mere geographical technicality. "We bought several phone com-panies, we bought the U.S. Post Office and a couple of airlines. I'd fly out for one day and fly back. We missed each other. We enjoyed each other. Allen would say I was on that westbound plane every twenty minutes, if there was a market opening or a leaf fell or something."

Betty's joy in her new marriage was tempered by several sad events, including, in 1963, the death of Horace White. "In six months, I moved to New York, Dad died, and all three dogs died. My mother's whole life fell apart. So we bundled her up and brought her back with us for a little while. Her life did an absolute hundred-eighty-degree turn."

Since the family was so close and Horace was not a socializer or party-goer, Tess had developed few outside friendships. After her husband's death, she began working as a volunteer at the hospital at UCLA and made friends immediately, but it was a painful and difficult period, until:

"Pretty soon she had so many friends, her social calendar made mine look like a bum. The last Christmas we had just a little party at home, and it was the last day she was even really able to be up for very long. And she got all dressed up in her red velvet robe and came into the living room with her wheelchair. We had an open house for her, mostly the Motion Picture Mothers friends. And everybody came by, and for a lady who had not been able to be up for that long, she held court for the whole time, and everybody was laughing and scratching. It was just a good last hurrah. I always like to remember that."

15 *When You Wish upon a Star*

The vicarious thrill attached to having a star in the family is greatly intensified in moms who once harbored their own ambitions, only to watch them slip through their fingers, either by choice or circumstance. Julie Powers insists that she did not cherish the notion that Stefanie would become a star, but it is certainly true that in finding fame, Stefanie Powers brought to fruition an idea of her mother's, an idea she had long since abandoned. Like George Hamilton's mother, Anne, Julie envisioned a career for herself on the silver screen, until she stumbled over the casting couch and bruised her dreams. But all those dreams cherished by all those moms did not disappear without a trace; their delightful imagery and aura of unfinished business must surely have seeped across the breakfast table into the subcutaneous layers of their children's very beings.

A hefty number of stars were putting their full weight behind a surface scratch that had been etched out by their mothers. Carol Burnett's mom sang. So did Bob Hope's. Sally Field's mother, Maggie, was an actress, as was Marlon Brando's mother, Dorothy, who passed on to Marlon a love of "beautiful pretense." Sometimes the influence was subtle: Paul Newman's mother, Teresa, was not an actress, but was a passionate theater-goer who came back from each performance exhilarated, spilling detailed accounts of the magic she had witnessed. Bing Crosby's mother struggled to raise five children in near-poverty but was a frustrated singer at heart. Stars like Robert Blake, Peter Sellers, Charlie Chaplin, Donald O'Connor, and Groucho Marx were stepping into territory previously trodden by their vaudevillian families.

Julie Powers ran the gauntlet of Hollywood's many pitfalls at age nineteen when she arrived fresh from New Hampton, New York, full of naive optimism. Her high hopes were rapidly dashed. She was not willing to sacrifice herself on the casting couch and she rapidly discovered that a dinner invitation from a studio executive invariably had strings attached. Julie's retort? She was not that hungry.

Years later, she had no inkling what lay ahead when, on a whim, she took fourteen-year-old Stefanie on a dancers' audition at Los Angeles's Greek Theatre, just to see how she would fare. Open calls are generally nightmarishly ruthless—look at *A Chorus Line*—yet Stefanie and her friend Kathy survived three hours of eliminations undaunted. What is more, they professed to enjoy the ordeal.

Julie's own run-in with the seamier aspects of the business did not deter her from encouraging Stefanie. Her daughter had one crucial advantage—a protective mother at her elbow. Already bored with Hollywood High School, Stefanie was a willing participant when her divorcée mom suggested they respond to a bulletin from the American Ballet School calling for dancers for a local production of "a thing called *West Side Story*." She was fifteen and on her way.

Julie is a bright, animated, and pretty brunette whose accent is undercut with an intriguing inflection of her native Polish, her sole language until she was eight years old. Her parents were born in Poland—her mother in the Russian sector, her father in the Austrian—but her family history is engulfed in the genealogical fog that clouds Eastern Europe, where so many records were destroyed during the wars. In the days when Julie hankered after seeing her name up in lights, many of her daydreams focused on what she would do for her mother if she became a star. Now, through Stefanie, she has been able to live out some of those fantasies.

Julie occupies Stefanie's Beverly Hills house, which Stefanie comes home to when she is not off nurturing her beloved wildlife in Africa, so mother and daughter are part-time roommates. The bond between them was forged early—Julie divorced before Stefanie was eight. They have fun together, and Stef's friends are so warmly accepting, Mom never feels like an intruder. She is not a clinging vine.

Early on in her career, Stefanie was sent on a press tour of thirteen European cities and Julie, worried about her inexperienced daughter going off alone, went too. They had been warned by publicity staff that European journalists (Parisiennes in particular) are a blasé bunch and impossible to impress. They eat lunch, ask a few questions, then leave. At one such event, Julie and Stefanie (who speaks six languages, including Spanish and French) were seated at opposite ends of the table and Julie was suddenly thrown in at the deep end, fielding questions from half the journalists. An unprecedented three hours later, the interchange was still going strong.

Julie clearly considers herself a useful adjunct to her daughter, not a liability—an opinion confirmed by Jack Cohen of Columbia Studios. "When he received the reports on the trip, he said, 'Look, from now on, we don't have to send Stefanie, we'll just send the mother.'"

On one occasion, an Italian correspondent interviewed Stefanie and by the end of the afternoon, he, Julie and Stefanie, were singing Italian songs and having a whale of a time. Despite the fact that his wife was expecting a baby at any moment, the journalist was reluctant to leave. For the duration of their stay, everywhere Stefanie went, there lurked the Italian scribe. "He became infatuated with her. He literally followed Stefanie around, writing her little love notes." At tricky times like that, Mom's presence can be downright useful.

In 1982 they visited Poland together. For Julie, the trip was poignant and nostalgic, bringing her closer than ever before to her family roots. Stefanie's success and the travel opportunities that came with it broadened Julie's horizons considerably. Their home is full of African artifacts, paintings, and objets d'art that bear witness to their globe-trotting. But long before William Holden catalyzed Stefanie's love affair with African wildlife (she now directs the William Holden Wildlife Fund on twelve hundred acres in Kenya), Julie Powers dabbled in a little animal welfare herself.

Stefanie and her brother Jeff's little white mouse, Petey, came to an icy end one especially cold night while sleeping in his usual spot, a goldfish bowl out on the service porch. Refusing to accept his frozen demise, Julie slipped him into a matchbox holder, put him in the open stove, and to the amazement of all concerned, he defrosted and came back to life.

Between acting jobs, Stefanie once performed as a bullfighter in Mexico, but now her efforts are purely conservational. Julie, having sampled Kenya's delights herself, totally understands Stef's willingness to distance herself from Hollywood. "She feels life and reality there. It's really getting back to basics, and back to real people, and she can be herself. She doesn't like this glitter. I shouldn't say this—it's too much of the same. And the competition of what you have to wear, what you have to do, where you're going, it's very shallow. She has too much to offer, and she has too much to enjoy, and she has too curious a mind to sit around and talk shop."

Julie has seen stars who have nary a critic among their friends and family, but she has not lost her ability to be objective about her star daughter. "Everybody says yes, yes, yes! They can do no wrong. And we *all* do something wrong, myself included. That goes for anybody. I try to be gentle about it, and I say this is for development and improvement. I understand no one likes to take criticism. It's funny, I've never felt, 'Oh, she's fabulous!' I'm happy that she does good work. I was her severest critic, and I am to this day, because I do it from the heart and I'm not in competition with her."

Teri Garr's mom, Phyllis, was one of the original high-kicking Radio City Rockettes—until she married vaudevillian comedian-impersonator Eddie Garr. Under Eddie's influence, she put away her tap shoes and switched her priorities to raising their three children: Edward, an orthopedic surgeon; Philip, who is in the boat business; and Teri. When work opportunities came her way, "Eddie said, 'No, please don't. Let's try to make our marriage different.' And we did." She retired without regrets.

Phyllis was athletic and sporty, but there were few less-likely careers than dancing for the daughter of Cleveland metallurgist Louis Lind and his wife Theresa. As a teenager, she earned pin money for chaperoning a couple of young children on the streetcar to their Saturday dance lessons. The die was cast. The elderly Russian teacher, who had noticed Phyllis's feet frustratedly tapping away on the sidelines every week, invited the would-be dancer to join his class. In those pretelevision days, the school sent a popular dance act out on the local circuits every summer, and Phyllis found her niche. When the act dissolved, she was sixteen and began pounding the pavement in New York.

She got her break in 1928 in the show *Rain or Shine*, joining the brand-new and yet-to-become prestigious line-up of thirty-six leggy Rockettes. Phyllis, who recently attended a Rockettes' fiftieth anniversary celebration in New York, was intrigued by the optical trickery that was utilized to create the illusion that a long line of girls of entirely disparate shapes and sizes were identical in height. They were first graded by height, the shortest at the ends, the tallest in the center; then all the hemlines were cut to break at precisely the same number of inches above the stage.

Phyllis's digs had a dormitorylike camaraderie as she and her roommates, fellow chorus girls, struggled to eke a living out of their meager salaries. With four, five, sometimes even six Rockette shows a day, fortunately there was little time for spending money.

In 1933, while in the show *Strike Me Pink*, Phyllis met Teri's father. Eddie Garr was a rising star, "the Rich Little of his day," who imitated W.C. Fields and Jimmy Durante. The other dancers warned Phyllis that he held a rather inflated opinion of himself. Phyllis found to the contrary: "He was actually so shy and amazed at his progress that he didn't pay any attention to the girls. But girls will be girls!"

After showtime, the cast members' ritual was to go en masse to a midnight movie in Times Square. Eddie latched onto their group and gradually he and Phyllis became a couple. Eddie, whose career was flourishing, traveled extensively, so it was not until 1936, three years later, that they found time to marry. They were engaged, but Phyllis seriously doubted the wedding would ever happen. Repeatedly, their plans unraveled at the eleventh hour.

It was not unusual for Eddie to break a night lunch-date (such was their topsy-turvy nocturnal world) with Phyllis and her sister Terry, and on one particular occasion Eddie had performed at a

Carnegie Hall benefit and was delayed. Then, in the wee small hours of the morning, Eddie's pianist began hammering on their door and would not be dissuaded, even when the sisters hissed out, "Go away!" Exasperated, they opened the door and the next thing they knew, they were being spirited off to Armonk, New York, near the Connecticut border.

Eddie's pianist informed the protesting Phyllis, who had a rapidly looming 7:30 A.M. rehearsal call, that she was going to be married. Certain it was one of Eddie's gags, she was amazed to find Eddie, a judge, and a couple of wedding rings waiting to greet her. "He said, 'I've been carrying these for a long time. Tonight's it,' " she recalls with a wistful smile. They scraped back into New York in time for her rehearsal and for Eddie to rush off to board a ship for London, where he was booked at the Palladium. Separated by over three thousand miles, their honeymoon had to wait.

The Garrs' fortunes changed after Eddie had an accident while touring the South Pacific with the USO. Phyllis learned that he had been injured via an item in Earl Wilson's newspaper column saying he was not expected to survive. Phyllis, of course, was devastated, but was unable to get any concrete information for a month. In fact, Eddie came home safely under a Navy escort, but the severity of his injuries was such that his career never recaptured its former glory. He had broken three vertebrae and suffered internal bleeding which led to a severe heart attack.

"That was the beginning of all his problems, frankly. He had to wear a brace. It was tough." Jobs he had breezed through became too much for him, and her "showstopper" husband could not follow his own act. The family felt the pinch financially; they were forced to sell their lovely home, and Phyllis Garr, who says, "Teri doesn't remember the good part of our lives," admits that things grew steadily worse until his death nine years later when Teri was eleven.

Phyllis had to find a way to contribute financially to keep them afloat and hit upon the idea of going into costuming. She began working on television shows as a wardrobe mistress, progressing to Hollywood film studios.

Teri was eight when she decided to follow in her mother's

dance steps, and was so keen that each afternoon after school she made a convoluted journey on five buses to get to her ballet classes.

On the way up, Teri lost more parts than she cares to remember because she was rated "not pretty enough." She was not the archetypal beauty. As her mom puts it, "She's not a sexpot." Phyllis Garr believes that insecurity, whether verbalized or not, is the name of the game, and in order to survive in show business, it is necessary to develop "a certain kind of hide. If you don't have it, you're not going to bounce back," she says matter-of-factly.

"All mothers think their kids are great, but I really thought she could do it if she had the desire," says Phyllis, who was not surprised by Teri's success. "I think I've traveled the road before. She's very deserving and she has been fortunate . . . she's one hundred percent into her work." Film critic Pauline Kael called Teri "the funniest neurotic dizzy dame on the screen." Mom agrees; Teri has a natural funny streak.

"She will call it as it is sooner [than she should], and sometimes when she shouldn't. But that's her nature. All my children are funny. When they are together, I would rather be with them than go to a show."

There have been times Teri has said things to the press which have startled Phyllis. She does not touch drugs or alcohol, but Teri once admitted to a two-year period in her life when she had a drinking problem, saying she thought it was in the genes:

"My father was an alcoholic, and I once went to meetings of Al-Anon, the group for families of alcoholics," Teri told Judy Klemesrud of *Cosmopolitan* magazine. "Anyway, I began drinking during a time in my life when I was surrounded by all these Academy Award winners. There I was, Little Miss Nothing. But I couldn't handle the booze. I'd get drunk on a single glass of wine. Finally, I stopped."

On Oscar night in 1982, when Teri had been nominated for Best Supporting Actress for *Tootsie*, Phyllis watched from afar, in her nonpushy style. But unlike Ron Howard's mom, Jean, this link to success has not given Phyllis a desire to perform again. "I think I got it out of my system!"

She was taken aback when the inevitable happened and her

daughter was cast in a film (Mel Brooks' *Young Frankenstein*) on which she also was working. She had not even known Teri was auditioning; the word had gone out that Mel was looking for a big-busted girl. "They got tired and hired Teri," she explains, grinning. Teri was far more nervous than Phyllis about the whole business. It was not accusations of nepotism that bothered them so much as the prospect of all the inevitable teasing from Mel Brooks and the crew.

"I said, 'When I'm near you, just call me Phyllis and we'll just keep going. You won't be nervous and I won't be nervous.' But I was afraid it would upset Teri, that's what worried me. I was afraid I would get in her hair and she would say, 'Mother!' "

Amazingly, halfway through filming, Mel Brooks (who does not miss a trick) was none the wiser about the mother-and-daughter team right under his nose. They almost pulled it off, but not quite. The game was up when Brooks' son, in from New York on vacation, overheard Teri yelling, "Hey, Mom!" when she thought no one was within earshot.

"The kid asked me, 'Are you her mother?' And I said, 'Oh a lot of people call me Mom,' and I kept right on going." Phyllis thought her bluff had worked until Mel Brooks confronted her saying, 'Phyllis, are you Teri Garr's mother?' I started sputtering, I said, 'Yes, in a way.' Of course, after that it was always 'Teri, stop it! Your mother's coming!' or some funny remark like that!"

Loretta Williams openly regrets the fact that she did not have the chance to sing professionally, as her son Billy Dee Williams, who got his first acting role at age seven, is well aware: "I feel as though I'm kind of living out a lot of those aspirations that she had, but she was always into her children." He tries to make it up to her; she says he treats her like a queen. When he was a presenter at the fiftieth Academy Awards, Mom was his date, and for Loretta, it was the next best thing to tasting success firsthand.

"I was so proud to hear thousands of people screaming, 'Billy Dee! Billy Dee!' I was so nervous, but still I felt so wonderful, I felt like a big star—because all of these years I wanted to be a movie star. Sonny introduced me to everybody, and oh, I felt so full!"

Loretta sees Billy Dee, who is devoted to her, almost daily. She lives in a comfortable home in the San Fernando Valley, the walls of which are lined with impressive family efforts with the paintbrush—including a self-portrait by Billy at age seventeen: "He had diarrhea and thought he was dying, so he decided to paint his last portrait!" There is Loretta's rendition of Billy Dee cleaning off his makeup on the last night of *Hallelujah Baby*, and a portrait of Loretta by Billy Dee's twin sister, Lady, who along with Billy won an art scholarship to what is now New York's High School of Performing Arts.

Lady began studying ballet at age six and was admitted to the American Ballet Theater School when she was fifteen. But the rheumatic fever and heart trouble she had as a baby eventually took its toll, and at eighteen she had to hang up her dance shoes for good. She studied business administration at NYU and later worked for the telephone company and Macy's.

Loretta knew Billy Dee truly had what it takes after seeing him on stage in *The Cruel World* at age seventeen. And with Billy Dee's success, life was fulfilling the promise that had drawn her parents from Montserrat, the smallest island in the West Indies. "Papa came to America to make a good living because he heard it was the land of milk and honey," she explains.

Loretta's mom, Annette Evelyn Lewis, being light-skinned and of the upper class—what was known as "high yellow"—was quite a prize for Patrick John Bodkin. The Lewises had property. Loretta's mother's maternal grandfather was a sculptor and maker of expensive coffins; Uncle Tom was captain of the cricket team and owned a tailor shop, a jewelry store, and a big department store. But despite his very dark skin and lower social standing, Patrick John Bodkin was handsome—and extremely snooty. So Loretta's father had no qualms about pursuing Annette and in 1910, when she was twenty-two, they sailed for New York where they were married.

Father, a shoemaker by trade, opened a grocery store on East 133rd Street. They lived in the back while he saved his money for a shoe factory; he eventually acquired two stores on Seventh Avenue, and made elegant footwear for an affluent clientele. One day, while standing outside, he got chatting to a Cuban who offered him entree into a new kind of lottery game—the numbers racket.

"Mother was against the idea, she called it gambling, and of course it was illegal," says Loretta, who was six at the time and remembers hearing her parents' arguments. "Mother said, 'I am going home to my family. This is racketeering! It's gambling and it's against God's laws.' He said, 'Oh, don't be so silly! It's just a small game. We would just be doing it in Harlem, it's very innocent.' She said, 'Well, I can see you're going to do it, whatever I say.'"

Loretta's mother did not leave, and the family fortunes rose dramatically with father's new business interest. Loretta recalls being driven to school in a chauffeured limousine; as a numbers banker's daughter you were "somebody."

The honeymoon came to an abrupt end four years later. Dutch Schultz moved into the area with his all-black Blue Gang and a white gang, both of which exerted a little ungentlemanly pressure over store owners. Loretta, who was ten, remembers gangsters tried to snatch her to "persuade" her father to join Murder Incorporated.

"One day I was roller-skating, and they drove up in a Packard car with shades and they opened up the shades and said, 'Come here, little girl.' I told them I wasn't allowed to go to anybody and I skated off. My father wanted out. He didn't want to get involved with any gangsters." Finally, he did leave, but not before the deaths of several of her friends' fathers who were similarly employed.

"After the Depression came, it was very sad. We never thought we'd ever see Papa in Thom McAn shoes. When he had money he always had the best Florsheim shoes. He used to look like Black Diamond Jim, but he couldn't afford the cashmere coats, the diamond rings anymore. Things got very bad for us, Papa lost all his money and Mama was right. That kind of money's no good."

After her father's death, Loretta was anxious to make some money to help support the family, since brother Bill was taking a pre-med course in college. She persuaded her mother to take her along to Dan Healey's glamorous Cotton Club after school one afternoon.

She passed her initial dance audition and was hopeful of filling a vacant slot in the chorus line-up. Two girls befriended her:

sixteen-year-old Lena Horne, and the late Winnie Johnson (who married Step'n'Fetchit), who offered to take her home and teach her the steps. "Most of the girls called me brown sugar," Loretta remembers. "Lena was brown, too, but she lightened up over the years."

Still hoping to land a job, Loretta began rising at three A.M. and heading for the Cotton Club just as the show was breaking. She would stand on the sidelines, entranced by the girls in their elaborate, expensive costumes and the gorgeous high-yellow boys. She then rehearsed until 6 A.M., ate breakfast and headed for school.

Her naïveté stood her in good stead—the others rallied to protect her from being drawn into prostitution, the club's sideline. "They said, 'They're not going to get ahold of you.' I asked, 'For what?' Lena's mother, Edna, and stepfather, Papa, were there every night. They beat Papa so badly because he wouldn't let Lena get involved in that sort of thing."

After practicing the Cotton Club dance routine for three months, Loretta learned the club was moving downtown into a white neighborhood—without her. "They took all the high-yellow girls but decided to leave back the brownies," she explains. "The only brownie they took, and she was dark, was Louis Armstrong's wife, Lucille Wilson."

Loretta then tried out as a dancer at Connie's Inn in Harlem, a swanky club built along similar lines, but being so innocent, she giggles, she did not swing and sway her hips in the appropriately seductive manner. Loretta did not altogether regret the outcome. Gang warfare and shoot-outs began soon afterward at the Cotton Club.

"Al Capone and them used to come in, shooting up the place," she recalls. "They were selling the girls to these white men, they didn't allow any black patrons at all. That movie, *The Cotton Club*, is not the true story. Lena told it right out in her book, she exposed it. I was very fortunate I didn't get into that sort of thing. Jehovah looks after me. I was always sort of religious inside and I felt God didn't want it, so I studied opera instead and studied to be a stenographer."

Billy Dee's father, William December Williams, was born in

1910 in Shepard, Texas. Loretta had yet to graduate from high school when they met, whereas Big Bill (as he was nicknamed) was twenty-five and a perfume salesman. Despite his lack of formal education, there was an appealing, genteel quality about Big Bill. He dressed in made-to-measure Ivy League clothes, a Homburg, spats, and Florsheim shoes. "He was quite a sport. He used to walk like Li'l Abner," Loretta says, laughing and imitating his jaunty swagger. "He had the big cigar sticking out of his mouth and dressed to kill, very dapper. That's where Billy gets it from."

The night they met, Loretta, who is now teetotal and a Jehovah's Witness, was initiated into the delights of sloe gin fizz at Mike's, a bar and grill where all the show people met after hours. From there, she and her friends went to Tillie's Kitchen Grill, noted for the world's best Southern Creole fried chicken and frequented by the top-hatted and evening-gowned social elite. By three A.M., the excitement Loretta felt at sampling this new, sophisticated world had given way to fear about being out so late.

They were tough times financially. But Big Bill Williams had serious intentions toward Loretta and managed to buy an engagement ring and wedding ring.

Mama and brother Bill had other ideas. Bill Williams, they decided, was not good enough for their Loretta, whom Mama had always envisioned marrying a doctor or a lawyer. Tactlessly, she informed her daughter, "You picked an illiterate ass." Although a wedding date was set to placate Loretta, Loretta's sister, Sylvia, overheard her mother and brother conspiring to stop the marriage and tipped her off.

Not to be outdone, Loretta reluctantly set about planning her own secret ceremony and was wed one evening in the chapel at St. James, Harlem's largest Presbyterian church. The bride wore a navy blue, fur-collared suit, and Big Bill's mother sent a cake for the celebration afterwards at the home of ex-Cotton Club dancer Billie Jones and her husband, Preacher Jones, the trumpet player. (Billie Jones and Loretta are still firm friends; nowadays, they have telephone conferences to discuss the progress of their favorite soap opera.)

Before they married, Loretta and Big Bill had secured an elegant three-room apartment on Harlem's exclusive Sugar Hill, but it remained empty. Loretta went home to Mama after her wedding, just as if nothing had happened. She even went back to high school. Bill visited her each evening, then returned to his lodgings.

A couple of months went by before Loretta was caught wearing her wedding ring concealed under kid gloves. Her mother was stunned but calm until Loretta's nineteen-year-old brother threw himself across the bed and "hollered." He made such a fuss that he stirred up Mama, who then became equally irate and insisted Loretta pack her bags and leave.

Crying, she ran out to the drugstore and telephoned her husband. "I told him, 'Please come and get me right away. But don't come in!' I waited outside for him, and I could hear Brother Bill crying. We got into the cab and went off to our dream apartment, but I didn't even enjoy it, because what was an apartment without Mama's blessings?"

Loretta was desperately lonely, and prayed to be pregnant. When she learned she was expecting twins, she felt sure that the news would heal the rift with her mother. Instead, "She said, 'Uhh, having more than one baby? Just like a dog!' And I was so hurt and bewildered."

She did not go back, and six months after Billy Dee and Lady were born, they had not been christened because Loretta kept waiting and hoping for a reconciliation. Finally, she relented and took the twins to visit. The building superintendent escorted her up to the apartment.

"She said. 'You stand behind me now, sweetheart.' My mother opened the door and said, 'Oh, Lucille! Where did you get these beautiful, gorgeous babies? Are they twins? Bill, come! Look what Lucille found! Whose babies are they?' 'These are your grandbabies,' Lucille said. My mother shrieked, 'Aaah! This boy is almost a red nigger!' Brother Bill put the babies on two pillows and said, 'Oh, we thought they were going to be like Bill Williams, but they're beautiful.' Because Billy Dee was very light with rosy cheeks, and his hair was blondish and curly, and Lady, who was born eight minutes earlier, was bald, with one black strand. She was sort of brownish-burnt color, like an Indian.

"That broke the ice. Right away we had to christen the babies and they even picked the godparents. Billy Dee was christened for his father, William December Williams."

By 1936, Big Bill was forced to wear paper in his shoes and they struggled to pay their thirty-five-dollar monthly rent. He even had to borrow a nickel from the subway cashier to go searching for work. They applied for welfare, and just as a parcel arrived, Bill found three jobs: chef at a Brooklyn restaurant, maintenance in an office building, and janitor. The welfare parcel was sent back. They were afraid that if they kept it, they might end up in jail.

Loretta and her family moved in with her mother and later, their apartment house (indeed the entire neighborhood) was taken over by prostitutes and dope pushers. Mama would shout out the window: "You're sinful creatures!" But the streetwalkers respected her and loved little Lady and Billy Dee. Loretta instructed Billy to take off his hat and say "good morning" or "good afternoon" to them. He remembers that to this day, saying, "My mother made me respect women."

Loretta was hired as an elevator operator at the Lyceum Theater. A trained stenographer, she was reluctant to take such a job, but needed the thirteen dollars a week. She stood no nonsense from her flirtatious passengers, nor did she stand on ceremony when the theater's owner, Max Gordon, visited the building.

"Max Gordon dropped his bags," she recalls with a twinkle in her eye, "and he looked at the bags and then he looked at me. I looked at the bags and I looked at him. I was very sweet, but I said, 'Are you Mr. Gordon? Well, pick your bags up and come in.' His eyes popped out of his head, but he said, 'Okay.' He and I became buddies. Georgie Jessel was running me all over the office trying to 'cootchie, cootchie, cootchie' me, saying, 'I'm engaged to your girlfriend, Lena Horne.' I said, 'Lena is Lena, and I'm me, Loretta. We're two different people, so you leave me alone.' I was crying, I was so annoyed with him. I met all the stars."

Kurt Weill was one of her elevator passengers. He and his wife, Lotte Lenya, were in a production of *The Firebrand of Flawrence*, the story of Benvenuto Cellini, the swashbuckling Italian painter.

For three years, a search had been underway for a little black boy with a high voice.

The late Ben Boyer (who became Billy's manager) suggested Loretta put seven-year-old Billy Dee forward. Resplendent in a zoot suit, he auditioned for Maurice Abravanel of the Manhattan Opera House to "oohs" and "aahs" from the chorus of beauties (one was the late novelist, Jacqueline Susann), who hugged and squeezed him. Billy was in heaven.

The Firebrand of Flawrence opened at the Alvin Theater in New York. During its run, the life-size picture of Billy Dee and Lotte Lenya that hung outside the theater was smashed. World War II was underway. Lotte Lenya was Austrian and Kurt Weill German, and German cast members were hardly an asset during wartime.

Billy was quite the little character and not always entirely popular, either. He earned no awards from the orchestra members on the night they asked him to keep watch for the fire chief while they retired downstairs for their customary game of cards and cigarette break—an activity which contravened fire regulations. "Billy thought they said to go get the fire chief!" Loretta recalls, giggling.

"Billy so liked walking across crying, 'Make way for the Duchess!' that he refused to leave the stage when he was supposed to. The ballet dancers complained and Kurt Weill said, 'We haven't got time for Billy's rudeness.' But John Murray, who staged the show, said, 'The Boss wants to walk across the stage, the Boss is going to walk across the stage. Walk across the stage, Boss.' "

When the show's six-month run drew to a close, the timing was, in fact, ideal. Billy was eating so much and growing so fast he would have soon burst out of his page boy costume.

"The Boss was getting spoiled," admits Loretta, who still treasures the red, gold-fringed cushion he carried. "One wardrobe mistress from the South said, 'Lord have mercy, Loretta! That child doesn't come and give me my kiss and hug anymore, he just done forgot about all of us now, they got him so spoiled.' One day I was making him up as a Moor, a half-Italian, half-African, and he was turning on his stool and saying—" she imitates Billy's childish profanities —" 'Dis Doddam tool! Dis Doddam tool won't move!' Jacqueline Susann told me to take him out of the show."

When Billy Dee was a teenager, Loretta scraped together the money to send him to acting classes given by Sidney Poitier. Loretta did not tell Big Bill about this little luxury, but she even borrowed thirty-five dollars from her mama (who hoarded her money in newspaper and a stocking under the mattress) to keep him in class. Soon afterward, Sidney Poitier landed the film *The Blackboard Jungle* and abruptly closed down the school. Loretta's mama sent Billy Dee racing to the airport by taxi to catch Sidney before he left town to get her money back. "Sidney told Billy, 'Oh, man, I'll be back.'" Loretta laughs. "I haven't met Sidney yet, but when I do I'll say, 'Where's the thirty-five dollars, Sidney?'

"Sidney did not ever reach out to help Billy. But then, I remember reading his story. Sidney said that in the West Indies, his mother always felt that they should stand on their own two feet, so she took him out in a boat and she threw him over and told him to swim back. Suppose he had drowned? He says he had to fight for his life. So, I figured that he threw Billy in the water. He told him he was going to make it on his own. And he did."

16   The Mythical Other Mother

There is another significant mother figure lurking in the lives of stars—in each of our lives for that matter. This other mother's influence is potentially so phenomenally powerful that one cannot overlook it when exploring what makes a star become a star. The "other mother" in question is movies and television. Not as bizarre as it might sound: the media's evocative images can affect entire lives.

It was movies that revealed to Michael Caine a world beyond the dismal East London slum where he was born in 1933, at a time when his fish-porter father was one of millions of British struggling on the dole. What happened to Caine exemplifies the power this "other mother" can wield:

"When I became an actor, I became absolutely, completely, and perfectly happy. In one day. It rescued me. The cinema started out as an imaginative escape from my surroundings. Eventually, it became a literal escape."

"Movies and television are a moving mythology and I believe they do inspire greatness in people," claims Dr. James S. Grotstein.

In the 1980s the continual media assault is so pervasive, so invasive, that it is impossible to distinguish quite where the influence of the true biological mother might end and that of the "other mother" begin. If, as Jack Nicholson observes, John Wayne had more impact on the mass psyche than any American president, it is very likely that he was also the catalyst that sparked a few thespian careers. Certainly ours is the first time in history when a man or woman can literally become recognizable right across the globe and live on in perpetuity. And Wayne, of course, is but one such influence. The most powerful celluloid heroes spring up when the realities upon which they were based are no longer available for inspection: James Dean, Rudolph Valentino, Marilyn Monroe.

Celluloid myths or images are literally larger-than-life and commensurately superpowered in the fantasies we attach to them. In terms of life inspiration, the cinema has an automatic edge over those shrunken versions piped into the television and consumed along with family interruptions and TV dinners. Inky dark cinemas which obliterate intrusions (well, most intrusions) are far more conducive to firing fantasies and precipitating the most potent kind of mind travel.

For thirteen-year-old Dorothy Faye Dunaway, in just one trip to a movie theater and a couple of hours in the thrall of Gene Tierney, the message was transmitted: this could all be hers. She saw her passport away from the dirt roads and the peanut farm in Bascom, Florida, where her mother, Grace Dunaway, had taken her and her brother when their father, John M. Dunaway, an Army career sergeant, left them.

In one fell swoop, this magical world of cinema promised to remove Dorothy Faye (who had been schooled in Texas, Arkansas, and Mannheim, Germany) from her poor, fatherless environment; from its unsophistication (they could not afford a phone); from its austerity and blatant struggle. Grace Dunaway's financial shortcomings so embarrassed Dorothy Faye that she would rather not invite friends home than have them find out how poor she was. Cinema transported her from her reality as "a lonely, frightened child."

Post–Gene Tierney, Dorothy Faye set up backyard pantomimes in which she of course starred, posing hair piled high, hand provocatively on one hip, emulating those movie stars whose immensely glamorous lives so captured her imagination. She soon progressed to playing a nurse in a community theater production of *Harvey*.

Cinema's "other mother" influence on Faye does not denigrate Grace Dunaway's own strong impact: mother and "other mother" work in conjunction with one another. In fact, Faye's famous intensity and perfectionism can be traced to Grace specifically. She infused both her children—Faye's brother Mac is a most successful Washington, D.C., lawyer—with that same drive. "My mother had a very important ambition for me—and it's the only thing I'd quarrel with her about—and that was to be the best," said Faye.

Grace, a determined woman who expounded the benefits of sheer hard work, was very much the devoted mother. She sensed that her children were destined for greatness. A devout Methodist, Grace was initially not keen on Dorothy Faye's plan to become an actress. Yet for all her religiosity, she ultimately found the goal that she be successful more pressing than her distaste for show business. "She was not a stage mother by any means, but she was totally seduced by what you'd call 'the American Dream,' " Faye observed.

Fame disappointed Faye in that it did not present her with the instant happiness she expected. Grace Dunaway, who remains close to her daughter, told David Lewin of the London *Daily Mail*, "I only hope that somehow at the end when she finds enough love, enough money, enough status—whatever it is that she needs—I hope then that she finds a little peace of mind."

Jessica Lange had an extremely active fantasy life as a child and with hindsight can see that she was seduced by the notion of story-telling. Although she is now close to her two older sisters, she was isolated as a child—voluntarily—and has fewer memories of playing with them than she does of being alone. If Jessie was missing, Dorothy Lange knew she was probably in the closet playing alone, or somewhere happily enacting scenes she had either created herself or stolen from films—and tackling all the roles. Her favorite was high drama from *Gone With the Wind*, and she alternately lay on the couch as the dying Melanie and sat up to play Scarlett. She did not allow others into her private world and felt very foolish if caught in the act.

Sylvester Stallone was an escapist child, journeying into fantasy books, devouring anything that dealt with adventure and heroism. A foreshadowing of Rocky and Rambo, perhaps? Jack Nicholson told Ron Rosenbaum, "I was always a fantasist. I always wrote my way out of trouble in school." Stardom was also a fantasy for Dustin Hoffman, who was named after cowboy star Dustin Farnum, and whose older brother was named after actor Ronald Colman. Hoffman's celluloid heroes were Marlon Brando and James Dean. He peered in the mirror wishing he could look like them, feeling sure he had their talent.

Marilyn Monroe's influence on Madonna spoke loud and clear to all who saw her in her first years of stardom, although she herself has since come to dismiss it. After she, too, became a superstar, it actively irritated her to be likened to the legendary Norma Jean, whom she blatantly imitated in the video for her hit record "Material Girl." It was as if she had suddenly looked behind the platinum vision and was not so sure the comparison was entirely complimentary. For unlike Marilyn, Michigan-born Madonna Louise Ciccone is not a victim, nor is she addicted to pleasing. And at this stage in her own fame, why should she relish being likened to anyone?

For Madonna, escaping into fantasizing and daydreaming was infinitely more pleasurable than dealing with her reality. Reality was not very pretty. Reality was her mother's death from breast cancer when Madonna was six years old, and the intense dislike she took to the "wicked stepmother" with whom her Chrysler engineer–father chose to replace Mom two years later.

The eldest girl in a family of six, Madonna's needs were fierce and overwhelming—both to break away from "the crowd" at home and to make her individual mark. She rebelled at school by going for outrage: she wore lipstick, a padded bra, and colorful underpants which she flashed at every opportunity. But behind the bravado, she felt abandoned, first by her namesake mother, then, when he remarried, by her father. She was lonely and empty. Had that void not been so immense, she would not have been so driven.

Teenager Melanie Griffith fantasized that her true mother was not Tippi Hedren, whose name was there in ink on her birth certificate, but Marilyn Monroe. Hedren, the blue-eyed blonde who was Hitchcock's favorite protégée and starred in *The Birds* and *Marnie,* gave birth to Melanie in August 1957, in the same New York hospital where Marilyn had recently been sequestered for a miscarriage. Melanie's flight of fancy (perhaps the hospital had made a mistake, she speculated, or God had switched her over when Marilyn briefly held her?) was therefore based on a modicum of reality.

The Marilyn idea first captured Melanie's imagination as a blossoming sixteen-year-old. She grew taller and curvier than Tippi—more Marilynesque. "I used to think maybe it was true. Just because I was real different from my mom," she admits. Now that the fantasy is far behind her, she obviously finds the topic rather embarrassing. Belatedly, she also recognizes the implied slight to her mom, of whom she is so proud. In fact, Mom was not offended. Tippi merely thought, "Melanie! Come on! I don't know what in the world prompted her to say that, it was ridiculous."

Even so, the effects of the fantasy seem locked in place in Melanie's wispy, breathy voice which sounds suspiciously like a long-since-absorbed emulation of Marilyn's. If the legendary Marilyn did give Melanie something, it does not detract from Tippi's legacy. Her mother's qualities are class, elegance (which Melanie sometimes forgets to practice), and loyalty (which she hopes she does not). She also received Tippi's strength and good survival instincts, which stood her in good stead when in her teens she got mixed up with drinking and drugs. "She gave me the ability to survive on my own. She taught me to trust in myself, encouraged me to be strong. I think Mom is really kind of one-of-a-kind, you know?"

Melanie also admires Tippi for the ladylike way in which she held her silence for twenty years about her ordeal with Alfred Hitchcock. The svengali director was so obsessed with Tippi that he put her under surveillance by crew members and became so proprietorial that he was angered if she did not check her personal social engagements with him in advance. Events came to a boiling point in the midst of the filming of Hedren's second Hitchcock film, *Marnie,* when, as Melanie puts it, "He basically said, 'You sleep with me or else!' But my mom never came out and said that, until Donald Spoto wrote *The Dark Side of Genius,* which I think is amazing, you know?"

(In fact, Hitchcock spoke of canceling Hedren's forthcoming part in *Mary Rose,* pointed out that she would no longer be able to help out her parents financially, and in effect threatened to ruin her in the business in which he had made her. When she refused to comply, he stopped speaking to her.)

Tippi Hedren grew up in Minneapolis, Minnesota, in a three-generational household that was formal but happy. Her American-born parents, Bernard and Dorothea Hedren, an accountant for a meat-packing company and homemaker respectively, were both strong influences. "There was never any backtalk. I was brought up to cook, clean, sew, and cope, with the 'life is tough, and if you can't take care of yourself it is even tougher' approach."

Hedren's paternal grandparents were stern Swedes, the maternal bloodline was German/Norwegian. "What my grandparents gave Mom," Melanie Griffith observes, "was strength and a home base. The courage to do what she wanted to do." Hedren's family was extremely poor and her secret ambition to be an ice-skater in the Ice Follies came to naught because there was never enough money for lessons. Her father's health precipitated their move to Los Angeles's warmer climes when Tippi was sixteen.

She was broken-hearted and truly thought her life was ruined. She had lost her friends and found herself in an alien world where she alone was in loafers, plaid skirt, and cashmere sweater, and all her high school peers wore short skirts, high heels, and an abundance of makeup. "My parents, hoping to reverse my apparent misery, sent me back to Minneapolis to live with the family for whom I had always babysat. I soon discovered 'there's no place like home.'"

She had won beauty contests and modeled for the Teen Club department in the Donaldson's store's Saturday fashion shows when, encouraged by her local success and by her parents, she boarded a train for New York with enough money for a month at the Barbizon Women's Hotel. She did not need the ticket back home; she signed with the Eileen Ford Agency and stayed for nine years.

While in New York, she married Peter Griffith (a commercials producer and director) and Melanie was born. Her marriage ended while Melanie was a baby, but she continued to model, then ventured into TV commercials, which brought her a step nearer to films—not that she craved them. She loved modeling;

it took her right around the world once and was highly lucrative. At one point she had ten television commercials running, for everything from refrigerators to makeup. One, for Sego, was spotted by Alfred Hitchcock, which led him to put her under contract and cast her in *The Birds*. She and her four-year-old daughter moved West.

"I think Hitchcock wanted an unknown because no actress in their right mind would have done it," she admits. Thankfully, Melanie was unaware of Tippi's collapse after being confined in a room for a week and having a succession of angry birds thrown at her. "It was a horrendous film to do. It was horrendous to watch. It was interesting getting to know his truly incredible 'IBM' brain, his knowledge of the industry, and his fantastic sense of humor. *The Birds* gave me an education that would have taken ten years to acquire." She is philosophical about what began as a wonderfully exciting opportunity and turned sour. "I really can look back and say that it enhanced my life tremendously, as difficult as it was."

Tippi strongly defends Mr. Hitchcock on one incident: the shocking gift he gave Melanie for her sixth birthday, an eerily accurate replica of Tippi in the form of a doll, lying in what looked for all the world like a mini-coffin. The gift was well-intentioned, Tippi insists, and not the weird joke it appeared. (Or "really sick," as Melanie has described it.)

"It was an enormously beautiful little doll, except that it was not just features of me—it *was* me!" Tippi explains. "In fact, they sent me to the makeup department for a mask. They had Elizabeth Taylor, every actress, in mask form, so it didn't surprise me. The ultimate result being this little doll for Melanie, dressed in clothes from *The Birds*. And unfortunately, it was in a pine box, not just a beautiful white gift box, but a wood kind. Melanie just went . . . it had a terrible effect on her. And we just put the doll away."

Tippi is now married to third husband Luis Barrenechea, a steel fabrication plant owner, and remains a most active fundraiser for her "Roar" foundation, which she began when she was married to Noel Marshall, the executive-producer of *The Exorcist*. They fell in love with lions and cheetahs while making two films in Africa and proceeded to raise twenty-five young cubs, "some right in our home." Tippi, who now travels as International Relief Coordinator for Food for the Hungry, explains that since the population on their ranch climbed to one hundred and fifty cats, the females have been on birth control.

To the strains of lions harmonizing in concert in the dusk outside, she admits she had misgivings about raising Melanie amidst the cats—indeed they call their plastic surgeon "the family doctor." No family member escaped injury, but she says cheerily, "It isn't serious unless you're dead!" It was also fun. Once they returned just in time to see the king-size mattress going out of the sliding door on its way to the pool, tugged by a little lion at one end and a tiger at the other. Her involvement with animals, she concedes, "borders a little bit on insanity. There's a degree of obsession here—I think any psychologist could have a field day with me!"

When Melanie Griffith was fourteen, she met Don Johnson and, she admits, applied the logic of adolescence: "If I love him, and he loves me, how could you tell me I can't be with him? I was very headstrong. I hope that I don't have a daughter like me!" Looking back, Tippi says, "I don't know that she was any wilder than anybody else, except that she happened to be in a situation of being a Hollywood brat, as the kids of actors are sometimes called. I certainly would handle it differently now, I would have been a lot stronger about it. But there was such a strong feeling for Don, I really didn't want to lose her friendship. You know, when you're damned if you do, and damned if you don't? It was just a terrible time for me, just awful."

Films grabbed Melanie rather than her grabbing them, she claims, and that same year she was approached to audition for Arthur Penn's *Night Moves*. Her first response was, "Thank you, but no thank you," because her interest lay in psychology and Greek history. Tippi almost dropped the telephone when the offer came in; she immediately worried that perhaps she had made insufficient effort to point out the heartbreak behind the glamour in the business. After all, Melanie had just seen mommy wearing pretty dresses. "You're constantly being looked at like a piece of meat," Tippi explains, but adds, "You also get to go to a lot of beautiful parties, meet interesting people, there's a lot of wonderful things." Eventually, the consensus of opinion was that it was too good an opportunity for Melanie to pass up.

To call Melanie outspoken would be an understatement, says Tippi who admits that the public attention focused on Melanie's now-resolved drug and drinking problem was painful. "Especially because at the time she was doing all that, I didn't even know it. I don't feel badly about saying that, because most parents don't know. It was never as bad as the press made it out to be, though. Never, that is just point-blank."

"It was a problem but it has been overblown," Melanie agrees. "I think that a lot of people have gone through that and I thought that I could maybe help some people if I admitted it—help other young women. I was saying it's okay to be fucked up, to admit it to yourself, and that you can get help, there are places to go." She is thoughtful for a moment. "Mothers and daughters are still two people, you know? So, I don't think I'm the kind of person who could live under any person's thumb. I know I put my mom through a lot of pain probably, but we're really close now, and that's what matters."

Maurice Micklewhite did not want to be who he was, he wanted to be somebody else, so Michael Caine lives, and Maurice Micklewhite is dead. That is how far Caine determinedly removed himself from the world he once occupied. It was a world in which Mr. and Mrs. Micklewhite, Maurice, and his brother slept in one room of their two-room tenement apartment and bathed in a tin tub in the other. Caine's mother (who is now in her eighties) worked as a cook, took in sewing, and scrubbed office floors after dark. The outside toilet had to suffice for eight people.

Maurice, a monosyllabic, closed-off boy who constantly had his nose buried in a book, would play hooky from sports to visit the cinema. Of one thing he was certain, he did not relish facing frozen cod and haddock at five A.M. every day for the rest of his life as his fish-porter father, grandfather, and great-grandfather had done before him. He wanted those other worlds, the ones he read about and saw on the screen.

While Maurice's devoted mom was supportive, his father was dismayed by his career choice, believing it to be a line of work which inevitably cast aspersions on his sexual preferences. Maurice married young and had a six-month-old daughter, Dominique, to support, but this did not stop Mrs. Micklewhite; she offered him her hard-earned life savings to tide him over while he tried his luck at an acting career. Sadly, Caine's father, who died suddenly and swiftly of liver cancer at age fifty-three, did not live to see his son's odds-defying transformation from a penniless, unemployed, would-be actor.

As Caine's star was rising, he invited his mother to attend the posh *Zulu* premiere in London with him, but she declined, saying she would not have felt comfortable. Michael arrived by chauffeur-driven limousine, and as he headed for the doorway, he heard a voice pipe up from the cordoned-off crowd, "Good luck, Maurice!" His dear mother had made the trip by bus and, along with all his other fans, waited patiently in the rain for two hours to see him arrive.

Mrs. Micklewhite's days of hiding from the rent man, and peeping out from behind the curtains, were behind her when Michael Caine became a star. But she is not given to lavish living or indulging herself, and when Caine asks her, "What do you want, Mum?" she says, "I don't want anything."

Carol Burnett cried the first time she saw James Stewart. To Carol, the warm, kindly, paternal figure represented the daddy her daddy might have been had he not left her and been an alcoholic. When Stewart spoke or smiled out from the screen, Carol felt his attention was focused on her alone. In the fantasies she spun around him, Carol invested him with greater power— this was her friend who would never let her down. For James Stewart, she could just as easily have substituted Robert Young of "Father Knows Best."

"The child whose environment is depressing or stagnant might set their sights on a screen image of how they would like their future to be, internalize it, and strive toward it, and that can be quite powerful," says Dr. R. Barkley Clark. "The image that comes across to the child is, 'That looks like someone who must feel very important and very good standing in the glittering lights and smiling the way they're smiling.' It says, 'That person is happy and that's what I want for myself.'"

For a child like Bette Midler was (a malcontent who always wished she was someone else), celluloid images can create something healthy to hang on to, a place to focus aspirations: "I decided I was going to be a legend, long before the public knew about me," said Bette, who, true to her word, affectedly took to calling those around her "darling" when she was seven. She planned her fame quite deliberately, determining it would come via a character she could hide behind: enter the Divine Miss M.

Ruth Midler, whom Bette adored, was a movie fan who once sold lingerie for a living. Ruth, to whom film fantasies and escapism meant so much, named her three daughters after her favorite stars: Judy Garland, Susan Hayward, and Bette Davis.

Ruth and Fred Midler moved to Honolulu from New Jersey before Bette was born in 1942, but it was hardly an island paradise. Theirs was the only white, Jewish family in their poor, shack-filled neighborhood in Hawaii. In the 1950s, Ruth was quite successful in the real estate business, but Bette cannot remember her parents enjoying the spoils of their labors.

Ruth's life was marred by the tragic death of Judy, her eldest daughter (a car exiting a garage crushed her against a wall), and her only son, Danny, was mentally handicapped. Yet Ruth always managed to encourage Bette's eccentricity, her entertainer side.

Although Bette had her show-offish, extroverted personality, she was an insecure, vulnerable young girl who was subjected to the taunts that befall an early developer endowed with big breasts. "I had my feelings hurt a lot as a kid and had built up a lot of armor and defenses." Yet Bette's internal picture of Bette was at odds with reality; initially she believed she was a ravishing creature, particularly when she had gone to town on her hair and makeup. Her positive self-image was shattered by the name-calling and by what she read in print (and what must therefore be true) about herself. Offstage she is suprisingly shy, restrained, and even ladylike. Still, she sees herself as a split, if not multiple, personality. The gutter girl, the librarian, the artist, the business-woman all vying for attention. What she calls the "look at me, I used to be nothing, now I'm a star" syndrome.

Ruth Midler died in 1979, a day before Bette's return from a work trip to Australia. Her sister Susan had nursed their mother during her two-year struggle with cancer—another reason for Bette, the absent, otherwise-occupied career girl, to feel delinquent as a daughter.

Even a few years after Ruth Midler's death, tears still sprang easily when she talked about the mom who had told her to go and make something of herself. Bette once remarked, "I just didn't want to die not having lived. My will not to be anonymous was so strong—and I don't understand where it came from, I really don't. I've always been grateful for my drive." Perhaps her success will become an "other mother" inspiration all its own. Certainly, she has now acquired the credentials that will one day secure her place among the legends that live on . . . and on and on.

17 It's All in a Name: The Show Business Dynasties

It is a debate that rages endlessly. Is a famous name a blessing or a burden? Diana Douglas's son Michael is the perfect example of an identity problem transcended. He successfully stepped into the hulking shadow of Kirk Douglas (a.k.a. Spartacus), but more than that, he created an identity all his own. Not that he managed it without trepidation or trying times: "I geared myself up for it knowing the comparisons were going to be made," he told Sue Russell in 1979. "It was very tough. I . . . always had the waste-basket and was puking backstage."

Michael Douglas succinctly summarized the negative side of being a second-generation star when he explained: "There is always a little piece of yourself which is not yours. A little piece of yourself that they take away from you, in terms of getting your full sense of satisfaction. The 'I did it.' "

Inevitably, those in show business families face physical comparisons: What do you know? Michael Douglas has Kirk Douglas's dimple! Also inevitable, the surrounding swirl of accusations of rampant nepotism. Those, Michael Douglas merely shrugged off, saying, "That's a reality, you deal with it, and it will go on forever." But Dorothy Bridges' son Jeff confronted his family name (and fame) with decided ambivalence. He was not comfortable with the nepotic element and was consumed by guilt about the ease of his success. Why had there been no suffering involved, no paying of dues? Why did his dad have all the right connections? Why was he so privileged?

It took years for Jeff to come around to his mother's way of thinking. Dorothy Bridges simply does not subscribe to the notion of nepotism. "It's so obvious [you can get a part or two]," she says emphatically, "but from then on, people are even more hypercritical when your parents are prominent in the business. We all love to see someone fail as well as succeed."

In fact, although show business families abound, the only true American acting dynasty is the Barrymores. The Barrymore connection is unique in that it stretches further back than the birth of films. When John Sr., Lionel, and Ethel cornered Hollywood's dynasty market in films in the 1940s, they were the third generation of actors in what was already a splendid theatrical royal family. (When John Barrymore went into films, it was considered tantamount to selling out.)

It was the next Barrymore generation that personified the negative aspects of the legacy of a label. For them, the Barrymore renown simply proved too much to live up to. John Sr.'s daughter, Diana, died an alcoholic before she was forty, and his son, John Drew Barrymore (Drew's dad), ducked out of the business in the 1970s without making an impact—aside from dubious headlines concerning public brawling and drug arrests.

Little Drew Barrymore was responsible for elevating the family stock once again when as an entrancing seven-year-old she had an auspicious close encounter with Steven Spielberg's extraterrestrial, E.T. Drew's Hungarian-born mother, Ildiko, was also an actress, and with Mom's assistance, Drew had made her debut in a burger commercial at eleven months. Ildiko was not surprised by Drew's achievement. "She has such concentration, it's spooky. You can't instill that."

When Mom or Dad is a star, growing up in their limelight can clearly become a seductive hook into the world of show business. Larry Hagman did protest too much as a teenager, when he talked about becoming a veterinarian and turned his back on opportunities that Mom pushed his way. But he was hooked by age seventeen. Janet Leigh and Tony Curtis were photographed for the cover of *Life* magazine clutching their daughter, Jamie Lee Curtis, when she was six weeks old. How about that for an early fix of fame?

Dr. R. Barkley Clark believes that having a famous parent need not be detrimental, providing that "behind the visible signs of success, the message gets across how a person becomes important, how a person becomes competent and successful. The parent's achievements can be very positive if the tools that it took to get there are shared with the child, if the child actually learns from the parent how to be successful." When a star has found success despite a parental shadow, Dr. Clark suspects that the parent was not a distant, elusive figure, but one who took the time and trouble to interact with the child, to show them what it takes.

Mary Martin's ambition took her away from Larry Hagman. But the moms of Michael Douglas and thespian brothers Jeff and Beau Bridges put their maternal roles before their own acting careers. Candy Bergen's mom, Frances; Teri Garr's mom, Phyllis; Diana Douglas; Dorothy Bridges; and Mia Farrow's mom, Maureen O'Sullivan, all kept the home fires burning, even when it meant sacrificing their own chances.

Dorothy Bridges got a huge thrill out of seeing husband Lloyd, sons Beau and Jeff, and grandson Jordan all united in *The Thanksgiving Promise,* a Disney movie which Beau directed—a bigger thrill than she would have had from an acting achievement that was hers alone. Theirs is a family that puts family first. They enjoy frequent gatherings at Dorothy and Lloyd's lakeside home in Bear Valley, 7,500 feet up in the High Sierras. They also have a house in Malibu, where their life-style revolves around the beach, long walks, and baseball, and much playing of Monopoly, Parcheesi, and Trivial Pursuit.

Perhaps it is the very dynastic aspect of the Bridges family's success that has played a part in keeping the feet of all its members firmly fixed to the ground. Or maybe, as the confidently jovial Dorothy suggests, it is because neither her husband nor her sons have reached Frank Sinatra or Marlon Brando–like dimensions of superstardom. (Of course, their unaffected attitude *could* stem from having a wife and mother who views them that way.) Dorothy's perspective: "This is just the work that you do."

Her father was a sailor from Liverpool. While on shore leave in Boston, he deserted ship to marry Dorothy's mother, a pretty minister's daughter with long blonde hair who had caught his eye in church. With admirable enterprise, he approached the minister, explained that he was far from home, and swiftly finagled himself an invitation to Sunday lunch. Nine months later, Dorothy's parents were wed. Her father, who lived to the ripe old age of ninety-three, was a self-educated man who eventually rose to an executive position with the Broadway department store.

The Bridges family is resolutely down-to-earth, and Lloyd and Dorothy, who have now been married for four decades, live in the old West Los Angeles neighborhood where both were raised and attended school. Their home is just a stone's throw from where they first met fifty years ago in a UCLA play; their old neighbors remain their closest friends. "I'm not trying to make us sound wonderful, that's just the way our lives have gone," says Dorothy.

She is insistent that although Jeff made what many would consider a premature acting debut at four months old, she did not imagine for one second that either Beau or Jeff would grow up to become actors. "Really, like a typical middle-class mother, I hoped one would be a doctor, one would be a lawyer. . . ."

Her disappointment was certainly ameliorated by her sons' success, but she has no illusions about the industry. "I've lived vicariously through the sorrow and insecurity of an actor's life. You're at the mercy of somebody hiring you and luck, having nothing to do with how capable you might be. I wouldn't *wish* that career on anyone. I worried about it. I never encouraged them."

It was she, however, who delivered a short, sharp pinch to baby Jeff to bring tears to his eyes during that first screen appearance. "I didn't pinch him very hard, but he still wouldn't cry," says the Dr. Spock devotee, sounding entirely unashamed of her un-Spockian action.

Two years before Jeff was born in 1950, Lloyd and Dorothy lost a three-month-old son in a crib death. A lot hinged on Jeff's arrival, yet it seemed headed for disaster. Midway through his delivery, Dorothy had a dangerous allergic reaction to the spinal anesthetic. She went into shock and labor stopped. A terrifying experience, given what had gone before.

"It was a miracle that he was okay. I knew I was in trouble. Once he was born, he was all right, but it was very touch and go. I finally begged them to let me sit up —you know how they strap you down? I made them untie me, and I just sort of panicked. They were very concerned. I thought how mad my husband would be if I either died or didn't have his baby. So I decided I'd better get on with it, and I did," she says matter-of-factly.

Early on, she instigated a policy of devoting an unadulterated daily hour to each of her three children, a technique she picked up from Dorothy Barouk's book *New Ways of Discipline,* which espoused the theory that if children felt they owned enough of their parents exclusively, they would not behave badly simply in order to gain attention.

"It seemed to work. Naturally it wasn't perfect harmony in our house at all times, there was always teasing and so forth, but relatively speaking I would say it worked very successfully. And they still talk about it, which makes me kind of purr."

The fact that Dorothy was a progressive mother and Lloyd was adept at changing diapers, bathing children, and getting up in the middle of the night, makes it especially ironic that both Jeff and Beau have been known to spout crazy tales in interviews—at Dorothy's expense. She remembers them once saying that they were beaten and told, "Now you're going to get it. Pull down your pants."

Unexpectedly, she does not skip a conversational beat when tentatively asked about Jeff's assertion that she beat him with a rhino penis. She fields the question in the unperturbed manner of one who is intensely familiar with the bizarre and off-the-wall.

"Well, first of all, I've never *seen* a rhino penis. I did come home from Alaska once with a—it was just a joke—a long piece of bone that was supposed to be the penis of, what's the mammal? A walrus? Then someone said, 'You were sold a bill of goods, because a penis doesn't have any bone in it.' But I've never taken it. . . . When I got *real* mad, I had a little bamboo switch and I chased them with it when I was trying to get a crack at their leg or something. But I rarely managed to catch them. It wasn't a rhinoceros, that's kind of bizarre!"

Many of Jeff's tales (not least, the rhino penis) have been if not manufactured, at least embellished, to amuse both himself and the journalist on the receiving end. However, Jeff did tell Claudia Dreifus of *Mademoiselle* magazine, in apparent seriousness, that he drove his father crazy with his smoking of pot. "He'd find the stuff, flush it down the toilet, and yell about how bad for me it was," Jeff said.

Dorothy glosses over any embarrassment she suffered during Jeff's rebellious period, which was itself, in her view, highly exaggerated. A *Rolling Stone* interview in the seventies stands out in her mind: "He made himself sound like a drug addict. When he was in high school, he and a group of friends, they were smoking pot . . . and as far as I know, that was the only drug they fooled around with."

True, he was girl-mad, and an erratic student, flummoxing them with grades like an A in physics one semester, a dismal F the next. But he did not drop out of school, or present his parents with any serious discipline problems.

His mother downplays the nepotism factor that caused Jeff so much grief, but she was aware of the pressure put on him by Lloyd's and big brother Beau's shadows. "I saw fame as a dream and a nightmare that came together all at the same time," Jeff once said.

"I always thought he was very good-looking, but that's not enough," says Dorothy, admitting it was fortuitous that at least the brothers did not look alike.

Jeff was born eight years after Beau (whom he worshiped) and four years before Cindy. And as Dorothy points out, the middle child in any family always has a hard row to hoe. According to psychologists, she reports, "he could have turned out to be a monster." Instead, he became one of the most loving, caring men she has ever met—and, upon occasion, one of the most outrageous.

When their father was in the television series "Sea Hunt" and occasionally persuaded the producer to cast them, the boys' reaction was underwhelming. They were neither interested nor impressed. Nor did they like it when, at the height of his "Sea Hunt" fame, their father attracted autograph-seekers who interrupted their fun on family trips to the zoo. They were resentful of the intrusion; why wasn't Dad with them, looking at the monkeys? On the plus side, they grew up with absolutely no fear of the camera whatsoever—something Dorothy feels helped them enormously as actors. Neither she nor Lloyd pushed Beau or Jeff or sought jobs for them; the opportunities that came up were simply family-type affairs. For instance, a friend cast Beau in his first film, *The Red Pony,* when he was four years old.

One definite contributory factor to Jeff's view that fame could be a nightmare was seeing his dad blacklisted for two years during the McCarthy era. For Dorothy, "It was a tough time, very disillusioning. We never even read Karl Marx. To this day, I couldn't tell you what the philosophical or political aspects of Communism were, and yet some group of nuts decided that if you had signed a petition saying you objected to Jews being kept out of a housing development, that made you suspect." They later learned that they had been turned in by a neighbor. They were not Communists and never had been, but their dossier noted that Dorothy had collected clothes for starving Russian women and children during the siege of Leningrad. Both Dorothy and Lloyd are liberal thinkers, but any passion they felt to become politically active and work for change was dampened by the whole traumatic affair.

Now a grandmother of eight, Dorothy explains that her daughter Lucinda, an artist, exhibited similar talent to that of her older brothers, but at sixteen she had a change of heart about acting. She married a young Frenchman with old-fashioned values who would only permit her to be an actress if she never kissed another man on the mouth. A prohibitive stipulation, Dorothy felt, considering that "today, the first thing they do is leap stark naked into bed. No, I'm exaggerating! But Lucinda is very much into motherhood, wifery. You can't do both, *I* don't think, completely."

Joel Douglas acted in a couple of college plays but rapidly determined that he hated being in front of the camera, neatly eliminating any sibling rivalry with Michael. Their mother, Diana Douglas Darrid, was born in 1923 in Bermuda, where her British barrister father, Tom Dill, was serving as attorney general. Diana was the last in a line of six children, and when she was six, Daddy transplanted his brood from its island paradise to the constriction of damp, foggy Britain. He was intent upon being called to the English bar (the Colonial version being its poor relative) and to facilitate this went back to law school at Lincoln's Inn in London.

The transition to gloomy British weather and pea-soup fogs from idyllic, blue-skied Bermuda, where they had lived alongside the water's edge and literally scampered barefoot, was, Diana admits, traumatic. Worlds apart. Each Bermudian day had begun with the rude awakening of her father's piercing reveille: "It was quite wild, he used to blow the bugle every morning at 5:30 A.M.," she says with a grin, her British intonations still dominating her speech pattern despite decades in the United States.

To ensure there was no loitering, Diana's discipline-inclined pater followed his bugle call by bellowing down the hall for good measure. It was the signal that the members of father's home-grown miniregiment were expected to leap from their downy couches and "even if it was January and pretty damn cold" jump straight into the bracing waters.

There followed a demanding calisthenics routine and finally the ritual of hoisting the flags: the Union Jack, the white ensign, the red ensign, and lastly the house flag. "Then, after we'd all exercised like mad, we were allowed to have some breakfast and go to school!" Diana says brightly, recalling that the journey was made by pony cart. On Sundays, father marched the Dill regiment along to the church, where it occupied an entire pew.

Diana has fond memories of her father, admiring his bright mind and quick humor, but notes, "He had the English lawyer's biting sarcasm which was *devastating*. We were all terrified of that, and if one dared to voice an opinion at the dinner table, you could be crushed immediately." Their American mother was, by contrast, warm and motherly. The personality combination worked; her parents' marriage was long and happy.

Each of the Dill children was dispatched to various points on the globe to pursue a serious education. Diana's siblings went variously to Cambridge University in England, and to schools in Switzerland, Canada, and the United States. Her own relocation was to a boarding school on the tiny Isle of Wight off the south coast of England when she was seven. "God, it was cold," Diana says, pulling a face. "Damp, everything was always damp, the sheets were damp."

By sixteen, she was determined to become an actress. Father was equally determined that she become a lawyer. He was not the easiest man in the world with whom to disagree. When World

War II broke out, Diana was vacationing with a Danish friend in Denmark, which is where, had they not hurled themselves onto the last boat out, she would have been stuck for its duration.

Once back in Harwich, England, Diana was terribly torn. Her pregnant sister Fan was staying on in England and loyal Diana would have liked to also—all her friends were joining the Wrens. But the parental edict was that she hotfoot it back to the States. Fortunately, Diana's late arrival meant she missed the *Athenia,* which sank. Instead, she boarded the *Aquitania,* which was loaded with three times its usual passenger quota, and zigzagged across the Atlantic to avoid hidden U-boats.

Since her father had always denigrated American law schools, Diana had the perfect excuse to escape *that* fate, at least temporarily. She was permitted to enroll at the American Academy of Dramatic Arts, "to get the damn foolishness out of her system. Then she'll come back to Bermuda like a sensible girl, marry some nice Navy type," Diana quotes, imitating her father's formal British speech.

Diana first set eyes on Kirk Douglas, whom she always calls Doug, while in her junior year at the Academy. His reputation with the ladies was such that she swiftly made a mental note to "stay away from that one." In their senior year their paths crossed more directly when they appeared together in *Bachelor Born.* Doug, who was about twenty-three and "frightfully cocky," was playing a very old schoolmaster and turned in, as Diana recalls it, a dreadful, clichéd performance which earned him a fierce reprimand for showing off. The severity of the dressing-down prompted young Diana, watching from her perch on a trunk in the wings, to burst into tears of sympathy.

After rehearsal, Doug confided his concern over consolatory apple pie and milk. His six sisters had all sacrificed to get him to drama school and now . . . well, he would probably have to go back to being a shoe salesman in Amsterdam, New York. Duly prompted by fear into some honest, hard work, Doug's acting shone.

He and Diana dated, but "I was not quite ready for all that intensity. Also I was very naive sexually, and knew that I wasn't ready for *that,* so I sort of bolted, which annoyed him no end."

She was stunned to be offered a stock contract by Warner Bros. after graduating. The idea of being paid to act was astonishing, and despite a twelve-page epistle from Doug begging her not to sell out to artificial Hollywood, she signed. "Actually it was very good advice, which I paid no attention to whatsoever." Nor did she answer his letter.

Diana moved to Hollywood with the grudging consent of her disapproving father, provided her sister chaperone her, "which was just as well because Errol Flynn had his eye on me as the youngest arrival, and Ruth was shooing him away all the time." Although Diana made an impressive one hundred dollars a week, to her immense frustration, she had barely a foot of film to show for it. A rare highlight was a small part in *Keeper of the Flame* with Hepburn and Tracy, whose romance was blossoming. ("You could tell the sparks were really flying like mad.")

Appalled by her lack of progress, the gamine-looking blonde started modeling at Saks department store, then headed back to New York where she swiftly landed *Vogue* and *Life* magazine covers. The latter was spotted by Kirk Douglas, who was by then in the Navy and renewed their acquaintance by writing: *My bunkmate doesn't believe I know you. Will you please write and say that I do?*

This time she wrote back—more than once. In truth, the opinionated young man had never been far from her thoughts in the intervening two years; his political awareness had stirred up her own. "I'd never met somebody who'd really grown up in a slum background and broken out of it," she explains.

Their first attempt at meeting when Doug was on leave was thwarted because Diana was a nurse's aide at Bellevue and unable to finagle time off. Eventually, they met for lunch and a matinee of *Kiss and Tell*. They were still together for dinner and finally wound up at the Penthouse Club, where Doug "announced that I was going to marry him no matter what." That seemed to be that. They were instantly inseparable, "madly in love and having an affair, the whole bit."

Their accelerated wartime courtship was halted all too soon. Doug was called to his ship in New Orleans. Diana, rather incongruously, headed for a modeling assignment in Phoenix, Arizona.

The young lovers burned up telephone wires, furiously wrote letters, and were married soon after in New Orleans, first in the Naval Chapel and then by a rabbi. Diana's mother broke this news to Diana's father gradually and with trepidation. "The idea that Doug was an actor was an absolute anathema, so she said he was a naval officer, which indeed was true."

In a manner of speaking, Kirk Douglas's naval exploits involved, one hopes, an unusually inept cast of characters. As Diana waved a fond farewell from the quayside, he left on a shake-down cruise to Miami. At his side was a crew of officers none of whom had been to sea before and an absent-minded skipper who had done so only once.

"Totally green crew. It was absolutely pitiful. So the chaplain blessed the ship, a brass band started playing, and they backed out and immediately sunk a little motor boat behind them— *bashed* into another boat. Doug, who was the duty officer, was running up and down saying, 'Let's go men, let's go!' and with that they'd crash into something else. Well! I just collapsed with laughter, it was the funniest sight I've ever seen in my life and I just howled. The skipper's wife never spoke with me again."

With obvious mirth, she reports that from there, Doug's vessel ricocheted in and out of dry dock, emerging from each repair session only to bash into something else. So much for the celluloid hero. (Fortunately, Doug also could see the funny side of it. His wild sense of humor was part of his initial attraction, and even when she was furious with him, he managed to make her laugh.) Finally, Doug's operation edged toward its ultimate destination, the Pacific.

"I thought, my God, they're never even going to find the Panama Canal, let alone get out in the Pacific," she exclaims, her eyes widening. Against all odds, they did and were en route to Hawaii when they thought they had come across an enemy sub and the skipper made another blunder. "Instead of saying, 'Drop the depth charge marker,' he said, 'Drop the depth charge,' and they blew themselves out of the water!" she says; howling by this time. Doug, who was flung across the ship, developed stomach problems, however, and was invalided out of the Navy in June 1944.

To contribute to the war effort, Diana worked for Squibb, testing penicillin and rabbits' blood, and it was there, sick to her stomach amidst frightful smells, that she first realized she was pregnant. They moved in with Diana's sister in New Jersey. She had recently divorced Seward Johnson of the Johnson & Johnson family, with whom she had four children. Her settlement was a rambling, Normandy castle–style abode too enormous to keep up, so she lived in the gardener's cottage. Diana and Kirk occupied the nursery in the big house until Michael's birth in September 1944, an event with which twenty-one-year-old Diana was "so thrilled, I couldn't see straight." Michael arrived ten months and three weeks into their marriage: "I saw my whole family go, 'Phew!' "

Doug's early release gave his acting career a head start; in wartime's dearth of young leading men, the work flowed. When Michael was one year old, they moved from Manhattan to California. Before Joel's birth in 1947, Diana secured an infinitely superior contract with Twentieth Century–Fox and continued to work spasmodically in films like *Sign of the Ram, Let's Live Again,* and *House of Strangers*.

The marriage lasted only until Joel was two, and they divorced in 1950, amidst pleas from Doug's family that Diana reconsider. Her own mother, on the other hand, took the news wonderfully well, and simply sent Diana off to buy some gin and vermouth to make a martini.

"Opposites attract, but like is much easier to be married to," Diana says, explaining that she initiated the separation after much careful thought, because she felt it imperative for her own mental health and her children's. "He was a deeply restless person, and even with his great humor he had a sort of almost Russian unhappiness which I found very frustrating. I felt a sense of failure that I could not make him happy. I realized later that nothing was going to make him happy . . . but it took me a long time to realize that."

She moved her sons to an apartment on Manhattan's Central Park West, within about four blocks of Michael's current home. It amuses her to see her son repeat the conventions of his own childhood by sending her grandson Cameron to a traditional school where uniform is compulsory. Her divorce from Doug affected both boys quite differently.

"Michael suddenly got enormously stubborn and would make

great big issues out of very small things. If we were walking in the park and I'd say, 'Let's go down this path,' 'No!' he'd say, and he'd get red in the face and his eyes would fill with tears. I was very worried and so I took him to a child psychiatrist." She was reassured that Michael was not seriously disturbed, but merely reacting to the loss of his father, and was advised to be less strict and to dole out lots of love. The remedy worked.

Since Kirk Douglas lived in California, the two boys commuted to see him during annual vacations. He remained an enormous presence in their lives, albeit looming from afar. He penned the frequent, long letters of admonition for which he is now famous. With hindsight, Diana wonders if her attempts to be fair to Doug about vacations worked to Michael and Joel's detriment. "It was unsettling for them. There were different sets of rules in each house, and Joel said he would weep on the way going out and weep on the way coming back. It was all too much."

Their father was in conflict too. "He was crazy about the boys, but he said, 'I can't live with them and I can't live without them.' He would spoil them like mad one minute and then clamp down like crazy the next minute," an inconsistency she feared was ultimately more damaging than either the discipline or Doug's high expectations.

This situation was alleviated considerably when Kirk Douglas married Anne Buydens, his wife of over thirty years. (They have two sons, Peter and Eric.) Anger dissipated, communication was facilitated, and with Anne's help, Diana was able to ensure that their stays in their dad's California movie star mansion bore more resemblance to home. The two women first met when Anne was Doug's secretary and Diana took the boys to his film location in Paris. She naturally envisioned that they would stay in a hotel. Unthinkingly, Doug expected them all to stay under one roof, which Diana pronounced "a perfectly ghastly idea," as did Anne, who was already rather fond of him. Diana suggested she and Anne have lunch, and she swiftly reassured her successor that she harbored no hopes of a reconciliation.

Diana married writer Bill Darrid in 1956, two years after Anne married Doug, and all four are firm friends. Diana and Bill's lengthy five-year courtship began while they acted together in a production of *Light Up the Sky*. "He had not been married before and was not sure that he wanted to be, particularly to somebody with two children," she explains. "But he was marvelous with them. God, he was good with them. They're very close now."

Unlike Joel, the giggler, Michael never was a great smiler, even as a baby, and although he was popular at school and a good athlete, he was reserved. "People would actually stand on their heads trying to make Michael laugh, because when he did it was absolutely like the sunshine coming out from behind the cloud."

Despite the enormous discrepancies in their backgrounds, there is no doubt that Michael inherited his father's enormous drive and ambition. When he was about seven, Diana had to step in and stop him from playing competitive games like Monopoly, because he was so unswervingly intense, so intent upon winning, no matter what. In prep shool, Michael always uttered an adamant "No" when asked if he would follow his father into acting. He intended to become a lawyer or go into real estate, something sensible.

From afar Kirk Douglas's influence was still actively felt. "He's a very emotional man," Diana says, explaining that if all was not well in his career, Michael and Joel sometimes bore the brunt of it. "He would call Michael up in college and bawl the hell out of him. Michael was like, 'What? Where did that come from?' But they learned to deal with it and realize where it came from, after a time. I think it was bewildering to them, some of those storms that seemed to come out of nowhere." Tellingly, Michael since has said: "I'm grateful to my father for not spoiling me in my growing-up years. He had to fight for what he got and he has not deprived his kids of that privilege."

It was not until he became an English major at University of California, Santa Barbara, that Michael joined a drama department. UCSB was something of a change from Choate, his private school, and that first year at state university, he performed so badly that the powers-that-be were not entirely sure they wanted him back. "It was the sixties and everybody was rolling around in wine vats, vine leaves in their hair," Diana explains, "so his grades slipped appallingly."

Her son spent over a year away from UCSB, during which time

he worked in a gas station (becoming "Mobil Man of the Month") and in the wardrobe department on one of his father's films. When he returned to college, Michael changed his major to drama and prepared to stand toe-to-toe with the giant. Diana vividly remembers seeing Michael in the role of an eighty-year-old king. He was onstage a full four minutes before she recognized him. "I thought, 'Who is that? If that's a young actor, he is really extraordinary.' Doug had seen it the week before and both of us got on the phone absolutely jibbering like idiots. He said, 'What a Henry V he'll make!' I said, 'Yeah, my God!' "

Diana had given little thought to the effects of Michael's stardom until, flying back from the Dominican Republic with him and his wife, Diandra, she was suddenly conscious of the way people watched him. It was a feeling she recognized from her days as Mrs. Kirk Douglas. "There was a strangely greedy look in their eyes, as though they wanted to eat him up, you know? It was weird. It was a frightening kind of thing, that kind of stardom." She gropes for a phrase, then describes it as "almost cannibalistic," as if stars were objects and not human beings, and it was okay to gawk at them as if they were unable to look back.

"I told Michael when he first came out to Los Angeles to do the first TV films, 'Look, you've been inoculated by going back and forth. You've seen enough of Hollywood. If you start getting a swelled head, there's absolutely no excuse for it whatsoever. So don't. Don't go Hollywood on me.' And he never has."

Did Kirk Douglas, then, go Hollywood? "A bit, yes," she admits. "Well, it was absolutely stunning for him. He was like . . . given the candy shop. He had suddenly come out here and everybody just kept telling him how wonderful he was. You know, 'I am, I am.' It was absolutely marvelous. And I was the loyal opposition saying, 'Oh, come down to earth, for God's sake!' And he didn't want to hear that particularly."

Her own life has changed little, save for a temptation, she admits, for people in Hollywood to view "Michael's mom" as an avenue by which to get scripts to him. Her policy is to immediately deflect inquiries to Michael's agent and to refuse to become involved.

She herself is in the throes of a new burst of ambition. Diana was a regular on the TV series "Paper Chase"; performed in

Hamlet with David Birney; did *Hedda Gabler* at the Huntington-Hartford Theater; and appeared in the soap opera "Love Is a Many Splendored Thing" for three years before it went off the air in 1973. Now she feels she has finally grown into the character parts for which she is best suited.

The Douglas dynasty could never have begun were it not for Kirk Douglas's mother, Bryna, after whom he named his film-production company in 1955. Kirk Douglas was the middle child amidst six sisters, all of whom worshiped him. So did Bryna, whom Diana describes as marvelous, sensitive, and sweet. She was also strong, and held the family together after Herschel Danielovitch abandoned them all when Doug was fourteen. The Danielovitch women were hard workers, the type who, if dissatisfied with the laundry's efforts with their husbands' shirts, would think nothing of laundering them all over again.

When Michael was young, he had to have his appendix removed in Albany, New York, where he was attending a cousin's bar mitzvah with his father. Diana collected him after Doug flew back to Hollywood and was so impressed that Bryna, who was then living in a ladies' retirement home, traveled miles just to say hello to her.

Like Kirk's father, Bryna was Russian-born and illiterate. "She was learning, she was trying to teach herself, she'd spell out things on the signs. She'd say, 'C-a-ris-co, Crisco!' It was lovely," Diana recalls.

Doug became strangely bossy around his family and once, when Bryna was visiting, demanded that Diana get him a sandwich. Unused to being given orders, she retorted, "You say 'please' and 'thank you' in this house, or you don't get a bloody thing!" Bryna, she recalls, looked quite terrified.

"She thought he was going to strike me, I think, because that was the way [Doug's father] behaved towards women. And finally Doug said, 'All right, I'm sorry. Yes. I agree with that, I'll make the sandwich myself.' I said, 'No, I'll be happy to make it for you. Will you just say 'please' and 'thank you'?" With that, showing true star mom quality, Bryna not only relaxed, she started to giggle. "It was very funny," Diana recalls. "She said, 'That's the way, Diana!' "

18 *In Their Own Right*

Some star moms defy the very description. They are the antithesis of stage mothers. Women who would fight to the last breath to retain their own identities. Women who refuse to exist solely via their connections to their star kids. Women who do not need to be star moms for legitimacy, a role, a sense of purpose, an identity. Women for whom being an appendage is a dubious blessing.

Charlotte Sheedy is a successful New York literary agent. She is also Ally Sheedy's mother. Make no mistake, it is not that role she objects to, merely the label and its inherent disregard for her own achievements. Her view is not dissimilar to Chatie Wagner's. R. J. Wagner's mom declined to be interviewed, saying that she had nothing to do with her son becoming a star. Charlotte's philosophy is that she does not want to accept any accolades for her children's success any more than she wants to be judged for their failures. She believes we are each responsible for our own life.

Sheedy is an intense, articulate woman in her fifties who is tied by an invisible thread of history to Gerry Dreyfuss (Richard's mom) and Brandy Foster (Jodie's mom). All three have been political activists whose beliefs propelled them into campaigning and marching for causes like peace and women's rights. All three participated in the Women's Strike for Peace movement back in the early 1960s—Charlotte Sheedy was arrested for lying down in the street in Washington, D.C., and has spent a night behind bars.

Sheedy's career landmark came in 1977 with the enormous

success of her client Marilyn French's novel, *The Women's Room*. She is scrupulously honest in her assessment of the way Ally's fame has affected her life, acknowledging that her position in the literary world has benefited from her stronger image in Hollywood, an arena where she is called upon to sell the work of the writers she represents. While she was always taken seriously, she concedes:

"I think there is certainly a different acceptance of me, and I don't mind that. What I find appalling is that I feel that I have distinguished myself in all kinds of ways, against all odds. And I would like to think that *my* efforts towards who I am legitimize me.

"The fact that I have Ally as a daughter dazzles a lot of people, and I can see it in their faces. I don't like to be introduced as 'Ally Sheedy's mother' because I do feel that I have another identity." She suspects that her name is added to party invitation lists because of her daughter, and at business lunches, the first topic of conversation is frequently Ally. What's Ally up to? "Even in literary circles, they're enamored of Hollywood's larger-than-life pull. The power of the silver screen, it's really quite astounding."

Philadelphia-born Charlotte Sheedy was one of four children of immigrant parents. Her father was a Jew named Baum, whose family fled Poland during the 1890s pogroms and who was recruited into the Chinese Army at age nine after being orphaned. When Charlotte's parents met, her Russian-born mother was widowed and very poor, and had two small children. She ran a grocery store in the cellar of her house, and Mr. Baum came by, selling fruits and vegetables out of his truck.

After their marriage, her mother remained the family's economical mainstay, however, and when Charlotte was four, their home burned down. Enterprisingly, her mother borrowed money and built a profitable business from a twenty-four-hour grocery store, doing a roaring trade in sandwiches with employees of a nearby defense plant. Her mother was also an active force in their community (they were the only white family), but after the war, she utilized her newfound affluence to move them to an upper-middle-class area.

For Charlotte, the move was a complete culture shock. Her

parents spoke English, but they were uneducated and illiterate, and when they dispatched her to her new academically stringent high school, she failed miserably. She developed a popular line of witty self-mockery, but although that earned her acceptance and friends, she was not one of them and was miserable. She felt abandoned emotionally. When she was sixteen, she was abandoned physically. Simply put, her mother told her it was time she fended for herself.

Inspired by books she had read and the film *La Ronde*, with the impudence of ignorance Charlotte headed for Paris with a meager seventy-five dollars in her pocket. She entirely overlooked the not-inconsiderable handicap of not speaking French in France. Writer Gwen Davis, a Bryn Mawr graduate, kindly facilitated her survival by taking her in as a roommate and loaning her money. Charlotte duly learned French and that universal language of female survival —shorthand and typing. Spongelike, she soaked up a new world populated with students, painters, sculptors, and writers. Although two years later found her back in Philadelphia, cooking at the Horn & Hardarts cafeteria steam counter, she was never the same again.

Financial pressure forced her to abandon the notion of college and she worked as a legal secretary in New York and went through a brief failed marriage before meeting John Sheedy, Ally's father. They were summer neighbors on Fire Island. She read Simone de Beauvoir, he read Camus. Hence a kind of literary liaison sprang up which slowly turned to romance. They lived together for a couple of years before marrying, during which time Charlotte opened an art gallery in their Manhattan apartment. Meanwhile, she was also employed as a secretary/editorial assistant at Dial Press, a small publishing house. (Her boss there, Jim Silberman, would later publish *The Women's Room*.)

She was "enormously ambitious," compulsive about details, and so enamored of working with authors that mundane tasks like filing their letters thrilled her. She put in long hours before returning to her little gallery. "I loved who I was becoming," she says candidly. "That was always part of what I was doing—being aware of my image, who I was, and how I wanted to move through the world."

She cannot remember not being political. Her early years in

that underprivileged, black neighborhood left her with a keen eye for social equity and a natural affinity for the efforts of the Fair Housing Committee. In the late fifties, she supported the Freedom Riders, then she campaigned against nuclear arms by joining Women's Strike for Peace, which grew out of the Ban the Bomb movement.

By 1964, she and John had two daughters, Ally and Meghan. Charlotte freelanced as a photographers' food stylist, a job which left time for the accelerating demands of her political activities. After Patrick's birth in 1967, she was so involved in antiwar activism that the only way she could also hold down her job as a cookbook editor was by working around the clock. John Sheedy, an advertising man, admired her efforts. The conflicts in their marriage sprang more from political discrepancies than her absences and obsession. As she grew more radical, so John became more conservative.

"He found my activities very threatening," Charlotte admits. "My name was in the papers, he felt it was a reflection on him, and so that then turned into a feminist argument. I said, 'I am not your appendage, I have my own identity.' So all of those kinds of issues that were emerging coalesced in some way in this marriage. It was most extraordinary. Our homelife became a sort of battlefield . . . and I don't mean abusive. I mean that we were constantly arguing and discussing."

She was depressed and despondent after the assassinations of Martin Luther King and Malcolm X. She had worked as a draft counselor, had seen the inside of a jail for passive resistance, and by 1969 was certainly not in the mood to teach middle-class women how to serve party food. She left the world of cookbooks and with the aid of fellowships and grants became a history major at Columbia University. She had separated from her husband and was heavily in debt when her fortieth birthday loomed large. Suddenly, the notion of going for her Ph.D. looked increasingly unrealistic.

Instead, to survive, she typed manuscripts at night for twenty-five cents a page. She rode a bicycle all over town—who had cab fare?—and grew more and more distressed with her situation. Teaching history was out, she was no longer in publishing, and a full-time job was not a realistic option with three children. "I wanted to be a presence in their lives," explains Charlotte, who has the utmost respect for her ex-husband whose support as a stable and wholly involved parent enabled her to cope.

Her study and work schedules caused resentment among her children, who were splitting their time between the two homes. John was more affluent and had a housekeeper. "At my house we had pizzas on those English muffins," Charlotte admits, with a wry smile. Fast food aside, Ally groused that she could hear her mom's typewriter clacking all night long.

While at Columbia, Charlotte had given a paper which led to the publication of her book, *Jewish Women in America* (Dial Press, 1976). She had also scouted books on campus for publishing houses, so an editor friend, brushing aside Charlotte's misgivings, suggested she become a literary agent, pursuing as clients those writers she knew. She began her agency in 1974 with no financial capital whatsoever; typically, she invested herself. Moonlighting, at night she typed, read manuscripts, and copyedited. During the day, she ran her agency and took care of her children: "You'd often find me crying from sheer exhaustion."

Two years later her efforts were rewarded with *The Women's Room*, the book that put her on the map. She devoured the monumental manuscript (which filled two boxes) over a three-day weekend. Immediately, she recognized her life. She stayed glued to the couch, with a jar of peanut butter and bottle of white wine for company, and read voraciously. "I would doze off, I'd go back to the book. It was the most extraordinary experience of my life. I felt that somehow this woman had captured it all."

Marilyn French was her literary lion, but Charlotte also had a literary cub in her twelve-year-old daughter Ally, whose book, *She Was Nice to Mice*, was published around the same time. For Ally, that first taste of youthful success threw her into a disconcertingly competitive situation with her peers. The reaction she read was, "Let's watch Ally and make sure she doesn't turn into a snob." She was teased mercilessly when the school authorities hung a newspaper interview up on the wall, so she asked to have it taken down.

The acclaim also put her under pressure. She was blocked with her writing, afraid she could not match her earlier achievement. Never mind being "Ally Sheedy's mom"; for Ally, there were times when being "Charlotte Sheedy's daughter" carried its own penalty. She knows Charlotte is a very good literary agent, but she began hiding her writing from her, admitting, "It's very hard to have your mother telling you what's wrong, and it would drive me nuts if she'd rewrite something I'd written and send it back to me and say, 'This is how it should be restructured.'"

Looking to the positive, the interesting environment her mother created had a tremendous impact on Ally. She grew up surrounded by writers, political people, teachers, and scientists, primarily liberals, and many of them brilliant women who were involved in the inception of the women's liberation movement at Columbia University. That is where Ally spent much of her time after school, learning of the tyranny of sexism. Ally was nine when her parents separated and sees that as the watershed period when Charlotte really came into her own. Her own watershed was moving to California as soon as she was old enough.

"My kids do have a lot of complaints to make about me," Charlotte readily admits. "And their descriptions of me sometimes hurt my feelings. But it's okay. They should do it, because I could not deny their experience of me. That's how they experienced me, and that's how I was—but my motives may have been vastly different from those that they assign me, because adults live in a very complicated world."

Ally's allegation that she was emotionally absent from their lives pained her greatly. She was always there for her children, she retorted indignantly—and indeed she was, in times of crisis. "Ally said, 'Is that really how you wanted to raise us? That the only time we feel we could get any attention is when we had a crisis?' I said that, no, it wasn't, and I was sorry that was the effect it had on them. I failed them. In their eyes I failed them."

Charlotte had to prove herself through her work. With her impoverished background, respect did not come as a birthright. But viewing society "from the bottom up" gives you an edge, she believes. And Ally's childhood, while considerably more affluent than her own, has not overridden the family ethos. Charlotte is now extremely proud to see Ally's political activities, and was delighted when she hosted a party to introduce young Hollywood actors to Jane Fonda and Tom Hayden. "She thrills me in every way. I admire her enormously. I love her values."

In her own right, Charlotte at fifty-one years old achieved the house of her fantasies: a ten-room Victorian mansion set on three acres in upstate New York that represents all she missed as a child, "family, status, roots, belonging."

"It symbolizes, I guess, for me, my movement through life from the little slum girl . . . to this Victorian mansion," she says, verbalizing a sentiment shared by many of the nouveau riche and of nouveau status, but voiced by few. "I had every intention of distinguishing myself, every intention," she adds forcefully. "As I said before, I wanted to be respected. And I had contempt for that value, but I really craved it."

It is hard for Ally's generation, she thinks, to comprehend the profundity and scale of the changes that marked her own—changes which she played her part in effecting. In asking Ally to forgive her, she told her, "I was living through very revolutionary times, and you were brought along with it. I have to tell you that I feel very proud of those years. I think the antiwar movement was responsible for stopping the war in Vietnam, and I think women were in the forefront of it and terribly important, and haven't yet been given their due."

Many years ago, Charlotte had two abortions in Cuba because she was unable to have them performed in the States. "The fear and the pain and the things that one went through! Sexism in all kinds of ways has been addressed and changed," she says. She points to the fact that when she began her business, although a mother of three, she was unable to get a bank loan or rent an apartment without a cosignature from her ex-husband—something she was unwilling to accept. Those intensely frustrating days, when twenty years as "Mrs. Somebody" apparently counted for naught in terms of giving a woman rights and identity, have also changed. Charlotte Sheedy may not be the perfect supermom, but she does feel she can share in a sense of pride in achievement.

Prior to the heinous murder of her eldest daughter, actress Sharon Tate, on August 9, 1969, by Charles Manson's disciples, Doris G. Tate had given little thought to issues like penal reform and victims' rights. Sharon was twenty-six years old and eight months pregnant with what would have been Doris G.'s first grandchild. A nightmare beyond imagining.

Slain with Sharon, in what she used to happily refer to as her love house on Cielo Drive in L.A.'s Benedict Canyon, were four of her friends. Coffee heiress Abigail Folger, Voytek Frykowski, Jay Sebring, and Steven Parent—Sharon's husband, film director Roman Polanski, was away in London. The Manson murders were staggering in their brutality; the victims had been shot, stabbed, and bludgeoned—Sharon had been hanged from a rafter before being stabbed to death, a knife had entered Voytek Frykowski's body fifty-one times. The very next day, Manson's disciples struck again, killing Leno LaBianca, the owner of a chain of grocery stores, and his wife, Rosemary. The entire Hollywood community was spun into a state of sheer terror. But for the victims' loved ones, life would never again be the same.

Out of this unthinkable situation has emerged what is for Sharon's mom a career from the heart. Over a decade later, Doris G. is entrenched in campaigning to keep the murderous likes of Manson and his family members behind bars. Through groups like Parents of Murdered Children, she also spends much of her time offering solace to other families whose lives have been devastated by the murder of a child.

At the time of Sharon's death, Doris G.'s daughter was a star in the ascendant—a bright, beautiful flame, extinguished before she had the opportunity to fulfill her promise. She was always a head-turner, according to her mom, and at just six months old was chosen as "Miss Tiny Tot" in Dallas, Texas. At sixteen, Doris G.'s increasingly stunning daughter won the "Miss Richland, Washington" and "Miss Autorama" titles. Once she turned professional as an actress, work began to flow and she appeared in "The Beverly Hillbillies," *The Americanization of Emily*, *The Sandpiper*, *The Eye of the Devil*, and *Valley of the Dolls*.

"Dear God, she was beautiful," Doris G. says, showing a photograph of her radiant daughter, serene in her pregnancy, shortly before her death. "Sharon was more beautiful as a teenager than she was in her twenties; in Europe people would turn around on the street just to look at her."

The Tates spent three years living in Verona, Italy, where Sharon's father, Colonel Paul Tate, was stationed with the U.S. Army Intelligence. Doris G. worried that their frequent moves were hard on her three daughters, Sharon, Deborah Ann (now thirty-four, with one child), and Patricia Gaye (now twenty-nine and a mother of three), but they adjusted without difficulty.

Sharon was sixteen years old when she was spotted walking in St. Mark's Square, Venice, and approached by a film crew member who thought she would be the perfect girl for Pat Boone to serenade in a gondola. Little suspecting she was American, he approached her in broken Italian. "Sharon just went right along with it. She got a big kick out of that!" her mom recalls, smiling.

Excitedly, Sharon had rushed back to Verona to ask her parents' permission to be in the film, but Doris G. had serious misgivings. Italy was then in the throes of converting to Communism, and with her husband's role in military intelligence, Americans always lived with the possibility of a kidnaping attempt. Sharon's enthusiasm was so great, however, that Doris G. finally relented. She was reassured by Pat and Shirley Boone's religious backgrounds and their apparent willingness to comply with her requests for security precautions: they agreed to post an Italian policeman at Sharon's door all night.

The episode gave her a tantalizing taste of the film business, and "She was hell-bent for the city lights," her mother recalls. Sharon left Italy for Fort MacArthur, California, her father's next posting, a few weeks ahead of her family. The idea was that she would start school on time, but she never got there. Within weeks, she had landed a contract with MGM Studios.

Fledgling film star or no, Doris G. remained a strict mother— unfashionably so for the liberal sixties. "I know I was horrible at times, I was. I really kept a tight rein on, I had to." Her worst fear of Hollywood and its ills was that someone might spike her daughter's Coke with LSD. "I felt fine about Sharon being a star, as long as I was close by," she explains. No one needs reminding of the bitter irony in that remark. "I was here!" she exclaims. "You cannot protect your kids, you just can't. There are twenty-four hours in a day."

When, after what seemed like an interminable wait, the Manson family members were finally caught and brought to trial, Colonel Tate was there, a heavy presence in the courtroom. Frustrated by the lack of police progress, Sharon's father had conducted his own unsuccessful undercover investigation on the streets of Holly-

wood, before their arrests. He was called as a witness and identi-
fied pictures of the bodies of Sharon and her fellow victims. Doris
G., however, was not at her husband's side. She could not have
borne it. She stayed at home.

In April 1971, Charles Manson, Susan Atkins, Patricia Kren-
winkel, and Leslie Van Houten were sentenced to death, as, in
October, was Charles "Tex" Watson. Charles Manson and family
members Bruce Davis and Steve Grogan were sentenced to life
imprisonment for the related murders of Gary Hinman and Donald "Shorty" Shea. For the parts they played in Gary Hinman's
murder, Susan Atkins was sentenced to life imprisonment and
Bobby Beausoleil was sentenced to death.

Justice seemed to have been served until on February 18, 1972,
the California State Supreme Court voted six to one to abolish
capital punishment. The Manson family murderers who were
awaiting the death penalty had their sentences automatically commuted to life imprisonment, a repercussion which meant that
after seven years they would be eligible for parole. That was not
justice, not to Sharon's family.

Doris Gwen Tate is a motherly woman, a hairdresser by trade,
whose warmth is immediately obvious. Over coffee in her home
south of Los Angeles, the Houston, Texas, native explains that
after her daughter's death, her means of survival was to sink her
energies into her hair salon. "Tate's" seemed a way of keeping
Sharon's memory alive. And naming the way they cut hair "the
Sebring method" was a tribute to Sharon's friend and fellow victim Jay Sebring.

For more than twelve years, Sharon's mother endured her suffering within the privacy of her own home and the bosom of her
family. The Tates' unspeakable grief was not for public consumption. Then, in 1982, her life changed dramatically. She can pin-
point it to the moment she learned of the imminent parole
hearing of family member Leslie Van Houten. The day Doris G.
thought there was a breath of a chance that the murderous Van
Houten might again walk the streets was the day on which she
began her personal fight for justice. Today, her spirit and determination are palpable, yet many long, painful years had to pass
before she could even begin to speak about Sharon's death.

"Until you have lost a child, you don't know what it is," she says slowly. "Parents are supposed to die first. When your child is gone before you for an abnormal reason, it creates a whole abnormal situation. But when I was needed, *really* needed, I was there."

She will never forget that telephone call from Steven Kay, then a district attorney on the Manson case, who was due to attend the annual parole hearings. Kay informed Mrs. Tate that he had in his possession a petition bearing around nine hundred signatures from those who apparently wanted Van Houten to be free to breathe fresh air and walk on green grass and enjoy all the things of which Sharon had been deprived forever. Doris G.'s reaction was swift and fierce: "Steven, if she can get nine hundred signatures, I'm sure I can!" Within one week she had gathered twelve hundred signatures of her own. Within six months she had culled 350,000 signatures and letters against the release of any member of the Manson family.

"I firmly believe that if I hadn't stepped in and started some sort of action, they would already have released Tex Watson and the girls," she says incredulously. "I always maintained that they could not turn people like this loose. Well, that was living in a bubble, honey! And thank God that I learned in time, because there's one thing that I am, I'm a fighter. If not, I could never have survived. I had to fight to raise my other two girls, who were ten and fifteen years old when Sharon went."

Once the emotional floodgates were opened and her rage was converted into positive action, there seemed no limit to her energy to work for what she believed was justice. Neither was there any end to the strength and support she was able to offer others, and in 1983 she began to do vitally important work with groups like Parents of Murdered Children (she became a director of the Los Angeles chapter), Justice for Homicide Victims, Citizens for Truth, and Crime Victims for Court Reform (she is the South Bay chairperson). She sold her twelve-employee-strong hairdressing business to conserve her time for these new causes, but still puts in about twenty hours a week coiffing loyal customers who will not let her go.

POMC's motto is Give Sorrow Words. "We exist to comfort, help, and educate each other," Doris explains. The philosophy is to speak out instead of holding in, to share instead of being solitary. When Sharon was murdered, Doris G. did not have the benefit of the support groups which exist today. POMC, for instance, which has a branch in each state, was founded in 1978.

During her years of private grief, Doris G.'s way of releasing her repressed feelings was to go off in a room alone: "If I wanted to cry I was going to cry, but I didn't want to disturb anyone else." She also found expression through a tape recorder which she kept beside her bed. "Every feeling that I felt, I put it on tape. Just started talking and let it all pour out. It was three years before I could even . . . I couldn't even look at Roman. Because, you see, I still expected Sharon to be with him, so I was playing games in my mind."

POMC first contacted Doris G. and asked her to participate fourteen years after Sharon's death. "I'd come over the hill, so to speak. My first public involvement was appearing at one of their luncheons, and that was the beginning, it snowballed from there. There are cases in this organization that would just chill your bones, and I want to let people know how the parents are affected, how some of them never come out of it. I want to do this. I feel a need to do it. There are so many horror stories."

Like a sixteen-year-old murderer who burned his victims—two small California girls—with cigarette lighters and sodomized them with a hammer. The girls' mother knew of Doris Tate's work and reached out to her. "She knew that I knew the feelings that were coming over her," Doris G. explains. "Since you've walked in these people's shoes, you know what stage they are in, these feelings of revenge they feel. If they want to be consoled in their most desperate time of need, that's what these services are for. And I cry right along with them."

Giving counsel is not a personally relieving or healing experience for Doris. Every time she consoles the parents of a murdered child, it is inevitable that she relives some of her own pain. "I only do it because I feel I have to," she says simply. "I am over this thing to the point that I can survive, but this person is not, and if someone like me doesn't go to help, who will? So what am I going to do? Turn my back? Each person has to come on in their own way through their stages of grief. A lot of them are on the road to suicide, and I am there if they need to talk."

Commonly, grieving is delayed while the family turns to dealing with immediate demands like cooperating with police, for instance. "You go through a disbelief stage where you can be active, but it's like it's happening to someone else, not you," Doris points out. "You haven't accepted it, because it's too horrible to accept. It's called denial."

Much of her work is an ordeal in its own way, stressful to her and her family and emotionally draining. Doris has grown used to receiving calls like the one from a woman whose live-in lover had murdered her daughter-in-law and two grandchildren. "She was desperate," explains Doris, who sat glued to the telephone one night from 11 P.M. until 2 A.M., doing her best to offer comfort.

"Who are they going to call who understands what the hell they are talking about? It's a show of strength on my part. They can say, 'She went through it and she's surviving, so it's up to me, I can do it.' Sometimes I don't *know* how I do it . . . but I can't turn these people off."

She accepts no credit or praise for her endurance. "I'll tell you where the strength comes from and you can take it with a grain of salt, or you can believe. The strength doesn't come from me. Number one, I'm Catholic. I'm very religious."

Heading home on the San Diego freeway one day, listening to the radio, the Tates heard that Susan Atkins had been bragging to a cell-mate about a job in Los Angeles. The "job," it transpired, was the inhuman slaying of their daughter and her friends. Who can even begin to fathom the suffering of a mother in Doris G.'s place? Who would presume to try? In her low-key manner, she says only this: "I can't tell you how mad I was. I wanted to kill her. And just about that time the thought came to me: it was as if I was two people, and the evil was on one side of me and the good was on the other. The evil was saying, 'Hey, all you have to do is wish it and it will happen.' And the good was saying, 'What makes you better than they are?' I was so puzzled."

She truly felt that had she at that moment wished the Manson family dead, had she been willing to make a pact with the devil, she would have got her wish. "I understood they were the disciples of the devil himself. I firmly believe that anyone who commits a crime like that, that's where it stems from. It's straight from hell."

Evil's strength is its ability to deceive and capture the soul, she says, to rob the sense of right and wrong. "You see, I knew the difference. Why didn't they?"

As soon as she arrived home, she flipped open the Bible. She does it again now, but on that particular day it fell open to a very pertinent page: "Revenge" was the first word she saw. She read on in Proverbs 24, and its message is still fresh in her mind: " 'When thy enemy shall fall, be not glad. And in his ruin let not thy heart rejoice. Lest the Lord see and it pleases him and he turns away his wrath from him,' " recites Doris, whose immediate thought was, "I don't want any of the Lord's wrath to be turned away from these people. I want them to get their full measure.

"This, to me, was proof positive. There's no way in hell that I could have flipped this Bible open to that. It says right up there at the top of the page, 'Revenge.' What was I tempted by if it wasn't revenge? Can you imagine that power? I never expect to go through anything like that again. No. But I know that it happened. And I could never have turned to that page in the Bible in a million years. It sits out so bold—'Revenge.' This to me was a blessing that I must share with other people."

For Doris G., her faith in Catholicism has been her salvation. "I believe in life after death," she says forcefully. "I believe in it so strongly. In cases like this, either you're going to find your strength or you're not going to survive. You're going to let that revenge just eat you up."

One of the hardest steps she has ever taken was, in the presence of a priest, to forgive her daughter's murderers, to make her peace with them. Not that she relinquished her ability to relate to the monumental rage and anguish which threatens to overwhelm the families she counsels. But she herself has come to the point where she can say, "If you really think about it, these murderers have given their souls to the devil, and they are to be pitied, in a way."

Doris has lost count of the times she has heard people ask why, if God is so good, He allowed this to happen to their child. Her faith is constantly tested and reaffirmed in her work. "They forget," she explains, "that Jesus Christ himself was crucified. He had no bed of roses while he was on earth. I feel we have two roads to travel, one is good, one is evil, and He will take over when something happens like what happened to me and Sharon.

I'm just as sure as I'm sitting here that Sharon is with Him. If I don't do my part, I'm not sharing, not using the gift that he gave me. You just have to go on faith, blind faith. I tell people, 'Read this in Proverbs,' because what ninety percent of our members feel is this revenge."

Much of the frustration stems from the fact that they cannot act out their vengeful feelings—not within the confines of the law. "A lot of the fathers will blow their brains out," Doris G. says quietly, noting that Charles Manson has stated that the only man of whom he is afraid is her husband, Paul Tate.

"Sharon's father has been in military intelligence all of his career and has been in three wars. It wouldn't bother him to blow this guy away. He went to the trials, I couldn't. They searched him for weapons of course. But you know how those dark eyes Manson has just sort of penetrate? Well, it didn't work on Sharon's father. Oh no. And Manson knows, he knows."

No loved one is exempt from problems: brothers and sisters sometimes attempt suicide too. They frequently withdraw, bottling up and hiding their pain, because they feel they must protect their grieving parents from more anguish.

From the way Doris G. lowers her voice from time to time in deference to the other occupants of her home, it is apparent that while her family supports her efforts, the climate her work creates is not an easy one in which to exist on a daily basis. These discussions serve as a constant reminder of the darkest days in each of their lives. Doris G.'s smiles shine through even weighty conversations, but "not everyone can do this," she acknowledges. "People want to put it behind them, get on with their normal lives, but I can't. Yes, it is hard on [my family], I realize that. But everyone works through their grief in their own way, and I feel that I must make something good come from her death." She suspects they would feel better themselves if they could reassure themselves that she had recovered. "Believe me, *they* aren't over it, so how can they expect me to be? And I feel that sharing what I have gone through has to be worthwhile. It *has* to be."

The strength of her belief that the Manson family members belong behind bars has in no way diminished. She reminisces about Sharon's promise as an actress, of awards she received, like

"Star of the Future," of the excitement with which she had been awaiting the birth of her first baby. All snatched away.

Sharon met film director Roman Polanski (*Chinatown* and *Tess*) in London in 1966. He has always lived on the brink of controversy. (In 1977 he was arrested on six counts of sex- and drug-related offenses involving a minor and subsequently fled to Paris.) He was even, for a time, a suspect in the murder of his wife and her friends. Devastated by Sharon's death, Roman in turn suspected friends like novelist Jerzy Kosinski and John Phillips of the Mamas and Papas. Unbalanced by the shock, he tested their cars for bloodstains and bought bugging equipment to leave in their homes.

Doris Tate did not doubt him for a second and cannot help feeling sorry for him. (She does not, however, condone his involvement with an underage girl, *any* underage girl.) "Roman really loved Sharon, I know that, and he was very, very grieved," she says, shaking her head. "He was supposed to do *Day of the Dolphin*, but he just couldn't do it." The only reason she did not rush to spend time with him after Sharon's death was because it was too agonizing to see him without her daughter at his side. When she goes back to Europe, she will certainly look him up because that, she knows, is the way Sharon would have wanted it.

"Sharon would have been one of the tops," says her mother. Then her look turns steely. "And that asshole Tex Watson sat there at the prison hearing and looked at me—him with two children—and he says, 'All I want to do is get out and raise my family.' When he said that, I was just boiling inside. I said, 'Mr. Watson, what you are asking for is the very thing that you denied my daughter.' I was looking across a coffee table at him, that close," she says, outstretching her arm to show that this monster who murdered her precious daughter was, for those minutes, literally within her reach.

"What was he going to say to me? What could he say? 'Oh no, I'm not going to kill again. I won't be influenced by another Manson'? You asshole, you can sit and rot in jail as far as I'm concerned! Watson did ninety-five percent of the stabbing. These people lose their rights to ever return to society."

It infuriates her to think that Tex Watson not only became an ordained minister, but began preaching in the prison to other inmates. The very idea that he should be entrusted with a power he could so easily abuse and turn to evil strikes her as ludicrous.

On December 31, 1985, Doris G. also braced herself and faced Susan Atkins (a.k.a. Sadie Mae Glutz) at a parole hearing. She cannot fathom how a woman who was a mother herself could show no glimmer of mercy to her pregnant daughter. Mrs. Tate said this to the parole board: "My daughter was sentenced to death without cause, and I was sentenced to life in prison without any possibility of parole. Should Susan Atkins' sentence be any less? I live with my daughter's screams and beggings for her life every day." In January 1986, Atkins' parole request was duly denied for a further three years. "She had absolutely no compassion. And I don't think she yet does. No, uh-uh. In fact I think Manson made the statement that if there's one hard cookie, that's her."

If, as was often suggested, Manson's murderous disciples had been brainwashed or subjected to mind games, that only makes Doris G. wonder about them all the more. It is one thing, she says, to think of Manson as "an idiot, or however you want to describe a man who is off his rocker, which I feel he is. But what do you think about the people that would listen to him and do his bidding? They have to be very weak in the first place. What kind of individual would listen to the mumblings of this . . . I can't even find a word for him? What causes that sixteen-year-old boy who murdered those little girls to be so cruel and unfeeling? These people have no feelings, no remorse."

She staunchly supports the death penalty, but first did some serious soul-searching. "I've really struggled with this. How can our judicial system turn these people free to walk the streets again, when recidivism is so high? There may be rehabilitation, it's very possible, but there is no way we can take that chance. Since we cannot take the chance of a convicted murderer committing this same crime on unsuspecting people, what are we going to do with them? It costs over forty-four thousand dollars a year to incarcerate them. It's not worth it. How about trying to rehabilitate those who have committed lesser crimes, those that possibly *can* be rehabilitated?"

She angrily points out that Tex Watson, Sharon's killer, has married and produced two children during the time he has been incarcerated. How rough is it, she wonders, in San Luis Obispo, when inmates are given conjugal visitation privileges? "You hear this 'life without possibility of parole.' Well, there's no such thing. You know what that means? That means thirty years. Why do they fool the public?" It is precisely because "life imprisonment" does not live up to its promise, that she feels we have no alternative but to execute the death penalty, if that is the sentence.

Is it ever effective in making killers think twice? She believes so, "if for no other reason than by virtue of the fact that it removes one individual's right to repeat the crime."

"I don't believe in executing people for no reason; we have a jury that convicts these people," she says, explaining that she does not view imposing the death penalty as "playing God." "*We're* not doing it. *I'm* not doing it. They did it to themselves! They convicted themselves when they committed the act. We're not responsible for sending them to the gas chamber, or the injection —which I think is great, that's a humane way of dealing with the death penalty—we're sentencing them to what they have already sentenced themselves to."

Despite the efforts of civil libertarians, she predicts that the death penalty will become active. She does not relish the prospect, in fact she considers herself the least bloodthirsty of the victims she knows, but she does believe this wholeheartedly:

"Until these people know that they must pay an eye for an eye, and a tooth for a tooth, they will continue murdering. So that is one way of saving innocent people, by putting those that commit these horrendous crimes to death. And it's just that simple."

Hearing that convicted murderers have been "born again" cuts no ice with Doris G. "Where do they get the idea that because you're a born-again Christian, you're automatically absolved of any duties that you have toward society? No way." She cannot think of a better place for such reformed characters to do the Lord's work than right where they are—in prison.

"It is possible that the people who murdered my daughter and her unborn child, and her friends, will be back on the streets during my lifetime. But I've had so many promises to knock them off that I don't think they'll get far. Isn't that awful?" she asks. Total strangers have volunteered those vows, entirely unsolicited. "I really don't know about an individual who would do that. Are they potential murderers too? What are they? That sort of worries me."

In 1984 Doris Tate was the Democratic nominee for the 51st assembly district in California, earning over forty thousand votes. Not a bad showing, since the mood of the country was heavily Republican. (She now thinks Republican herself, having parted company with the Democrats' liberal party-line.) She doubts she will run for public office again, believing she can work just as effectively from the outside to counter her major enemies: the "flaming liberals" in the California Supreme Court, and the American Civil Liberties Union. She has seen progress:

"I feel that we have pushed the judicial system, the California Supreme Court, over to the victims' side. I want to get all of the organizations I work with under one umbrella into a coalition. That is where the strength lies, the exchange of information. The work is so important. Every day I feel I have achieved something. Every day. Because if you can talk to one person and make them understand, if you can open up cases that have been wrongly closed, then it is worthwhile. But the ACLU," she complains, "is so busy working for the criminals, that they don't know that there's victims left. And that is the truth."

She sees her God-given role in all this as trying to convey what it would be like to walk a mile in her shoes. "There is so much to be done. I don't know how I got this job, but I got it and I have to live with it." As an activist and campaigner, she is well aware that through Sharon's fame (and Manson's notoriety) her name carries a certain weight and she will use that to help her reach her goals. The pain never stops, but there are redeeming, worthwhile moments every day. "I have to do what I feel is in my heart. If not, Sharon's died in vain."

19 . . . *And When Fame Leads to Pain*

Arnold Schwarzenegger's mom was upset. She telephoned from Austria specifically to tell him so. Mom wanted to know, what was this she read about Maria Shriver (with whom her son had been romantically involved for five years) shopping for a wedding dress in New York? Arnold laughed. "If so, she must have sneaked out of L.A. without me knowing about it!" he replied. In fact, they did not marry for two more years, but on another occasion Mom telephoned, highly indignant, because she had read that Maria and Arnold had actually tied the knot. "She said: 'I read it in the paper. It must be true.' I had to try to de-program her completely," he recalls, chuckling.

Schwarzenegger grew up simply but happily on a farm in a tiny village outside Graz, where his stern but affectionate father was a policeman. The highlight of his teenage life was watching an hour's television once a week in the local restaurant: "That was big-time." Infinitely more sophisticated by the time he was in his thirties, he had become all too familiar with the ways of the press.

For three years after meeting Maria at a tennis tournament in New York, he had read how much the Kennedy family hated him. In fact, though Schwarzenegger was a staunch Republican infiltrating the first family of Democrats, the opposite was true. The welcome mat always was out. He did not take offense at the gossip. Everyone expected Maria Shriver to date a Washington lawyer or a political aspirant and was confused; so explained the green-eyed giant who, as a teenager, gave his mom cause for concern about his sexual proclivities when he suddenly began papering the walls of his bedroom with pin-ups of bare-chested musclemen.

Like Schwarzenegger, Joan Collins has the press survival philosophy perfected: "Nobody has it easy, not even the Queen, so why should I expect that there aren't going to be people who are going to knock me?" says Collins.

But stars and those around them rapidly learn that media coverage is a double-edged sword. Behind the names in the headlines, there are real people with real feelings who feel real pain. There is heartache in having your family put under the critical glare of the spotlight.

When the relative of a star—most commonly an embittered child—is driven to put pen to paper and give the family linen a public airing, it is obvious that they are seeking something: love, approval, or perhaps the vindication they believe they deserve. Yet such intimate revelations simply do not lead to popularity for their authors. This spilling out by "a relative of . . ." is invariably perceived by the public as an act of betrayal against the star, with the ironic result that it often precipitates the most painfully public rejection of all for someone already living in the shadows. Be it Joan Crawford's adopted daughter, Christina, writing *Mommie Dearest*, and claiming her book was not intended to crucify her mother, simply to exorcise the demons plaguing an abused child; be it the acid tome from Bette Davis's daughter, B. D. Hyman— the outcome is predictable. Fans simply will not believe that which they prefer not to.

The fact that the public so resists its heroes and heroines being tipped from their pedestals only serves to reinforce the star's power in the family hierarchy.

On the other side of the coin are revelations made by the stars themselves, which can be devastatingly hurtful or embarrassing to their families—and few family members fight back publicly. While stars run the gamut from loose-lipped interview-hounds, who will talk to anyone bearing a notebook, to the reticent Robert De Niro, what they do share is an autonomy about what they will and will not say to the press. Yet many of them do not feel that that freedom of speech should extend itself to their families. They believe their fame confers upon them the power to make those decisions for them.

The moms of Diahann Carroll, Tina Turner, and Natalie Wood have all been hurt in one way or another by their daughters' autobiographies.

Maria might not say so herself, but she was less than thrilled about Lana's decision to tell all in *Natalie: A Memoir by Her Sister*. (R. J. Wagner was even less so.) Maria does insist that Natalie loved both of her sisters, Lana and Olga. She also points out that it was Natalie who bought Lana her first car—a Corvette.

Tina Turner wrote in her autobiography, *I, Tina*, that her mom, Zelma Bullock, did not love her, and gave the impression she left her quite callously. "My mother wasn't mean to me," Tina wrote, "but she wasn't warm, she wasn't close, the way she was with Alline. She just didn't want me. But she was my mother, and I loved her."

A number of star mothers have an ax to grind at the way the press has treated them, not least of them Joanna Moore, whose pretty heart-shaped face mirrors daughter Tatum O'Neal's. She was prompted to give Sue Russell an interview in 1985 to clear up the muddy record. "I'm sick of the lies," Joanna said, referring to the bad press she, Tatum, ex-husband Ryan (they were divorced when Tatum was two), and son Griffin had been getting. Joanna is the first to admit that her relationship with Tatum has not always been the proverbial bed of roses, but among the thorns in Joanna's flesh were reports that still labeled her an ex–drug user, fifteen long years after she had successfully beaten a dependency on prescription diet pills.

She was hurt by stories that Tatum had a stomach ulcer by the time she was seven years old. Untrue, Joanna said vehemently, as were reports that Tatum could not wait to get away from her and that her children were snatched from her. In fact, there was a fair amount of to-ing and fro-ing between Joanna and Ryan, and Tatum not unnaturally spent more time with her dad after she started appearing in films at age eight. But there was no more to it than that, insisted Joanna, who has lost count of stories like the one printed when Tatum first met John McEnroe, which claimed that McEnroe's folks did not like Joanna's daughter. Not to mention the report that had Tatum hurling obscenities at McEnroe and locking him out of the house when he asked her to pose for a picture. The list goes on.

"It's been fifteen years and it's accumulated little by little," Joanna Moore explained in desperation. "It's hurt me all along, I'd be lying if I said it hadn't. A lie can start to become an entity as if it's the truth, and that's why I feel a responsibility to say, 'Hey, it's a lie!'"

Joanna does not deny her dependency upon Dexedrine back in the late 1960s, but she was never a desperate junkie, roaming the streets looking for drugs, which is the picture sometimes conjured up. "Those particular pills were dispensed like sweets at the time. You're really dependent before you realize—then it's too late. I'll bet you will find any number of women my age that went through that with prescription diet pills. And I never had a street drug in my life!"

The truth of the matter, said Joanna, is that she approached her ex-husband Ryan and told him that she had a problem with the pills and needed his help. She asked him to take the children while she went to a hospital for treatment. "Ryan was terribly sweet about it. He is a kind man and he felt for me, he really did. And I think he appreciated and respected the way I did it." After seven weeks in the hospital, she went into therapy, which helped her start to build a new life. "That," she said emphatically, "is exactly what happened."

Joanna, who met Ryan before he was a star, was devastated by their divorce. It was bitter, it was ugly, and Joanna, as a Catholic, did not want a divorce at all. "There were pulls and tears in my break-up with Ryan that really shouldn't have been," she admits. "Right or wrong, I was trying to get around without legs for a number of years, and I think that translated itself to the children in a certain helplessness too."

Joanna Moore was a fairly successful actress herself once upon a time. One day, seven-year-old Tatum sauntered into her bedroom dressed in Joanna's negligee and brandishing a cigarette holder. Without seeing Joanna, "she walked through the bedroom and said, '*I'm* going to play Joanna Moore.' So I said, 'I quit, that's it! *You're* going to play Joanna Moore! I'm your mother!'"

Joanna's snap decision to stop acting was, however, rapidly followed by Tatum's professional debut, and at ten, the precociously talented young thespian won an Oscar for *Paper Moon*. In Joanna's view, Tatum was too young to be in the business, and while Ryan was encouraging her to act, she repeatedly tried to persuade her to go to school. She knows that her ambivalence hurt Tatum.

"Believe me, it hasn't been easy for her. If anybody tells you that a child as famous as Tatum has an ordinary life, it's just not true, it's not even a possibility. There was plenty of excitement and pizzazz, but at the same time there was a deep loneliness because she was isolated from the ones she desperately wanted to be with—just children her own age. And for the most part *they* found it difficult to be with her, that's what hurt me. It's easier for an adult, but children don't handle fame well at all. Her childhood was far, far from the norm, and emotionally exceedingly difficult, just because of being so famous when she was so young."

When the press either misrepresents the truth or blatantly disregards it, Joanna tries to laugh it off, and has succeeded up to a point, but all the coverage has clearly been a source of embarrassment. Much as "you don't want to be upset by comments that aren't kind," she would be lying if she said she was not. "Everybody likes to be liked and loved."

Most mothers can only watch helplessly if their children are subjected to cruel and unusual punishment at the hands of the press. Elizabeth Taylor has collected enough insults in her career to compile a dictionary of snide remarks. Rarely have writers had a better target for their verbal prowess. She's been called everything from "overweight, overbosomed, overpaid, and undertalented" by David Susskind, to "plump as a Christmas fowl" by Anne Pacey to, in Rex Reed's eyes, "a hideous parody of herself —a fat, sloppy, yelling, screaming banshee."

Richard Dreyfuss took his mother to Italy on a European press tour when he was awarded the Donatello (Italy's answer to an Oscar) for *The Goodbye Girl*. Richard was not married and had no special girlfriend, so he invited his mom and his secretary to accompany him. "The press, especially the German press, thought that he must be homosexual," says Gerry Dreyfuss, with a wry smile. "Who else travels with his mother? They gave him a hard time."

Rod Stewart's mother made tactless remarks about his ex-wife Alana once the couple's pending divorce came to light. "I could never understand why he married her. There's always an atmosphere when Alana's around. My husband always said he wished Rod had married a Scottish girl. He'd have been a lot better off," pronounced the senior Mrs. Stewart. Alana was forgiving—especially since it was Rod's infidelities that wrecked the marriage.

Joan's dad, theatrical agent Joe Collins, has voiced his true feelings on Joan's men, saying that her disastrous first marriage to the abusive Maxwell Reed caused unheard-of, serious friction between him and Joan's late mother, Elsa. Joe claims the marriage to Reed set an unfortunate precedent for Joan's future relationships: "Joan's relationships with men have often left me astonished at her naïveté. She has never manipulated any man, nor played off one man against another. In this respect, Alexis would despise Joan as a stupid little ninny."

Paradoxically, along with that wish of the public's not to have illusions shattered about longtime legends, there is their desire to depose stars from their pedestals. A perverse delight is taken in a star's fall from grace. When Sylvester Stallone had marital problems with first wife Sasha, he says the press "jumped on it like it was the greatest thing since Watergate or the exploding of the neutron bomb. They jump out of trashcans, they follow you on airplanes, they piece a story together so that there's no way you can look honest. . . ."

Sting upset his parents, Audrey and Ernest Sumner, by referring to them as losers. Audrey (who succumbed to cancer in 1987 after a two-year battle) was a hairdresser. Ernest, who died six months later, was an engineer who later worked as a milkman. The Sumners raised their children in Newcastle, an industrial port in England's depressed Northeast. One childhood home had a view of a tanker-building shipyard. By contrast, Sting now lives in the Highgate, London, house which once belonged to Yehudi Menuhin.

In 1980, Sting got into hot familial water by unthinkingly telling Kristine McKenna of *Rolling Stone*: "I suppose part of my egocentric drive is an attempt to transcend my family. I come from a family of losers—I'm the eldest of four—and I've rejected my family as something I don't want to be like." He did not decry his parents' occupations or financial and social standing, rather what he colorfully called his "piss-poor family life."

Three years later he would tell McKenna that some of the things he had said about them hurt his family deeply. "I learned a big lesson there and had to work very hard to repair the damage done by the article." He blamed his own thoughtlessness and arrogance.

Sting, who transcended his working-class background and first career as a schoolteacher to become a star, has since realized that his dearth of fond childhood memories had less to do with his parents and more to do with his own psychological makeup, which made his growing-up years very painful. Now he feels gratitude for the background that gave him his fighting spirit.

Diahann Carroll's autobiography, *Diahann!*, revealed the psychological pain she had suffered stemming from being left by her parents for more than a year when she was one and a half years old. It was not until her late twenties, after undergoing LSD therapy to try to find out why she strongly feared rejection in relationships, that the episode came to light. Yet nothing could have been further from the mind of her mother, Mabel Johnson, than abandoning her little daughter.

It is true that she and her husband, John, left Diahann with Mabel's sister in North Carolina, but they did so reluctantly, and only to enable them both to work full-time in New York. They could never have eked a babysitter's pay out of their salaries, and it was not uncommon practice for young couples to send a child back to their families. Admittedly, the separation stretched on much longer than intended. But the sin did not seem so great.

Mabel grew up on a cotton and tobacco farm in Bladenboro, North Carolina. Her father died at age thirty-six when she was just six, leaving Mabel's mother, Rebecca Faulk, to raise nine children, the oldest of whom was fourteen. Mabel believes she inherited Rebecca's strength and determination, and that Diahann has in turn received that legacy from her.

"My mother did all the planting, and my fourteen-year-old brother took over the plowing and the things that would automatically fall to the father of the group, and we came through, I don't know. People used to come and want to adopt us, and she said, 'No, I want to bring them up together.' She had suitors, men who would have liked to have her hand in marriage, but she would say, 'No, I have my children. I have to raise my children.' "

When Mabel was twenty, she met Diahann's father on Long Island, where she was seeking summer employment. They married within a few months, and she worked as a domestic until Carol Diann was born, thirteen months later.

"I wished I had stayed home with my baby," she says, her strong demeanor shaken by the memory of that unhappy interval and its effect on Diahann. "I didn't realize at that time what it was doing to her." She brushes away a tear.

To make the transition as easy on her baby as possible, she took Diahann's own crib to her sister's home—at least that would be familiar. That night, she put her to bed as usual; then, once they were sure Diahann was sound asleep, they slipped away. Since Diahann was so young, Mabel just assumed she would adjust to her absence without difficulty. Sure enough, she did not cry or scream, and far less was known then about the profound long-term impact of such events on terribly young children.

"I thought she'd just wake up and see that I wasn't there and then attach herself to my sister. It probably still haunts her. She felt abandoned," Mabel says sadly, shaking her head. "I really didn't have any choice, because my husband's salary was so meager. I figured we'd feather the nest, and we'd go back and get her to a better-feathered nest. I used to cry every day almost about my baby being away from me."

Diahann wrote that she did not see or hear from her parents in over a year. But she was so young it is understandable they did not write her letters, added to which, Mabel did not want to risk upsetting her once she was settled with her aunt and uncle. When Mabel was finally able to retrieve Diahann, she believed that her daughter recognized her: "I wanted to feel so strongly that she knew me." Diahann barely did and wrote that she was so devastated on her return to her parents' home that she was too scared to sit on the toilet—she was afraid she would be flushed away. One day they walked to the nearby dentist's office where Diahann had her teeth checked.

"When we came out of the dentist's office to the sidewalk, she took a running spell. The street we were going down at that time was very, very long, and she ran, I guess, about two blocks, me running after her. And I couldn't catch her, she ran so swift.

"When I caught her, it was at a corner she would have had to cross, and that's what stopped her. I think she was probably looking for my sister and thought if she ran away, she might get back to them. I don't know why she did it. When I caught her she was just trembling," Mabel says, wiping at her eyes.

"But then is when I realized what a mistake I had made. Because material things were not worth it, not worth it, what I had done to her mind. She had to work it out after she grew up. But she never offered any problem that I knew of while she was growing up."

It seems particularly ironic that Mabel's innocent decision to move up in the world toward a better life should cause so much pain and grief, for in every other respect she was a model mother. Diahann is the first to admit that her doting parents gave her a fairy-tale childhood. As far back as she can remember, her family fell into the "haves," not the "have nots." They owned a brown-stone and drove a new Chrysler car, and Mabel had the luxury of staying home and devoting herself to raising Diahann while her husband went off to work as a subway conductor.

Mabel dressed Diahann's hair each night, putting on Vaseline, then wrapping individual curls in grocery bag paper to make her look pretty in the then-fashionable Shirley Temple vein. The Johnsons had rules, discipline, and values—and high hopes for Diahann. Mrs. Johnson is an enormously dignified woman and Diahann proudly recalls her mother's ladylike handling of brushes with racism.

Diahann's parents were there whenever she needed them, and she now understands why she needed them and their adoration quite so badly. But as the years went by, the separation was never referred to; nothing bad was ever discussed in their home.

When Diahann finally broached the subject with her parents, she met first with denial, then with tears and an unleashing of their pent-up feelings of guilt. None of this remotely changed Diahann's love for them—it merely explained why she felt the way she did.

"We're a very close family," Diahann says. "My parents were

married for thirty-seven years, and because of their stability in the home, I was very well-prepared for many of the knocks and periods of time that were extremely difficult, I didn't take them personally. The sense of being loved and cared for was there; it was instilled since I was a child, that self-confidence."

Maria Gurdin, Natalie Wood's mother, suffered the sharp end of press attention at an excruciatingly agonizing time in her life. She was awakened from a fitful sleep by the ringing of the telephone at eight A.M. on Sunday, November 30, 1981. It was just a couple of hours since waves of sheer exhaustion had finally won their battle against her insomnia. A free-floating anxiety, a bad feeling somewhere deep inside, had kept her tossing and turning all night. Maria's first thought was to quiet the ringing so that it would not wake her daughter Lana, whose night had been equally sleepless. She answered the telephone, rapidly dispensing with the caller, Lana's friend Sheri Herman.

Peace reigned—but all too briefly. The intrusive ringing again. Maria remembers being irritated on hearing Sheri's voice. Lana was still asleep, she chided Sheri, did she want Maria to wake her? No, Sheri said, but she had to tell Maria something she just could not hold in any longer. "She said, 'Natalie's dead.' Just like that."

For a fragment of time Maria thought this was the cruelest joke imaginable. She was just about to slam down the receiver in disgust when Sheri spoke again. This time Maria could not dismiss what she heard: "She said, 'Natalie's drowned, it's all over the radio, it's all over the TV.' And that's all I remember. I pass out."

Lana, on hearing her mother scream, grabbed the receiver and listened while Sheri repeated the words that had caused Maria's collapse. As is frequently the case, the media had spread the news of a tragedy to the public before it had been broken to the immediate family. This time, radio broadcasts robbed Natalie's husband, R. J. Wagner, of his opportunity to break the news gently. Lana's daughter Evan, who was seven, was so scared to see her grandmother unconscious on the floor that, sobbing, she ran and locked herself in the bathroom.

Maria's body temperature dropped so fast that Lana was afraid she was dead. While she was waiting for the paramedics, a horrified Lana telephoned Natalie's house and the Wagners' longtime British secretary, Liz, confirmed that there had been no mistake, her sister was dead. In shock, Lana went off to wash her hair. "Imagine that?" Maria says, eyes wide.

Maria next opened her eyes in a hospital bed and was soon railing in angry disbelief against a nurse who was insisting that yes, it was true, her Natalie was dead, her body had been washed up on the beach off Catalina Island. "I said, 'You liar! Everybody's a liar!' I just went wild. I said, 'I want to go and find Natalie. She's alive! She's alive!' I don't believe anybody. I was a basket case."

Discharging herself against doctor's orders, she rushed back to Lana's two-story townhouse, only to find her eldest daughter, Olga, waiting with Lana. (Olga, her husband, Alexi, and two of their three sons had flown down from San Francisco immediately upon hearing the news.) There it was, the unthinkable confirmed.

Determined to say her private good-byes, Maria visited Natalie's body armed by concerned doctors with "some sort of shot in my unmentionable." Similarly fortified, she numbly endured the funeral of the daughter who had meant more to her than anything in the world. Natalie was buried in the same Westwood cemetery as Marilyn Monroe. Natalie's death, at forty-three, came just a year after Nicholas, Maria's husband of forty-five years, succumbed to a major heart attack. For Maria, although the double loss was almost unbearable, there was one blessing. "I am glad he was not alive when she died, because that would really have killed him right there and then."

What haunts her most is the thought that Natalie might be alive today had she joined her, R.J., and Chris Walken on their sixty-foot yacht, *Splendour*, that weekend. Maria had spent Thanksgiving at Natalie and R.J.'s Beverly Hills home just a couple of days earlier, and as she was leaving the festivities, Natalie had extended an invitation. Maria, mindful that Lana believed she loved Natalie more, decided she must honor her prior commitment to babysit for her granddaughter Evan.

Looking back, Maria attributes her sleeplessness on the night Natalie drowned to a premonition. "I think I knew that she was gone, yes. Always, if something happened to my children, I will always know." Lana had briskly dismissed it as her mother's overactive imagination playing tricks, but at five A.M., Maria had telephoned Olga. "I said, 'Olga, is everybody all right? My grandsons are all right?' And she said, 'Fine, Mother. Are you having nightmares or something?' I said, 'No, I didn't go to sleep yet.' " She did not, however, telephone Natalie. "I wouldn't dare to call Natalie at five o'clock in the morning, you know, and wake her up? They were planning to relax."

The day after Natalie drowned, Maria wanted to see R.J. and visited him with Lana. "He was in bed, his eyes were swollen, he just hugged both of us." She asked him if Natalie had suffered. He assured her she had not. That made her feel better.

To this day, Maria does not know the exact details of the circumstances of that night. Fearing for her health, R.J. spared her that pain, she explains. But it strikes her as a particularly cruel twist of fate that Natalie should drown. Natalie loved sailing with R.J., and their second marriage ceremony in July 1972, which captured the hearts of romantics the world over, was a gloriously romantic affair held at sunset, anchored off the Malibu coastline. Yet throughout her life, Natalie shared Maria's own abiding fear of deep, dark waters. "Then they bought *Splendour*, and that is the boat that took her away. Oh why, oh why, did they have to buy that boat?"

Maria vividly remembers the day that ten-year-old Natalie first set eyes on Robert Wagner, the young star of *Prince Valiant*, and promptly announced, "When I grow up, I'm going to marry him!"

Maria has never for a moment doubted R.J. She has not asked where he was, why he was not able to save Natalie, nor has she ever felt anger toward him.

"Never, never. Never come to my mind, never. He loved Natalie so much. The first thing I said was, 'How is R.J.?' I thought, 'Oh my God, he is going through a hard time like I am.' I love R.J. I wanted a son, so he just become my son. In fact Natalie told me he said to her [after she filmed *Brainstorm*], 'We have to have another honeymoon.' She loved him very much too."

Natalie was like a bright light in Maria's life, and with that light extinguished, she readily admits she did not want to go on. She could not sleep, she plunged from one hundred and thirty pounds down to one hundred and three with alarming rapidity, and she could not have been less interested in her deteriorating health. "I didn't want to live. I couldn't live without her. She was my whole life, she was so much part of me."

It took Maria's Russian Orthodox priest to deflect her from her downward spiral of despair. "He said, 'You better snap out of it, and you better don't cry about Natalie. You drowning her with tears. That's bad, very bad, when person's dead to cry all the time. You can cry maybe a little bit to relieve yourself, but you hurting her.' That did it."

So, she would live. Almost seven years have gone by, but at ten o'clock each morning a shadow passes over Maria's mood—wherever Natalie was, studio soundstage or beauty parlor, that is the time she telephoned her mother, just to check in with her.

Maria has nothing but praise for R.J.—as a man, a father, a son-in-law, which is why she took so to heart much of what was printed after Natalie's death. She recalls a tabloid claim that R.J. would not let her see her granddaughters, Courtney and Natasha. "I just got mad at that paper—how dare they? Because R.J. is such a wonderful man and I love him so much that it hurts me. It just hurts me when they say that, even though I know it's not true."

In that instance, R.J. telephoned Maria hoping to warn her about the erroneous story. "He said, 'Isn't that ridiculous?' I said, 'It sure is!' I always saw the children. Even Father's Day, or something, R.J. says, 'We won't be happy if you don't come.' All the big family affairs, I still go. You know when he travels, he call me from Rome . . . wherever he is, he call me all the time. He worry about me."

He frequently informs Maria if he has spotted one of Natalie's old films coming up on television. Traditionally, Maria and R.J. celebrate their February birthdays together, but since Natalie has been gone, the venue has been changed. It is simply too painful to go to Trader Vic's, Natalie's old favorite, without her.

20 The Power and the Glory

Timothy Hutton's mere presence in his grandmother's Connecticut neighborhood prompted a reaction something akin to that generally reserved for the Washington Monument. The stunned young Oscar-winner in the decrepit blue jeans was shocked to see Grandma's friends and neighbors come driving by just to catch a glimpse of him. Which is to say right away that well-intentioned family members have as much to do with the way stars handle stardom as do stars themselves.

Years ago, Diahann Carroll looked to her parents to take the reins in her confrontation with Sidney Poitier, with whom she was entrenched in a painful love affair that she finally hoped to resolve. Diahann was disappointed. Her usually imposing mother, Mabel Johnson, far from reiterating her frequent maternal complaints about Diahann's out-of-wedlock arrangement, "was too dazzled to say anything" once in the presence of Sidney Poitier, The Star.

In her autobiography, *Diahann!*, Carroll described the insidious process of being swallowed up by the sheer glamour and luxury of fame. In her case, it happened in the late 1960s. She was consumed by the attention that sprang from her hit TV series, *Julia,* and from highly lucrative nightclub performances in Las Vegas. It was all so seductively magical that she did not care to know that the home she bought from Barbara Hutton's son Lance Reventlow was way beyond her financial means. She did not wish to face the fact that she was wealthy, but not *that* wealthy. Instead, she blithely stepped even further from reality, signing on an entire team of workmen to glamorize her new abode. "I was so caught up in the fantasy that no one was able to get through to me," Diahann admitted. "Not even my own parents. They were as bedazzled by my success as I was."

Why did they, too, lose sight of reality, those strong, achieving parents of whom she was so proud? Why did Mabel Johnson, a woman who has never ceased to inspire awe in her daughter, lurch on her pedestal? In the blaze of Diahann's success, the Johnsons also lost their bearings. They began to doubt their perspective. It was not that they felt they knew *nothing*, rather that perhaps Diahann knew better? After all, it was she, not they, who had risen to these exceedingly lofty heights.

Diahann became unavailable to her friends and ignored their frank counsel. She was deaf to young daughter Suzanne's bona fide gripes about the nurse in whose care Diahann left her. She was also remiss in offering support and comfort to her mother when, in the early seventies, her parents' marriage broke down irretrievably after thirty-seven years. Their real-world problems threatened to chew away a corner of Diahann's glamorous, fairy-tale existence that she was simply unwilling to yield.

"It is sad for me to think that my friends were more helpful to my mother than I was during that awful time." With rare candor, she admitted, "There wasn't much give and take with me during those years. It was always I, I, I, me, me, me."

And so it begins. Fame, without doubt, creates havoc in the status quo, even if only temporarily. Along with star status comes an increase in authority and power—financial, personal, and emotional. Goldie Hawn's sister, Patti, who believes it is naïve to imagine that it could be otherwise, observed to Oprah Winfrey, ". . . having a major star in a family has to change the dynamics of a family."

When the thrust of power shifts and changes hands, an unnatural hierarchy kicks in. It is as if there is a new head of the household almost overnight, and the change is all the more marked if a star is footing all the bills, literally putting a roof over the heads of parents and family members. "Suddenly you have this all-powerful star who not only has the biggest bank balance, but also has an almost superhuman dimension via their public image," says Dr. R. Barkley Clark, who acknowledges that it can be an unhealthy state of affairs when "that person becomes almost idealized by the family and elevated on a pedestal."

But who can blame them if they succumb to the temptation to treat this new power figure with more deference than they would normally show the breadwinner/head of the household? As Madonna's sister, Paula Ciccone, told Oprah Winfrey: "It's not really a natural power, because the power that they get outside the family tends to come home with them. You have to get through the barrier, then you can start talking to them. And let's face it, when you get in a situation where you're being treated, you know, really well a lot . . . it's really hard to put it aside and just be a person. And it's also hard to talk to that person as a person if they're not willing, you know."

Some stars manage to hang on to their sense of reality, but far from all are strong enough to resist the dizzyingly heroic proportions of their own images. Be it the thrill of going onstage and mesmerizing thousands; be it the intoxicating, larger-than-life proportions of their cinematic selves; or be it the breadth and width of TV fame with recognizability from here to Rumania—it is tremendously tempting to fall for the mythology.

Leslie Caron believes that if you caught Warren Beatty off guard in the middle of the night and quizzed him on what he truly wanted to be, he would say, "President." Well, the next best thing is "Star." Fame is a revered commodity in the western world in general and America in particular, and like power, it is deliriously heady, highly seductive, and potentially addictive. The appetite for its excitement, once whetted, frequently grows into a craving. Its withdrawal can lead to major depression and loneliness. Once a star is hooked on the adulation of the masses, it is virtually impossible for any mere mortal to meet their needs. How could one person match the seductive applause of thousands?

Babies know they are the center of the universe. Two-to-five-year-olds demonstrate their belief that they are kings of their households (if not the world) with their exhibitionistic, grandiose behavior. Over time, that huge ego naturally deflates. (Hopefully.) And most of us emerge from childhood having successfully subsumed the painful knowledge that the world does not revolve around us, and that our happiness does not hinge upon being the most important person in the world. Well, stars face an extra, unsettling twist in this natural progression: they become the center of the universe for a second time. They find themselves in what Dustin Hoffman calls a suspect position.

The tiny kernel of grandiosity that lingers on in each of us jumps at the chance to flourish again in the fertile ground of fame. It is natural for stars to believe that everything revolves around *their* work, *their* desires, *their* wants and needs. They are citizens of a different world, one effectively removed from reality as we know it, and are exempt from the usual chain of cause and effect. Imagine a traffic cop tearing up a ticket and settling for your autograph? Perhaps not a daily occurrence, but it has happened to stars.

Normal rules no longer apply when your face is your calling card. There is no waiting in line, no jostling for seats on buses or subways, no struggling to see the cinema screen over rows of burly shoulders, no battling for service in stores and restaurants. Bette Midler has blithely voiced the opinion that tantrums are acceptable "because I pay the bills." She was half-joking—maybe —but Sting was not when he observed that "when you're a rock star, you're allowed to be a petulant child, and many other things you're supposed to grow out of."

"The state of being famous," Dustin Hoffman told Mel Gussow of *Cosmopolitan* magazine, "affects everything around you, most strongly the house you live in and your family. Invisible gas wipes everyone out once in a while. It's a little like drinking strained orange juice. Being a celebrity removes the pulp from life. You lose a lot of nutrients. It's nice not to wait in line, to be treated with great deference, but you're lifted out of the common life."

And then there is the adulation. Ally Sheedy has watched women run screaming after her male peers Judd Nelson and Emilio Estevez. She likens the fuss to an ultimately meaningless visit to an amusement park: "You're in a ride screaming and you know it's just a ride, but when it's happening it's fun. Nothing to take seriously and nothing that should be too frightening." Even so, just imagine having your every mundane little move recorded for posterity? From the lifting of a glass to the scratching of your nose? Inevitably, the attention of a hundred popping flashbulbs distorts the drinker or the scratcher's perspective on his own importance. It is back to the center of the universe.

John Lennon's Rolls-Royce regularly took a pounding from a hoarde of overexcited adolescents yelling his name. Undaunted, he would lock himself inside and carry on reading. When his chauffeur became indignant, John reprimanded him, explaining that since the fans had bought his car, they had a perfect right to smash it up. Few stars view things quite that way.

Mother, along with the rest of the family, is cast in the role of the custodian of common sense, rational behavior, and the value system. Past efforts hopefully pay dividends (if not immediately, at least in the long run), but weaknesses and cracks are magnified. To even hope to handle the sheer volume of attention, a star must have a rock-hard grip on reality *and* a family and friends who are ready, willing, and able to keep a grasp on it too. It is not only stars who cannot handle recognition and its ramifications; Sylvester Stallone noticed changes in his friendships which he did not instigate. After moving into his first palatial, post-Rocky home, he invited an old buddy over to visit. Within ten minutes, Sly was itching to eject his guest.

"He was giving off such a negative, hostile, jealousy-type aura, I couldn't believe it!" Instead of being pleased about his friend's good fortune, "It was 'Does it rain much out here? I guess you paid a lot of money for this place. I guess you can really throw it around now.' And if he's going to be jealous, imagine what a so-so acquaintance would do?"

Stallone's frequently tactless mother, Jacqueline, refuses to tip-toe around her son just because he is a star. She is the only mom to own up to both pride and jealousy being at work in their relationship. "It's just basic human instinct to say, 'Hey, I gave this kid everything. Maybe I could've been that, but I guess I didn't have the opportunity or the breaks.' It's been pretty turbulent. I'd say every smile's been drenched in gallons of tears. It hasn't been all sunglasses and autographs."

Stallone swiftly weeded out those who emerged hoping to capitalize on his success, but the problem has not disappeared. In his view it is realistic, not paranoid, to remain aware that unsuspected enemies lurk in the shadows. "There are definitely more people that wish me woe and self-destruction than people that wish me well." When someone inquires about a film's box office progress, he sometimes senses insincerity thinly masked behind the congratulations. He can feel it, he can smell it; the mouth smiles, but the eyes lie.

Mick Jagger occupies an inconspicuous limestone house on New York's Upper West Side and prides himself on the Rolling Stones' "streetness." His mother Eva agreed to be interviewed for this book without feeling obliged to first seek her son's permission. Yet, novelist Jay McInerney visited Jagger in a recording studio in 1985 for *Esquire* magazine and witnessed the power play at work:

"Everybody is very cool, but one can hear the change in the register of voices when Jagger enters or leaves the room, a kind of systole and diastole of self-consciousness." Later, when those assembled headed for the Ritz, McInerney noted that no one moved until Mick said, "Well . . . ," and rose. Suddenly, everyone else was ready. If Jagger does not demand this deference, he simply commands it by virtue of his star power. It's a case of "Long live the king"—whether he wants the crown or not. Sycophancy flourishes, especially, but not exclusively, among those for whom there is a pay-off like a salary and perks.

As fame tightens it stranglehold, mothers can find themselves shunted aside to make way for those who parrot praise and reinforcement. It takes a strong family to resist caving in to the presence of these influences. Stardom's artificial reality is much like that in the story "The Emperor's New Clothes." The healthy degree of skepticism with which an average family would normally greet egocentric behavior from within is replaced by this pseudocommunication. The lack of what Goldie Hawn calls a "truth person" takes its toll. Janet Leigh agrees that it is crucial to have people in your life who will tell you the truth, however painful. She and daughter Jamie Lee perform that function for one another in their two-star family. "If it's done in love, then it's not criticism," she says.

But many of those in a star's orbit literally become frightened to relate to them normally. They fear that if they fail to toe the line, they may find themselves ejected from the royal court. Mothers are not exempt from this syndrome. And it occurs for a not-insignificant reason, according to Dr. Grotstein, who sees no villain in the situation, but merely questions who is using who.

"We need him to be our star—he's manipulating us while we're manipulating him, therefore we dare not tell him the truth. So I think that the star is caught in a bind with his retinue. They lie to him, he lies to them. And they keep a myth going, and the myth serves both."

Fame, then, is just as potentially addictive to those sunning themselves in the reflected glory as it is to the stars themselves. So when someone has a shaky sense of self, is dissatisfied or uncomfortable with his or her own identity, and the opportunity avails itself for fame-by-association, it can open up the floodgates.

John Lennon admitted as much to Jann Wenner of *Rolling Stone* magazine in 1970. The Beatles, he pronounced in typically forthright fashion, were bastards. How could they not be, first to have made it and secondly to survive under such pressure? But the image of the Fabs as four nice boys remained untainted because those around them were unwilling to wave the bandwagon good-bye.

"We were the Caesars," Lennon told Wenner. "Who was going to knock us when there's a million pounds to be made? All the hand-outs, the bribery, the police, all the fucking hype, you know. Everybody wanted in, that's why some of them are still trying to cling on to this. Don't take it away from us, not a portable Rome where we can all have our houses and our cars and our lovers and our wives and office girls and parties and drink and drugs. Don't take it from us, you know, otherwise you're mad, John, you're crazy. Silly John wants to take all this away."

To Lennon, it was a kind of trap. He was a guest at a party where he played emperor and was given limitless wine, women, drugs, power, and praise. Who, voluntarily, would extricate themselves from all that? Ringo Starr saw a different side of the coin: "It's like if you had sweets every day, you'd get sick of them." In Ringo's case, his mom, Elsie; his dad; his ex-wife, Maureen; and his "three brothers" provided his lifeline, the essential voice of reason. "We all went over the edge," Ringo admitted to Sue Russell. "I remember going over the edge and the other three saying, 'What's all this shit? What's going on? You're going crazy.' And it was that honesty and support (that kept us sane)."

John Lennon's father resurfaced after years of silence when his son became a superstar. So did Pierce Brosnan's. "Because I get some fame and fortune, he comes out of the woodwork," Pierce noted to Diane de Dubovay of *McCall's*. Tom Brosnan deserted him when he was just two. The "Remington Steele" star's mom left him in Ireland with her parents and went off to nurse in London. After his grandparents died, Pierce was ferried between various relatives, finally rejoining his mom when he was eleven. He says he does not know what he would be if he had had a normal childhood. "It's easy to criticize now but my mother did her best for me," he says. He looks less kindly upon his father, who, after their meeting, ungraciously told a London tabloid: "Pierce Brosnan, Pierce bloody Brosnan . . . I'm sick and tired of hearing about Pierce Brosnan! Who does he think he is? Royalty?"

To stars, it can appear that everyone around them, including those they previously trusted implicitly, suddenly has lights in their eyes spelling "meal ticket."

Shirley MacLaine and Warren Beatty consistently kept their parents out of the spotlight, yet as inveterate showmen, one wonders, might Mr. and Mrs. Beaty not have enjoyed sharing a chink of their limelight?

Maria Gurdin, Natalie Wood's mother, only felt free to be interviewed for this book after getting Robert Wagner's blessing. Christopher Reeve was not thrilled when his journalist mother wanted to overstep her maternal bounds and write about him. He told her she could be a reporter or mother, not both.

The effects of stardom can extend way beyond family power struggles. When stars feed off the excitement of having a constant diet of reinforcement and praise, of having everyone agree with them, when that becomes the motivating force in their life, then really close, *equal,* and nourishing relationships suffer. Without the ability to have an intimate, sharing, honest relationship with another person, stardom is ultimately a very unsatisfying experience.

Just as stars can be in a bind with their retinues, so moms can be in a quandary with their stars. If they call them on their behavior rather than simply toeing the party line, will they even be heard? Gerry Dreyfuss and her husband, Norman, did not rein in their feelings when Richard's stardom brought about some foolish behavior on his part. They criticized him for doling out what to them were vast sums of money to people they felt sure would never repay him; they chastised him for extravagances like keeping a costly limousine on call for which he often had no better use than ferrying a secretary off to Bloomingdale's. But they might as well have held their tongues. Their commonsense philosophies not only fell on deaf ears, they were read as interference by Richard.

"He would get very defensive," Gerry recalls, "and then, it was true, it was none of our business. So we had to just stop. But there was a separation . . . because we were Depression-oriented people, we couldn't accept that kind of *waste*."

Richard Dreyfuss, happily, has risen Phoenixlike from the wreckage of the old life to which his mother refers. The turning point came on October 11, 1981, when he lost control of his Mercedes 450-SL convertible rounding a bend at two o'clock one morning. He crashed into a palm tree and ended up pinned beneath his overturned car, held in place by a seat belt he had no recollection of fastening, his feet pointing skywards. Incredibly, he sustained only mild injuries (a separated rib), but after being freed by firefighters and rushed to Cedars Sinai Hospital, vials were found in his clothing and he was duly arrested and charged with possessing .75 grams of cocaine and thirty-one tablets of the prescription painkiller Percodan.

Gerry Dreyfuss, who divorced Richard's father in the late 1970s and does not like to sleep alone, leaves her radio playing softly all night long. She learned of Richard's accident via a news bulletin while she was in bed, and promptly pulled on her clothes and rushed to the hospital. To her amazement and relief, she found her son without a scratch on him. To Gerry and Richard alike, the crash was a blessing in disguise, a miracle warning that certainly changed—and most likely saved—his life.

Richard had not been overtly suicidal prior to the accident, but he was on a disastrous course. He could have gone behind bars for up to six years for drug possession and driving while intoxicated. But with no prior convictions, he was eligible for a two-year rehabilitation program which included attending at least one Alcoholics Anonymous meeting a week, and felony charges were later dropped.

"I don't know how bad it was for him," Gerry Dreyfuss says of those days, shaking her head and looking pensive, "but I know the results were *terrible* for him. He was drinking, he was taking pills, I was not aware of any of that stuff, and he really went downhill. He spent all his money . . . sort of throwing it away like he didn't want it." Dreyfuss, though interview-shy, speaks with his mother's candor and plenty of self-directed sarcasm when he offers this account: "Taking twenty Percodan a day, two grams, six quarts of alcohol, that's pretty suicidal. But I never said, 'I want to kill myself.' I'm not a shmuck."

In fact, Richard first dabbled in drugs when he was fifteen. He began with marijuana, progressed past cognac and amphetamines to cocaine, and by the time of his first taste of success in *American Graffiti* in 1973 and *The Apprenticeship of Duddy Kravitz* in 1974, his substance abuse had begun to escalate. It accelerated further when he had the mega-hits *Jaws* and *Close Encounters of the Third Kind*, and the scales were tipped entirely with *The Goodbye Girl*, which won him an Oscar in 1977 when he was just twenty-nine. After the Oscar, Gerry's son was in serious trouble.

When he seemed so blessed, why did his life go so badly wrong? On the surface, Richard appeared to bask in his success, as did Gerry, who still recalls a lot of the loving attention he received from appreciative fans as very beautiful. It was not nearly so simple. Dreyfuss was a brash, cocky young star who rubbed many the wrong way (behavior which would haunt him later, when it came time to climb back), and whose fame, money, and success were too much, too soon. Success did not come for him as early and speedily as for some, but irrespective of that, as Gerry Dreyfuss says, "he did not handle it well at all."

The world labeled Richard Dreyfuss a movie star, but he would call himself a commodity, or any self-deprecating thing he could dream up, rather than acknowledge that. He had never suffered hardship. He had had a happy, love-filled childhood. He was plagued by the little voice of the real Richard inside him, muttering that maybe he did not deserve his success? Perhaps someone would discover he was not worthy of it and snatch it back? At his ten-year high school reunion in 1975, instead of making his planned movie star entrance, he was so scared he did not venture beyond the coat room.

He was obsessed with work; without it he felt nothing. Not until his arrest in the emergency ward was perspective restored, dissipating the so-called humiliation of the failure of his films *The Big Fix, The Competition,* and *Whose Life Is It Anyway?*.

To hear Richard Dreyfuss describe celebrity, it is hardly surprising that it is disruptive. "Fame is bizarre, because you never wait for a table in a restaurant, and that's great. And you do get beautiful girls who walk by and—" he imitates a feminine come-hither look "—*that's* great. But what's bad about fame is the exact same thing.

"I stood at a restaurant for a moment and they said, 'Oh, right away, Mr. Dreyfuss.' And I heard—" he pauses and gives an imitation of background noise of hissed whispers. "And I sat down and I was all very cocky and filled with myself. Then I heard —" he repeats the hissed whispers "—and I turned around and Claus Von Bulow was right behind me. *That* will put fame in its perspective. And by the way, every time a girl walks by and goes like that—" he repeats the come-hither glance "—her boyfriend walks by too and goes, 'Hey, motherfucker!' So, it's got, you know what I mean, yin and yang?"

With all these conflicting emotions, he was not a happy man. He was in such a state of confusion about his feelings that, he says, "the only way I could contain them was to take drugs. So that's how it all started. By the eighties I was gone." Richard now likens trying to get through to his blinkered, pre-crash self to approaching a baby boy. "If he doesn't want to talk to you, he's going to go 'bladadadaada.' Well, I'd been doing that for ten years. I couldn't talk to anybody, I wouldn't listen to anybody," he admits.

"I was in big trouble. It wasn't like relationship trouble, you know, which is bullshit. It wasn't like, 'My friends don't like me.' It wasn't like, 'Oh, what do I do for dinner?' It was *real trouble*. It was real world trouble. It was cops, it was law, and it was the public humiliation of it. And it was horrible. And that was the beginning, what led to my changing."

Richard Dreyfuss speaks in defense of stars who find themselves curiously alienated from the world around them. For him, the most disturbing, shattering realization was that his own family appeared to have swallowed the movie star mythology whole. They had stopped behaving as if he were Richard, and had begun treating him as a star.

Gerry Dreyfuss concedes that this was so, but she does so briskly and unapologetically. She reasons that some changes simply were inevitable. A down-to-earth, jovial, and spirited woman, she approaches the subject with a lack of guard and pretense. There is nothing self-serving about her response to Richard's citations. Gatherings at Gerry's home (of a vast array of uncles, aunts, cousins, and assorted offspring) exemplified times when he was made to feel different, he said. Those were occasions that compounded his paranoid feelings. She shrugs dismissively and replies:

"It was *impossible* not to treat Richard differently, because he was in Hollywood. What were we? One [relative] was a grocery clerk . . . there was nobody in this glamorous thing called Hollywood, so naturally they would ask him questions [about the stars]. They wouldn't treat him the same way they treated their other cousins. He hated it and he stopped coming."

She does admit she was shocked when she later learned the extent to which this contributed to Richard's emotional discomfort. Showing little concern for currying favor with her son, she continues, saying, "It was tough. We didn't realize, but there was no other way. He *was* different. He was jetting all over the country, he had a limousine carry him to places if he needed it. Who else lived like that? There was nothing anybody could do. It was *his* problem. Nobody asked him for money, nobody asked him for favors. If your relative was Robert Redford, could you talk to him the same way you talked to your cousin who was working in Vons market?"

(Interestingly, Redford once revealed that his kids swiftly serenaded him with "R . . . R . . . Superstar. Who the hell do you think you are?" whenever he snapped his fingers for a taxi or behaved remotely like a star. "Conceited! The humor in our family is savage," Redford said.)

Gerry Dreyfuss will accept blame for tolerating bad behavior from Richard because he was busy, for stretching the limits, for making too many allowances on too many occasions. She overlooked, for example, broken lunch dates which had less to do with his supposedly extraordinarily busy life than with the rude, hard-to-swallow fact that in his self-absorption he simply forgot to meet his mom. It did not dawn on Gerry until much later that Richard had a point. "I didn't have to take that. There was no excuse for that. I wouldn't take bad manners from my other children, Lorin and Cathy . . . and they wouldn't have given them," she says.

Richard was too preoccupied with stumbling through his identity crisis to spare a thought for the fact that his mother had also to adjust to his fame. She noticed a subtle undercurrent, even in long-term relationships:

"I got 'recognition' from people that I knew all my life as Gerry," she says, with a chuckle. "I was suddenly being introduced by them to other people as Richard's mother, and that was a little funny. All of a sudden I had another identity. I was Richard Dreyfuss's mother and not just Gerry—which was enough for them in the past. I like to be known as his mother at times, but I have an identity of my own. And I have friends that still think of me as just me—and they like me anyway!" She laughs.

The negative repercussions of fame were pointed up for Gerry on a cruise she took with Richard. A fellow passenger, considerably younger than she, paid her a lot of attention. She was mildly surprised, but naturally rather flattered and excited—until she learned his ulterior motive. "I discovered he had a book he wanted Richard to read with the possibility of making a movie out of it . . . and I didn't know." She laughs wryly. "But nothing ever came of it, and I just realized that's one of the things that could happen." It was her sole experience of that kind, but it made her angry. "That was a little disconcerting—I am a woman. I thought how nice this young man was. Oh, well . . ."

Dr. James Grotstein believes the quality which best enhances the chance of any star's survival to be a degree of humility. In the interests of sanity, stars must recognize that although they are gifted, their gift is not there because they deserved it, they are merely its conduit. A singer acknowledges and respects that by saying, "I'm in good voice today."

"They do their best to develop and preserve it—but the gift is from somewhere else. And it can disappear," Dr. Grotstein explains. "One cannot and should not use humility to deny one's gifts. Gifts should be out and celebrated. But one should be careful *how* it's celebrated and not get drunk on it."

Dr. Grotstein believes that a star does not always change as drastically as it might appear. Stars are often manipulative personalities. "Some of them are great con artists. Sometimes fame caters to or helps to develop a certain psychopathic and narcissistic element in the personality. Especially when they see that they are above the rules, they get carried away. They actually *believe* that they are famous, and I think that's really the beginning of the danger."

A conscientious objector during the Vietnam War, Richard Dreyfuss grew up on a diet of political dinner table conversation. His mother was invariably its initiator.

Growing up in Brooklyn, Gerry was expected to deliver straight-A grades and was scolded by her strict father (with whom she simply never got along) when she did not. Gerry's mother was a longtime member of the American Jewish Congress, yet Gerry questions the depth of her influence, primarily because she cannot recall any communication, conversation, family intimacy, or shared activities. However, Gerry does remember her mother telling her that before World War II she had gone with a group to confront New York's telephone company to discover why they were not hiring Jewish people.

"They gave her some stupid answer—like Jewish girls' arms aren't long enough to reach the switchboard. She went to Washington with a contingent to speak to President Roosevelt about that. She didn't get to see him, but she took it seriously enough to go."

Gerry married lawyer Norman Dreyfuss in 1941. She was twenty, had no college degree and, although she had shown enterprise by establishing a children's play school, no plans for her future. Yet her political awareness was firmly established, and with the Depression, and then Adolf Hitler riding roughshod over Europe, the time for activism could not have been riper.

Gerry does not imagine herself standing still for an invasion, so cannot in all honesty claim she would have been a conscientious objector. The fair-weather pacifist was nevertheless astonished when her husband voluntarily enlisted in the infantry in 1944. (Norman studied German at Johns Hopkins University, and had already entered the ASTP, a program preparing American soldiers for the postwar army of occupation.) It was simply beyond Gerry's comprehension that a man would volunteer to kill . . . and face being killed.

With Norman overseas, and her new knowledge that American G.I.'s who were putting their lives on the line for their country were not being permitted to cast election votes by absentee ballots, Gerry Dreyfuss was driven to take her first political step. She became involved in the formation of the Wives, a group which went to Albany, spoke to Governor Dewey, and successfully secured the vote for servicemen. For her trouble, Gerry was also branded a Communist.

She joined the Consumer's Board in Brooklyn, New York, exerting patriotic pressure over her fellow Americans not to buy black market. She stood outside supermarkets with her son Lorin (who was born while Norman was overseas) in his baby carriage, urging shoppers to use their ration books and food stamps and not to encourage profiteering. Once again, she was labeled a Communist, but she ignored the name-calling. She considered it an unavoidable eventuality, "any time you tried to do anything more than going to the voting booth, any time you stuck your neck out."

Gerry was raised amidst Brooklyn's ethnically mixed communities in a religiously nonobservant Jewish family. Somehow she grew up without setting foot inside the home of a non-Jew, yet she was well aware of anti-Semitism: the very next apartment building on Eastern Parkway bore a hard-to-ignore placard: *No Jews or dogs allowed*. "We just took that sign for granted because it was there," she says, with a shrug. "It was very, very insulting, but it was so common. It wasn't until the middle forties, I guess, that that changed."

She also knew of companies—banks, insurance companies, advertising agencies—who would not be willing to employ her because she was Jewish; and yet her focus settled on redressing other inequities. The causes closest to her heart were peace and women's rights. As a twelve-year-old Girl Scout she had met Mrs. Roosevelt, and did not for a second doubt that a woman would one day sit in the White House. Against this activist heart of her life, and entirely by accident, Gerry also carved a lucrative career niche for herself as a demonstrator of a different kind. She showed kitchen gadgets, cleaning fluids, and cosmetics in department stores and dime stores.

The births of Cathy (now a public defender in Los Angeles) and Richard rounded out her family, and after 1958, Gerry sank her not-inconsiderable energies into causes like the League of Women Voters, Women's Strike for Peace, Another Mother for Peace. Many groups of women were initiated in her living room, which hosted a constant stream of meetings, fundraisers, and parties.

The involvement in Women's Strike for Peace sprang out of a study group in which she and her fellow activists uncovered an article expounding this theory: throughout civilization there had been three taboos, cannibalism, incest, and individual murder. It was now time for a fourth—war. As The Women for the Fourth Taboo, they each chipped in twenty dollars for stamps, corraled their children into stuffing envelopes, and fired off hundreds of letters to the media.

Their efforts were fruitless, save for a suggestion that they join a Santa Barbara resident who was at that moment endeavoring to stir the mothers of America into being angry enough about Vietnam, Strontium 90, and weapons testing, to strike for peace. When in November 1961, three thousand women marched to Los Angeles's downtown state building with the Women's Strike for Peace, Gerry and her friends were in the thick of it. Once again, the response was underwhelming.

"Churches told us to get lost, synagogues told us to get lost, we got no cooperation from most women's groups," she recalls, shaking her head. "I want to tell you, driving downtown that day, all of us who were used to wearing denim jeans, we got dressed up—silk stockings, clean underwear, gloves, hats, we really were Beverly Hills ladies. We were going to be noticed.

"When we were interviewed, we picked out some of the most elegant women to speak because we wanted the country to know we were not riff-raff. And we weren't, we were very proud of what we did because it did bring attention to the fact that nuclear weapons—there's just no way. We didn't stop the war. Sometimes I'd say to myself, how many marches do I march, and how many demonstrations do I go on? And the war kept on, all through the sixties. I never lay down in front of an army truck, that I never did, but I did go on all the marches. I just felt I couldn't stay home."

Gerry and her husband faced what she politely terms a dichotomy when he bought a business which manufactured fiberglass gun-shields for the Navy. Norman's position was that this was a defensive, life-saving product. "That was his, I guess, apology," she says with a chuckle, "because one time I threatened to put a picket line against his factory. We didn't fight about it, though. He helped support me."

When Gerry went to Washington to march for civil rights, he even paid for her trip. (The Dreyfuss's separated in 1976 and divorced in 1980.)

Gerry is a lively conversationalist with a good sense of humor and is intrinsically curious. She has traveled Europe, been to China, and visited Cuba "to see what Castro was all about." She was once asked to run for the Senate as a peace candidate in a loss seat and considered it, fleetingly. But these days she is a rather sedate armchair activist. She sold her concession for engraving jewelery in department stores after a 1970 check-up at Scripps Institute uncovered cancer of the thyroid, which led to radical surgery; she also required a second cataract operation.

The Dreyfuss family made the shift to the West Coast in 1950, when Lorin was twelve, Richard nine, and Cathy four. But it was not proximity to Hollywood that sparked Richard's interest in acting. He began seriously talking of an acting career in New York, when he was about seven. In Gerry's view, while there was nothing wrong with it, being an actor was "kind of silly." Yet she encouraged him.

Richard was a good student, albeit the only student in his high school to get a D in Algebra, then an F when he re-took it. She remembers that when he was in fifth or sixth grade, he came home crying, asking her if he was a coward. "He said, 'Is it because I don't know baseball and football, is that what a coward means?' I said, 'You're not a coward. You're not afraid to go swimming, to do anything.' He said, 'The kids think of me that way, but I know more about the Civil War than they do.' I said, 'Well, they may be cowards, they're afraid to learn about the Civil War.' And that was the end of that. But he was different."

When they settled in California, Norman changed, she says. The man who had never been interested in making money, who preferred playing guitar, acting in an amateur group, socializing and parties, became house counsel for a manufacturing company, then segued into real estate and became highly successful.

So Gerry, who thought lemons grew in grocery stores when she was a girl, was suddenly a Beverly Hills homeowner with a swimming pool in her backyard.

One of Gerry Dreyfuss's happiest moments came in March 1983 when Richard married Jeramie Rains. He met his wife in January, a few months after his accident, and Gerry, who was in Florida at the time, will never forget his call. "He said, 'Mom, I went to a party, met a woman, and I want to mmm-mmm mmmerrmmerr.' I said, 'What are you saying?' He said, 'I want to get mmmm.' I said, 'Listen, if you can't say it, you can't do it.' He hung up. That was in the morning." Five or six hours later, he called back. "He said, 'Mother, I went to a party about ten days ago and I met a woman, and I love her and I want to marry her.' I said, 'Well, that's different.' "

Despite the whirlwind speed with which their romance accelerated, Gerry had no misgivings. "None, as soon as I met her . . . she was not an airhead, she was not a flake. I had met *lots* of girls! No, his girlfriends were always very nice people and they're still friends, he has never lost them, a lover has become a friend and they're even friends of Jeramie. I don't know anything about women he was with once or twice . . . but the women that were meaningful in his life are still in his life and in Jeramie's life. It's nice."

Jeramie, an ex-actress from West Virginia, was a promo-producer for CBS prior to the birth of Emily in 1983. (Benjamin was born in 1986.) They wed at a quiet ceremony at a friend's Beverly Hills home, followed by a massive bash for 750 thrown by Gerry on a Burbank Studio soundstage, with the likes of Steven Spielberg, Teri Garr, Raul Julia, and Brian De Palma in attendance.

Columbia Pictures gave her free use of the soundstage and her choice of decoration . . . but omitted to tell her that she would have to pay for the decor to be put up and removed. By the time she had paid golden-time Sunday union wages for the necessary firemen, nurses, electricians, and carpenters, it was so costly that she jokes she might as well have been running the studio for a day. Caterer Arthur Sargent transformed the party setting into nighttime Manhattan, complete with backdrop, Tavern-on-the-Green, fairy-lights, a subway kiosk, and park benches. There was a black and white art deco theme, a white piano, and full orchestra. Six food stations served tempura, Italian food, roast beef, magnificent seafood. A rabbi closed the proceedings filmmaker-style by declaring, "It's a wrap."

It was a major achievement for Gerry and she was proud of her efforts. "They told me I could have produced a movie after it was done. It was fabulous!" Better still was the welcoming into the family of her daughter-in-law: "Jeramie's the best thing that ever happened to Richard—the best thing that ever happened to anybody!"

21 *Splendid Isolation*

It is not entirely surprising if a star sometimes feels driven to retreat from a world where, as Meryl Streep complains, she can no longer go shopping without people peeking to see what size underwear she buys. There are two kinds of isolation and this one can be labeled "necessary withdrawal." Stars are forced to isolate themselves from the public to a degree, if only to avoid interruptions twenty-four hours a day. Even the approachable Betty White—who cannot bear it when fellow thespians with overinflated egos sweep past their fans with their noses firmly tilted skywards—is forced to admit, "You don't want to hang out, you learn the tricks to expedite it as much as you can." It goes too far in the opposite direction, she believes, when stars suddenly have teams of agents, managers, and publicity people advising them which projects are beneath them and warping their perspective. "They get a little coterie around them, a guard-all wall, which is such a mistake."

Lily Tomlin would doubtless agree, after an incident that befell her mother, Lily Mae, a native of Kentucky, on a visit to Los Angeles. They were out on a drive, Lily reports, when Mom spotted a major movie star on his bicycle. "She got so excited! We slowed the car and she called out, 'Hello!' And this big star threw her the finger. She was crushed by that!"

Isolation is all a matter of degree, and some stars carry the self-imposed seclusion to extremes, literally living what is tantamount to a non-life-style, for which Elvis set the tone—fenced off, surrounded by bodyguards, entourages, nannies, household staff, secretaries, high walls, and electronic fences and gates.

Irrespective of whether the isolation is merely rational or wildly excessive, families can suffer. One superstar mom, who shall remain nameless, likens trying to see her star child to obtaining an audience with the Pope, the obstacles to their meeting are so legion. It is inevitable that the priorities in a star's life shift away from hearth and home into a global arena. Diana Kind, who allows that she has forfeited time with her daughter Barbra Streisand, has a very clear picture of the star's role in life: "Oh, yes. You're out there for the world to be pleased, and you hope they will be."

When Barbra's son, Jason, was small, she was moving full steam ahead on her flourishing career. Had Grandma not been employed full-time as a school secretary, Diana feels sure Barbra would have preferred her to take care of Jason, rather than hiring an outsider. As it was, Diana was determined to keep close ties to her grandson, work or no, and visited him frequently. For a while, they even lived in the same house. But Diana admits there were times that keeping up that contact through the barrier of officious personnel was done only with difficulty.

"Sometimes these maids don't even let you go upstairs. 'Oh, you will disturb this, you will disturb that, it is his bathing time, this is suppertime,' you know. You feel like hitting them in the head. But you can't cross them either, when they are adamant about things. But I did not enjoy it as far as Jason being in that position. They really need family folks."

When Grandma does take the reins, she must concern herself with security precautions. Laura Hawn admits there is little carefree or spontaneous time for a star's children in Hollywood; everything has to be carefully planned and monitored. Because of this, she was all in favor of Goldie's decision to move to Aspen, Colorado, in the shadow of the Rockies.

"It's hard on the children. You have gates, and you have to make arrangements for other children to come and play with them. It's awful, really, it's not a free kind of thing." She is proud to say, however, "Goldie doesn't let being a star disrupt her life."

Diana Kind admits that when Barbra is approached by fans, "sometimes she will be amenable, and sometimes she would be a little cross." Like most people in the limelight, Streisand is drawn simultaneously by opposing tides: the wish for fame, and the desire for anonymity. She resents being treated like an object, a thing, she hates flashbulbs popping invasively. She has also likened the world in which she lives to a cocoon.

When stars remove themselves from the likelihood of brushing up against the real world, they remove themselves from the very people whose presence is essential for them to keep their view of themselves in perspective. It is tragic that when Elvis was in his sad decline and most in need of voices of reason and truth in his life, he did not have them handy. Gladys had died, Priscilla had divorced him. He had both engineered himself and been engineered into a position where he was ever more isolated from those who might have told it like it was.

Where Elvis led, Michael Jackson and Eddie Murphy followed. Elvis was Murphy's boyhood hero, and now he himself has taken Presley-style refuge.

Murphy's entourage has grown to immense proportions and all of this has come about in a stunningly short space of time. Eddie's police officer father died when he was three years old, and although his mom, Lillian Lynch, remarried, the household lacked financial security and Murphy became a chronic worrier. "I miss going to the mall, hanging out with friends, being like everyone else," he admits, but on balance, he will stay as he is.

Buffering himself or being buffered? Isolating himself or being isolated? Robin Williams puts seeing old friends in the same category of necessity as scraping barnacles off the side of a ship that has been at a standstill.

Sometimes the separations between star and mom are compounded by geographical distances. Inveterate traveler George Hamilton keeps his insomniac mom company by proxy. Anne watches his old movies on television at 4 A.M. While it is hard to imagine Eva Jagger bopping to the strains of "Too Much Blood" or "Sympathy for the Devil," she does have a soft spot for the Stones' melodical oldies like "Ruby Tuesday" and "Lady Jane," and very occasionally, when she is lying in bed late at night listening to her favorite radio program, the host will pop on a favorite. "What's that one? Something horses?" she asks. " 'Wild Horses,' yes. And if I haven't seen Mick or spoken to him for a long time,

I'll think, 'Oh, isn't that nice.' I'm lying in bed listening to him, and it's really lovely."

Sometimes fame itself is so devastating that it precipitates the isolation. Being a teen idol brought David Cassidy to what was tantamount to a nervous breakdown. Somehow—and for this he blames no one but himself—he was not able to reach out to his mother, Evelyn Ward, or to any of his loved ones. He isolated himself more and more as his pop-idol image devoured so much of the real David that he became "an emotional cripple."

"You couldn't go anywhere without police escorts and chaos and being thrown in trunks of cars. You couldn't even go out of your room." But, he notes, for all the adulation, "No one really is looking at you, loving you. You *know* what they're loving, they're loving this 'thing.' " Cassidy fell prey to what USC literature professor Leo Braudy described in his book, *The Frenzy of Renown,* as being "created by others before one can create oneself." A particularly treacherous trap for youthful stars, and Cassidy admits, "I didn't handle it well at all. I don't think I left my house for nine months. It's very dark and it's very black to me, and I don't remember much about it, except being alone in my room."

David's stepmother Shirley Jones married his father, the late actor Jack Cassidy, when David was seven. Although David continued to live with his mother, he was close to his half-brother Shaun, and Shirley Jones admits that when it came time for Shaun to follow in his footsteps as a teen heartthrob, her son certainly benefited from David's prior experience. Shaun was more down-to-earth about it, knowing fame could fall as fast as it came. The whole phenomenon was more devastating to David, who, Shirley says, at first "was fascinated, and then became so frightened of all the girls."

The TV series "The Hardy Boys" led to Shaun's own turn in the spotlight and a string of hit pop records, but Shirley, who had also been a young star, remained unimpressed and the vital great leveler: "If somebody had told me 'Da Doo Ron Ron' would be a hit record, I'd have said 'You're crazy,' because it just sounds like a bunch of gibberish to me."

While she was and is happy to sign autographs at the proper time and place, she rapidly grew impatient with the army of fans who saw her as a link to Shaun and David and stood vigil outside her home. "I do resent them knocking on my door, ringing my doorbell," she told Sue Russell back in the late seventies, when her blood was still boiling, "because that's my one moment of privacy and they wouldn't like me getting them out of a shower . . . and I tell you, I cannot abide it. I have no humor or patience and I'm very angry when it happens. I've thrown more people off my lawn, as calm as I seem to be. I've had years of it, more than my share. That goes beyond . . . my home is sacred."

When stars fear for their personal safety and employ body-guards, an extra-impenetrable wall is erected between them and the real world. These hopefully intimidating heavyweights serve another purpose by saving stars from lawsuits. Stallone has called them a buffer between him and the people who come up and want to start a fight, hoping to provoke him into retaliation. He knows if he hits back, it is a sure legal action. Michael J. Fox tells the tale of a man who approached hockey player Wayne Gretzky. "He said, 'Are you Wayne Gretzky?' and he said, 'Yes,' and the guy went and smashed his own face into a wall, and turned around and said, 'Why did you do that to me?' He was creating a situation where he could sue Wayne. It's a little weird. If it had happened to me, I'd probably say, 'While we're at it . . . and if I'm going to get sued for it . . .' "

Fox credits his mom, Phyllis, and father, Bill, with his low-key approach to fame; he does not have an entourage. "I'd rather be on the same level as everybody else. You set yourself up on a throne, eventually you're going to get knocked off it." He gestures to the extras in the bar where he is filming and says, "I can imagine it's pretty damn frustrating. I can imagine if they saw me sitting in a big chair with someone lighting my cigarette . . . *I* would risk a few days in jail to come over and set me straight on what it feels like to hit the ground!"

Marvin Gaye was a tragic example of how isolation and paranoia can build, the havoc they wreak badly compounded in his case, of course, by drug addiction. Alberta Gay, Marvin's idolized mom, died in 1987 at age seventy-four from a form of bone cancer. Three years earlier, Marvin (who added the *e* to Gay) had been gunned down by his own father, Marvin Gay Sr., in the horrific culmination of a lifelong battle waged between father and son. Father had consumed vodka, Marvin was under the influence of cocaine, and the combination, stirred with their history of antagonism, was positively lethal.

Gaye had received his share of death threats over the years, but a relative told *Rolling Stone* writer Michael Goldberg that Marvin feared being killed, and his paranoia about being poisoned had reached such a degree that the day before he died he asked a member of his family to go and buy him a hot dog, only to throw it in the bushes when it was brought to him.

There were happy times, though, and perhaps the proudest moment in Alberta's life was May 1, 1972, the day declared Marvin Gaye Day, when her son was handed the key to the city of Washington. Alberta and her husband rode with Marvin, who sold 30 million records during his lifetime, in the open-car motorcade that followed marching bands and all the paraphernalia of celebration in his honor.

The story was dreadfully bittersweet, however: and ultimately more bitter than sweet. Marvin Gaye died in debt, paranoid, in terrible physical and mental condition from drugs and exhaustion, and was given to suicidal moods shortly before his death.

Alberta was a constant source of love and support for Marvin; she encouraged her son's music, slipped him money when he was struggling. In return, her son idolized her, but her love could never cover the cracks in Marvin's personality wrought by a cold, unloving father whom he was incapable of pleasing. The Gays exemplified those family dynamics: Mother could never compensate for Father's negative input.

Marvin Sr. who was jealous of Alberta's love for Marvin Jr., abused his son throughout his childhood. The beatings were worse if Alberta tried to intervene, and while she harbored thoughts of leaving her husband, loyalty and a deep knowledge that this was a man in trouble kept her at his side.

She was, however, realistic in her view of the father-son relationship and when the adult Marvin voiced his wish that his father could express love for him, Alberta said he should put that thought out of his mind and comfort himself with the knowledge of all who did love him. Perceptively she observed to David Ritz,

"Marvin didn't believe me. My son didn't really believe that anyone loved him." The scars ran too deep.

Alberta Gay was a kind, generous, hardworking mother who rose before daybreak and took pride in the fact that her labors as a domestic kept the family afloat. She was also a sacrificing woman, who stood unflinching in snowfall waiting for a bus to take her to work while knowing that her husband lay idle at home. Not to be underestimated either was that she was fearful of Marvin Sr., and her strong beliefs dictated that she obey him, come what may.

Marvin Pentz Gay was a minister (although never officially trained or ordained) when Alberta met him in 1934, soon after arriving in Washington with her young son, Michael, from Rocky Mountain, North Carolina. Marvin Sr., one of thirteen children of sharecroppers, was raised in the House of God, a Pentecostal church which housed the wild, emotion-laden, hand-clapping, fervent gospel music that would later inspire his son.

Just as Elvis wanted to become a star so Gladys would be taken care of in the manner to which she was unaccustomed, so Marvin talked of robbing a bank so his mother would not have to work so hard. Marvin Gaye also had the savior complex. Indeed, as soon as he was able, he moved his family out of the projects in Washington, D.C., buying them a home in a middle-class neighborhood. In her son, Alberta found the provider she had never had in Marvin Sr. Marvin Jr. was resentful that his caring for his mother benefited his father and his entire family, but paradoxically he relished the power too. Alberta was proud of the fact that never a fortnight went by without a phone call from Marvin, nor a month without him sending her money, from the time he left home at nineteen.

In 1973, Marvin moved his parents up in the world once more, buying them the 1930s Tudor-style home in L.A.'s Crenshaw district where they lived with his sisters Jeanne and Zeola, brother Frankie, and assorted nephews and nieces. It was the home to which he would retreat in those last troubled months preceding his death on April 1, 1984.

The bond between Alberta and Marvin remained unsevered throughout Marvin's life. When his fears of performing drove him into seclusion, only Alberta was capable of cajoling him into going on stage.

"If Mother hadn't traveled with me, I'd never have the nerve to do live performances again," Marvin said after one of his depression-induced withdrawals. He once survived a suicide attempt in Hawaii: "In one hour I snorted up a full ounce of pure coke and knew I was dead. I called Mother to tell her. But God wasn't ready to take me. I was saved that day, to suffer the next."

Singer Bobby Womack said, "Marvin had a lot of love, more than normal, for his mom." It could also be said that Alberta was not tough enough on her son for his own good. (Marvin's friend Mrs. Price told David Ritz: "I love Mrs. Gay, but she was never firm or frank enough with Marvin. He was so good to her, she was afraid of angering him.")

Yet, speaking of the time, just months before his death, when she tried to persuade him to check himself into a hospital and he flatly refused, Alberta observed to Ritz: "The people around him should have forced him to go, but they did whatever he wanted. That's the way it had always been."

In November 1983, Marvin Gaye made the fateful decision to move back into his parents' home. His drug use was at such a pitch that his mother was forced to watch tearfully as he consumed them in front of her very eyes. All pretense was gone. He barely ventured out of his room. Alberta saw her pitiful, frightened little boy transformed into an undeniable crazy man. But her pleas that he flush the drugs down the toilet were to no avail.

When her son was gone, loyal to the last, Alberta bailed her husband out of jail. Only then did she file for divorce from the man for whom she could no longer find it in her heart to pray. Her daughter Jeanne told David Ritz that she believes Marvin's end was exactly as he would have chosen it (and perhaps did choose it), bringing relief to him and to his mother by freeing her of his father, and sentencing his father to eternal unhappiness.

The story of Tina Turner and Zelma Bullock is infinitely more uplifting. Their not-always-happy alliance ("The fact is, I had no love from my mother or my father from the beginning," said Tina) has given way some forty years later to a warm, loving mother-daughter relationship. Both Tina and Zelma have come a long way from the cotton and strawberry fields of Nut Bush, Tennessee.

Zelma proudly gives a guided tour of the house that Tina gave her, an impressive contemporary abode with high sloped ceilings, cozy wood beams. The abundant greenery on the outside pours inside visually via enormous windows. As a little girl back in Tennessee picking cotton in the fields, Tina wanted desperately to be part of the school principal's daughter's world which was so far removed from her own unhappy home life. At the core of that fantasy was having a home where her whole family could be together. Nestled in a woodsy Los Angeles canyon, this is it.

Zelma's health forced her to Los Angeles in 1979 and she does not mind admitting that it was a major adjustment. The ultimate irony, and the not-atypical lot of a star mom: now that Zelma is in Los Angeles, Tina rarely is. Zelma soon had itchy feet. She had worked hard all her life and could not get used to sitting around the house. Tina helped her find a job in the beauty parlor of a Beverly Hills department store, mixing hair colors, making coffee, and the like. Sociable Zelma was in her element; she was popular and no one knew she was Tina's mom, at least not at first. But eventually she gave in to Tina's requests that she retire; it did not seem right to Tina to have Ma working. Strong, proud Zelma was in a foreign world, a big, unfriendly, sprawling city, and without her job, she was even more isolated.

"When I first moved [to Los Angeles] I couldn't hardly stand it," she explains. "I was raised to say 'good morning' or 'good afternoon,' and I would say it to people and they'd just look around at me. I thought it was the coldest place I'd ever been in my life. They're just not as polite as the people in St. Louis, but I'm adjusting."

For Zelma, seeing Tina is the highlight in her life. "You never get tired of being around Tina, not ever. She spent the night with me recently and I was so happy, I really felt good. I miss her when she's away and I miss Alline too, both my daughters are very close. We go shopping and out to dinner when Tina has time, I see her when she's home . . . but that's very seldom, because she's a go-getter."

Zelma, a devout Baptist, was the daughter of sharecropper Josephus Currie and his wife, Georgianna. Josephus was three-quarters Navajo and a quarter black, Georgianna was three-quarters Cherokee and a quarter black: enter Tina's cheekbones. Georgianna's paternal aunt was Martha Mae, and between them they inspired Tina Turner's real name, Anna Mae Bullock. Zelma's own childhood was quite comfortable and happy, her social activities revolving largely around the church. "I had six brothers and I was the only girl, so they all spoiled me. But once you get married that unspoils you," she says with a shrug.

She refers to her turbulent marriage to Tina's father, Floyd Richard Bullock, a deacon in the Woodlawn Baptist Church and farm overseer. Where the Bullocks were staunch, strict folk, Zelma was definitely a little wilder; she started smoking cigarettes and firing off .45's when she was ten, she loved to party and have fun. Her firstborn, Evelyn, was the result of a teenage pregnancy prior to her marriage, and the baby was taken under Georgianna's wing. Alline was Zelma's first child from her loveless marriage to Richard Bullock. Then three years later, in 1939, Anna Mae/Tina was born, just as Zelma had been drawing close to leaving her husband. Anna Mae seemed to bear the brunt of the lack of warmth and affection between them. She never felt that Zelma loved her like she did Alline. Perhaps Zelma blamed Anna Mae's arrival for the fact that she had to stay with Richard.

On the surface, Anna Mae/Tina's childhood was far from deprived. While her parents had no formal education, father was head man on the farm and the girls each had their own bedrooms; they had nice furniture and brand-new clothes each year. Their home was always alive with music—blues, jazz, spirituals, all kinds—and according to her mom, Anna Mae started to sing just as soon as she began to talk.

"I would take Anna Mae to the movies and she'd come back and act the part—like falling out on the floor and holding her breath. I'd tell her to get up and she'd say, 'But that's what the lady did!' Every Saturday night Anna Mae and Alline would go to the movies. I had a friend named Edith Willis, so she says, 'This girl is gonna be something when she grows up!' I just said, 'Oh.' But still, deep down, I thought she would be, because when she started pulling herself up on a chair before she started walking, I'd turn the radio on and there she'd be—dancing to the music! I'd catch her by the hand and dance around the floor with her to the radio. I went to church a lot, and Tina sang in the choir when she was real small—she was the smallest one. I liked dancing also. I did it all, including the jitterbug. There was a guy called Slim, worked at a bank in St. Louis when I lived there, and I went as his guest to a party at the bank and we stole the show. Everybody else stopped dancing and sat down and clapped to us.

"When Anna Mae was just so high, she tried three or four times to climb on this stool in front of my dressing table. Finally she made it and she pulled both mirrors together so she could see herself all the way round. Then she'd make these thick braids and play the piano and sing. She used to put my high-heeled shoes on, my bra, and my hat. She didn't have anything to go in the bra, but she would put it on anyway and walk along in the high heels. Tina was always active, always. Anything she'd attempt to do, she did it well, regardless. Everything. She would try, try, try until she got it exactly like she wanted it. She was strong and she had determination."

The ritualistic, theatrical aspect of some religious denominations can spark a fascination in children, sow a seed which is eventually reaped in a very different but not totally unallied field like music or theater. And children who have been steeped in religiosity from a very early age often have a strong sense of discipline in their lives, a capacity to keep their noses to the grindstone, to delay gratification and to work very hard toward accomplishing goals—all characteristics which Anna Mae/Tina would later exhibit in abundance.

In 1942, Zelma and Richard Bullock left the farm in Nut Bush for a fresh start after securing jobs at the nuclear research plant that was built near Knoxville. They left—their children did not. Alline was packed off to live with grandmother Georgianna, while Anna Mae was sent, much to her dismay, to the somber, dull, disciplined abode of her paternal grandmother, Roxanna Bullock. On a visit to their parents' new home the following year, she and Alline briefly sampled the delights of the bright lights of the city of Knoxville where Anna Mae was introduced to the comparative wildness of the local Pentecostal church. She watched the women popping their fingers and dancing to blues and jump rhythms, and rapidly picked up the dance of the Holy Rollers. The gospel influence was always evident in Tina's stage persona, in the swaying of her body, the throwing of her head.

In 1945, the family was reunited, but her parents' marriage was more turbulent than ever. She was ten when Zelma left and moved to St. Louis. Anna Mae fully expected her mother to send for her and Alline. As a little girl, she did not comprehend that Zelma simply could not have made her escape from her unhappy marriage if she had taken her daughters with her. She could not afford to find a place of her own. To Anna Mae, however, Ma's disappearance was an abandonment and another bitter disappointment. She shed many tears and each day checked the mailbox, hoping for some word. She loved Zelma so much, but at that stage, she hated her too.

When Anna Mae was thirteen, Richard Bullock, with whom she had never been close, went off to Chicago, and her and Alline's lives were disrupted once more as they were shuttled between various friends and relatives until, in their midteens, they were able to join their mother, who had work as a cleaner in St. Louis. It was an uneasy reconciliation. Anna Mae was rebellious; having grown used to fending for herself, it was hard for her to get accustomed to being under her mother's eye again.

When Tina Turner launched her singing career, it was without the knowledge of Zelma. She was still in school at the time and also working part-time as a nurse's aide, but she and Alline went to the Saturday jam sessions held by Ike Turner and his band, the Kings of Rhythm. Once Tina jumped up to sing, there was no looking back. Zelma found out by accident.

"One day Ike's piano player came to the house and wanted to know where Tina was," Zelma recalls with a smile. "I said, 'She's gone swimming with a friend, what do you want with her?' So she says, 'She's late for rehearsal.' I said, 'Rehearsal for what?' And that's how I found out! Tina came home and I said, 'Annie Mae has been here looking for you.' She looked at me with these big eyes!" Zelma learned that Ike's piano player, Annie Mae, had been accompanying Zelma's underage daughter and posing as her guardian so she would be admitted to the clubs where she performed.

"They thought Annie was her mother, that's how she got in. It was quite some time before people realized that I was her mother, not Annie Mae. We were in Chicago one night at the Millionaire's Club and a lady introduced me as Tina Turner's mother. This lady says, 'No, that's not Tina's mother. I know Tina's mother, she's short and she's fat and she's fair like Tina!' It was really funny!"

Zelma had reservations about Tina's musical career: "I didn't like it really. I wanted her to be a nurse. But I wanted her to do what she wanted to. That way she would be good at it. If you force a child to do something, it goes the other way. I saw Ike and Tina perform in St. Louis when they just got together and I said, 'She will be good one day.' I said that to myself, to no one else. It's unbelievable what happened when Tina got out on her own. I was kind of afraid, but thank God, she made it. Did she ever!"

Mom is quick to confirm that the real Tina is vastly different from the tigress onstage, the wild and sexy warrior woman, the dynamo stomping the stage in specially reinforced spike heels. "She is very modest, and conservative to a certain extent. But she's always been flamboyant onstage, that's why people like her. Tina's very down-to-earth, really down-to-earth. She believes in getting things done around the house. She's never been any problem whatsoever, she's very level-headed."

Zelma, a staunch Baptist, remembers praying hard for Tina when at seventeen she went out on the road with Ike Turner. The staunch Baptist now finds herself with a Buddhist daughter. Tina became interested in Buddhism while still embroiled in her marriage and embraced it wholeheartedly after she left Ike; its cause-and-effect philosophy helped her come to terms with the hardships and problems in her life. She chants several times a day, visits psychics, and believes that she lived in Egypt many lives ago.

Her change in faith does not bother her mother: "I feel like, whatever religion you desire, just be a good one if you can. So if Tina wanted to be Buddhist and she thinks being Buddhist helped her, I think it helped her. I know Baptist helped me. If Tina feels like she lived in Egypt, she did. That's how I feel. I've never been to psychics myself, but I do like psychic movies!" She laughs, the happy laugh of a woman who may be a little lonely in Los Angeles, but who can warm herself with thoughts of Tina and the wonderful way things are between them.

22 *Facing Fear*

The lunatic fringe, seemingly drawn to the bright lights of celebrity with increasing regularity, is ever present in the lives of stars. Prior to Cher's appearance as a presenter at the 1984 Academy Awards, since various threats were leveled against her, she made her arrival presidential-style, her limousine wedged between others fore and aft, each car in the convoy manned with armed guards. Cher's personal six-foot-three, 240-pound security guard (as much a part of her life as her makeup and gowns) perched on the roof of her limousine.

To her mother, who rode with her and who was unprepared for any of this extraneous entourage, it presented a scary sight. "I was a nervous wreck," Georgia Holt remembers. "You cannot check crowds, you definitely cannot frisk them, and you can never, ever, be sure. Kids always mobbed [Sonny and Cher's] concerts. There's a picture of them in an old Cadillac convertible where it is literally a sea of bodies. It's macabre, there are bodies everywhere, like a bunch of cockroaches going through a piece of pie. It can be scary."

Billy Dee Williams owns a gun, and offered to arm his family and send them for firearm training too. His mother Loretta, a devout Jehovah's Witness, would hear of no such thing. "Jehovah is our gun. We call on Him for any help we need, and for you. Your house is protected too," she admonished Billy Dee.

Eva Jagger says that security fears, although they do pop up, are not a constant, preoccupying thought in England. America, particularly after the fate of Mick's compatriot and peer-superstar

John Lennon, is more worrisome, but she is pragmatic. "You could worry about your kids being out in a car and getting killed, or in a plane, couldn't you? So you just don't think about it."

In 1980 Mick Jagger asked a reporter from *US* magazine, "Whatever happened to John Lennon? He lives like ten yards from me, but he stays in his place cloistered like a nun." A gruesome irony, yet despite John's death, Mick's philosophy remains firm: you cannot live in fear.

Lest anyone should be under the delusion that it is only the controversial inhabitants of the rock netherworld (or bare-midriffed attention-lovers like Cher) who are preyed upon, witness the case of Annette Funicello.

Who, you might wonder, could be more wholesome and innocent than the not-especially-pretty, twelve-year-old brunette who won her way into the hearts of Americans as a Mouseketeer? With benefit of hindsight, Virginia Funicello admits that she and her family were ill-prepared for Annette's phenomenal transformation into an "American institution" receiving five thousand fan letters a week. It took Virginia and Joe Funicello—down-to-earth, family-oriented folk and total strangers to the entertainment industry—entirely by surprise. Virginia, who was a thirty-year-old, pony-tailed housewife when Annette became a Mouseketeer, suspects that their naïveté, their openness, made Annette more vulnerable. "We were so dumb, we didn't know show business," she readily admits.

A case in point: when Annette was thirteen, she was sent a highly extravagant Christmas gift by an enthusiastic young male fan. As briefed by the Disney executives, who issued strict guidelines to all their Mouseketeer moms, Mrs. Funicello telephoned the boy's mother and explained that it would be absolutely impossible for Annette to accept the diamond wristwatch. Unfortunately—enter naïveté—Virginia allowed the boy's mother to weaken her resolve with her pleas that her son would be heartbroken and had worked after school for a year to save up for the gift.

Months later, when the watch was long forgotten, a nicely dressed seventeen-year-old boy became a seemingly innocent but constant presence at the Mouseketeers' tour stops in Connecticut. Curiosity aroused, Virginia Funicello was prompted to speak to him. She did not know him, but he knew her, said the boy who had saved a whole year to buy Annette a watch and who now would like a date with her, please. Virginia told him the truth: Annette did not date. He said, "Well, the least she can do is talk to me."

So the famous thirteen-year-old was instructed by her mother to treat the young man nicely, to be courteous. Virginia invited the boy to ride on the bus with the company so he could meet the Mouseketeers and accompany them to the Mayor's presentation and some local TV stations. She went out of her way for this loyal fan and remembers being somewhat embarrassed because the girls paid no attention to him. "They were cutting up and laughing and telling jokes. They ignored him completely, left him to me. You know kids!"

When the time came to say good-bye at their hotel door, the boy once again pressed Virginia for a private date with her daughter. It was, of course, out of the question. Annette Funicello would not go out with a boy she did not know, even if her mother had been willing to give her permission, which she was not.

"Annette went up to her room, and he went home and tried to commit suicide," Mrs. Funicello says flatly. "Shot himself. The kid must have been a little mental, I don't know. We had moved on to the next city and all of a sudden it was all over the newspapers, in headlines, 'Annette Accepts Diamond Wristwatch But Spurns Boy's Love.' On and on and on, how horrendous these kids were that accepted these gifts—and the boy was dying. Poor Annette, she was so innocent."

Disney executives arranged for their young star to telephone the boy in his hospital bed, an enormously difficult call for a teenager to make to a stranger.

"The boy lived. Thank God he lived, that would have been a terrible thing for Annette. It was all over the papers, very derogatory. Now Disney got after me. We were so upset. I was so nice to him. I liked him a lot, he was a nice, clean-cut kid, but he had emotional problems. Because he was in love with her, he thought she'd love him back. The kids from the mental hospitals, all of them fell for her. They'd watch [the Mouseketeers] every day, madly in love with her, and think she loved them back. Then they would hitchhike out here and try to find her."

An escapee from a psychiatric ward once slept outside Annette's bedroom window for three nights in a row, without the Funicellos' knowledge. During daylight hours, he sat on the curb across the street from their home, jotting down notes—the times the various family members arrived at the house and left again. Virginia was aware of (and was bothered by) his presence but was not unduly concerned. Not enough to stop her from popping out for an hour to take nine-year-old Joey to the dentist, leaving Annette at home looking after two-year-old Michael. How could she have known?

"Well, he tried to break down the front door. He saw me leave with Joey, knew she was alone in the house. She was hysterical." Fortunately, Annette had the presence of mind to immediately telephone her father, Joe Funicello, who was at his garage a mere five-minute drive from the house.

The police swiftly arrested the young intruder, who, it transpired, occupied a tiny room in downtown Los Angeles. He had plastered the walls of his living quarters with pictures of Annette which were defaced and covered with obscenities. He was sent back to his psychiatric hospital—which did not erase the family's terrible fear that he might one day return.

The Funicellos' lives had changed irrevocably in 1954 when Annette was singled out by Mr. Walt Disney himself. Uncle Walt spotted the petite preteen dancing in *Swan Lake,* after seeing literally thousands of children as he scoured the country for his twenty-four Mouseketeers. The immensely popular daily TV show, which kept children enthralled while moms made dinner, was a mixed blessing for shy Annette. "She auditioned, got it, didn't want it, cried her eyes out, hated every minute of it—until she got in there. Then she loved it. She had a ball."

In fact, Annette signed two seven-year contracts with Disney, her fan following outstripping that of all other Mouseketeers. "I think everybody associated with her because she was so natural, so down-to-earth, not a show-off, not pushy," explains Virginia, who hates spoiled children and insists Annette did not change. "Nope, didn't affect her at all, not one iota. She's here every single day with her mom and dad. We do all our shopping together. She got the same allowance as the boys did. She never knew how much she was making, never cared, never asked. We didn't spoil her with expensive things." At sixteen, she received a used T-bird, just like her brothers Joe and Michael.

Annette was smacked if she was nasty to her brothers. "She got cracked in the head with a frying pan from me," Virginia says matter-of-factly, explaining that her daughter and Joey fought a lot. "She didn't know she was any different. She didn't know, believe me." (Joe Funicello is now forty-three and a vice-president at ICM, the theatrical agency. Michael, the baby, is thirty-six and works at Disney Studios in the research department.)

Virginia was a rather reluctant stage mother. She loathed setting the alarm for 4:30 A.M. so she could take her youngest son to the baby-sitter in time to take Annette to the set. She spent what she considered to be many wasted hours on studio lots, with housework piling up at home, but Mr. Disney was adamant that his minors be accompanied at all times. Occasionally, the guard at Disney Studios' front gate was persuaded to cover for Virginia when she had no choice but to sneak off and collect her sons from school or had to pop home to cook the boys' dinner.

Later, when Annette made a dozen beach-party films, she was not permitted by Disney to taint her wholesome image with a two-piece bikini, nor was she allowed to wiggle provocatively. "They used to be so wild, some of those girls," Virginia recalls. "Poor Annette, always with the schoolteacher and me, her old mother!"

In fact, the Disney code of discipline was not overly restrictive as it was not far removed from the Funicellos' own family and moral standards. "That's why Mr. Disney was so in love with her, because he knew what kind of a background she had. He was very shy and she was shy. And I was always hiding somewhere—all the other Mouseketeer mothers were trying to push their kids, to get in the front."

Life as a Disney protégée was first-class all the way, but the studio got value for money. It was relentlessly hard work, seven days a week, including holidays. Touring especially disrupted family life. Annette was so timid she refused to go anywhere without Virginia, who admits, "I neglected my boys so terribly." She could not see much glamour in spending three months in England separated from her two small sons and shed many a tear.

On the plus side, Annette graduated with a tidy nest egg and how many women can claim to have received their high school diploma onstage with the Rockettes?

Yet Virginia persists in her claim that the financial rewards were minimal after they deducted extra hidden costs they would not have incurred had Annette not been working, like buying their daughter the extensive wardrobe she needed. Paying baby-sitters for the boys and eating cafeteria lunches at the studio were both extra costs the family court would not allow the Funicellos to recover from Annette's income. Every few months, Virginia and Joe were required to make a humiliating appearance in front of a judge with their itemized expenditures. "You feel like a freak, like you're stealing her money," Virginia recalls.

She was once instructed by Disney to find Annette a new dance routine, for which the choreography fees ran into hundreds of dollars. Virginia deducted a portion each week from Annette's money as shown by the Disney lawyer. "The judge said, 'Who paid for her dancing lessons before she worked?' I said, 'Your Honor, we did,' and I was so scared, the room was full of people." The Funicellos were ordered to repay the money into Annette's bank account forthwith and a lien was put against it. "He made me feel like a cockroach! So it wasn't all peaches and cream."

Virginia Funicello, like her husband Joe, is of Italian stock. Her father was an immigrant, unable to speak English, who regularly lined up overnight in an effort to get work. Virginia was the seventh in a family of nine daughters and one son. Her mother died when she was fifteen and the burden of supporting them then fell to her father who was variously employed as a garbage man and a farmer. He was, partly of necessity and partly by nature, exceedingly strict.

Virginia fell madly in love with Joe Funicello when she was eighteen. It was wartime, they were afraid that Joe (who was fixing army trucks) would be drafted, and so they eloped. Given that Virginia was subjected to a 10 P.M. nightly curfew and was forbidden to date, this was more complicated than it sounds. The young couple was married in a Catholic church, after dark, with the aid of a friendly and understanding young priest. By way of celebration, they then devoured a mushroom stew sandwich (all the rage during World War II) before Virginia rushed home to comply with her curfew.

The newlyweds kept up the charade and their marriage remained a secret for five whole months. Each evening they returned to their respective homes as if nothing had happened. When Virginia finally plucked up the courage to break the news to her father, he reacted much as anticipated, hurrying off to fetch his big shotgun and demanding, "Who is he? Who is the man?" She is convinced he would have taken a shot at Joe had he set eyes on him at that moment, but when the dust died down, because money was so tight and Annette was on the way, Dad let Joe move in with the family.

In 1945, when Annette was almost four and their son Joey ten months old, Virginia and Joe left Utica, New York, for the sunnier climes of California. They journeyed cross-country, desert included, at the height of summer in a sweltering hot Dodge that pulled their three-room trailer, which repeatedly tipped over and veered off the side of the road. "It was the worst nightmare of my life. The children all had heat rash," Virginia recalls.

Miserable or not, she refused to turn back—their families were already taking bets that they would not last six months. That trusty old trailer, lodged in a park in Sun Valley, became their home for eight months, by which time Joe's services as a mechanic were sufficiently in demand to enable him to open a gas station and garage.

In 1984, Annette Funicello's pristine image took a turn for the controversial. She released a country-and-western album which included her composition "Sin City"—a little ditty that went down like the proverbial lead balloon in the Funicellos' hometown, although Annette did not mention Utica by name. Uticans clearly felt the shoe fit (many years earlier, the town had been tagged "Sin City" because of purported connections between some residents and the Mafia), and were outraged by Annette's presumed slight on their moral standards. The ex-Mouseketeer was accused of destroying the city that made her a star—although, as Virginia notes, she did not become a star for eight whole years after leaving Utica.

Annette was so upset by this unexpected venomous reaction

that she refused to go on a Utica phone-in radio program. In a move that was at once cheeky and supportive, Virginia stood in for her. Their voices are so similar that no one was any the wiser. Virginia sweetly fielded antagonistic phone calls, littered with names like "brat" and "wop," merely responding mildly: "Well, I'm sorry, I didn't mean to offend Utica." After an hour under fire, Virginia's sister (also duped) came on the line and said, "Annette, honey, don't you believe all these bitches. They're all crazy."

"Boom! They hung up on her," Virginia recalls. "To this day my sister doesn't know I did the interview!" Her mom is so attuned to the way Annette talks that she could predict what her every response would be, which she did so effectively, she also contrived to fool another caller: her sister-in-law.

By the end of her ordeal-by-phone, Virginia was drenched with perspiration. Annette, on the other hand, was "wetting her pants laughing . . . howling" at her mother's mimicry. Annette has sinced lived up to her vow to stay away from Utica, and refused to relent even when the town's mayor vowed to make amends by instigating "Annette Funicello Day," offering his personal assurance that nothing nasty would happen to mar the auspicious occasion. "Annette said, 'I'll probably be riding on a float and somebody will take a shot at me,'" her mom explains.

It is almost three decades since Annette's first boyfriend, Paul Anka, wrote "Puppy Love" for her, yet the attention she receives has not diminished—doubtless courtesy of almost a decade of Skippy Peanut Butter commercials. She was just twenty-one when she married her first true love, agent Jack Gilardi. But what should have been the most perfect day in her life became memorable for all the wrong reasons. She had ignored the missives of a serviceman stationed in Germany until he wrote informing her that he was coming home on furlough and if he could not have Annette, then nobody could have her: he would kill her on her wedding day.

A romantic occasion was rapidly transformed into a top-security event during which Annette even had to be accompanied to the bathroom. The Funicello home was surrounded by policemen, the church was encircled by more policemen, and intensive security checks were carried out. Each pew was searched, every individual invitation was closely scrutinized at the door by a Disney employee. Security was so tight that when Virginia tried to deliver Annette's fur coat to her hotel so she could take it away with her on her honeymoon, she was not allowed her own daughter's room number.

The Funicellos' flippant reaction—they laughed hysterically—sounds strange but was a not-atypical response to intense stress. Virginia even found herself quipping, "Annette, you and Dad are going to be walking down the aisle, and ping, Daddy will go down," and all these years later, she laughs again, as if still unwilling to truly acknowledge that the danger her daughter faced was serious. "It was a nightmare," Virginia then concedes. "Her wedding was ruined. We were scared. We were afraid." When Annette's would-be assailant was arrested within days, it did not alter the fact that he had successfully spoiled the bride's big day.

The Funicellos remain a resilient, uncommonly tight-knit family. Virginia and Joe considered moving—often—but have occupied their comfortable ranch-style home for over twenty-five years, just as Annette has lived in the nearby home she now shares with second husband Glen Holt for more than twenty years. Why should they be driven away?

But Virginia cannot help ruminating on the terrible fate of Connie Francis, a constant source of concern because Virginia and Annette are very close to Connie and her mother. (Connie was raped repeatedly in a hotel room and has never fully recovered from the ordeal.) The security worries are real.

Brandy and Jodie Foster have been forced to survive their fame-induced ordeals in a considerably more public fashion than the Funicellos. Through no fault of her own and regardless of the magnitude of her future accomplishments, Jodie Foster's name will do down in history inextricably linked with that of John Hinckley. For the benefit of amnesiacs, Hinckley is the man who made Jodie the target of his misguided and psychotically obsessive affections. He is also the man who on March 30, 1981, shot President Ronald Reagan, his aide James Brady, and two others, with six Devastator bullets from a .22 caliber pistol.

Brandy Foster first heard of the attempt on Reagan's life while breakfasting in a restaurant. She then sat in a Beverly Hills salon having her hair and nails beautified for a forthcoming trip to Yale, peacefully unaware that the presidential assailant and the man who had been harassing her daughter with threatening letters were one and the same. Driving home, tuning her car radio to the news, that bubble of tranquility burst forever. Brandy heard only fleeting mentions of an Ivy League school and a gunman intent upon impressing someone; no names were given—and yet "something snapped inside of me; I automatically knew there was something wrong. Something just made me frightened."

With the help of her son-in-law and Jodie's then-boyfriend Jamie Rosenfield, Brandy packed hastily and rushed off to catch the red-eye flight east. She knew that Hinckley was safely under lock and key; her fear was for her privacy-loving daughter, she had to be at Jodie's side. "My first reaction . . . was, of course, wanting to protect my child, who was the absolute innocent in the whole thing, and the one who I think was hurt the most by it."

It must be said that Brandy was not brimming with sympathy for the President, believing the possibility of an attempt on his life to be part and parcel of the presidential territory. Then again, this is a woman who will never get over a country having a B-movie actor for a president. "I feel very bad for his press secretary, Brady. But it didn't touch me at all what happened to those people. I was only concerned with my daughter."

Like her mother, Jodie Foster learned of the assassination attempt on Ronald Reagan in an undramatic fashion—in her case, via the Yale campus grapevine. Also like her mother, Jodie initially had no idea of her own involvement in the nightmarish story that was unraveling. A telephone call from Yale's dean later that night shattered her peace of mind instantaneously: it seemed that when arrested, John Hinckley had been carrying photographs of eighteen-year-old Jodie, along with her address.

Hinckley had written, Brandy Foster now knows, hundreds of letters to her daughter. They arrived at a postal box in Hollywood and were destroyed without being seen by either her or Jodie. This was Brandy Foster's longtime fan-mail policy, based on her belief that such mail is not psychologically beneficial to its recipient—particularly if that recipient is a child or youngster. Occasionally, Brandy read Jodie's mail, heeding warning signals such as an untoward amount of communication from one source, but neither she nor Jodie had been aware of John Hinckley's existence until a few letters filtered through to Jodie directly, at Yale, in October 1980. She showed them to her dean. The dean in turn alerted both the FBI and Yale's own top-notch police department (long accustomed to caring for famous offspring bearing names like Kissinger and Shriver) to the fact that a student's life might be in danger.

The fuss then died down until approximately one week before the attempt on Reagan's life, at which juncture Hinckley resurfaced and, to Brandy's consternation, began slipping letters underneath Jodie's door at Yale. Obviously, he was alarmingly close. Brandy Foster assumes that from that moment on, mail to Jodie was intercepted. She can only assume and presume, since throughout the entire affair she and Jodie were told irritatingly little. Hinckley, it transpired, had sat quietly in the audience through two performances of *Getting Out,* the play in which Jodie was appearing on campus, prior to his attempt on Ronald Reagan's life.

Six days after the presidential assassination attempt, mother and daughter were forced to confront a more sinister reality. It was not merely Hinckley who posed a threat to Jodie's safety; they had also to contend with the risk of danger from those Brandy describes as "all the nuts who came after." Yale police stayed in attendance for the play's few remaining performances, keeping vigil in the auditorium and frisking the audience for cameras. Nevertheless, one evening Jodie heard the menacing, all-too-familiar clicking of a camera's motor-drive. Pinpointing its origin, she was unnerved by the "emotionless stare" of the man at its source and by his presence in the audience again the following night.

During one intermission, a note mysteriously appeared on the bulletin board threatening that Jodie would be dead by the end of the performance. To this day, Brandy Foster does not know whether the man Jodie saw with the camera was the author of that threat. Neither does she know if it was he who outsmarted security and sat in the audience during two or three performances bearing a loaded gun. The existence of this theater-goer came to light when, just days after the closure of the play, Jodie received an inescapably ugly death threat via a note in the hallway of the master's house. She instructed Brandy, who was visiting her, to hold it carefully by the corners, then together they called the police.

"This guy had pictures with blood crossed over her and Mr. and Mrs. Reagan," Brandy Foster recalls. "It said, 'death to the fascist pigs' or something. All of a sudden it was Secret Service everywhere, as if they were coming by helicopter. The guy apparently slept down in the basement of one of the buildings that night."

Yale furnished a round-the-clock bodyguard for Jodie and moved her—much to her disgust—from her own niche, to another dormitory which she called the "psycho single": it was reserved for emergency security risks. "I've never seen people come to the rescue like they did at Yale, from the president to the head of the board of directors on down, they were fantastic," Brandy Foster reports, defending the precautionary measures taken and explaining that this second incident was even worse than Hinckley because it was an actual threat on her daughter's life.

Within twenty-four hours, the suspect was quietly apprehended at the New York Port Authority. He was armed and, he told the arresting officers, on his way to Washington to carry out his threat to kill Ronald Reagan. Jodie, he had concluded while repeatedly sitting in the audience of her play, was too pretty to kill after all. "His mother said he was crazier than a loon. He was out on good behavior in six months."

Naturally that knowledge angers Brandy Foster, as does the fact that she and Jodie were kept so in the dark: no one confided in her how subsequent letters were being handled and whether or not action was being taken to protect Jodie from further incidents. She was ired by the FBI's law-unto-themselves approach; little care is taken to offer comfort to those terrified folk whose lives it is that are on the line, by keeping them in the picture.

When Jodie was nominated for an Oscar for *Taxi Driver,* Martin Scorsese, the film's director, received a telegram saying that if she won, he would be killed. Maureen Reagan telephoned Mr. Scorsese to console him, but although the threat was equally devastating emotionally to young Jodie, at no point did anyone from the White House or the Reagan family afford her the courtesy of a similar call. Jodie was angry about that, but to Brandy, it merely reinforced the sad conclusion she had come to about those she once excused as naïve. She now concludes, "It's just downright ignorant and just being ill-mannered."

After all that happened, who could blame Brandy for being overwhelmed by a desire to scoop up Jodie and whisk her off to the Paris apartment they have had for fifteen years on the Ile St. Louis? "My immediate reaction was to say, 'Let's get the hell out of here,' " she readily admits. "Everybody on the island knows us —the vegetable lady, the butcher, the cleaners—and I knew that those people would be so protective that nobody going there would find out where we live." Another attraction was that Brandy's daughter Lucinda and two of her grandchildren live in Paris, where Brandy herself would happily live full-time were it not for her obligations as Jodie's manager and her emotional ties to her three children and five grandchildren in Los Angeles.

Despite Brandy's urging, Jodie refused to budge. "She said, 'No, I'm not going to allow this to disrupt my life,' and she didn't. She stuck it out." That difference of opinion notwithstanding, Jodie has openly admitted how crucial her mother's support was to her through the dark times that inevitably followed the Hinckley incident. Brandy, too, felt her share of fury, of course:

"I was angry that she had tried so hard just to be anonymous and that was completely blown. Two weeks after it happened, she went with a boyfriend into Manhattan to the Russian Tea Room. People stood up and clapped. Well, if you know her! She almost died."

When she walked down the street, total strangers would call out, "Hey Jodie, you're getting fat!" She was recognized as the target of Hinckley's obsession by folk who had never seen her act. Brandy says that while Jodie never minded strangers approaching her to make some comment about her work, "to have this fame and this notoriety for something that she had absolutely no control over, it took its toll. Paparazzi would run up in a pizza place and stick a camera in her face, which she resented terribly."

Jodie wondered why she and not someone like Brooke Shields

had been singled out for such obsession. "Of course Jodie said, 'Why me?', because she had always been so low-key," her mother explains. Jodie is very generous and quick to pick up restaurant bills, but is not acquisitive, hates shopping, does not want the responsibility of good jewelry, and wants no more clothes than can fit in two suitcases. She was hardly what you would call a glamour queen, nor was she a party-goer or a social butterfly. Her life was quiet; she was happy with a bed, a desk, and a word processor.

The Hinckley facet of Jodie's fame does not please mother or daughter, but they realize they are stuck with it. They have slowly come to terms with that which cannot be changed. Even so, Brandy cannot help complaining: "What bothers me most about the Hinckley thing is that when they write about Jodie, why do they always write about Hinckley? That's in the past. Why do they still concentrate on *Taxi Driver* which she did when she was twelve years old? She has done so many other things since then."

To prove her point, she reels off a list of Jodie's achievements, which include a couple of prestigious British Academy Awards, an American Film Critics' Award, and a New York Film Critics' Award. "She did five films while she was at Yale and graduated cum laude. Does anybody ever ask about that? No they don't. They only ask about Hinckley or *Taxi Driver*," she says, with understandable frustration.

That summer of 1981, the always-companionable mother and daughter went off to Germany to lick their psychic wounds. Returning to her German-Irish roots is something Brandy finds revitalizing and therapeutic. The relief was merely temporary. Once back in the U.S., their trials continued. Jodie was required to give her deposition, supposedly in private. Even Brandy was not allowed to be present, so she waited back in their Washington, D.C., hotel room, entirely unaware that Jodie was enduring yet another ordeal for which she was entirely unprepared—confronting John Hinckley face-to-face for the first time. A painful, and one would have thought unnecessary, incident. For the slowly recovering Jodie, it was yet another cruel and disturbing blow. Her admirer had to be escorted from the courtroom "raving."

Fragile and newly suspicious, she came to liken being photographed to being shot. When a Yale senior she had not met sold his tale of her campus habits to *People* magazine, it was a betrayal by a stranger, but it confirmed her deep dread that she had never really been one of the crowd at Yale, that she had been watched all along. Other students could even remember what she had worn when they first set eyes on her. As she wrote in *Esquire* magazine in 1982, the Hinckley ordeal did not destroy her anonymity, only her illusion of it. (She had worked one summer at *Esquire* as a trainee editor and got a close-up glimpse of what she now considers a cutthroat, back-stabbing world, which rapidly dissolved her vision of one day becoming a high-powered publishing executive, her mother says.)

She wrote that she returned to Yale in the autumn of '81, aware of the two Jodie Fosters. The screen-sized, self-assured Jodie the public had watched. "But the second Jodie was a vision only I knew. She was shrouded in bravado and wit and was, underneath, a creature crippled, without self-esteem, a frail and alienated being."

The intervening eighties have been something of a salve, according to Brandy, and Jodie no longer looks over her shoulder at every turn. "You cannot live your life being suspicious and afraid all the time," she explains, "and I think it is something that just time has healed. I think it's like disaster. Each time it's repeated, it just becomes easier to take. You build up a certain defense system." Or as Jodie herself put it, "After a period of death-dodging you learn to believe that you've been picked for survival."

Jodie was just twelve when she played Iris, the prostitute in *Taxi Driver*, and the film which originally fueled John Hinckley's deranged fantasies was a controversial project from the word go. The Child Welfare Board deemed the subject matter unsuitable for portrayal by a minor. Brandy, who normally concurred wholeheartedly with the board's efforts to protect child performers and ensure that they were not overworked, on this occasion hired a lawyer to fight its decision. Her contention then, which has not weakened in the light of subsequent events, was that while it was indeed the board's task to monitor the welfare and education of her child, she herself was the best judge of Jodie's mental health and of what she did and did not know about sex.

"Jodie was in no danger physically," Brandy explains. "She was in no moral danger as far as I was concerned, because she was very well able to accept the division of fantasy and play-acting, and acting and real life. I was not a mother who held back answers about sex. I always felt that it was easier for me to answer questions about sex than it was to answer them about God. I was more *comfortable* with sex than I was with God," she adds, laughing. "So what I simply did was to say, 'Look, I think that the subject is embarrassing you perhaps more than it would Jodie.' So yes, I went tooth-to-nail with them."

Obviously, Brandy prevailed and Jodie duly made the film in New York, with a Welfare worker present at all times. "I have absolutely no regrets about *Taxi Driver*," she says emphatically. "I think Jodie has had two films that if she had never done anything else, she could be very proud of. *Taxi Driver* is one, and *Bugsy Malone* has to be my all-time favorite."

New York-born Brandy Foster grew up in Rockford, Illinois. She was adopted and lived alone with her mother, a divorcée she found herself taking care of, instead of the other way around: "Every time it would thunder and lightning, I'd have to sing to her because she was scared to death." Hers was not a bad childhood, but it was an existence so bland and bourgeois that she could not wait to escape it. If Brandy envies Jodie anything, it is her hundred-thousand-dollar education, the best that money could buy. (Being able to afford it without student loans was one major payoff of Jodie's career as a child actor.) Brandy was not afforded the same opportunities: "Fifty years ago, it was, 'Get married kid. Forget it.' "

Brandy began her career in New York, working for the man she considered the finest pretelevision publicist, the late Arthur Jacobs. She married an Air Force colonel, and when, about eighteen months into their marriage, he left the service, the family moved to Los Angeles. Just one month after Brandy filed for divorce in 1962, she learned that she was pregnant with her fourth child. Everyone kept advising her to go back to her marriage. "No way!" was her defiant response. "If I can get along without him with three, I'll make it with four."

Jodie Alicia Christian Foster (to give Jodie her full name) was born when Lucius "Buddy" Foster was six, Connie was eight, and

Lucinda was nine. Brandy laughingly describes herself in those days as "a cop who did dishes. I was a very strict mother, I had to be. At one time, I had three kids in cribs, three in diapers, and three on bottles. I think if I had it to do all over again I'd just shoot myself. You don't know how you do it. I would like to have been softer, but when you have four kids and they're all waiting for you to break down, you can't."

She frequently vacuumed at three A.M. Exhaustion all but prohibited dating, and when she did venture out, the children invariably managed to scare off the gentleman in question. She struggled financially, buying candy before going to drive-in movies because it was cheaper, bringing home the box-lunches the children were given when they worked on commercials for family dinners.

Each year she took her four children to San Diego for a vacation, booking a single motel room as far from the office as possible. When no one was watching, the brood would pile out of the car with their sleeping bags. They rose early to slip out before the maid arrived to clean the room. Brandy and Jodie still reminisce about those times.

Without a doubt, Brandy's children's work in show business alleviated a considerable amount of the financial pressure on her. It was just prior to Jodie's third birthday when Brandy took her along on an audition of Buddy's because "I certainly couldn't leave her in the car in 110 degrees. Guess who got the commercial?" Jodie's career began with a cute, bare-bottomed Coppertone TV advertisement.

Jodie, who taught herself to read, was enrolled in the gifted program immediately upon entering the public school system and was writing constructive poetry at age seven. She had made over forty commercials by the time she was eight, the last being "Look Dad, no cavities." Brandy charted her career with a sure touch. Once she broke into television in 1971 (appearing in, amongst other things, "My Three Sons"), Jodie did no more commercials. The following year she made *Napoleon and Samantha*, the first in a small string of Disney films, and in 1974 appeared in the TV spin-off of the film *Paper Moon*. Once her foothold in films was secured, Brandy turned down all TV work for Jodie.

After graduating from the Elysée Français, Jodie was accepted at Yale, Harvard, Princeton, Columbia, and Stanford. She chose Yale more for its proximity to New York City than because her father (and his father before him) was a Yale graduate—Jodie has only seen him a couple of times in her life. For all her academic achievement, Jodie's interest in acting has not waned.

Brandy, who now operates from a large home in Calabasas, California, believes that deciding to manage Jodie's career herself was "the best protection in the world for a child. I always felt I was building her career, I never just took everything that came along." She is still highly selective and turned down script after script rather than have Jodie appear in frat-house romps or films like *Weird Science*. "I just cannot see her pandering to twelve-year-olds, and that's literally what this business has become."

A soft-spoken but clearly determined woman, Brandy learned to stand up for her daughter's rights on her very first commercial. She protested vociferously when Jodie, in complete body makeup, was expected to stay in a hotel room with no bathroom. "I would scream and holler when producers didn't give me what I wanted," she admits. "They'd see me coming, I'm sure, and they weren't happy." Always, her priority was on her children's education. Show business was fun, but would go away some day. "I don't think about her being a star, never have," she says today. She did, however, recognize that Jodie had a unique personality, a wonderful gift of speaking correctly, and an unusual voice. Even as a young girl, Jodie hated dresses with a passion, yet her timing was immaculate there too. It was the beginning of women's liberation and she personified the new look in her little jeans and sweat shirt.

Having passed through the troublesome teens into womanhood, Jodie is once again able to work at full tilt and the mother-daughter team has a production company. "Doesn't everybody?" quips Brandy, admitting it is a meaningless label. "Too many vipers in this business to think that I'm going to be a producer. I wouldn't kid myself about that," she says sharply.

She does, however, consider herself a shrewd negotiator on Jodie's behalf and does not believe she has ever been taken advantage of. She has never been sidetracked into accepting nebulous deferments rather than money up front. "If the dressing room wasn't good enough, that was taken care of before we started," Brandy says, explaining her policy. "It was always a matter of contract. I have never asked for any more than I contracted for, but I sure as hell don't want any less. And when you have in your contract 'preferential treatment,' that's what it means."

She decries the notion of stage mothers, a stereotype she feels died of natural causes along with the studio system. There was never any place for stage mothers in Hollywood anyway, no way for them to survive, she says. "It's like gossip. It travels and gets bigger as it rolls along. It's like the smallest Peyton Place in the world."

Brandy, who is very political and fiercely antiwar, took her children with her on civil rights freedom marches in the 1960s. Before Jodie was born, she was one of the original members of the antinuclear group, Mothers for Peace, and marched against the Vietnam War. Travel, opera, and architectural history are her great loves. She is a supporter of the architectural division of Los Angeles's Museum of Contemporary Art, and of New York's Metropolitan Museum, Museum of Modern Art, and Whitney Museum, and she enjoys helping her daughter Constance, who is an architectural interior designer. She laughingly claims to have read every script ever written and to have seen every film ever made—all in the line of duty.

She is proud of Jodie's fluency in French, Italian, and Spanish and hopes she will eventually attend graduate school for a Ph.D., but she does not push. Like her mother, Jodie is very much her own woman.

"I'm very proud of being Jodie Foster's mother," she says firmly, "as I'm proud of being Lucinda Foster's mother, Connie Foster's mother, and Buddy Foster's mother. I'm very proud of being her mother, but I'm also a person myself.

"To know that you can't get a reservation in a restaurant unless they know that I'm Jodie Foster's mother, that makes me very angry. I never use that. It kills me more than anything to go to an art opening and have somebody say, 'Oh, this is Jodie Foster's mother.' I turn beet red." She makes a deliberate effort to stay in the background. "We are never photographed together, because I have always felt that it was *her* career, it is not my career."

23 Bring on the Magic

For which lucky mom did superstar Diana Ross host an intimate, elegant birthday dinner party? Which mom has gifts lavished upon her so expensive that her daughter has first snipped out the designer labels so she will not "give her hell" about her extravagance? Which mom arrives at her doctor's office in a chauffeured limousine? Which mom's proudest moment was seeing her longtime superstar son enthrall a throbbing, capacity crowd at Madison Square Garden? Which mom had great fun playing screen mom to her real-life son in *Down and Out in Beverly Hills*? And which deliciously spoiled mama was instructed to start thinking like a millionairess? Cher's, Goldie Hawn's, Billy Dee Williams', Mick Jagger's, Richard Dreyfuss's, and Pia Zadora's, respectively.

None of the above are exactly everyday experiences, yet those are the kind of heart-stopping thrills, luxuries, and perks of which star moms are the recipients. You could call it getting their just deserts; those are the highlights that balance out the pain and the sacrifice . . . and hopefully make it all worthwhile.

When Pia Zadora married Meshulam Riklis ten years ago, he was in debt to the tune of $650 million. Now that he is out of arrears, Pia's mom, Saturnina Schipani, fully expects to hear that he has given her granddaughter Kady four New York city blocks.

Pia and Meshulam Riklis live magnificently, and so, now, does Saturnina. Before her father died, Pia bought her parents a Manhattan apartment so vast that Saturnina claims, "I would have to holler from one end to the other to get my husband." She is treated royally, has a full-time chauffeur at her disposal, and is loudly reprimanded should she try anything sneaky like boarding a bus. She is also chastised for opting for "nice, cozy, and comfortable" clothes rather than splashing out on silks in designer boutiques.

"I am going to have to think like a millionairess, it's going to be tough," she says cheerfully—and miraculously, one is not tempted to hit her. Saturnina is endearingly reminiscent of a lottery winner who is slightly dazed by it all. She confides a cardinal rule recently broken: she must never tell Pia and Riklis if she sees something she likes—in this case a gorgeous little white two-seater Porsche. "Do you want it?" they asked. "No! No, thank you! I have a Seville that sits in the garage. Please no, not another one."

Eva Jagger is not unfamiliar with magic, not after two decades of Rolling Stones wizardry. But Madison Square Garden in 1981, that was in a thrill league all of its own. Somehow the thunderous reception that a second generation of young folk felt stirred to give the Stones, well, "it's something you never dream . . . and it sort of chokes you." Better still, Eva observes matter-of-factly, the histrionic screaming has stopped and you can even hear the music. ("Unfortunately I have got sensitive hearing and I really don't like it loud. It does things to my ears.") At Madison Square, Eva could dispense with ear plugs and relish a unanimous standing ovation. "You think, 'There's my son. It's him! It's our son! What is it? Why is it?' And I don't know the answer, really."

There is another reason Eva Jagger is not sorry that the climate has changed a mite from the days of dreadfully deafening screams and sobbing nubile maidens. Mick used to precipitate enough teenage tears to launch the *Queen Mary,* and that always rather upset Eva, who just could not fathom what all the crying was about. "I had never experienced emotions like that. I would go up and try and comfort them, it was ridiculous. I felt such a fool, really!" she laughs.

"I'm not saying Mick hasn't got magic. He's got to have, otherwise he wouldn't be where he is today after all these years. There's *something.* But I'm not the person to say, really, what it is, am I? I could say he takes after me, couldn't I? Or he takes after his father? He takes after both of us!"

Bill Cosby was all of nine years old when he promised his dearly beloved Mama that when he was grown, he would do all the things Daddy had not done for her. And, says Anna Cosby, with unconcealed pride, "You know, he kept his little promise? I've been on many cruises, to many places, yes. And gee whiz, all the goodies that's come my way, it's been wonderful."

After extensive globe-trotting with Bill and Camille, it is easier to say where Anna's passport has not been stamped: Hong Kong. Quite a revelation it has all been too, particularly the lack of racial distinction she found when they took a world cruise. "Exciting? Was it ever. Very educational too, seeing how other people lived. We'd get off the boat and the men and women would grab us, even Camille and I, and kiss us, as if it was nothing. I said, 'Oh boy, this is the only way to live.' "

The night the generally unflappable Laura Hawn says she "fell apart" over the enormity of Goldie's success came at the 1970 Oscars when Goldie had been nominated for Best Supporting Actress for *Cactus Flower*. Laura and Rut had opted to watch the ceremony alone at home on television. No guests, Laura insisted, "because I thought maybe they would talk. I really didn't want anybody talking." She was convinced Goldie was going to win, which is precisely what worried Rut.

"He said, 'You haven't even seen the other films, they are all good.' I don't know what I would have done if she hadn't won. I was lying on the sofa, and when the moment came I got up, involuntarily I think, and stood right at the television. They announced that she had won. *I* was fine—but I had to get my husband off the ceiling." The aftermath was equally exciting; all the Takoma Park residents knew Goldie, and the Hawns were inundated with congratulatory phone calls and wires.

One day, just for fun, Laura plans to line a wall of her home with all the photographs she has of herself alongside Goldie's handsome leading men. "They are so funny. They are so gorgeous and *I* look like I don't know what!" Warren Beatty would take pride of place because he has been a friend of Laura's since they met at his high school graduation—the Hawns' goddaughter was in Warren's class. Laura is no aspiring actress, but does extra work periodically, in Goldie's *Swing Shift*, for instance, just to top up her hospitalization insurance. Casting around for a role, she once endeavored to use her contacts; would Warren please give her a job? "He said, 'I can't use you because I just do dirty pictures.' I said, 'Warren, I have no problem with that. You might have a problem with that, but I don't.' "

Since Laura does not drive and is a frequent traveling companion of Goldie's, Goldie lays on the limousines to ferry Mom around while she is tied up in meetings. Witness one New York trip when the limousine deposited Laura and her companion at the theater door for an evening's entertainment. The driver informed madam that he would be waiting when the curtain came down.

"We had dinner reservations at Sardi's. Now, I didn't know New York. Well, we got out of the theater and the fella is standing there with the car, saying, 'Do you want me to walk you or drive you?' Sardi's was next door! I was hysterical. This great big production with the chauffeur and the outfit and the whole bit and it was next door! Goldie is a very sweet daughter. She does nice things for me. And she hasn't changed, thank God, with all that has happened."

Never in her wildest fantasies could Georgia Holt have imagined that her wayward teenage daughter, Cher, would grow into a world-class actress and entertainer. Let alone that she would one day take her as her date to an exclusive restaurant like L.A.'s Ma Maison, where they both would exchange dinner-table chitchat with the illustrious likes of Barbra Streisand, Steven Spielberg, George Lucas, Teri Garr, and Sydney Pollack.

And how many moms can reminisce about the night Diana Ross hosted an elaborately chic birthday dinner party in their honor in her very own home? Diana and Cher were inseparable buddies during the early seventies, and, Georgia recalls, the evening was stupendous. "The table was set with exquisite silver and crystal and magnificent antique Oriental plates. But what I loved about Diana was the way she said, *I* didn't do it, I don't know a thing about table settings. My secretary did it all and we borrowed her mother's things because we wanted everything to be perfect for you.' Cher presented me with beautiful diamond earrings that night. She was so proud and I was so thrilled."

If she has not done so already, Cyndi Lauper should give serious consideration to buying her mom, Catrine Domenique, a big fur coat. On second thought, make it a raincoat. Catrine has more attacks of chills (albeit the thrilling variety) and tears (the happy variety) than the average mom. Catrine vividly remembers her customary cynical response when, back in the anti-establishment 1960s, Cyndi and her sister Ellen were always talking of making it a better world: "How can one person do anything?" Catrine used to scoff.

Well, what do you think ran down Catrine Domenique's spine the first time she watched the "We Are the World" video for U.S.A. for Africa and heard her daughter Cyndi giving unique voice to those very same ideals? And what do you think poured down Catrine's cheeks when in concert, Cyndi dedicated her song, "I'm Going to Be Strong," from her days with Blue Angel, to her mom? "When she hit the last notes, the tears would just flood down my face, I just couldn't hold back because of the depth of her feeling in that song."

Catrine was reluctant, to put it mildly, when Cyndi first asked her to fry up some eggs in front of the camera for the video for her record "Girls Just Want to Have Fun." She had never appeared in a simple school play, let alone a video. "I was very shy in that respect. I still am. Then I thought, 'How could you do that to your daughter? If she has the guts to get in front of a camera and sing, you could at least break eggs!' The director, Ed Griles, was so sweet and made it very easy for me. And my daughter, she would say, 'It's just you and me. You're in the kitchen, Ma, as you always were.' And we had a ball."

"Time After Time," the next video, was intended to be an artsy production, Cyndi told her, in which Catrine would again play her mom and would also have to turn on the tears. When Catrine saw the frumpy outfits provided for her to wear, she said, "You're not kidding, I will cry!"

She will never forget the emotional impact when they taped the segment where Cyndi and her boyfriend drive up as mom is sweeping the stoop. "She's saying good-bye because she's leaving town, and her face puckered up and tears came into her eyes, and it brought back when she left home and we were separated, and it hit us both so strongly, I just couldn't stop crying. I was actually sobbing and I had completely forgotten that there were hundreds and hundreds of people around. After the director said, 'Cut,' there was dead silence. You could hear a pin drop, then everybody broke out into applause . . . that's when I came out of it and realized where I was."

By the time Cyndi did the video for Steven Spielberg's "Goonies," Catrine was a staple presence, and on that occasion was elevated to playing a sea hag, which necessitated her wearing an exquisitely outrageous layered costume, a cape with huge shellfish and lots of netting. But "Goonies" was different from the other videos—it was more like stunt work and downright terrifying for Catrine. "First, my daughter was on this log suspended over rocks and a lagoon. I was going out after her and I was frightened because I could just picture myself falling in, but I was also frightened for Cyndi. Then when the waterfall gushed down on her, I was terrified. My heart was in my mouth, because I said, 'How can she breathe under all that water?'

"She's such a gutsy girl, she really is. Sometimes she amazes me. No matter what Cyndi does, no matter how outrageous, the funny thing is, I can't wait for the next one because I think she's so terrific."

Catrine Domenique could be speaking for all stars and all star moms when she says, "Cyndi had her dreams, and she wouldn't let reality destroy them, and that's why she and others like her are so special. And that's really beautiful, you know? There aren't that many dreamers in this world anymore."

Chapter Notes

1. THE THRILL OF IT ALL

Author's own interviews with Martha Selleck; Lillian McEdward; Olive Abbott; Anne Hamilton; Margot Warren; Betty White; Maxene Reynolds; Bob Cosby; Anna Cosby; Laura Hawn; Eva Jagger. Other sources include Fran Erwin, *San Fernando Valley Living;* Kathleen Hendrix, *Los Angeles Times; Milton Berle, An Autobiography,* by Milton Berle; Fred Robbins, *McCall's;* Roger Laing, *Woman* magazine (United Kingdom).

2. THE DYNAMICS OF INSPIRATION

Author's own interviews with Neile McQueen Toffel; Dr. R. Barkley Clark, Assistant Clinical Professor of Psychiatry at the University of Colorado Health Sciences Center and Psychiatric Consultant to the Denver Public Schools; Martha Selleck; James Grostein, M.D., Clinical Professor of Psychiatry at U.C.L.A.; Ringo Starr (1980); Charlotte Sheedy; Sally Field (1982). Other sources include *My Husband, My Friend* by Neile McQueen Toffel; Nancy Collins, *Rolling Stone;* "Superstars Salute Their Moms," Dick Clark TV special; *Elizabeth Taylor, The Last Star,* by Kitty Kelley; *Call Me Anna: The Autobiography of Patty Duke,* by Patty Duke and Kenneth Turan; Paul Donovan, *London Daily Mail; The Mother Book,* by Liz Smith; *Penthouse;* Chaim Potok, *Esquire;* Lawrence Grobel, *Playboy; Lennon* by Ray Coleman; *Lennon Remembers: The Rolling Stone Interviews,* by Jann Wenner.

3. MAY THE FORCE BE WITH YOU

Author's own interviews with Zsa Zsa Gabor (1984); Dr. James Grostein; Maxene Reynolds; Debbie Reynolds; Bob Cosby; Anna Cosby; Bernice Janssen; Barbara Voight; Jon Voight. Other sources include *Fatherhood,* by Bill Cosby; *The Lady, the Legend, the Truth,* by Lana Turner; *Lauren Bacall, By Myself,* by Lauren Bacall; John Mariani, *Viva* magazine; Claire Saffran, *Redbook.*

4. Laughter Lines: You Don't Have to Be Crazy, but It Helps

Author's own interviews with Laurie Williams; Anne Hamilton. Other sources include Lawrence Linderman, *Playboy;* "Superstars Salute Their Mothers," Dick Clark TV special; Kurt Loder, *Rolling Stone;* Sue Reilly, *People;* Craig Modderno, *Playgirl;* Debra S. Davis, *Cosmopolitan.*

5. Stars in the Making

Author's own interviews with Laura Hawn; Dr. James Grostein; Sara Taylor; Margot Warren; Mary Allen Rowlands; Other sources include "The Oprah Winfrey Show"; Timothy White, *Rolling Stone;* Celeste Fremon, *Playgirl; Elizabeth Taylor: The Last Star,* by Kitty Kelley; *"Elizabeth, My Daughter,"* by Sara Sothern Taylor, *Ladies' Home Journal,* 1954; Larry Grobel, *Playgirl; Symphony for the Devil: The Rolling Stones Story,* by Philip Norman; *Joseph Cotten: An Autobiography, Vanity Will Get You Somewhere,* by Joseph Cotten; *Lennon* by Ray Coleman; *The Beatles: The Authorized Biography,* by Hunter Davies; *A Twist of Lennon,* by Cynthia Lennon; *Savrola,* by Winston Churchill.

6. When Pain Leads to Fame

Author's own interviews with Saturnina Schipani; Britt Ekland; Loretta Williams; Elvera Davis; Greta Peck; Ringo Starr (1980). Other sources include Bob Greene, *Esquire; Past Imperfect,* by Joan Collins, *Cybill and Bruce: Moonlighting Magic,* by Barbara Siegel and Scott Siegel; Barbara Lovenheim, *McCall's;* David Rosenthal, *Rolling Stone;* Jane Hall, *People;* Arthur Bell, *Cosmopolitan;* Paul Donovan, *London Daily Mail;* Nancy Collins, *Playboy; Vivien Leigh* by Anne Edwards; *Barbra Streisand: The Woman, the Myth, the Music* by Shaun Considine; Brad Darrach, *People;* Colin Dangaard, *Woman* magazine, (United Kingdom); *Cher!* by Mark Bego; *One More Time,* by Carol Burnett; *Julie Andrews* by Robert Windeler; Ivor Davis, *Woman* magazine, (United Kingdom); Lynn Barber, *London Sunday Express Magazine;* Edwin Miller, *Seventeen;* Carl Arrington, *People;* David Lewin, *US;* David Wigg, *Woman* magazine (United Kingdom); Fred Hauptfuhrer, *People; Yes I Can,* by Sammy Davis, Jr., and Jane and Burt Boyar; Diane de Dubovay; Gary Smith, *Rolling Stone;* Iris Schneider, *Rolling Stone;* Phyllis Battelle, *Woman* magazine, (United Kingdom); David Thomson, *Playgirl;* Sharon Rosenthal, *US* magazine; *The Reluctant Superstar,* by Diana Maychick; *Bob Hope* by Joe Morella, Ed Z. Epstein, and Elinor Clark; Mel Gussow, *New York Times Magazine;* Ross Benson, *London Daily Express;* Michael Leahy, *TV Guide; Fonda, My Life* by Howard Teichmann; *People;* Douglas Thompson, *Sunday* magazine, (United Kingdom); Mark Morrison, *Rolling Stone; US;* Richard Sanders, *People;* K. W. Woods, *Playgirl;* Guy Flatley, *Cosmopolitan; Warren Beatty: His Life, His Loves, His Work,* by Suzanne Munshower; Martin Torgoff, *Interview;* Donna E. Haupt, *Life;* Susan Edmiston, *McCall's;* Jeffrey Wells, *US;* Jim Jerome, *US;* David Hutchings, *People;* Christopher Connelly, *Rolling Stone.*

7. MOM'S MISFITS

Author's own interviews with Mary Fletcher; Catrine Domenique. Other sources include Mary Fletcher, *Woman* magazine (United Kingdom); Nancy Collins, *Rolling Stone;* Wendy Leigh, *London Daily Mirror;* Michael Neill, *People;* William E. Geist, *Rolling Stone; Woody Allen: A Biography,* by Lee Guthrie; Frank Rich, *Esquire;* Joe Klein, *GQ;* Richard Schickel, *Time;* Mark Rowland, Playgirl; *Company* magazine, (United Kingdom); Guy Flatley, *Cosmopolitan;* Claudia Dreifus, *Playboy;* Wayne Warga, *Cosmopolitan;* Lewis Grossberger, *Rolling Stone;* Nancy Collins, *Playboy;* Kurt Loder, *Rolling Stone.*

8. ROUGH ROADS, RICH REWARDS

Author's own interviews with Mary Fletcher; Teddy Quinn; Zsa Zsa Gabor (1984); Rona Newton-John (1981); Dr. James Grotstein; Sylvester Stallone ('78); Linda Evans (1982); Hilda Owen; Janet Leigh; Jamie Lee Curtis (1980). Other sources include Elliott Sirkin, *Good Housekeeping; My Heart Belongs,* by Mary Martin; Mary Fletcher, *Woman* magazine (United Kingdom); Eric Sherman, *Ladies' Home Journal; Lauren Bacall, By Myself,* by Lauren Bacall; David and Victoria Sheff, *Playboy;* Judy Gillespie, *US;* David Thomson, *Playgirl;* Michelle Green, *People;* Arthur Lubow, *People;* D. Keith Mano, *People;* Bob Colacello, *Woman* magazine (United Kingdom); Lawrence Grobel, *Playboy;* Joyce Haber, *Los Angeles Times;* Robert Windeler, *People;* Robyn Flans, *US;* Lynn Norment, *Ebony;* Joanna Ney, *After Dark;* Lesley Thornton, *Cosmopolitan; Katharine Hepburn, A Hollywood Yankee,* by Gary Carey; *Is That It?,* by Bob Geldof with Paul Vallely; Aimee Lee Ball, *Redbook;* Roger Ebert, *Esquire; Judy Garland,* by Anne Edwards; *My Story,* by Ingrid Bergman and Alan Burgess; *Star Profiles* by Marc Wanamaker; *Vivien Leigh,* by Anne Edwards; *Richard Burton: The Actor, the Lover, the Star,* by Paul Ferris; *A Christmas Story,* by Richard Burton; *The Beatles: The Authorized Biography,* by Hunter Davies; *Rock Hudson, His Story,* by Rock Hudson and Sara Davidson; *Idol: Rock Hudson,* by Jerry Oppenheimer and Jack Vitek; *The Mother Book,* by Liz Smith; *Blessings in Disguise,* by Alec Guinness; *Survivor; The Authorized Biography of Eric Clapton,* by Ray Coleman; Fred Schruers, *Woman* magazine (United Kingdom); Chris Chase, *Cosmopolitan;* Diane De Dubovay, *Woman* magazine (United Kingdom); *Jack Nicholson,* by Derek Sylvester; Ron Rosenbaum, *You* magazine, (United Kingdom); *There Really Was a Hollywood,* by Janet Leigh; Colin Dangaard, *US;* Judy Markey, *Cosmopolitan;* Roberta Plutzik, *US.*

9. RICH MOM, POOR MOM

Author's own interviews with Dolly Parton (1979, 1986); Frances Bergen. Other sources include Marie Brenner, *Vanity Fair;* Clarke Taylor, *Los Angeles Times;* Alan Ebert, *US;* Scot Haller, *People;* Roger Ebert, *Esquire;* E. Graydon Carter, *TV Guide; Knock Wood,* by Candice Bergen; Guy Flatley, *Cosmpolitan;* A. E. Hotchner, *McCall's;* Andrea Chambers, *People.*

10. Troubled Waters

Author's own interview with Shirley MacLaine (1984). Other sources include *Conversations with Joan Crawford,* by Roy Newquist; *Jazz Baby,* by David Houston; *Rock Hudson, His Story,* by Rock Hudson and Sara Davidson; *Idol,* by Jerry Oppenheimer and Jack Vitek; *Cary Grant: A Touch of Elegance,* by Warren G. Harris; *Marlon Brando: The Only Contender,* by Gary Carey; *A Portrait of Joan,* by Joan Crawford with Jane Kesner Ardmore; Celeste Fremon, *Playgirl;* Ross Benson, *London Daily Express;* David Wigg, *London Daily Express;* Phyllis Battelle, *Ladies' Home Journal;* Michael *Leahy, TV Guide;* David Lewin, *Woman's Own* magazine, United Kingdom; Phyllis Battelle, *Woman* magazine (United Kingdom); Adam Edwards, *Woman* magazine (United Kingdom); *Dancing in the Light,* by Shirley MacLaine; David Thomson, *Playgirl;* Leo Janos, *Cosmopolitan;* Adam Moss, *Esquire Film Quarterly.*

11. The White Picket Fence

Author's own interviews with Patty Micci; Eva Jagger; Dr. R. Barkley Clark; Dr. James Grotstein; Julie Powers. Other sources include Elizabeth Kaye, *US* magazine; *Kate: The Life of Katharine Hepburn,* by Charles Higham; *Katharine Hepburn,* by Anne Edwards; Joan Barthel, *McCall's;* Diane de Dubovay, 1980; *Cybill and Bruce; Moonlighting Magic,* by Barbara Siegel and Scott Siegel; Michael Leahy, *TV Guide;* Roger Laing, *Woman* magazine (United Kingdom); Duncan Falowell, *Playgirl; Symphony for the Devil: The Rolling Stones Story,* by Philip Norman; *The True Adventures of the Rolling Stones,* by Stanley Booth.

12. Negative Reinforcement: Weathering Its Storm

Author's own interview with Dr. R. Barkley Clark; Diana Kind; Mabel Johnson; Charlotte Sheedy. Other sources include: Joan Barthel, *Cosmopolitan;* David Thomson, *California* magazine; *Barbra Streisand: The Woman, the Myth, the Music,* by Shaun Considine; Lawrence Grobel, *Playboy;* Brad Darrach, *People* magazine; *I, Tina,* by Tina Turner and Kurt Loder; Wayne Warga, *McCall's; Bing Crosby: The Hollow Man* by Don Shepherd and Robert F. Slatzer; William E. Geist, *Rolling Stone;* James McBride, *US;* Judson Klinger, *Rolling Stone;* Michelle Green, *People; Katharine Hepburn: A Hollywood Yankee,* by Gary Carey; *Star Profiles,* by Marc Wanamaker; Aaron Latham, *Rolling Stone.*

13. Stage Mothers: An Extinct Species?

Author's own interviews with Maria Gurdin; Jean Howard. Other sources include: *Pin-Up: The Tragedy of Betty Grable,* by Spero Pastos; *Pretty Babies* by Andrea Darvi; *The Mother Book,* by Liz Smith; *Parade* magazine; *Hollywood Revisited,* by Sheilah Graham; Ivor Davis, *Woman* magazine, (United Kingdom); Lynn Barber, *Sunday Express Magazine* (United Kingdom); *Call Me Anna* by Patty Duke and Kenneth Turan; *Judy Garland,* by Anne Edwards; Henry Schipper, *Playgirl.*

14. Dearest Mommie

Author's own interviews with Betty White; Dr. James Grotstein; Dr. R. Barkley Clark; Maria Gurdin. Other sources include: *Goodness Had Nothing to Do with It,* by Mae West; *People* magazine; *The Mother Book,* by Liz Smith; *Elvis and Gladys,* by Elaine Dundy; *The Private Elvis,* by May Mann.

15. When You Wish Upon a Star

Author's own interviews with Julie Powers; Phyllis Garr; Loretta Williams. Other sources include, *One More Time,* by Carol Burnett; Timothy White, *Rolling Stone;* Paul Rosenfield, *Los Angeles Times;* Jonathan Black, *Mademoiselle; Paul Newman Superstar,* by Lionel Godfrey; *Bing Crosby: The Hollow Man,* by Don Shepherd and Robert F. Slatzer; Lawrence Linderman, *Playboy;* Wayne Warga, *Los Angeles Times; Star Profiles,* by Marc Wanamaker; Jeff Jarvis, *People;* Judy Klemesrud, *Cosmopolitan;* Pauline Kael, *The New Yorker.*

16. The Mythical Other Mother

Author's own interviews with Dr. James Grotstein; Melanie Griffith; Tippi Hedren; Dr. R. Barkley Clark. Other sources include: Pat Jordan, *Mademoiselle;* Stephen Schiff, *Vanity Fair;* Jesse Kornbluth, *Vanity Fair; Faye Dunaway,* by Allan Hunter; Amy Gross, *Vogue;* David Lewin, *London Daily Mail;* Bob Greene, *Esquire;* Ron Rosenbaum, *You* magazine (United Kingdom); Sandra Shevey, *Playgirl;* Carl Arrington, *People; The Dark Side of Genius,* by Donald Spoto; Joan Barthel, *Cosmopolitan; One More Time,* by Carol Burnett; Simon Kinnersley, *Woman's Own* magazine (United Kingdom); Joan Goodman, *Ladies' Home Journal;* Gloria Steinem, *MS;* Nancy Collins, *Rolling Stone;* Mark Morrison, *US.*

17. It's All in a Name: The Show Business Dynasties

Author's own interviews with Michael Douglas (1979); Diana Douglas, Dorothy Bridges. Other sources include Claudia Dreifus, *Mademoiselle;* Patricia Morrisroe, *New York; My Heart Belongs,* by Mary Martin; Kathy Mackay, *People; Star Babies,* by Raymond Strait.

18. In Their Own Right

Author's own interviews with Charlotte Sheedy; Gerry Dreyfuss; Brandy Foster; Ally Sheedy (1986); Doris G. Tate. Other sources include *Helter Skelter* by Vincent Bugliosi with Curt Gentry; Peter Lester, *People; Los Angeles Times Magazine;* Anne Heller and Susan Schneider, *US.*

19. ... And When Fame Leads to Pain

Author's own interviews with Arnold Schwarzenegger (1984); Joan Collins (1982); Joanna Moore (1985); Gerry Dreyfuss; Sylvester Stallone (1978);

Mabel Johnson; Diahann Carroll (1984); Maria Gurdin. Other sources include: *Natalie: A Memoir by Her Sister,* by Lana Wood; *I, Tina,* by Tina Turner and Kurt Loder; Anne Pacey, *Daily Herald,* (United Kingdom); David Suskind; Rex Reed; Margaret Langham, *Sunday* magazine (United Kingdom); *A Touch of Collins,* by Joe Collins; Kristine McKenna, *Rolling Stone,* 1980 and 1983; *Diahann!* by Diahann Carroll and Ross Firestone.

20. THE POWER AND THE GLORY

Author's own interviews with Dr. R. Barkley Clark; Ally Sheedy (1986); Sylvester Stallone (1978); Janet Leigh; Dr. James Grotstein; Ringo Starr (1980); Gerry Dreyfuss; Richard Dreyfuss (1987). Other sources include: *Playboy; Diahann!,* by Diahann Carroll and Ross Firestone; "The Oprah Winfrey Show"; Aaron Latham, *Rolling Stone;* Mel Gussow, *Cosmopolitan;* Kristine McKenna, *Rolling Stone; Lennon,* by Ray Coleman; Nancy Collins, *Rolling Stone;* Jay McInerney, *Esquire;* Nancy Collins, *Cosmopolitan; Lennon Remembers,* by Jann Wenner; Diane de Dubovay, *McCall's;* Donald MacLachlan, *Woman's Own* magazine (United Kingdom); Frank Candida, *Los Angeles Herald Examiner;* Tom Seligson, *Parade Magazine;* Stu Schreiberg, *USA Weekend.*

22. SPLENDID ISOLATION

Author's own interviews with Betty White; Diana Kind; Laura Hawn; Anne Hamilton; Eva Jagger; David Cassidy (1987); Shirley Jones (1978); Michael J. Fox (1986); Zelma Bullock. Other sources include: Jeff Rovin, *Los Angeles Herald Examiner;* Tom Burke, *Cosmopolitan;* Chaim Potok, *Esquire;* Eric Sherman, *Ladies' Home Journal;* Lois Armstrong, *People;* Simon Kinnersley, *Sunday* magazine (United Kingdom); *The Frenzy of Renown* by Leo Braudy; Nancy Collins, *Rolling Stone; K. W. Woods, Playgirl;* Divided Soul, by David Ritz; Michael Goldberg, *Rolling Stone; I, Tina,* by Tina Turner and Kurt Loder.

23. FACING FEAR

Author's own interviews with Loretta Williams; Eva Jagger; Virginia Funicello; Brandy Foster. Other sources include: Richard Sanders and Ray Bonici, *US;* George Carpozi, Jr., *US;* Jodie Foster, *Esquire;* Tom Morganthau, *Newsweek;* Donald Martins, *US.*

24. BRING ON THE MAGIC

Author's own interviews with Laura Hawn; Loretta Williams; Eva Jagger; Gerry Dreyfuss; Saturnina Schipani; Anna Cosby; Catrine Domenique.

Index

Index

PHOTO CREDITS

417

ABOUT THE AUTHORS

GEORGIA HOLT, entertainer and former beauty queen, is the co-executive producer of the first and second annual Mother's Day television special, "Superstars and Their Moms," in which she appeared with her daughter Cher.

PHYLLIS QUINN, president of Motion Picture Mothers and former president of Screen Smart Set, is the co-executive producer of "Superstars and Their Moms."

SUE RUSSELL is an internationally syndicated reporter who has written for *Redbook, Us,* and *Family Weekly.*

Exciting Lives—
Memorable People
from St. Martin's Press!